BUSH LEAGUE

*A History of
Minor League
Baseball*

BUSH LEAGUE

A History of Minor League Baseball

ROBERT OBOJSKI

Macmillan Publishing Co., Inc.
New York
Collier Macmillan Publishers
London

Macmillan Publishing Co., Inc.
866 Third Avenue, New York, N. Y. 10022
Collier-Macmillan Canada Ltd.

Library of Congress Cataloging in Publication Data

Obojski, Robert
Bush League
    A history of minor league baseball.

    Bibliography: p.
    1. Baseball clubs—History. I. Title.
GV875.A1026   796.357'64'09   74-16345
ISBN 0-02-591300-X

FIRST PRINTING 1975

Printed in the United States of America

Contents

PREFACE   ix
ACKNOWLEDGMENTS   xi
FOREWORD   xiii

PART ONE

1   THE MINORS FROM 1877 UNTIL THE END OF
        WORLD WAR II: A Brief Historical Survey   3

2   THE MINORS FROM THE EARLY 1950s TO THE
        PRESENT   26

3   BRANCH RICKEY: The Father of Baseball's Farm
        System   39

4   FRANK SHAUGHNESSY AND THE SHAUGHNESSY
        PLAYOFFS   46

5   GEORGE WEISS: The Last of the Empire Builders   49

6   HENRY J. PETERS: An Interview and a Look into
        the Future   55

PART TWO

7   THE AMERICAN ASSOCIATION: The Fastest Minor
    League in the Midwest   61

8   THE INTERNATIONAL LEAGUE: The Senior Minor
    League   94

9   THE PACIFIC COAST LEAGUE: The Long Season
    and Giantlike Statistics   137

10 THE TEXAS LEAGUE: Baseball Deep in the Heart
    of Texas   177

11 THE SOUTHERN ASSOCIATION AND THE SOUTH-
    ERN LEAGUE: Baseball Way Down South in Dixie   214

12 THE EASTERN LEAGUE: Fifty Years of Professional
    Baseball   248

13 THE MIDDLE ATLANTIC LEAGUE: The Toughest
    Class C Circuit in the History of Organized Baseball   269

14 BASEBALL IN MEXICO   287

PART THREE

15 GREAT MINOR LEAGUE PLAYERS   295

16 OUTSTANDING MINOR LEAGUE RECORDS 299

17 CITIES AND TOWNS THAT HAVE HAD PROFES-
SIONAL BASEBALL TEAMS IN REGULARLY OR-
GANIZED LEAGUES 306

APPENDIX: Rosters of the Minor Leagues Since
1902 320

BIBLIOGRAPHY 401

INDEX OF NAMES 405

INDEX OF THE MINOR LEAGUES 412

GENERAL INDEX 417

Preface

The Baseball Encyclopedia, published by Macmillan in 1969, and revised in 1974, is a landmark in baseball literature since *every player* who was active in the major leagues (even for a single game) is listed, together with his complete record.

Only the major league records are given and still the book runs to 1,552 pages. However, only looking at a player's major league record often can mislead us in evaluating his total career. We shall cite three examples here:

Walter Alston, long-time manager of the Brooklyn and Los Angeles Dodgers, is listed for a single game and a single time at bat for the St. Louis Cardinals in 1936. Alston, incidentally, ignominiously struck out in his brief brush with the majors. However in a thirteen-year playing career in the minors (1935–47), Alston, strong as an ox, was an authentic power hitter. He lead the tough Middle Atlantic League in home runs no less than four times and hit a professional career total of 176 circuit clouts.

Perhaps it is even more important to emphasize that Alston began managing in the minors at the comparatively youthful age of twenty-eight (in 1940). He proved that if a potentially successful major league manager can sharpen his leadership skills in the minors, he doesn't necessarily need major league playing experience. After all, they play the same game in the bushes as they play in Dodger Stadium or Yankee Stadium.

Oscar Eckhardt, according to *The Baseball Encyclopedia,* played in a total of twenty-four National League games for Boston and Brooklyn in 1932 and 1936, producing a mere ten hits for an anemic .192 average. Nonetheless, "Ox" Eckhardt was one of the greatest sluggers in the Pacific Coast League, which was rated by many baseball experts as the premier minor league circuit. A big bruising Texan, he led the PCL in batting a record four times, achieving three of those titles in succession while playing for Mission (a district of San Francisco). He hit for .369 in 1931, .371 in 1932, and .414 in 1933 (a record in the 70-year history of the PCL). Then in 1935 he beat out Joe DiMaggio for the championship .399 to .398. It's hard to say why Eckhardt never established himself in the majors, but in the PCL there was nobody better.

Arnold "Jigger" Statz compiled a pretty respectable record while playing the outfield for a total of eight years for three National League clubs (New York, Chicago, and Brooklyn) between 1919 and 1928. During that time he slammed out 737 base hits and batted .285. In his best season, with the Cubs in 1922, he hit safely 209 times while averaging .319. His American League career consisted of two games with Boston in 1920. Nevertheless, Statz's big league service forms only a small part of his professional career.

Statz played with the Los Angeles Angels in the Pacific Coast League for eighteen years (from 1920 to 1942, with time out for major league play) and established a hatful of records. He played in 2,790 games, came to bat officially 10,657 times, scored 1,996 runs, amassed 3,356 hits, and cracked out 595 doubles and 137 triples (all PCL records), while batting .315. A little fellow, standing only 5 feet 7-½ inches and weighing 150 pounds, Jigger Statz starred in the Coast League until he was forty-five! More will be said about Statz in the chapter on the Pacific Coast League.

In short, the purpose of *Bush League: A History of Minor League Baseball* is to complement *The Baseball Encyclopedia*. It is all intended as a tribute to all of the professional players who for the past century have entertained fans all over North America, from the tiniest towns in the low minors to the sprawling metropolises of the majors.

Acknowledgments

Special thanks are due to Don Avery, director of research for the National Association, who helped us immeasurably in compiling the rosters of over 225 minor leagues listed in the Appendix. He also allowed us to examine many official records and documents at the National Association headquarters (then located in Columbus, Ohio), which were of great value in writing the text of this book.

We also received a great deal of cooperation from Clifford Kachline, historian at the National Baseball Hall of Fame Museum and Library, Cooperstown, New York; Joe Reichler, director of public relations, and Monte Irvin, special assistant, at Baseball Commissioner Bowie Kuhn's office in New York City; Jim Castor, baseball writer for the *Rochester Democrat & Chronicle,* Sam Lippa, promotional manager for the Rochester Red Wings, William B. McKechnie, Jr., former president of the Pacific Coast League, and Paul Mac Farlane, an associate editor of *The Sporting News.*

Finally, we wish to thank the scores of minor league presidents and team executives from across the nation, who took time out to answer our many questions either personally or by letter or telephone.

Foreword

If the minor league baseball program in the United States should ever be cut back drastically from its present level, the quality of major league play would decline so sharply that baseball would soon cease to be the national game. There is certainly no question that the minors are absolutely vital to the majors as the prime source of player talent.

Whenever major league teams have tried to develop alternative sources of player talent, they have generally failed in the attempt. For example, those organizations which have tried to utilize the colleges for that purpose, discovered that collegiate players gain only limited experience on varsity nines. The colleges simply don't play enough games and the competitive climate is substandard. Now and then we'll see a youngster come right off the college campus and star in the big leagues, but such cases are highly unusual. The great majority of ballplayers need a good strong dose of seasoning in the minor leagues, where they get a chance to play every day under highly competitive conditions, before they're ready to take that big step into the majors.

The minor leagues are almost as old as major league baseball itself, as this book so clearly points out. Teams in the majors, from the very outset, had to face the problem of what to do with the young player of real potential who was almost totally inexperienced. Since the big league clubs were in the business of trying to win games, they could not gamble by placing a youngster with only raw talent in their lineup. Out of sheer necessity they hit upon the idea of "farming" him out to a team in a lower professional league, where he could work on fundamentals under the guidance of experienced coaches. And for a century now, the minor leagues have been the great schools of baseball and their alumni the game's most noted stars.

Every so often, baseball critics tell us that the game has lost some of its appeal among the general public. Reports of attendance figures at professional games belie that sort of criticism. In recent years the two major leagues combined have drawn in excess of thirty million paid admissions annually, and the minor leagues have drawn an additional eleven million plus. No other professional team sport attracts paid attendance of that magnitude. This is to say nothing of the tens of millions who watch professional baseball on television.

It is only natural that the minors are completely overshadowed by the activities of the big leagues. For the most part, minor league games are thinly covered in the media, while the majors get almost saturation coverage by all branches of the media: the newspapers, magazines, radio, and television. Despite all this we have no doubt that our games—and maybe I can speak best for the International League in this regard—are as exciting and well played as they are in the majors. Our pitchers can throw just as hard and our batters can hit the ball just as far as their major league counterparts. Maybe we're not as well known, and maybe we don't have superstars in the quantity the majors have, but our game continues to improve all the time. Just look at the number of times major league teams recall players from the International League, as well as from the other minor circuits, during the course of any season.

Today, as perhaps never before, the quality of play in the high minors more closely approximates that of our "big brothers." This phenomenon has probably occurred because the major leagues have expanded in recent years from sixteen to twenty-four teams. Consequently, the minors have had to do an even bigger job in training and supplying the additional required talent. We've found, in fact, that the majors wanted us to cut the apprenticeship time players had to serve before being called up to the big show.

International League teams frequently take on clubs from the majors in exhibition games and, happily, we win a lot of them. In one of our season highlights, the International League All-Star team plays a major league club and it is always a highly spirited game. This contest has been played annually for the past eighteen years, and currently the International League holds the edge over the major leagues, ten games to eight.

Yes, the minors are alive and kicking! They are doing their job of providing talent for the major leagues, and it is talent of the highest caliber.

I am particularly pleased to write this foreword to Robert Obojski's *Bush League: A History of Minor League Baseball*. He has made a significant contribution to baseball literature, since most baseball histories and reference books say little about the minor leagues. It has been refreshing to read such a thorough history of a subject so close to me.

George H. Sisler, Jr.,
President International
League of Professional
Baseball Clubs

PART ONE

1

THE MINORS FROM 1877
UNTIL THE END OF
WORLD WAR II:
A Brief Historical Survey

The National Association of Professional Baseball Leagues in St. Petersburg, Florida, has a file card on every ball player who has played professionally under the rules of Organized Baseball since 1911. There are more than 200,000 cards. Unfortunately, the National Association has no detailed records of players prior to 1911, when a fire destroyed the National Association headquarters (then in Auburn, New York).

We can conservatively estimate, however, that an additional 75,000 men played professionally between 1876, when the National League was organized, and 1911. The number of professional players would be higher still if we counted those who were active in the National Association of Professional Baseball Players from 1871 to 1875. If we go back even further, we can include in our count members of the Cincinnati Red Stockings of 1869–70, the first professional team, and individual players such as Alfred J. Reach. When Reach, a left-handed second baseman, was sold by the Brooklyn Atlantics to the Philadelphia Athletics in June 1864 (the first player transaction in history), he was put on a salary of $25 per week, reputedly becoming baseball's first professional player. Reach, who went on to found the noted sporting goods firm bearing his name, was one of the many star players of the 1860s given a salary by a city eager to have an outstanding team.

From the above evidence we may conclude that *there have been more professional baseball players in the United States than professional players in all other sports combined.* Professional football and basketball leagues, for example, developed many years after baseball was firmly established on the American sporting scene. We may also conclude that *many more persons have paid to see pro baseball games than have paid admissions to witness all other U.S. pro sports contests combined.*

After the Civil War the so-called amateur baseball teams started traveling widely, and "baseball fever" began to sweep the country. The Washington Nationals were considered to be one of the strongest of the teams that took to the diamond before the formation of the Cincinnati Red Stockings. (The Red Stockings went through their entire sixty-nine-game schedule in 1869 without sustaining a single defeat. They chalked up 68 victories and 1 tie.) The fame of the Washington Nationals spread far and wide. According to a contemporary account:

> In 1867, the Washington Nationals made the first trans-Allegheny tour, playing games at Columbus, Cincinnati, Louisville, Indianapolis, St. Louis, and Chicago against the local clubs. At Columbus, the scene of the first game, the Nationals were received with demonstrations of marked fervor and most profuse hospitality. On July 12, they met the Capitals nine on a very poor field in the suburbs of the city. Two namesakes were pitted against each other as pitchers in this contest—J. Williams, afterward secretary of the American Association, appeared for the Capitals, while W. Williams filled the pitcher's box for the Nationals. The Western [Capitals'] Williams did not make good in this game, a total of twenty-seven base hits being made from his delivery, while the Columbus team got only ten hits from the Nationals Williams. The score at the end of seven innings—which were quite enough to satisfy the spectators and players—was 90 to 10 in favor of the Washington club, an unprecedented score . . . up to that date.[1]

THE FIRST MINOR LEAGUES

From a historical viewpoint the story of the minor leagues begins in 1877 with the formation of three different minor league circuits: the International Association, the League Alliance, and the New England League. The first two leagues acknowledged an allegiance to the National League, while the New England League did not establish formal ties with the only major circuit of the time.

In selecting 1877 as the start of the minor leagues, we ought to state the simple fact that there must be a major league before there can be a minor league, and discounting the short-lived National Association, we

[1] From a document in the Archives of the National Association of Professional Baseball Leagues, St. Petersburg, Florida.

must regard the establishment of the National League in 1876 as the real start of major league baseball as we know it today. Thus, any league ranked below major status—and operated within the framework of Organized Baseball—is entitled to be called a "minor league."

The International Association: Of the three original minor leagues, the International Association probably did the best job of record-keeping; season's standings and other statistical data pertaining to its inaugural season have been preserved. Arthur "Candy" Cummings, whose niche in baseball history is secure because he is credited with having invented the curve ball in the late 1860s, was one of the founders of the International Association, and he served as president of the loop during the first year of its brief two-season history.

Organizational meetings for the International Association were held at Pittsburgh, Pennsylvania, and concluding agreements were signed on February 20, 1877, by the representatives of seven teams, two from Canada and five from the United States. The teams included the Tecumsehs of London, Ontario; the Maple Leafs of Guelph, Ontario; the Alleghenys of Pittsburgh, Pennsylvania; the Live Oaks of Lynn, Massachusetts; the Buckeyes of Columbus, Ohio; the Rochesters (also called "Hop Bitters") of Rochester, New York; and a Manchester, New Hampshire team, which apparently had no nickname.

The league was really only a weekend enterprise, since games appear to have been played only on Saturdays and Sundays. The players all held other full-time jobs and regarded their affiliations with the various teams only as an avocation.

No team played more than nineteen games, with the London Tecumsehs winning the championship. The season standings for the International Association in 1877 were as follows:

	Won	Lost	Pct
London Tecumsehs	13	4	.756
Pittsburgh Alleghenys	13	6	.684
Rochester Rochesters	10	7	.588
Manchester	9	10	.474
Columbus Buckeyes	7	11	.389
Guelph Maple Leafs	4	12	.250
Lynn Live Oaks	3	9	.250

The twenty-nine-year-old Candy Cummings had a busy year in 1877. In addition to serving as league president, he was Lynn's regular pitcher. He had his troubles on the mound, however, posting a 1–7 record; still his single victory was a shutout. And he also found time that season to pitch for Cincinnati in the National League, winning 5 and losing 14.

Cummings, who began his competitive pitching career with the Fulton, New York, Hercules in 1866 in an independent league, went on to become one of the greatest hurlers in the National Association. With four different teams from 1872 through 1875, he compiled a formidable 124–72 record. He was 33–20 with the New York Mutuals in 1872; 28–14 with the Lord Baltimores in 1873; 28–26 with Philadelphia in 1874; and 35–12 with Hartford in 1875. In addition, he compiled a 16–8 record for Hartford in the National League in 1876, the League's inaugural year.

A frail-looking fellow who carried only 120 pounds on a 5-foot 9-inch frame, Cummings, nevertheless, was one of the toughest and craftiest moundsmen in baseball's early days. He won election to the Hall of Fame in 1939 for his achievements as a player and as a baseball pioneer.

The International Association operated for a second and final year in 1878 as a reorganized ten-club circuit playing the usual short schedule. London, Manchester, Pittsburgh, and Rochester remained in the league; while Guelph, Lynn, and Columbus dropped out. Teams were added at Buffalo, Hornellsville (now Hornell), Syracuse, and Utica, New York, and at Hartford, Connecticut, and Springfield, Massachusetts. Buffalo won the league crown—most of the other records for this particular season are lost.

Among the future stars who played in the International Association was pitcher James "Pud" Galvin, who was with the Pittsburgh Alleghenys in 1877 and with Buffalo in 1878. No won–lost records are known, but he played in nineteen games for Pittsburgh and in thirty-eight games for Buffalo. Galvin, dubbed "The Little Steam Engine," pitched in the majors from 1879 to 1892 and became the first 300-game winner in the big leagues, compiling a 361–309 record. He was elected to the Hall of Fame in 1965.

In 1879, four cities from the International Association (Manchester, Pittsburgh, Rochester, and Springfield) joined the National Association, which had been formed in 1878 and became a 12-club circuit in the following year.

Similarities in league names can often be confusing. For example, Tom Burns, a star National League infielder from 1880 through 1892, played for Hornellsville in the International Association in 1878 and for Albany in the National Association in 1879. But some baseball guides simply list the 1878 league as being the National Association.

The League Alliance: The League Alliance also lasted for two seasons from 1877 to 1878. In its first season it operated thirteen teams—

an unusual number—in such cities as Brooklyn, Buffalo, Indianapolis, Memphis, Minneapolis, Philadelphia, Providence, St. Paul, and Troy. In its second year the Alliance cut its roster of teams to six: Brooklyn, Buffalo, Memphis, Minneapolis, St. Paul, and Troy.

The New England League: The New England League operated sporadically from 1877 until 1949, and like most of the early minor circuits, it began upon a foundation of amateur and semi-pro teams. The semi-pro New England Association, which began serious play just after the Civil War, included many towns that later became mainstays of the New England League: Brockton, Fall River, Haverhill, Lawrence, Lowell, Lynn, New Bedford, Quincy, and Worcester, Massachusetts; Manchester and Nashua, New Hampshire; Portland, Maine, and other cities.

Innumerable major leaguers got their professional starts in the New England League, including scores of nineteenth-century stars, for example: Tommy Corcoran (Lynn, 1887); Patsy Donovan (Lawrence, 1886–87); Billy Hamilton (Worcester, 1888); Joe Kelley (Lowell, 1891); Larry Lajoie (Fall River, 1891); and Wilbert Robinson (Haverhill, 1885).

OTHER EARLY LEAGUES

The Northwestern League: In 1879, the Northwestern League began play, earning the distinction of being the first minor league established in the western part of the country. At the outset the league had teams in just four cities: Davenport and Dubuque, Iowa; Omaha, Nebraska; and Rockford, Illinois. The growth of the Northwestern League made a tremendous impact on baseball since it developed into the powerful Western League, with both the American Association and the American League stemming directly from the Western.

Eastern Championship Association: Another early minor league of some importance was the Eastern Championship Association, a six-team circuit formed in 1881. There were three clubs from New York City (the New Yorks, the Metropolitans, and the Quicksteps), along with the Philadelphia Athletics, the Brooklyn Atlantics (Brooklyn was then an independent city), and the Washington Nationals. Only three clubs finished the 1881 season, and the New York Metropolitans, who won 32 and lost 13 games, had the best record.

The association pulled itself together for the 1882 season with another six-club roster. The New York Metropolitans again dominated play in yet another incomplete season. While the Eastern Championship Association folded after only two incomplete campaigns, all the cities in it continued to field teams in a variety of leagues.

Professional baseball was so popular in populous Brooklyn and New York at this time that both cities could easily support teams in several leagues simultaneously. In 1882, for example, Brooklyn also was represented in the newly-founded American Association (considered as a major league) and in the newly-organized Inter-State League (a minor circuit). However, the Brooklyn franchise in the American Association was shifted to Baltimore early in the season.

It should be emphasized that soon after the first minor leagues were established almost every responsible executive in professional baseball recognized that a spirit of cooperation must exist between the minor circuits and the major teams of the National League. The administration of professional baseball at all its levels eventually came to be so carefully structured—after early trials and tribulations—that it won the admiration of business and political leaders throughout the nation.

The National League did struggle through its first season under its first president, Morgan G. Bulkeley, later governor of Connecticut and a U.S. Senator. In his book *Historic Facts Concerning the Beginning, Evolution, Development, and Popularity of Base Ball with Personal Reminiscences of Its Vicissitudes, Its Victories, and Its Votaries,* Albert G. Spalding, Chicago's manager and star pitcher in the league's inaugural year, commented that the teams did not have regularly scheduled series, but rather depended upon local secretaries to arrange games for each club. Thus, when the season ended the teams had played an uneven number of games.

Bulkeley, a distinguished man who agreed to serve as league president for one year only (he won election to the Hall of Fame for his efforts), was succeeded by William A. Hulbert, president of the Chicago White Stockings, who brilliantly directed the affairs of the circuit for five years until his untimely death in 1882. When Hulbert took office he immediately addressed himself to the task of drawing up set season schedules for all teams, and since that time, all professional leagues have followed the procedure of publishing set schedules before the season opens.

The majors have always looked to the minors, of course, as a solid source of top-drawer talent. This is why the National League fostered the formulation of the International Association and the League Alliance at the very beginning. From that point the National League went right on encouraging the development of minor professional circuits.

At first there were no formal plans as to how a major league club could obtain a minor league star; in the beginning there were all too many cases of a major team blatantly "raiding" the roster of a good minor league outfit. Early National League teams derived much of their revenue from exhibition games with minor league and independent clubs across much of the East and Midwest. And after the game it was not unusual for an NL team to sign up one or more of the best players of the local organization and take them away! In his book Spalding recalled a particularly flagrant "raiding" incident, which seems to have occurred in 1877:

> I recall one instance where a National League club visited St. Paul and took from the Red Caps of that city [the St. Paul Red Caps were in the League Alliance] *five* of their finest players, practically breaking up the team. A great outcry, of course, was raised over this high-handed proceeding, and while there was no league rule forbidding such action on the part of League clubs, it became evident to the far-sighted Hulbert that, unless this custom was stopped, discredit would be reflected not only upon the league, but upon the game itself. He at once set about to institute reforms in this direction.

But Hulbert's efforts to stop the raiding were not entirely successful. In fact, the National League clubs in their first years of existence almost had to raid in order to survive. Spalding made this observation:

> Now at this time in the history of baseball, it was not customary during the season's play to carry on trips around the circuit a lot of utility players, as at present. Ten, or at most eleven men, constituted the limit. It was, therefore, of not infrequent occurrence, when players became ill or incapacitated through accident, to fill the team from the ranks of professionals in cities where visiting teams happened to be.

Through a set of directives, Hulbert urged all professional players in both the major and minor leagues to stand by their contracts, but he found that contract jumping was almost impossible to stop.

Hulbert was especially concerned about the problem of major league players jumping from one National League club to another. At his insistence all clubs in the league agreed not to employ a player who jumped the club with which he had contracted. He fostered the principle that a contract is a sacred document and must be kept inviolate by all parties.

While he was president, Hulbert worked out with the National League club owners, the basic precepts of the "reserve clause," a foundation principle which has become the cornerstone of professional baseball. Under the reserve clause, a player *must remain* with the team he has contracted with unless he is sold, traded, or released. Though critics of the reserve clause concept say that it "enslaves" baseball players, there's no question at all that it has given the professional game its basic stability over the past century.

Hulbert also strongly maintained that baseball and gambling cannot mix. All too often gamblers tried to fix games in order to win large bets. Weak and dishonest players became their victims. Whenever Hulbert and his associates found a player involved in gambling, that player was suspended from baseball—both from the majors and minors—for life. Above all, he felt it was vitally important that public confidence be maintained in the integrity of the game.

Although William A. Hulbert has never been elected to the Hall of Fame, his influence on Organized Baseball has been permanent. In recent years, incidentally, there has been a movement among veteran baseball writers to effect Hulbert's election to baseball's shrine at Cooperstown.

Colonel A. G. Mills, a successful Washington, D.C. lawyer and former professional player, succeeded Hulbert as National League president and proved to be an able administrator. Almost immediately after taking office, Mills and his associates went to work formulating the "Tripartite Agreement," which was officially adopted in the fall of 1883.

The Tripartite Agreement, popularly referred to as the "National Agreement," involved the National League and the two most important of the minor circuits (the American Association, and the Northwestern League). Under the provisions of the agreement, the National League recognized the American Association as a major league, and all three organizations were to maintain a proper respect for each other's territorial rights. Moreover, the pirating of players was to be stopped. In order to settle disputes, an arbitration committee was established with Colonel Mills as chairman.

The National Agreement, often called the "Magna Charta" of professional baseball, was amended many times over the years, but its basic tenets—the sanctity of player contracts and territorial rights—gave the game a strong sense of direction.

The number of minor leagues continued to increase throughout the 1880s and 1890s as professional baseball became the nation's number one spectator sport.

The International League (originally known as the Eastern League) commenced activity in 1884, and now after more than ninety consecutive years of play, it is the oldest minor circuit having a continuous history (see Chapter 8).

One year after the International League was launched, the Southern League began play, and from the old Southern League the modern Southern Association was organized in 1901. Chapter 11 on the Southern

Association relates the story of professional baseball's great popularity south of the Mason–Dixon Line.

Professional baseball came into its own in California in the early 1880s, as is seen in Chapter 9 on the Pacific Coast League. Although the league was not organized until 1903, its origins go back many years before that.

The Texas League began operations in 1888 (an era commonly referred to today as "The Stone Age of Baseball"), and although this league had rough going in its early years, it developed into one of the country's finest minor circuits. In Chapter 10 on the Texas League, it is shown that more than 100 cities in the Lone Star State hosted professional baseball teams at one time or another.

Following is a list of other important minor leagues that flourished in the 1880s and 1890s, along with the dates in which they began play: Connecticut State League (1884); Iron and Oil Association (1884); Virginia League (1885); Northeastern Connecticut State League (1885); Ohio State League (1886); Three-I League (1886, Illinois, Indiana, and Iowa); Pennsylvania State League (1886); Central Pennsylvania League (1887); Kansas State League (1887); Central Atlantic League (1888); Central Inter-State League (1888); Central League (1889); Tri-State League (1889, including Ohio, Indiana, and West Virginia); Atlantic Association (1889); Eastern Inter-State League (1890); Michigan State League (1890); Montana League (1891); Nebraska State League (1892); Pacific Northwest League (1892); Iron and Oil League (1895); Northwestern League (1895), including teams from Washington State and British Columbia); Atlantic League (1896); Canadian League (1899, mostly teams from the province of Ontario).

This is by no means a complete listing of the minor leagues that made their imprint on the professional baseball scene in the two decades prior to the twentieth century. A comprehensive account of minor league baseball during the 1880–1900 period would easily fill a thick volume, even though records for many leagues and teams have been lost.

Many famous names in baseball are associated with the leagues in the above list. A tall, slender twenty-one-year-old catcher named Cornelius McGillicuddy—better known as Connie Mack—made his professional debut with Meriden in the Connecticut State League in 1884. He moved over to Hartford in the Northeastern Connecticut State League the following year. Connie Mack, of course, gained his greatest fame as manager of the Philadelphia Athletics for a half-century, and when he retired in 1950, at the age of eighty-eight, he had been in the game for sixty-seven consecutive seasons, one of the longest careers in history.

John Peter "Honus" Wagner, perhaps the greatest shortstop in the history of baseball, played in four different minor leagues in his first year of pro ball in 1895 when he was twenty-one-years old. He began with Steubenville in the Inter-State League, and then he saw service with Mansfield in the Ohio State League, Adrian in the Michigan State League, and Warren, Pennsylvania, in the Iron and Oil League. Ed Barrow, who organized the Atlantic League in 1896, brought Wagner over to his Paterson, New Jersey, franchise in that year. Wagner also played for Paterson during the first half of the 1897 season (he hit .379 in 74 games) before Barrow sold him to Louisville of the National League. "The Flying Dutchman" remained in the National League for twenty-one years and during the course of that period he set many of the circuit's most important batting records.

Other future Hall of Famers who began their careers in these minor circuits during the 1880s and 1890s include: Sam Crawford (Chatham, Ontario; Canadian League; 1899), Ed Delahanty (Mansfield, Ohio; Ohio State League; 1887), Hugh Jennings (Allentown, Pennsylvania; Eastern Inter-State League; 1890); and Denton T. "Cy" Young (Canton, Ohio; Tri-State League; 1890). Tommy Leach and Al Orth never made the Hall of Fame, but they are among the many solid big leaguers who started their careers in the old Virginia League in the 1890s. Leach, a National League third baseman–outfielder for nineteen years, played for Petersburg–Hampton in 1896; while Orth, a right-handed pitcher who became known as "The Curveless Wonder" while compiling a 202–189 record in fifteen big league seasons, hurled for Lynchburg in 1894–95.

Because minor league records up to the time of the formation of the National Association in 1901 are often so spotty, the baseball historian can easily become frustrated. For example, Connie Mack's and Honus Wagner's early minor league batting and fielding statistics are virtually unknown. And the statistics can never be "reconstructed" for too many of the early box scores have been irretrievably lost.

Moreover, the National Association takes no responsibility for minor league records and statistics accumulated prior to its formation in 1901. The Association has had enough problems keeping straight the mountains of records piled up by some 225–250 minor leagues after that time.

In compiling our rosters of the various minor leagues, we had to, in most cases, begin in 1902, the first full year in which the National Association functioned. It is possible to compile accurately the rosters of cities in the larger minor league circuits active in the latter part of the nineteenth century (for example, the International League, the Southern League, and the Texas League); but it is impossible to reconstruct fully the rosters of teams in many of the more obscure leagues, simply because complete records are no longer available.

For example, in respect to early minor league records being spotty, the history of the Three-I League begins in 1886, but *The Sporting News Official Guides* list league champions only since 1901. The reason for this is that the Three-I League was completely reorganized in 1901; and during the fifteen years prior to 1901, the league's history is not continuous.

As another example, the Virginia League began play in 1885, but *The Sporting News Official Guides* list pennant winners only since 1906. As in the case of the Three I-League, the Virginia League was not active in every season during the first fifteen or twenty years of its history.

In studying the history of the minors we will discover that there has been a plethora of circuits bearing the same name, especially with names like "Tri-State League" and "Inter-State League." These two names came into vogue in the 1880s and were used almost up to the present. Some of the Tri-State and Inter-State circuits were related, while others were not. "Keeping all the Tri-State and Inter-State Leagues straight can be a real problem," said Don Avery, long-time research director for the National Association.

THE ESTABLISHMENT OF THE NATIONAL ASSOCIATION OF PROFESSIONAL BASEBALL LEAGUES

Despite the existence of the National Agreement, which was supposed to guarantee the legality of player contracts and territorial rights, minor league club owners still complained that their players were being taken over, without payment, by major league teams. The situation began to climax in the late 1890s, when a group led by Ban Johnson began a drive to launch a new major league. Johnson and his associates were successful in their drive, and their new major circuit, the American League, claiming major league status effective with the 1901 season.

The National League strongly opposed—as always—the creation of another major league, for they desired, above all, to retain sole possession of big-league status in baseball. And in August 1901, during the consequent struggle between the entrenched Nationals and the fledgling Americans, the National League announced abrogation of its agreement with all the minor leagues. The struggle for topflight playing talent was now so intense that the National League felt it simply could not follow the old established rules that had governed the sport.

When Thomas Jefferson Hickey, the ambitious and hard-driving president of the Western League, heard of the National League's decision to nullify the National Agreement, he immediately sent telegrams to all minor league presidents informing them of the league's move. The minors were now without protection, and any of their players could be taken away from them *by either the National League or the American League —without compensation.* In his telegram, Hickey implored the minor league presidents to attend an emergency meeting that he was arranging at Chicago's Leland Hotel for September 5. The response to Hickey's call was a thundering "Yes," with all eleven of the regularly organized professional leagues agreeing to be represented either in person or by proxy. The Western Association, as well as the Eastern, Western, Pacific Northwest, Three-I, New England, and New York State leagues all sent their presidents; while the Connecticut, North Carolina, Southern, and California leagues sent proxies. Hickey presided at the meeting, and as one of the first orders of business, the group decided to call itself The National Association of Professional Baseball Leagues. The organization has endured to this day with the same name.

The seven league presidents who attended the National Association's first meeting are called the "Founding Fathers." They were, in addition to Hickey of the Western League: William Meyer, Jr., Western Association; Patrick T. Powers, Eastern League (later to become the International League); W. H. Lucas, Pacific Northwest League; Michael H. Sexton, Three-I League; T. H. Murnane, New England League; and John H. Farrell, New York State League. Farrell, whom we will encounter later as the first president of the new Eastern League, was named Secretary–Treasurer of the National Association at its September meeting. He retained that post until he retired in 1931. (By the time the 1902 season began, the Western Association disbanded and was largely absorbed by the new American Association.)

Tom Hickey was offered the presidency of the association at the Chicago meeting, but he declined since he was heavily involved in plans to form a new league, the American Association. Pat Powers, energetic head of the Eastern League, was then elected as the association's first president, a post he held for eight years.

For the first time in baseball history, the minors had banded together into a cohesive organization. The organization's primary purpose, of course, was to prevent their rosters from being raided by the two warring major league circuits. But at its second meeting (held in New York City on October 24–25, 1901), the organization adopted a long list of rules and operating procedures in order to stabilize the entire minor league establishment.

Among the most important procedures adopted was the *classification* system. The minors were divided into four classifications: A, B, C, and D. The main purpose of the classifications was to assure more equal competition among the teams in a given league. Those leagues operating in the smaller cities and having teams made up of relatively inexperienced players (young men usually in their first year of professional baseball) were given the D rating, while leagues operating in the big cities and having the most experienced players (including veterans with big league experience) were given the A rating.[2]

Size of team rosters and player salaries (both minimums and maximums) also depended upon a league's classification. When the system went into effect in 1902, a Class D team, for example, could carry no more than fourteen players on its roster, while an A team was permitted eighteen players.

The National Association also adopted a strict reserve clause, making it illegal for a player to break his contract and jump from one minor league team to another. The fines were graded according to classification: for example, Class D deserters were fined $300, while Class A deserters were fined $1,000. A rule was also adopted prohibiting the farming of players by any club to a lower class league.[3]

Henry Chadwick (1824–1908) is called the "Father of Baseball" because he published baseball's first rule book and developed the box score system still in use today, and although he was approaching eighty

[2] Throughout the years the classification system has been revised many times. In 1908, the AA rating was used for the first time, and the three most important leagues, the American Association, the Eastern (International) League, and Pacific Coast League "graduating" from single A to double A. The National Association awarded the A-1 rating, a halfway rank between A and AA, to both the Texas League and Southern Association in 1936. AAA ratings came into being in 1946, and in 1952, the Pacific Coast League became the only circuit to have been awarded the "super rank" of Open Classification. Then, in 1963 the classification system underwent major revisions; the B, C, and D ratings were abolished in favor of the new "rookie" league. Special "instructional" leagues had been set up by the majors in 1958, and these circuits, which are completely outside the regular classification system, remain in operation to this day (see Chapter 2).

In 1943, during the height of World War II, the National Association's only Class E circuit was organized. This was the four-team Twin Ports League, with three clubs in Duluth, Minnesota, and one in Superior, Wisconsin. Called a "kindergarten league," the circuit was restricted to players with no professional experience, and only four games per week were scheduled. However, the league was beset with all manner of ill-fortune, particularly financial ill-fortune, from the outset, and it was forced to cease operations on July 26, or about midseason. There have been no other Class E circuits.

[3] The rule prohibiting the "farming" of players to lower classification leagues was all but waived in later years, especially since the mid-1920s when major league farm systems were being developed. Major league executives like Branch Rickey shifted players from one minor league club to another at will. And the Class C Middle Atlantic League for all intents and purposes operated the Class D. Pennsylvania State Association as a farm system.

years of age at the time, he was a member of the National Association's first Playing Rules Committee. He also offered wise counsel in many organizational areas, and at his urging, the Association published its own *Official Guide* [4] and adopted a uniform contract for all players. In fact, every minor league contract must still be approved by the association, and a copy must be kept on permanent file at its offices.

From the time of the National Association's establishment, all leagues that operated under its aegis became a part of what is called "Organized Baseball," or "O.B." for short. Any professional league that did not join the association and play according to its rules came to be called an "outlaw league." During the days of the old National Agreement, circuits that did not become signatories to the agreement were usually called "independent" rather than "outlaw."

When the 1902 season started, six additional leagues joined the original nine National Association members: the reactivated Texas League, the Cotton States League, the Iowa-South Dakota League, the Missouri Valley League, the Northern League, and the Pennsylvania League. (All other leagues listed in Part Three as being active in 1902 were not National Association members.) Ironically enough, the American Association (which Tom Hickey had put together in time for the start of the 1902 season), was not admitted to the National Association because of protests from the Western League (which Hickey had headed) that it was invading its territory. Within two years, however, the differences were settled, and in 1904 the AA was awarded full association membership. It has held its membership ever since, except for six years in the 1960s when the league did not operate (see Chapter 7).

Because of a dispute, the California League, the predecessor of the Pacific Coast League, withdrew from the National Association in 1902. As the Pacific Coast League, it rejoined the organization in 1904.

PEACE ON THE BASEBALL FRONT

The National Association was formed just when the popularity of baseball was increasing tremendously throughout the United States. As a concrete indication of this phenomenon, the number of member leagues finishing the season had increased from fifteen in 1902 to nineteen in 1903.

During the course of the 1903 season, events of momentous importance occurred. The warring National and American Leagues called

---

[4] The National Association did publish its own *Guide* during its first two years of existence, and since 1904, it has produced a *Guide* in conjunction with both major leagues.

a truce, and they together with the National Association signed a tripartite agreement through which the three organizations were to be considered as equal partners in administering the professional game.[5] Among the many provisions of the new Major–Minor League Agreement, the most important bore on the protection of player contracts and territorial rights. Another important provision dealt with a "selection" system; for example, a minor league team would draw up a selected list of players, with those players being subject to a draft by the major league clubs. The majors would then pay an agreed upon sum for those players selected for their rosters. Higher-class minor league teams could also draft players from the low minors and pay an agreed upon sum for them.

The Major–Minor League Agreement, which undergoes periodic examination and revision, remains to this day as a key governing instrument of Organized Baseball. Only one gap (1919–20) occurred in the history of this agreement.

The National Association experienced many periods of turbulence during its long history, particularly in its early years. Upper classification leagues feared that the smaller circuits might run amuck and destroy valuable franchises by unwise legislation. In order to prevent catastrophes of this nature, the high minors demanded, and eventually obtained, additional seats on the association's special Board of Arbitration.

Once a crisis of great magnitude occurred when both the American Association and Eastern (International) League requested permission to withdraw from the association. They were voted down, but they marched out anyway. For a few tense weeks, it appeared that a rival association was in the making. The rest of the member leagues, however, appealed to the National Commission (the three-man governing board of the major leagues), and after a short while, the matter was resolved peaceably by giving the complaining leagues a higher classification. It was in 1908, after the dust settled, that the American Association and the Eastern League (together with the Pacific Coast League) became the first circuits to achieve double A status. The temporary withdrawals of the two leagues from the National Association were, incidentally, stricken out of the official record. There were a few subsequent situations where some of the top minor circuits threatened to leave the fold, but again they were mollified through arbitration. For some sixty years now, no league at any level has seriously considered leaving the Association.

Despite the conflicts, the National Association continued to grow in power and prestige as the number of member leagues increased. In 1907,

[5] As part of the truce, the National and American leagues agreed to play the first World Series at the end of the regular season in 1903. The Boston Red Sox of the "upstart" American League defeated the Pittsburgh Pirates 5 games to 3.

thirty-six leagues in 244 cities completed their seasons, and the association processed more than 4,300 player contracts. By 1914, forty-two circuits started the season and no less than thirty-nine finished.

WORLD WAR I AND THE MINOR LEAGUE CRISIS

While the National Association membership enjoyed a good measure of prosperity during the decade or so before 1917, changes in society together with the outbreak of World War I had a great impact on professional baseball. New forms of popular entertainment—including movies, automobile driving, billiard parlors, and various other spectator sports (including basketball and football)—became enormously popular at this time, and they came into direct competition with baseball for those dollars spent for recreation. Moreover, the United States was at war in 1917–18, and everything else became secondary to ending the horrendous conflict in Europe as quickly as possible.

In 1917, only twenty leagues started the season, and a mere twelve leagues remained intact to complete their schedules. Every minor league in the country suffered from lack of interest and patronage to such an extent that Michael H. Sexton, the association's president, and all club owners seriously became concerned as to the very health of the game. In 1918, a scant nine minor leagues started the season, and only one circuit, the International, managed to finish.

At its annual convention (held at Peoria in the fall of 1918), the National Association raised a number of objections to the Major–Minor League Agreement, particularly in regard to the prices big league clubs could pay for drafted minor league players. The objections continued, and in January 1919, the agreement was rescinded. However, in November 1920, when the old three-man National Commission was abolished and Judge Kenesaw Mountain Landis became commissioner of baseball, a new agreement was signed. This agreement providing for, among other things, more equitable payments for drafted players. Judge Landis, baseball's first "Czar," had jurisdiction over the entire spectrum of the professional game, and he had urged that all differences be ironed out. Since that time there has been no break in the relationship under the agreement between the major and minor leagues.

THE POST WORLD WAR I ERA

Membership in the National Association came back up to fourteen in 1919, the first postwar year, with thirteen leagues completing their schedules. Within a relatively short time baseball recovered its prewar popularity. Both the number of leagues and overall attendance increased steadily despite all the other diversions the American public could choose from.

With a plethora of baseball heroes dominated by Babe Ruth (who changed the nature of the game by driving tremendous home runs over distant fences), the Roaring Twenties became one of baseball's really great eras from the lowest minor leagues right up to the majors. By 1925, the number of leagues had risen to a healthy twenty-five, and approximately that same number continued to operate through the rest of the decade.

Also during the 1920s, the majors began exercising greater control over the minors through the development of "farm systems" (see Chapter 3).

Judge Landis consistently opposed the farm system, but the movement toward almost total amalgamation of the two major leagues with all the minor leagues was inexorable. Landis, a slight, white-maned, tough-talking ex-federal judge first gained nationwide attention in 1905 when he fined the Standard Oil Company of Indiana a staggering $29,240,000 in a freight rebate case,[6] but he was ever zealous in his defense of the rights of the player. The commissioner believed that the farm system gave the big league clubs too much control over the destinies of too many young players, and he often took carefully aimed shots at what he termed the plan's "monopolistic tendencies."

THE DEPRESSION AND THE 1930s

The severe economic depression that struck the country after the stock market crashed in October 1929 deeply affected every strata of American life, including baseball. The minors struggled as never before to survive the lean years of the early 1930s. While twenty-five leagues had completed the 1929 season, only twenty-one survived 1930, and by 1931 the number dropped to 16.

The situation became so serious that, at the annual National Association meeting held at West Baden, Indiana, in December 1931, minor league executives decided to inaugurate an all-out revitalization campaign. Michael H. Sexton, who had capably served the association as president for twenty-two years, retired shortly before the West Baden meeting, and the organization's administrative duties passed into the hands of the newly-formed executive committee. The committee, which governed the

---

[6] The fine was later rescinded on appeal.

association for a full year, was comprised of such respected minor league executives as Warren C. Giles, general manager of the Rochester Red Wings; J. Alvin Gardner, president of the Texas League; and Judge William G. Bramham, president of the Piedmont League, who served as chairman. William G. "Billy" Evans (long-time American League umpire and then general manager of the Cleveland Indians) and Branch Rickey (general manager of the St. Louis Cardinals) were appointed as representatives of the majors to help and advise the committee.

In late 1932, the executive committee unanimously elected Judge Bramham as National Association president and gave him sweeping powers over the minors that corresponded to those Judge Landis held over the majors. Bramham was no stranger to baseball since he had served as president of four leagues simultaneously—the Sally, Virginia, Piedmont, and Eastern North Carolina—and had been a member of the National Board of Arbitration for many years. A native of Hopkinsville, Kentucky, Bramham came to Durham as a young man, studied law at the University of North Carolina where he received the LL.B. in 1905, became active in Republican politics, and enjoyed a long and successful career as a corporation lawyer. Bramham never served on the bench, though many thought he did because of his title, "Judge," which he used for his entire adult life. The title was bestowed upon him by his law school classmates because of his serious demeanor.

In one of his first official actions, Bramham moved the National Association headquarters from Auburn, New York, where they had been located for many years, to Durham. He then proceeded to institute fundamental reforms. One of his first targets was the so-called "shoestring operator," a club owner, usually in the lower classification leagues, who started out with little or no capital, staggered through until the Fourth of July doubleheader, pocketed the gate receipts from that event, and then dissolved the operation and quickly left town.

He insisted that all club owners show integrity by backing up their operations with a guaranty deposit equal to one-half of the teams' monthly payroll. This regulation protected player salaries for two weeks in the event the owner skipped town and could not be located on pay day. Any part of the deposit which was left intact at the end of the season would be returned to the club.

By rigidly holding all teams to the provisions of the deposit rule, Bramham succeeded in placing the minors on a more solid foundation. The stability of all circuits improved markedly as fly-by-night promoters were eased out of Organized Baseball. If one occasionally slipped through the net, he did not last very long.

Bramham's strict controls showed immediate results. During the National Association's annual meeting (held at Columbus in December

1932), only five league presidents said their circuits would definitely be ready to go for the 1933 season. But as spring approached fourteen leagues had entered the fold, and *all* of them finished the campaign. The North Carolina lawyer did everything in his power to encourage legitimate club owners in their organizational efforts, while at the same time he discouraged operators of "firecracker" circuits from disturbing the Organized Baseball front.

Moreover, Bramham did everything he could to promote minor league baseball wherever it was played. He was the prime mover in establishing the association's promotional department, which served as a clearinghouse of information for members of the press and radio who required materials for news and feature stories dealing with individual players, teams, leagues, etc. Minor league club owners also could call upon the promotional department in regard to promoting professional baseball in their respective towns.

Joe F. Carr, a veteran baseball man and long-time association official, was named as the first promotional director. He established headquarters in Columbus, Ohio, and served ably in the post until his death in 1939.

Bramham also encouraged such innovations as night baseball, which played a vital role in improving minor league attendance during the 1930s. Night baseball was introduced by the Des Moines, Iowa, club of the Western League on May 2, 1930, and before the decade was out, night games became so popular throughout the minors—and so very profitable to the club owners—that the majority of weekday games were played under the arc lights.

Bramham also gave support, reluctant though it was, to Frank Shaughnessy, general manager of the Montreal Royals in the International League, who conceived the Shaughnessy Playoff Plan in the early 1930s (see Chapter 4). In one form or another this plan was eventually adopted by all the minor leagues.

Bramham's far-reaching organizational reforms led to the minors becoming stronger than ever during the several years preceding World War II. The number of leagues went up to nineteen in 1934 and went all the way up to thirty-seven in 1938. There were forty-one leagues in 1939, and forty-three in 1940. Then the number dropped off a bit, to forty-one, in 1941.

Paid attendance also began to reach record levels. In 1938, National Association teams played to what was believed to be an all-time high of 15,500,000 paid admissions. (There is no accurate attendance figure for 1914 when thirty-nine leagues finished, but it is thought the 1938 figure was not reached.)

A wide variety of promotional campaigns were staged by both the majors and minors in 1939 to celebrate baseball's centennial. (According to legend Abner Doubleday "invented" baseball at Cooperstown, New York, in 1839.) Each of the forty-one leagues was invited to send one of its star players to Cooperstown to participate in special "National Association Day" ceremonies, scheduled for July 9. The forty-one players were split into two squads and played a spirited All-Star game.

Total paid attendance soared to more than 18,000,000 in 1939 and approached 20,000,000 in 1940, but it dropped off to 16,000,000 in 1941 because of grave international tensions and the possibility of America's entry into World War II.

BRAMHAM FIGHTS ROWDYISM ON THE FIELD

During the 1920s when he was a league president, William Bramham backed umpires to the limit in disputes with unruly players, coaches, and managers. Commissioner Landis issued an edict in 1927, which set the minimal penalty for assault upon an umpire as suspension, without pay, of ninety playing days; and as National Association president, Bramham demanded enforcement of the regulation. League presidents who backed away from invoking this minimum, for lack of courage, politics, or other reasons, gained no respect from Bramham. He was quick to override their decisions when they failed to levy the ninety-day suspension.

He regarded umpires as representatives of the league, the National Association, and the commissioner. Moreover, Bramham thought physical attacks on umpires were cowardly and reprehensible, and he would go to the limit to prosecute any violator.

In one of his most widely publicized cases, Bramham suspended Ben Chapman, former big-league outfielder and playing-manager of Richmond in the Piedmont League, for an entire year when he slugged umpire I. H. Case on September 16, 1942. Chapman was forced to sit out the 1943 season, but he returned to Richmond in the following year. Later he managed the Philadelphia Phillies and several other minor league clubs.

JUDGE LANDIS FREES THE SERFS

We have already indicated that Judge Landis relentlessly fought the evils of the farm system, though it was a fact of life that farm clubs had become an integral part of the entire major league operation. Landis in particular cracked down on "cover-up operations," "secret working agreements," and any type of illegal manipulations of minor league playing contracts.

In a spectacular case in April 1937, Landis decided that the Cleveland Indians were "covering-up" (that is, holding in the minor leagues too long) a hard-hitting young outfielder named Tommy Henrich, who was with the New Orleans Pelicans in the Southern Association. Landis thereupon declared Henrich a free agent, and in the rush by major league clubs to grab him, the New York Yankees got there first with the most money. They paid Henrich a hefty bonus of $25,000 (a lot of money in those days), farmed him out to Newark (where he hit .440 in seven games), and then brought him up to the Yankees. He starred for New York through 1950, when he retired.

In 1938, Commissioner Landis reprimanded the St. Louis Cardinals management for maintaining "secret working agreements" with three minor league clubs, and he declared seventy-three players to be free agents. The Cardinals and the three farm teams all drew fines.

Then in 1940, Landis zeroed in on the Detroit Tigers for illegally manipulating the contracts of players on a number of teams. Cover-up operations were rampant in this case, and in a sweeping decision, Landis declared ninety-one players, valued well in excess of $500,000, as free agents. All were restricted from re-signing with Detroit or any of its minor league affiliates. Among the players of top major league caliber that the Tigers lost to other teams were Benny McCoy and Roy Cullenbine.

WORLD WAR II: THE MINORS STRUGGLE TO STAY ALIVE

America's entry into World War II sharply curtailed minor league operations. That the game was played at all during the war was largely due to President Franklin D. Roosevelt's letter to Commissioner Landis. In his letter President Roosevelt, an ardent fan himself, expressed the feeling that the continuance of baseball served as an important morale booster during the crisis.

In spite of the green light, minor league club owners found it difficult to maintain operations because so many young players entered the armed forces and because of wartime travel restrictions. The number of leagues dipped to thirty-one in 1942, to only ten in 1943 and 1944, and to twelve in 1945.

The National Association, along with the major leagues, did its share in aiding the war effort by contributing portions of gate proceeds to the Army and Navy Relief Funds, the Red Cross, the U.S.O., and other wartime agencies. Thousands of baseball kits, consisting of bats, balls, and gloves, were sent to armed forces in all parts of the world, enabling the fighting man to get a little recreation whenever it could be permitted.

Lieutenant Gordon Houston of the Army Air Corps became the first professional player to lose his life in World War II. He was killed in a plane crash near Tacoma, Washington, on February 10, 1942. He had been with the Texarkana club of the East Texas League before he joined the air corps.

The first player to be killed in combat was William Hebert, who had been with Merced of the California League and had enlisted in the navy. He was wounded in action at Guadalcanal and died on October 30, 1942.

THE POST WORLD WAR II ERA

With the end of the war, baseball began to prosper again immediately, as forty-two leagues signed in with the National Association for 1946. By 1949, there were fifty-nine leagues, but then their number began to decline sharply again, largely because of the impact of television upon minor league baseball.

In December 1946, Judge William G. Bramham, who had guided the destinies of the minor leagues for fourteen years and who had spent nearly a half-century in the game, announced his resignation as president because of ill health at the National Association's annual meeting, which was held at Los Angeles. After he delivered his farewell speech, he received a standing ovation from convention delegates, and then he retired to his home in Durham, where he died on July 8, 1947.

Bramham's legacy consisted primarily of a strong and well-organized National Association. Moreover, all presidents who succeeded him inherited his broad powers as the "Czar of Minor League Baseball," powers which Bramham had maintained were essential in keeping the association alive and well.

GEORGE M. TRAUTMAN SUCCEEDS TO THE NATIONAL ASSOCIATION PRESIDENCY

George M. Trautman succeeded William G. Bramham as National Association president upon Bramham's resignation in December 1946. He established a notable record in that office for sixteen years, until his death in 1963. Trautman, a native of Bucyrus, Ohio, had pitched for the Ohio State University baseball team in his college days and had a long association with the game before he became president. He had coached amateur teams in Columbus (where he became a business executive and civic leader), and then in 1933 had become president of the old Columbus

Red Birds in the American Association. He had served so well in that post that his colleagues in the AA had elected him league president in 1936, a post he held until 1945 when he was named general manager of the Detroit Tigers. He had been in Detroit for just over a year when the National Association's Executive Committee elected him president by a unanimous vote. In one of his first moves, Trautman moved the association's headquarters from Durham, North Carolina, to Columbus.

Trautman administered the National Association during its critical adjustment period when the number of member leagues went down from fifty-nine to eighteen. All through the 1950s Trautman played a key role in getting the major leagues to assist the minors financially so that the association would have a minimum strength of at least a hundred teams, a number deemed sufficient to keep the majors supplied with top caliber talent (see Chapter 2).

"Red" Trautman was equally adept at handling problems big and small, whether it was persuading big league executives to part with many hundreds of thousands of dollars to keep the minors afloat, answering a schoolboy from Pocomoke City, Maryland (who wrote to his office requesting information for a classroom baseball project), or answering a boy from Provo, Utah (who wanted to know how he could get into professional baseball). He always kept a particularly close watch on all minor league playing contracts in order to make sure that all players were legally signed and fairly treated. Throughout his tenure as president, he always maintained close liaison with the major league commissioner's office, and he managed to work well with both A. B. Chandler and Ford Frick.

Phil Piton, longtime chief assistant to Trautman, succeeded to the National Association presidency in 1963 and held the post until he retired in 1971. Piton, who served in the office of Judge Landis before he came to Columbus, was generally recognized as the top U.S. authority on Organized Baseball's laws and procedures. Piton wrote much of the "Blue Book" legislation by which baseball is governed, and for years whenever a new rule was required to cover a particular situation, Piton was generally called upon to do the drafting.

Henry J. Peters, former farm director for the Cleveland Indians, has been National Association president since 1971. Peters gives his views concerning problems confronting the professional game today in Chapter 6.

2

THE MINORS FROM
THE EARLY 1950s
TO THE PRESENT

THE MAJOR LEAGUES AID THE MINORS

Ever since the health of the minor leagues was seriously threatened by blanket television of major league games across the country in the early 1950s, the majors have been trying to work out schemes to keep the minors operating at a productive level. No serious student of the game has yet questioned *the indispensability of the minors to the basic health of the majors.* Not since the dark days of the early 1930s had the minors faced such great economic difficulties as they encountered in the 1950s.

To state the case directly, for the past twenty years the minors have required substantial financial support to meet the salaries of players, to pay necessary travel expenses, etc. Minor league teams in the 1950s were not as independently organized to operate in a free-wheeling manner as some teams were in the 1920s, when an owner like Jack Dunn of the Baltimore Orioles in the International League could hold onto a phenomenal pitcher like Lefty Grove for five years until he got his asking price from a major league club (in the Grove case the price was $100,000, and he got it from Connie Mack's Philadelphia Athletics).

The minors, in general, experienced great prosperity in the immediate post–World War II period. (Evidence of this prosperity, particularly in the realm of high attendance figures, is given in the various histories of individual leagues in Part II.)

In 1949, when the minor leagues reached their peak, there were fifty-nine leagues with 464 teams in as many cities. Rosters of these teams included over 9,000 players and paid attendance for the fifty-nine leagues soared to a total of nearly 42,000,000. The accompanying chart shows that fifty-eight leagues were still active in 1950, but attendance dropped off by more than 7,000,000. By 1950, televised big league games had become an important factor all across the baseball spectrum and had begun to pull fans away from minor league parks in alarming numbers.

Minor League Attendance Figures [1]

Year	Paid Attendance	Number of Leagues
Year	Paid Attendance	Number of Leagues
1947	40,505,210	52
1948	40,949,028	58
1949	41,872,762	59
1950	34,534,488	58
1951	27,518,837	50
1952	25,301,253	43
1953	22,183,821	38
1954	19,585,819	36
1955	19,042,825	33
1956	17,031,069	28
1957	15,496,684	28
1958	13,184,836	24
1959	12,171,848	21
1960	10,974,084	22
1961	10,100,986	22
1962	10,047,568	20
1963	9,963,174	18
1964	10,313,823	20
1965	10,193,819	19
1966	10,061,252	19
1967	10,087,152	19
1968	10,033,142	21
1969	10,182,223	21
1970	10,978,967	20
1971	11,443,489	19
1972	11,140,577	19
1973	11,248,399	18

[1] Includes both regular season and playoff games.

From 1950 until the early 1960s, the number of leagues, as well as paid attendance, dropped steadily and sharply. In 1963, only eighteen leagues remained and total attendance dipped to less than 10,000,000. The league total rose a bit in succeeding years. There were twenty-one in 1968–69, but in recent seasons the number of those in operation has stabilized itself at eighteen or nineteen.

In 1973, the National Association list contained eighteen minor leagues on its rolls, including two in Mexico. The 136 teams in these eighteen leagues listed approximately 2,500 players on their rosters, or less than 30 percent of the total number of players active annually in the minors' peak period of 1948–50. Moreover, the eighteen minor leagues in 1973 were the prime source of player talent for twenty-four big league teams, while the fifty-nine leagues had only sixteen teams in the majors to be concerned with. But back to all this later.

During the early 1950s a number of baseball observers said that the minors could do a far more effective job of developing players with fewer leagues and teams. Gerry Hern, for years a baseball writer on the old *Boston Post,* maintained that the minors would be stronger and more efficient if only sixteen to twenty leagues operated instead of forty, fifty, or more. In an April 1954 *Baseball Digest* article, entitled "There Are Still *Too Many* Minors!" Hern claimed that too many youngsters at the Class D level played high school-caliber baseball under the guise of being called "professionals." Hern also charged that numerous Class D leagues were organized almost solely because of local pride and boosterism. He concluded:

> A man in a small town owns a franchise in a doddering league. He likes being a small town celebrity, so he wants to keep baseball going. So he huffs and he puffs and he digs up a few more teams, and finally by stretching and scrimping, he announces that he has a league and the townspeople will have to support it or he will take it away from them Twenty years ago, the same man would have been satisfied to own a semi-pro team which would play the neighborhood teams, but not now. Everybody has to get into Organized Baseball.

Minor league executives all across the country quickly rebutted Hern's assertions, however, calling them "nonsense."

THE $500,000 STABILIZATION FUND

By the mid-1950s, major league owners as a body realized that positive action had to be taken to strengthen the minor leagues. In 1956, the number of leagues had slipped to twenty-eight, and no one knew where the descent would stop. Various proposals to help the minors came forth. One idea, proposed by the Brooklyn Dodgers' president (Walter O'Malley), called for a series of major league all-star games to be played in a dozen top minor league cities as fund-raising events. But minor league operators gave this proposal a frosty reception.

At the August 2, 1956, major league meeting, Commissioner Ford C. Frick set up a "Save the Minors Committee" so that definite plans could be drawn up for aiding the National Association membership. Arnold Johnson (Kansas City's president) became the committee's chairman. Joe Cronin (Boston's general manager) and George Medinger (Cleveland's vice-president) were to represent the American League; while Gabe Paul (Cincinnati's general manager), Horace Stoneham (New York Giants' president), and Bob Carpenter (Philadelphia Phillies' president) were to represent the National League.

The committee recommended that a "stabilization fund" be established, and on October 11 Commissioner Frick announced that during a special meeting held during the World Series the owners had agreed. A fund totaling $500,000 would be established, with most of the aid earmarked for clubs and leagues in lower classifications. The money was made available by equal contributions of $31,250 by each of the sixteen big-league clubs.

William O. DeWitt, veteran baseball executive and then assistant general manager of the New York Yankees, was named administrator of the fund, and he officially assumed his duties on January 1, 1957. He continued in that post until September 30, 1959 (the fund was augmented by the interest it drew and by additional contributions), when he became president of the Detroit Tigers. At about the same time as DeWitt moved to the Tigers, the majors discontinued the stabilization fund plan and drew up an entirely new plan. A fund of $1 million would be raised to finance both a player development and promotional program for leagues in the National Association. John W. Galbreath, Pittsburgh Pirates' president, was one of the chief promoters of the new $1 million fund, which proved to be a real shot-in-the-arm for the minors as a whole. Big league executives worked closely with National Association president George M. Trautman in administering financial aid to the various minor league circuits during the critical period of the late 1950s and 1960s.

THE NEW PLAYER DEVELOPMENT CONTRACT PLAN
AND THE RECLASSIFICATION OF THE MINORS

On May 18, 1962, major league owners convened at the Savoy-Hilton Hotel in New York City and took a series of decisive steps to shore up the very foundations of minor league baseball. They voted unanimously to accept a new "Player Development Plan," which guaranteed the operation of at least 100 minor league teams in 1963. (The owners were, of course, concerned with the high mortality rate of minor circuits in recent years, but in 1963 the situation was not all that frightening; a total of 130 teams were operating in eighteen leagues.)

The plan, two years in the making, is perhaps the most significant development in minor league history since the National Association itself was organized in 1901. The plan, calling for increased financial aid to the minors as well as for a restructuring of the entire O.B. setup, was formally adopted at the annual minor and major league meetings (held at Rochester, New York, and New York City, respectively, later in 1962). A twelve-man Player Development Committee, having representation from both the majors and minors and headed by John W. Galbreath of Pittsburgh, had prepared the entire program.

The plan called for reorganizing the minor leagues into four classifications instead of seven. Class AAA remained unchanged, but the former class AA and Class A leagues together became Class AA, while the B, C, and D leagues were all grouped in Class A. At the same time a new "rookie" classification was established so that major league teams could place their youngest prospects into a freshman professional circuit.

The man point of the entire reorganization plan was that baseball executives agreed that it did not make much sense to maintain the old system of seven classifications with only eighteen to twenty leagues operating. Moreover, the majors agreed to support a minimum of twenty clubs in AAA, twenty in AA, and sixty in the A and rookie leagues. This classification system is still operative.

As part of the overall plan, the Player Development Contract (PDC) was instituted to modify the old Working Agreement between major and minor league clubs. The principal provisions contained in the Player Development Contract were : (1) the major league organization must reimburse the minor club for each farmhand's salary in excess of $800 per month in Class AAA, $150 in AA, and $50 in Class A; (2) the parent club assumes all spring training costs of its minor league players; (3) the majors pay the full salary of the minor league manager, with a maximum liability of $7,500 when Class AAA team names a pilot of its own choosing.

Except for the four new expansion clubs (the New York Mets, the Houston Astros, the Washington Senators, and California Angels), each major league team was committed to support at least five farm teams under the commitment of backing the minimum of 100 minor league clubs. (It was understood that the expansion teams would support a minimum of four minor league clubs.) Major league executives were in general agreement that this plan would adequately take care of player development requirements.

The 1962 plan has remained substantially intact, although various provisions have been modified in recent years. The major league teams now assume a greater share of the responsibility for paying player salaries for those minor clubs they work with on a Player Development Contract basis. (The term "Working Agreement" is still used interchangeably with PDC.) In Class AAA the parent club now pays the farmhand's salary in excess of $450 per month, in Class AA it pays everything above $150, and in Class A and the rookie leagues it pays all player salaries in full. When a major league team owns a farm club outright, it assumes, of course, all the financial obligations. Also a major league club can now take the responsibility for supporting as few as four minor teams, as opposed to the five originally called for in the plan.

A substantial share of a major league organization's budget and manpower is directed toward the area of player development. Teams ordinarily do not like to release the exact figures they spend on their farm systems, but when we interviewed Phil Seghi (then director of player personnel and now general manager for the Cleveland Indians), he said: "We spend a minimum of $250,000 per year on player development. We may develop as many as three or four players in one good year for our major team or maybe one or even none in a given year. Thus, if you figure the *per player cost* of development talent, this is a very expensive proposition." In recent years the Indians have been supporting four minor clubs, one each in AAA, AA, A, and rookie.

THE NEW YORK METS: BIG SPENDERS FOR PLAYER DEVELOPMENT

The New York Mets today rank among the really big spenders for player development. The Mets, who have plenty of cash available because their owners are wealthy and because the team usually draws well over two million paying customers into Shea Stadium every season, have been supporting six minor league clubs in recent years.

"We spend well over a million dollars a year on our farm system,"

Joe McDonald, director of minor league operations for the Mets told us. McDonald said that items such as travel expenses for a club like Visalia in the Class A California League, which the Mets own outright, add up to a considerable sum. Of course, with their substantial budget for player development, the Mets are in a position to offer sizable bonuses to the country's most talented young players with whom they have negotiation rights under the provisions of the Free Agent Draft.

In the course of numerous trips to gather information for this book, the author traveled to places like Batavia, New York, where the New York Mets have an entry in the Class A New York–Pennsylvania League. The Mets sponsor the Batavia Trojans on a PDC basis, but the club itself is locally owned by the Genesee County Baseball Club, Inc. Arthur H. Roth, the enterprising young general manager of the Trojans, told us in an interview:

> The Mets are an excellent organization to work with . . . for example, they make sure our team has the best uniforms and equipment available, and we travel the circuit in a modern air-conditioned bus and not in old rickety vehicles we've seen other teams use in years past. The distances between towns in the league aren't too great, so it wouldn't make much sense to fly.

Roth also indicated that the Trojans always have several high bonus players, youngsters usually eighteen to twenty-one years old, who drive big Cadillacs or Chrysler Imperials around Batavia and its environs. These are the young plutocrats. How many of the young prospects make it all the way to big league stardom is problematical. Some of the kids are unconditionally released after their first season, while others like Tim Juran, a left-handed pitcher who had a 5–3 record for the Trojans in 1972 along with 100 strikeouts in 80 innings, are promoted to teams in higher classifications and get that much closer to a position on the Mets' roster. (No one can build up really big statistics in the New York–Penn League because the seasons consist of only seventy games.)

Players who sign a contract calling for a small bonus or none at all are generally the first to be cut, since the parent club has little or no "investment" in them. The parent club naturally will stick with a high bonus player a good deal longer because it has an investment to protect. Baseball may be a sport, but it is also a very serious enterprise calling for hardheaded business decisions.

Joe McDonald of the Mets is also a great booster of the Instructional League, first organized in 1958 and since that time an integral part of the major leagues' training program for young players. "Every dollars we've allocated for our Instructional League teams down in Florida has been money well spent," emphasized McDonald.

Each year some sixteen to eighteen Instructional League teams operate, usually four in Arizona and twelve to fourteen in Florida. These teams serve as a proving ground for the rawest prospects and since these circuits begin their schedules after most professional leagues have concluded their seasons (play begins about September 20 and continues for two months), players already on the rosters of other teams are often assigned Instructional League work in order to work on fundamentals.

In fact, players on big league rosters are sometimes placed on Instructional League rosters to work on a specific phase of their game. Tommy Hallums, a fine New York Mets' infield prospect, for example, played in the organization's farm system in 1973, spent all of September of that season on the Mets' active roster, and then was assigned by Joe McDonald to see further action with the Mets' Instructional League team in St. Petersburg for a period of intensive tutoring during the months of October and November. "Those major league teams that don't participate in the Instructional League program are missing an excellent method by which to develop young players," McDonald concluded. And since the primary purpose of these circuits is to instruct, statistics compiled by players while performing on Instructional League teams are not included on their total professional records.

In Florida, Instructional league teams usually have been based in cities like Bradenton, Clearwater, Dunedin, Sarasota, Tampa, or St. Petersburg. In Arizona, they have usually been based at Mesa, Phoenix, Scottsdale, and Tucson. Instructional League parks and facilities also are used as spring training sites by the parent major league teams.

THE MINOR LEAGUES IN 1974 AND THEIR MAJOR LEAGUE AFFILIATIONS

Team	Type of Affiliation	Parent Club
The International League, Class AAA		
Charleston, West Virginia	PDC	Pittsburgh
Memphis, Tennessee	PDC	Montreal
Pawtucket, Rhode Island	PDC	Boston
Richmond, Virginia	Owned	Atlanta
Rochester, New York	PDC	Baltimore
Syracuse, New York	PDC	New York, AL
Tidewater, Virginia (Norfolk and Portsmouth)	PDC	New York, NL
Toledo, Ohio	PDC	Philadelphia

| | Type of | |
| Team | Affiliation | Parent Club |

American Association, Class AAA

Team	Affiliation	Parent Club
Denver, Colorado	PDC	Houston
Des Moines, Iowa	PDC	Chicago, AL
Evansville, Indiana	PDC	Detroit
Indianapolis, Indiana	PDC	Cincinnati
Oklahoma City, Oklahoma	PDC	Cleveland
Omaha, Nebraska	Owned	Kansas City
Tulsa, Oklahoma	PDC	St. Louis
Wichita, Kansas	PDC	Chicago, NL

Pacific Coast League, Class AAA

Team	Affiliation	Parent Club
Albuquerque, New Mexico	Owned	Los Angeles
Honolulu, Hawaii	PDC	San Diego
Phoenix, Arizona	PDC	San Francisco
Sacramento, California	PDC	Milwaukee
Salt Lake City, Utah	PDC	California
Spokane, Washington	PDC	Texas
Tacoma, Washington	PDC	Minnesota
Tucson, Arizona	PDC	Oakland

Texas League, Class AA

Team	Affiliation	Parent Club
Alexandria, Louisiana	PDC	San Diego
Amarillo, Texas	PDC	San Francisco
El Paso, Texas	PDC	California
LIttle Rock, Arkansas	PDC	St. Louis
Midland, Texas	Owned	Chicago, NL
San Antonio, Texas	PDC	Cleveland
Shreveport, Louisiana	PDC	Milwaukee
Victoria, Texas	PDC	New York, NL

Southern League, Class AA

Team	Affiliation	Parent Club
Asheville, North Carolina	PDC	Baltimore
Birmingham, Alabama	Owned	Oakland
Columbus, Georgia	PDC	Houston
Jacksonville, Florida	PDC	Kansas City
Knoxville, Tennessee	PDC	Chicago, AL
Montgomery, Alabama	PDC	Detroit
Orlando, Florida	Owned	Minnesota
Savannah, Georgia	Owned	Atlanta

Team	Type of Affiliation	Parent Club
Eastern League, Class AA		
Bristol, Connecticut	PDC	Boston
Pittsfield, Massachusetts	PDC	Texas
Quebec City, Quebec	PDC	Montreal
Reading, Pennsylvania	PDC	Philadelphia
Thetford Mines, Quebec	PDC	Pittsburgh
Three Rivers, Ouebec	PDC	Cincinnati
Waterbury, Connecticut	PDC	Los Angeles
West Haven, Connecticut	PDC	New York, AL
California League, Class A		
Bakersfield, California	PDC	Los Angeles
Fresno, California	PDC	San Francisco
Lodi, California	PDC	Baltimore
Modesto, California	PDC	St. Louis
Reno, Nevada	PDC	Cleveland
Salinas, California	PDC	California
San Jose, California	PDC	Kansas City
Visalia, California	Owned	New York, NL
Carolina League, Class A		
Kinston, North Carolina	PDC	Montreal
Lynchburg, Virginia	PDC	Minnesota
Peninsula, Virginia (Hampton and Newport News, Virginia)	Co-op [2]	
Rocky Mount, North Carolina	PDC	Philadelphia/Texas
Salem, Virginia	PDC	Pittsburgh
Winston-Salem, North Carolina	PDC	Boston

[2] "Co-op" means that two or more major league organizations share PDC arrangements with one minor league team.

Team	Type of Affiliation	Parent Club
Western Carolinas League, Class A		
Anderson, South Carolina	PDC	New York NL
Charleston, South Carolina	PDC	Pittsburgh
Gastonia, North Carolina	PDC	Texas
Greenwood, South Carolina	Owned	Atlanta
Orangeburg, South Carolina		Los Angeles
Spartanburg, South Carolina	Owned	Philadelphia

Team	Type of Affiliation	Parent Club

Florida State League, Class A

Team	Type of Affiliation	Parent Club
Daytona Beach, Florida	Owned	Los Angeles
Fort Lauderdale, Florida	Owned	New York, AL
Key West, Florida		Chicago, NL
Lakeland, Florida	PDC	Detroit
Miami, Florida	Owned	Baltimore
St. Petersburg, Florida	PDC	St. Louis
Tampa, Florida	PDC	Cincinnati
West Palm Beach, Florida	PDC	Montreal
Winter Haven, Florida	Owned	Boston

Midwest League, Class A

Team	Type of Affiliation	Parent Club
Appleton, Wisconsin (Fox Cities)	PDC	Chicago, AL
Burlington, Iowa	PDC	Oakland
Cedar Rapids, Iowa	PDC	Houston
Clinton, Iowa	PDC	Detroit
Danville, Illinois	PDC	Milwaukee
Davenport, Iowa (Quad Cities)	PDC	California
Decatur, Illinois	PDC	San Francisco
Dubuque, Iowa	Co-op	
Waterloo, Iowa	PDC	Kansas City
Wisconsin Rapids, Wisconsin	PDC	Minnesota

New York–Pennsylvania League, Class A

Team	Type of Affiliation	Parent Club
Auburn, New York	PDC	Philadelphia
Batavia, New York	PDC	New York, NL
Elmira, New York	PDC	Boston
Newark–Wayne, New York	PDC	Milwaukee
Niagara Falls, New York	PDC	Pittsburgh
Oneonta, New York	PDC	New York, AL

Northwest League, Class A

Team	Type of Affiliation	Parent Club
Bellingham, Washington	PDC	Los Angeles
Eugene, Oregon	Independent	
Kennewick–Pasco–Richland, Washington (Tri-Cities)	Independent	

Team	Type of Affiliation	Parent Club
Lewiston, Idaho	PDC	Oakland
New Westminster, British Columbia	Independent	
Portland, Oregon	Independent	
Seattle, Washington	PDC	Cincinnati
Walla Walla, Washington	PDC	San Diego

Appalachian League, Rookie

Bluefield, West Virginia	———	Baltimore
Bristol, Virginia	———	Detroit
Covington, Virginia	———	Houston
Elizabethton, Tennessee	———	Minnesota
Johnson City, Tennessee	———	New York, AL
Kingsport, Tennessee	———	Atlanta
Marion, Virginia	———	New York, NL
Pulaski, Virginia	———	Philadelphia

Pioneer League, Rookie

Billings, Montana	———	Cincinnati
Great Falls, Montana	———	San Francisco
Idaho Falls, Idaho	———	California
Ogden, Utah	Co-op	

Gulf Coast League, Rookie [3]

Chicago, AL
Chicago, NL
Cleveland
Kansas City
Pittsburgh
St. Louis
Texas

[3] The Chicago (AL), Cleveland, Kansas City, and St. Louis and Texas teams are based at **Sarasota, Florida;** the **Chicago (NL),** and Pittsburgh, teams are based at Bradenton, Florida. The Kansas City Royals have two teams represented games in this circuit. (Note: The Baseball Academy was closed at the end of the 1974 season.)

| | Type of | |
| Team | Affiliation | Parent Club |

Mexican Center Class A [4]

Team		Parent Club
Aguascalientes		Mexico City Tigers
Ciudad de Valles		Poza Rica
Ciudad Mante		Tampico
Ciudad Victoria		Monterrey
Durango		Saltillo
Ebano		Mexico City Reds
San Pedro		Union Laguna
		(Gomez Palacio)
Zacatecas		Guadalajara

[4] Both the Class AAA Mexican League and Class A Mexican Center League are members of the National Association, but they maintain no direct affiliation with clubs in the U.S. major leagues. All eight teams in the Mexican Center League are, however, affiliated with clubs in the Class AAA circuit. For a list of teams in the Class AAA circuit see Chapter 14.

3

BRANCH RICKEY:
The Father of Baseball's
Farm System

Since Branch Wesley Rickey ranks as one of the prime movers in the development of professional baseball in the twentieth century, it is almost impossible to adequately summarize his lengthy and varied career in a relatively short essay. Therefore, we shall concentrate on his work in structuring the farm system, which prepared players for the major leagues, as well as give an assessment of his overall contributions to baseball. In Chapter 10 on the Texas League, we shall touch on his playing career in the minors and majors as a catcher. No one, including Rickey himself, ever claimed that he was an outstanding player, yet he went on to master every phase of the game from the way it is played on the field to the technicalities of running an entire organization from either the general manager's or president's office. He became considered as the best judge and shrewdest trader of baseball talent on the entire professional scene.

A descendant of pioneers, Rickey was born on a farm at Lucasville, Ohio, on December 20, 1881. His parents, Jacob Franklin and Emily Brown Rickey, were known to everyone as "Uncle Frank" and "Aunt Emma." As farmers, they were not too well off financially, but they were recognized for their piety and for Frank Rickey's talents as a wrestler. "Weck," as young Branch came to be called, was brought up in the strict Wesleyan tradition. The second of three brothers, he was never known to drink, use profanity, or work on Sunday, although he did indulge in cigars when he reached maturity.

The boy read widely, and after graduating from the local grammar school–high school, he was hired to teach in a neighboring schoolhouse eighteen miles from his home. He bought himself a bicycle on which to travel, and from his $35 per month salary, he bought books from which he taught himself Latin, rhetoric, and higher mathematics. Within two years he also managed to save $100 or so for college, and in 1900, at the age of 18, he entered Ohio Wesleyan University at Delaware. A good athlete, Rickey organized football and baseball teams. On the baseball team, he was always the manager and catcher. As catcher he could view the entire diamond and give directions to his men.

Rickey paid his way through the university as a professional athlete, playing baseball in the summer and football in the fall and winter. He played semi–pro baseball at first and then broke into Organized Baseball with Terre Haute in the Central League in 1903. He finished that campaign with LeMars, Iowa, of the Iowa–South Dakota League, spent the 1904 season with Dallas of the Texas League, and then from 1905 through 1907 played for St. Louis and New York in the American League with another stopover at Dallas. From that point his playing career was over, except for a one-game appearance he made with the St. Louis Americans in 1914. While catching for the New York Highlanders in the June 28, 1907, game, he had permitted Washington to steal thirteen bases in one game—an all-time American League record!

While doing all this playing, Rickey doggedly had pursued his studies. He had received his bachelor of literature degree in 1904 and his bachelor of arts degree in 1906 from Ohio Wesleyan. Then in 1911 he took a degree in civil law from the University of Michigan. While studying law at Michigan, he also coached the baseball team, and it was there that he discovered George Sisler whom he recommended to the St. Louis Americans.

In 1913, Rickey became a scout for the St. Louis Browns, covering particular teams on the Pacific coast. Late in the season he was appointed field manager, a post he held through 1915. In Rickey's two full years as pilot, the Browns finished in fifth and sixth places, whereas in the preceding four years they had landed in the basement three times and finished seventh once. When the ownership of the Browns changed in 1916 and Phil Ball became president, Rickey gave up managing and moved up into the front office as vice-president and business manager (the term "business manager" in effect meant "general manager").

Meanwhile, a group of St. Louis businessmen had formed a syndicate to purchase the St. Louis Cardinals in the National League, and they wanted Rickey, now a popular figure in town, to take over as club president. Rickey, none too happy working under the abrasive blustering Ball with his high voltage adjectives, accepted the offer. Ball refused to release his vice-president, but Rickey, a skilled attorney, went to court to prove that his contract allowed him to switch positions if a better one was offered. (Several years later, when Donald Barnes bought the Browns from the Ball estate, Rickey represented both parties and received a reported attorney's fee of $25,000.)

Rickey was to spend the next twenty-five years with the Cardinals. He took on managerial duties in 1919 and held those reins until June 1, 1925. In the meantime Sam Breadon succeeded Rickey as president in 1920. After Rickey gave up his field duties, he ran the club's day-to-day operations as vice-president–business manager until he went to the Brooklyn Dodgers as president in 1942.

At first Rickey had tough sledding financially with the Cardinals, who had not won a National League pennant since they entered the league in 1876! In 1919, the club was nearly $200,000 in debt and could hardly meet basic operating expenses. "We didn't even have the money to send the club south for spring training," Rickey recalled years later, "so we trained at home. We even wore the same uniforms at home and on the road. . . . I had to pass up my salary to meet the payroll. It was really rugged." On one occasion Rickey purloined a rug from his own house, without his wife's knowledge, to brighten his bare office when important visitors were expected.

The Cardinals' financial difficulties soon became widely known throughout baseball. Of course, the situation put Rickey at a tremendous disadvantage when he tried to obtain talent from the minor leagues. For example, a minor league executive whom Rickey approached would wire a richer team, indicating that if Rickey was after a certain player that player must be good, and the other organization would be in a better position to make an offer for him. And all too often when Rickey turned over a hot prospect of his to a minor league team for seasoning, the minor team's general manager would double-cross him and sell his discovery to another team in the majors. "That kind of thing drove me mad," declared Rickey, "I pondered long on it, and finally concluded that, if we were too poor to buy, we would have to raise our own."

During that fateful 1919 season, the Cardinal chief decided on an action that was to eventually transform the entire minor league organization by establishing the "farm system," with the major league teams owning or controlling a hierarchy of clubs in the minors. Rickey began on a modest scale when he quietly bought eighteen percent of the Houston Buffaloes in the Texas League early in 1920. (The Cardinals eventually gained control of Houston while Rickey tried not to make public this acquisition. See Chapter 10.) Then later in 1920 he acquired working control of Forth Smith, Arkansas, in the Class C Western Association. After Sam Breadon took over the Cardinals' presidency

Rickey held only the title of field manager, but he continued to have almost a *carte blanche* in expanding St. Louis' farm holdings.

The "Mahatma," as Rickey came to be called, soon discovered that part ownership was unsatisfactory—there were too many chances for conflicts to develop—so he had Breadon buy up minor league teams outright. In *The St. Louis Cardinals* (1944), Frederick G. Lieb, said, "Rickey even went so far as to back entire leagues, and at one time he controlled the entire player supply in the Nebraska State and Arkansas–Missouri Leagues." But all this was too much for baseball commissioner Kenesaw Mountain Landis. An opponent of Rickey's farm system idea from the start, Landis limited the Cardinals to one club in each of these leagues. But "Farmer Branch" went right out and found big league sponsors for the rest of the teams in order to keep the leagues going.

As we saw in Chapter 1, Commissioner Landis fined the Cardinals in 1938 for maintaining "secret working agreements" with three minor league clubs. In handing down that ruling, Landis also declared seventy-three Cardinals farmhands as free agents.

The whole farm system idea was first ridiculed and then vitriolically attacked as "Rickey's chain gang," but it produced a legion of players who became stars in the big leagues. Within a few years, however, those very teams which had derided Rickey's farm system were organizing their own and at the same time were willing to pay handsome prices for *surplus* farm-bred Cardinal players. Branch Rickey raised so much top caliber talent that he couldn't use it all.

By 1940, the Cardinals owned thirty-two clubs outright and had working agreements with eight others, involving a total of more than 600 players. The only Class D league in which St. Louis fielded no entry was in Canada. Thus, Rickey directed a baseball empire that was approximately thirty percent as extensive as the entire minor league operation in 1973 when 136 teams were active in 18 leagues. In order to understand the magnitude of the Cardinals' farm system in the 1930s, we might indicate that in 1973 no team in baseball owned outright or had working agreements with more than seven teams (the Kansas City Royals led the list with seven), while one team owned outright or had working agreements with only three teams (the San Diego Padres). A usual practice for big league teams today is to work with only five minor league clubs, the ideal setup being to have one team each in the Class AAA and AA circuits as well as either one in Class A and two in the rookie leagues or two in Class A and one in the rookie leagues. In 1973, the New York Mets, who have a bigger than average budget for player development, had one team each in Class AAA and Class AA, three in Class A and one in the rookie league. All this pales in comparison with the scope of the Cardinals' farm operation before World War II.

Strangely enough, Rickey never had great success as a field manager —at least he never lived up to expectations in his stewardship with the Cardinals. He never finished higher than third (he did that twice, in 1921 and 1922) came in sixth in his last full season as pilot (1924), and had his Cardinals firmly lodged in eighth place on May 31, 1925, when he was succeeded as manager by his star second baseman, Rogers Hornsby. (Rickey and Hornsby never got along, and relations were particularly strained after the two had a fistfight during the midst of the 1923 season. To make matters worse, Hornsby spent a good part of the time on the bench that year despite his .384 batting average.) Rickey moved up to the post of vice-president and general manager and directed the team's fortunes from the front office.

As a manager Rickey was criticized for employing "too much theory and too little practice." Roy Stockton, St. Louis baseball writer, once said, "There wasn't anything wrong with Rickey's baseball theories. Major league managers adopted many of Rickey's innovations—blackboard talks, sliding pits, plays to catch runners off base, and others—but his players often could not understand or execute his ideas."

Still, Rickey's greatest contribution was in getting those players who won pennants for the Cardinals under his general managership in 1926, 1928, 1930, 1931, and 1942. Moreover, in the nonchampionship years his teams were usually contenders—a remarkable achievement considering that historically St. Louis had been a National League doormat. Rickey's estimates of players were not always without error–he touted many prospects as sure-fire stars, only to see them flop under big league fire—but his overall track record for judging talent had no peer.

Only a few weeks after the Cardinals won the 1942 World Series, Rickey suddenly switched over to the Brooklyn Dodgers as president and general manager. (Sam Breadon did not renew Rickey's contract primarily because he was averaging over $75,000 a year with his salary and bonus arrangement, the highest income in baseball at the time. Breadon said he could no longer afford the expense.)

At the time Rickey took over the Dodgers' organization, the farm system was extensive, thanks in part to the efforts of Branch Rickey, Jr., who had been the Dodgers' farm director since 1939.

While serving as major domo at Brooklyn for nine years (1942–50), the senior Rickey saw the Cardinal teams he had built up through his farm system win three more pennants (in 1943, 1944, and 1946) and remain a respected power even in those years when the team did not get into the World Series.

Rickey went on to improve further the Dodger's farm system as well as to strengthen the entire organization. In 1945, for example, he effected a major extension in the team's minor league operations by purchasing the Fort Worth Cats in the Texas League. He succeeded in establishing a dynasty; since 1942, the Dodgers, both in Brooklyn and after their move to Los Angeles in 1958, have won the National League pennant ten times. His signing of Jackie Robinson to a 1946 contract with Montreal—the Montreal Royals at the time ranked as the Dodgers' top farm club—resulted in the breaking of the game's color line, an act which had a tremendous impact on baseball (see Chapter 8).

From 1951 through 1959, Rickey served with the Pittsburgh Pirates first as vice-president–general manager and then as chairman of the board of directors. The Pirates won no pennants while Rickey was in the front office, but they did become a National League power in the 1960s and early 1970s, largely with the players he had obtained from other teams or developed in his farm system. Roberto Clemente was one of Rickey's prime acquisitions. Rickey then served as president of the ill-fated Continental League, which he envisioned as a third major league circuit. Though the Continental never came into existence, it forced the expansion of the American and National leagues to ten and then twelve teams each.

He spent the remaining two years of his long career in Organized Baseball (1963–65) with his old team, the St. Louis Cardinals, as a "special consultant" to the president, August A. Busch, Jr. Rickey suffered a heart attack on November 13, 1965, at Columbia, Missouri, while in the midst of a speech accepting his induction into the Missouri Sports Hall of Fame. He died at Columbia on December 9 of that year.

George "Sparky" Anderson, the very successful manager of the Cincinnati Reds, recently made the statement that Rickey's influence upon the National League is still clearly apparent. Anderson gave Rickey credit for enabling the senior circuit to catch and then pass up the American League as the dominant force in major league baseball.

American League fans may not agree with this assessment, but Anderson maintains that the National League has star players in much greater depth than the junior circuit. Anderson bases his contention partially on the fact that the Nationals have won 22 of the last 27 All-Star games, and 11 of the last 12. Asked his reason for the National League's supposed superiority, Anderson replied:

The only solid reason I can point to is that one man ran through this league and never touched the other league: Branch Rickey. He built the Cardinals, the Dodgers, and the Pirates and his influence is still around. There are a lot a people around who are Rickey's disciples who are still doing things his way.

Doing things Rickey's way means well-organized scouting and a good system of farm clubs. Mr. Rickey always put the highest priority on speed. He always wanted players who could throw hard, run fast, and play defense. That's the kind of players we have in our league.

In paying tribute to Rickey after his death, *The Sporting News,* generally conservative in offering opinions, said; "Branch Rickey over a period of many years demonstrated *true genius* as a baseball executive."

In 1967, Branch Wesley Rickey was voted into baseball's Hall of Fame at Cooperstown, an honor that many baseball men thought was long overdue.

4

FRANK SHAUGHNESSY AND THE
SHAUGHNESSY PLAYOFFS

Frank "Shag" Shaughnessy (1883–1969) ranks as one of the great figures in minor league history. He is perhaps best-remembered today for having devised the so-called "Shaughnessy Playoffs," which are generally acknowledged to have saved the minors from almost total financial ruin in the depression-ridden 1930s.

Prior to the early 1930s many minor leagues conducted no postseason playoffs at all. A league's championship team was determined solely by the teams' positions in the won–lost column, at the end of the season. Other leagues played split-season schedules, with the first- and second-half champions meeting in a postseason playoff for the overall league title. There was no playoff, of course, if the same team won both the first- and second-half titles.

Under the Shaughnessy plan, four teams in an eight-team league qualify for postseason playoffs. Teams finishing first and fourth would meet in a semifinal series, while the second- and third-place finishers would engage at the same time. Then, the winners in the semifinals logically would meet for the league crown in the finals. The International League placed both the semifinals and the final on a best of seven games basis, while other circuits set the semifinals at the best of five games and the finals at the best of seven.

The International League instituted the Shaughnessy Playoffs in 1933, and many other circuits across the country adopted the plan at the same time or shortly thereafter: the Texas League in 1933, the Southern Association in 1935, the Pacific Coast League and the American Association in 1936, and the Middle Atlantic League and the Eastern League in 1937.

The Shaughnessy Playoffs had an immediate positive impact on the participating leagues. No longer would fans lose interest in a pennant race if a team took a big early lead and walked away with the percentage championship. Interest could now be sustained for the entire season with the race for *fourth place* being hotly contested, since that was the last playoff spot. Heretofore, fourth place meant next to nothing, but with the advent of Shaughnessy's system, there are many cases where two teams finished the regular season in a fourth-place tie, necessitating a single-game playoff to see who would get that last precious playoff position.

Playoffs generally drew very well, with full houses becoming common occurrences for these games. One team could take part in as many as fourteen postseason contests if it had to go the full seven in both the semifinals and finals. Since one team could play seven of those playoff games at home, it could increase its season's paid attendance by perhaps as many as 100,000 paid. This might easily make the difference between finishing deep in the red or well into the black ink. This is exactly what happened to the Rochester Red Wings on several occasions.

Despite the instant popularity of the playoffs, there were still a great many people who did not like them at all, including National Association president William G. Bramham. The Shaughnessy plan came in for bitter attacks later when some leagues chose to award the pennant to the winner of the postseason series. There were numerous cases where a club had battled hard all season to finish on top of the heap only to be knocked out of the postseason series in the first round. Buffalo, for example, finished fourth in the International League in 1933 at under .500 (.494), but went on to win the playoffs and represent the circuit in the Junior World Series. Still, the league keeps a dual listing of champs: Newark as the 1933 pennant winner at .622 and Buffalo as the playoff winner.

Other leagues did not even bother with dual listings since the official championship trophy was awarded to the percentage (pennant) winner. The Shaughnessy Playoffs were considered only as an extra afterpiece. The Pacific Coast League is perhaps the most important minor league to have handled the Shaughnessy plan in this manner.

The recent trend has been to split leagues into two divisions ("eastern–western," "northern–southern," etc.). The PCL now has a simple playoff plan in which the two division winners meet for a best out of five series and that's it. The International League is not quite so simple. In its divisional plan, inaugurated in 1973, the leaders of the American and National divisions meet for a best of five, as do the second-place finishers. The winners of the semifinals then meet for the league crown and the right to represent the circuit in the Junior World Series. In 1973, Pawtucket, a second-place finisher in the American Division, came on to win all the marbles in the playoffs and then went on to victory against Tulsa of the American Association in the Junior World Series.

FRANK SHAUGHNESSY

Frank Shaughnessy, the man who succeeded in making the minor leagues playoff-conscious, enjoyed an Organized Baseball career that spanned some sixty years. A native of Amboy, Illinois, he had experience in all aspects of the game—as a player, as a manager and as league president.

Shaughnessy, an outfielder, saw brief major league service in the American League—he was with Washington in 1905 and Philadelphia in 1908—but he spent many years as a player and manager in the minors. While serving as player–manager for Roanoke in the Class C Virginia League in 1909, he led the circuit in home runs with the majestic total of five. He had the distinction of winning six pennants in four different leagues: with Roanoke in the Virginia League (1909), with Fort Wayne in the Class C Central League (1912), with Ottawa in the Class C Canadian League (1913, 1914, 1915), and with Montreal in the Class AA International League (1935).

"Shag" Shaughnessy spent the better part of his long tenure in Organized Baseball in the International League. He managed Syracuse, Providence, and Reading in the 1920s; became general manager of Montreal in 1932; and served as the Royals' field manager from 1934 through 1936. He then was elected a president of the International League, a post he held until his retirement in 1960 at the age of seventy-seven. It was while he was general manager at Montreal that he devised and sold his playoff plan to the minors.

In the 1950s Shaughnessy strongly recommended a flat ban on all major league television into minor league cities, a recommendation that was not followed. He died at Montreal on May 15, 1969, at the age of eighty-six.

5

GEORGE WEISS:
The Last of the Empire Builders

George Weiss (1894–1972), one of baseball's most successful executives at both the minor and major league levels, earned induction into baseball's Hall of Fame solely on the strength of his front office talents. Weiss did play a few games of baseball as a high school student, but even in his adolescent years he was more interested in promoting games than in participating in them.

A native of New Haven, Connecticut, Weiss became business manager of the New Haven High School team while a student there. Then after graduation he turned the club into a semi-pro outfit. While a junior at Yale in 1915, he became manager and director of the New Haven Colonials, a fast semi-pro team that soon rivaled the New Haven entry in the professional Eastern League. Weiss' Colonials often outdrew the local professionals.

The New Haven professionals did not play on Sundays because of Blue Laws that affected Organized Baseball, and Weiss proceeded to fill the Sunday afternoon vacuum by scheduling numerous attention-getting opponents for his Colonials. He imported a Chinese team, a "bloomer girls" team, and a major league all-star team led by the great Ty Cobb (who would appear while his Detroit Tiger teammates were idle in either Boston or New York).

At first Cobb, a shrewd businessman in his own right, insisted on a $350 guarantee to make the trip to New Haven. However, when Weiss voluntarily gave him a check for $800, Cobb was so impressed that he came back frequently—with no written guarantees.

Weiss loaded his Colonials' lineup with top college athletes, like Charley Brickley and Eddie Mahan of Harvard and big leaguers like Wally Pipp of the New York Yankees. In a game in mid-October 1916, the Colonials defeated the Boston Red Sox, who had Babe Ruth playing first base. The Red Sox had won the World Series against Brooklyn just three days earlier!

In 1919, the owners of the New Haven franchise in the Eastern League decided that competing with Weiss for local support was too difficult, and they offered him the club for $5,000. "I had to borrow every bit of the $5,000," Weiss later recalled, "but I realized this was an opportunity that could not be passed up."

Weiss operated the New Haven club for ten years, and during that period, he used his business and professional skills to help the entire Eastern League during the 1920s. He built a new ball park, appropriately named "Weiss Park," in New Haven, and at its opening in 1920 the publicity proclaimed "the park is insured against fire, wind, rain, and earthquake."

Early in 1929, the directors of the Baltimore Orioles in the International League invited George Weiss to become the club's general manager. Sensing a challenge, he accepted the offer and sold his holdings in New Haven. Weiss had a tough act to follow for he succeeded Jack Dunn, the long-time Orioles' president–general manager. Dunn had died the previous October after falling from a horse.

The Depression struck soon after Weiss began his tenure in Baltimore, but he managed to meet expenses by selling a dozen or so players to various clubs in the majors over a three-year period. He also tried all kinds of promotional schemes, such as "ladies' night," to draw more people into the park. After his first ladies' night, Weiss recalled, "It would have been considered a success if fifty ladies turned out, but 5,500 showed up!"

In the fall of 1931, Weiss met Colonel Jacob Ruppert, owner of the New York Yankees, at the annual minor league meeting held that year in West Baden, Indiana. Ruppert induced him to join the Yankees as farm director, a position that Weiss formally accepted in February 1932. Ruppert was greatly impressed with the St. Louis Cardinals' success in establishing their farm system under Branch Rickey, and he too wanted to enter the "chain store" business of developing talent.

Ruppert had just purchased the Newark Bears of the International League (his first venture in owning a farm club). He wanted to add others to his holdings, and he thought that Weiss was the best man to run the operation. Ed Barrow, the Yankees' general manager who recommended Weiss to Ruppert, said, "He knows as much about minor league baseball as anyone in the country. He knows the International League especially."

Weiss remained with the Yankees for twenty-eight years, the first fifteen as farm director and the remaining thirteen as general manager. During that span the Yankees won nineteen pennants, and Weiss is given much of the credit for that record because of his ability in developing the organization's highly-productive farm system and because of his overall baseball expertise.

By the mid-1930s, Weiss built up the Yankees' farm system to a total of some fifteen teams which New York either owned outright or sponsored on a working agreement basis. He carefully constructed the system with the foundation being several Class D teams, where a promising young player was introduced into professional baseball. He then made sure that the Yankees had representation in every other minor league classification right through to the Class AAA level, where the player was given his final grooming before being sent into the big league wars.

Weiss often shifted affiliations and sometimes got down to nine or ten teams. Just before World War II his system included nine teams. There were three Class D clubs: Butler in the Pennsylvania State Association, Wellsville in the Pony League, and Fond du Lac in the Wisconsin State League. Ranging just above were two clubs in Class C leagues: Amsterdam in the Canadian–American and Joplin in the Western Association. Then came Norfolk in the Class B Piedmont League and Binghamton in the Class A Eastern League. Finally, Weiss topped off his farm system with two Class AA teams: Newark in the International and Kansas City in the American Association. (The AAA classification did not then exist.)

George Weiss had a hand in signing virtually every player who saw action with the Yankees during the 1932–60 period, whether the player was brought along in the farm system or obtained from another major league team. We could hardly begin to mention all the Yankees Weiss signed in his long career, but we might at least cite one specifically: Lawrence Peter "Yogi" Berra. Weiss prepared Berra's first professional contract in late 1942 (Yogi was just seventeen at the time), a contract calling for assignment to Norfolk, Virginia, in the Class B Piedmont League for the 1943 season. The contract stipulated a salary of $90 per month and $500 bonus "to be paid if retained until September 20, 1943." Berra was retained for over twenty years, and he eventually made well in excess of $60,000 per year.

GEORGE WEISS AND CASEY STENGEL

After the Yankees lost the 1960 World Series to Pittsburgh, both Weiss and manager Casey Stengel (whom he had recommended for the pilot's post in 1949) were "retired," as the New York front office switched to what was described as a "youth movement."

Weiss did not stay retired for very long; in early 1961, he was appointed as the first president of the newly-organized New York Mets. In one of his first acts he hired Stengel as his manager, a move that helped insure the team's popularity, even though the Mets began by foundering and playing clownlike baseball. Weiss held the Mets presidency for more than five years, retiring on November 14, 1966, at the age of seventy-two.

When Weiss won election to the Hall of Fame in 1971, his admirers pointed to the fact that while with the Yankees he was chosen as Major League Executive of the Year a record ten times. He died at Greenwich, Connecticut, on August 13, 1972.

Casey Stengel, who first met Weiss in 1925 when he was player–manager at Worcester in the Eastern League, made the following comments after he learned of the death of his old boss:

> Whenever I was discharged that fine fellow George Weiss would find out about it and would reemploy me. . . . He was successful and great and capable in every way, shape, and form. He was high class. He didn't talk rough, and he wanted you to have three clean uniforms, but play hard enough to slide when you had to. He wasn't a terrific mixer, but George sure knew how to pick men. Why, you can't stay in baseball that long by pulling players out of an icebox.

THE FREE-AGENT DRAFT

George Weiss had his critics as well as his admirers. Some critics blamed him, at least in part, for the Yankees' slide which began in mid-1960s and gave him little credit for the Mets' almost sudden rise to power. They said the Yankees had been seriously weakened by his resistance to big cash bonuses for promising young players. He was also accused of having been tightfisted in general.

In reply, his supporters pointed out that the Yankees could always depend upon a steady stream of talent from the farm system personally built by Weiss. The Yankees, they stoutly maintained, really had been undermined by a series of new rules designed to strengthen the weaker clubs and to channel more talent their way.

The new rules are embodied in part in the Free-Agent Player Draft, which went into effect on May 1, 1965. Under the provisions of this legislation, clubs are no longer permitted to sign free agents at will, but must *select for the right to negotiate,* the same as in professional basketball and football. The regulation applies only to players who are residents of the United States.

At first, players were drafted at three selections meetings annually, but now selections are held twice yearly, at a winter meeting in January and at a summer meeting in June. "Free agents" are roughly defined as those players not under professional contract. For example, college athletes, sandlot players, and others generally referred to as "raw talent," are "free agents."

Both the January and June sessions are conducted in two phases. One covers the regular group of eligible players and the other, known as a "special phase," embraces those who were drafted at a previous meeting but did not sign. The key provision in the regular phase is that clubs draft in the *reverse order of their standings of the previous season* (priority in the special phase is determined by lot). Thus, the Kansas City Athletics, who finished in last place (tenth place) in the American League in 1964, had first choice in the first Free-Agent Draft held in 1965; while the New York Mets, the National League's cellar dwellers in 1964, received second pick. The American and National leagues alternate each year as to the first pick.

According to the provisions of the draft agreement, as written in 1965, major league clubs may select just one player in each phase of each meeting, while Class AAA teams are permitted two selections, each Class AA team four, and each Class A team as many as desired. Since virtually every minor league club in the United States has a big league tieup, all selections in effect are made by the parent organizations.

At the first free-agent draft meeting held at the Commodore Hotel in New York City on June 8–9, 1965, the twenty major league organizations selected negotiation rights to 814 players. The Houston Astros' organization made the most selections, seventy-two.

Once a club drafts a player, it has exclusive negotiating rights with him until fifteen days before the following winter or summer meeting when a "closed period" begins. A selected player who fails to sign before the closed period goes back into the "pot." Of the 814 players selected in the first draft, 426 signed contracts before the fifteen-day closed period preceding the January 29, 1966, selection meeting.

A number of revisions have been made in the free-agent selection system during the past decade, but in essence the plan still works under the original guidelines.

The Free-Agent Draft was also designed to eliminate heavy bonus bidding for raw talent. Before the system went into effect, the Los Angeles Angels (now the California Angels) paid out the biggest bonus in baseball history—a reported $200,000 plus—in June 1964, to land Rick Reichardt, a twenty-one-year-old outfielder and University of Wisconsin junior. Further evidence of heavy spending came when Charles O. Finley, Kansas City's owner, disclosed that the Athletics paid out $634,000 in bonuses during the same year to sign eighty players.

The new system did not eliminate bonuses altogether. In 1965, the Athletics had to come across with $104,000 to sign their number one choice, Rick Monday, highly-touted nineteen-year-old outfielder from Arizona State University. Several other high draft choices also received substantial, though smaller, bonuses. With the elimination of the general bidding contest, however, most clubs effected a considerable reduction in their outlay for new talent.

There is no question that the draft system has resulted in a more equal distribution of promising young players all across the big league front. The wealthy clubs can no longer dominate the raw talent market through the use of their fat bankrolls as they once did.

It should also be noted that Kansas City (now the Oakland A's) and the New York Mets, both of whom were in a position to pick the cream of the crop in the early draft sessions because of their low standings at the time, have fielded powerful teams in recent years. In an ironic touch, it was the A's and the Mets who clashed in October 1973 for the World Series title.

In recent years the rules have also been changed so that the amount of time a major league organization can control the contract of a minor league player is reduced. If a player is not promoted to the major leagues after three seasons in the minors, he becomes subject to the draft by any higher classification club. No longer can a major league organization "bury" a potential star within its farm system for six or seven years as once was possible.

Thus, it is now impossible for any big league club to control a huge pool of top talent as it was during Weiss' tenure with the New York Yankees. With the institution of this significant new body of rules and regulations strictly governing the administration of professional baseball, George Weiss is properly called "the last of the empire builders."

6

HENRY J. PETERS:
An Interview and a Look into the Future

We interviewed at length Henry J. Peters, National Association president, concerning the future of the minors as well as primary problems concerning the professional game. Following are three of our questions and Peters' replies.

(Q) "What is the outlook for minor league baseball for the future, at least for the decade ahead?"

(A) "I believe the future of minor league baseball is a solid one. I base that opinion on two factors. First, the fans around the country have proven by their attendance at minor league games that they enjoy professional baseball and want it in their communities. Secondly, the relationship which minor league baseball has with the major leagues. It is my opinion that the physical and mental demands required of a player to perform successfully in the major leagues are such that very few players can move right from the amateur ranks to the major leagues. These players need to develop their skills and gain maturity by performing in the minor leagues. Therefore, even though the major leagues don't particularly like to spend large amounts of money on player development, no one has yet devised a way for a player to develop other than by playing competitively in the minor leagues. As long as the minor leagues continue to provide the highly-skilled and mature players and as long as there is a need for player talent in the major leagues, the minors are here to stay."

(Q) "What are the greatest needs of the minors? Better parks? A different relationship with the majors? Better promotion by club owners?"

(A) "Certainly we must recognize that minor league clubs are in competition for the entertainment dollar available in their communities. People today are more *quality conscious* than ever before, and when they spend their dollars, they want the best. For this reason we can't expect to attract fans to parks that are not comfortable and properly maintained. We must continue to do all we can to improve facilities throughout the minor leagues. It's almost impossible to do this solely with private capital, although there have been a few cases where parks have been built or greatly improved with private moneys in recent years.

"I happen to believe that a community would be wise to invest its tax dollars by updating or providing new multipurpose stadium facilities that can accommodate professional baseball teams as well as teams in other sports or activities apart from athletics. I happen to believe that every community needs its park and recreational programs. Cities spend generous amounts of tax dollars to build and maintain swimming pools, tennis courts, hockey rinks, and many other types of recreational facilities. I really don't see why a stadium, simply because it is used by a professional baseball club, should be excluded from tax dollar support.

"Business management of minor league clubs is another important area of concern. Yes, we have many fine operators in minor leagues of all classifications, but unfortunately not enough. Eventually, we hope to implement a program which will attract more top-caliber administrators to Organized Baseball, men who will want to spend their careers in club management. A good sound business manager, or general manager, conducting a well-executed promotional program can expect to show excellent financial returns from his operation.

"While the major leagues have continued to contribute substantially to the support of minor league baseball, I do believe that it is time for the relationship to be reevaluated. For example, the minor leagues can do even more in certain areas in assisting the major league teams in carrying out their player development programs. At the same time the big leagues can do much more in helping the minors with their problems, including in the area of promotional activities."

(Q) "What are some of the major problems facing the president of the National Association?"

(A) "One particularly nagging problem we have—and it is a continuing one—has to do with the negative attitude of many groups of people, particularly those in the news media, toward minor league baseball as a whole. Yes, the minor leagues have struggled in the past, and they will always have to struggle to survive, but professional baseball below

the major league level today doesn't present as bleak a picture as some so-called sports 'experts' make it out to be. The minor leagues in the 1970s are certainly alive and well. In fact, the entire minor league apparatus today is much more streamlined, more efficient, and healthier than it was in the past."

Of the approximately 12,000 men who have played in the big leagues during the past century, only a comparative handful never served an apprenticeship in the minors. Stars like Walter Johnson, Mel Ott, Bob Feller, and Al Kaline, who arrived in the majors directly from the sandlots or high school, are rare in the annals of baseball.

In recent years we have also seen Dave Roberts, a twenty-one-year-old infielder, jump directly from the University of Oregon to a regular spot in the San Diego Padres' infield (in May 1972) and David Clyde, an eighteen-year-old fastballer, take the giant leap from the Houston Westchester High School to the Texas Rangers' regular pitching corps (in June 1973). These are rare occurrences and bring banner headlines in the sports pages. Part of the headline stories naturally deal with the fat bonuses young phenoms like this receive for signing contracts—Roberts and Clyde are reported to have received approximately $100,000 each.

Nevertheless, the preponderant majority of all the great stars of the game have spent time honing their skills in the minors before they earned promotion to the majors. Ty Cobb, Babe Ruth, Rogers Hornsby, Lou Gehrig, Jimmy Foxx, Joe DiMaggio, Stan Musial, and Hank Aaron all served in the minors. Carl Hubbell and Dazzy Vance, two Hall of Fame pitchers, both spent long years beating the bushes before they reached the majors, Hubbell six years and Vance nearly ten.

While there may not be nearly as many minor leagues today as there were twenty to twenty-five years ago, we can say with certainty that college baseball has filled at least part of the vacuum. Dozens of colleges throughout the country—especially those located in the warmer climes of the South, Southwest, and California—maintain topflight baseball programs. Eddie Stanky, veteran major league player and manager, for example, has been head baseball coach at the University of Southern Alabama in Mobile ever since he left the professional wars in 1969.

Even some of the northern schools like the University of Michigan manage to play some serious baseball as early as March and April by taking three or four-week "spring tours" down south.

Arizona State University at Tempe has one of the top baseball programs of any higher institution of education in the country. They play some sixty-five to seventy-five games per year, or about as many as some of the Class A and rookie professional leagues. Arizona State's place in the sun as a collegiate baseball power drew wide attention when Bobby Winkles, its head diamond coach for thirteen years (1959–71) became manager of the California Angels in 1973. Never before in history had anyone jumped from the collegiate coaching ranks into major league managing. Winkles piled up a brilliant 524–173 won–lost record at Arizona State, but he prepped for his coaching assignment by playing minor league ball for seven seasons in five different leagues: the Western League, the Three-I League, the Southern Association, the American Association, and the Texas League. Winkles, who coached Rick Monday and many other future big leaguers at Arizona State, spent a year as an Angels coach before moving up to the pilot's post.

For the past several years, the Kansas City Royals have been experimenting with a Baseball Academy in Sarasota, Florida. The Kansas City organization operates the Academy as a training ground for promising young players that it expects to place on the rosters of its various farm teams and eventually on the roster of the parent club.

The academy, which is really a "college for ball players," has so many coaches and instructors around that they almost bump into each other. The "students" play plenty of intramural games, with the top performers getting to see action with the academy's team in the Gulf Coast Rookie League. If the student does "A" work in the rookie league, then he is permitted to take "postgraduate" work with Kansas City's farm teams in higher classifications, such as San Jose in the Class A California League or Jacksonville in the Class AA Southern League.

Even the academy's best instructors admit that a player's most valuable training comes while he's on the playing field engaged in a professional game. Bobby Winkles, the premier college baseball coach of the current era, has often admitted that his finest Arizona State players, Rick Monday included, needed a good dose of additional seasoning with professional teams before they could take that big step into the major leagues. (Note: The Baseball Academy was closed at the end of the 1974 season.)

PART TWO

7

THE AMERICAN ASSOCIATION:
The Fastest Minor League
in the Midwest

INTRODUCTION TO PART TWO

Author's Note: Seven minor leagues were chosen for detailed discussion in this book, including the six top circuits based in the United States today: the three Class AAA leagues (the American Association, the international League, and the Pacific Coast League) and the three Class AA leagues (the Texas League, the Southern League—including its predecessor the Southern Association—and the Eastern League). Of the more than 250 minor leagues which have passed from the baseball scene, the Class C Middle Atlantic League was selected, primarily because it served as a training ground for some 400 major league players—plus dozens of big league managers, coaches, and executives during its quarter century of operations—from 1925 through 1951. No other lower classification minor league has been that productive.

ROSTER OF AMERICAN ASSOCIATION TEAMS
CLASS A, 1902–07; CLASS AA, 1908–45,
CLASS AAA, 1946–   ) [1]

Team	Years in Operation
Charleston, South Carolina	1952 (Charleston took over the Toledo franchise on June 23), 1953–60
Cleveland, Ohio	1914–15
Columbus, Ohio	1902–54
Dallas, Texas	1959
Dallas–Fort Worth, Texas	1960–62
Denver, Colorado	1955–62, 1969—
Evansville, Indiana	1970—
Fort Worth, Texas	1959
Houston, Texas	1959–61
Indianapolis, Indiana	1902–62, 1969—
Des Moines, Iowa	1969—
Kansas City, Missouri	1902–54
Louisville, Kentucky	1902–62
Milwaukee, Wisconsin	1902–52
Minneapolis, Minnesota	1902–60
Oklahoma City, Oklahoma	1962, 1969—
Omaha, Nebraska	1955–59, 1961–62, 1969—
St. Paul, Minnesota	1902–60
Toledo, Ohio	1902–13 (franchise shifted to Cleveland for 1914–15), 1916–52 (franchise shifted to Charleston for 1953–55)
Tulsa, Oklahoma	1969—
Wichita, Kansas	1956–58, 1970—

The American Association was for many years recognized as the epitome of stability in Organized Baseball. From 1902, the league's first season, until 1952, its membership remained the same, except in 1914–15 when the Toledo Mud Hens operated temporarily in Cleveland. For this period of a half century, the AA's stability matched that of both major leagues, which had not experienced a single franchise shift during the same time span. The first permanent break came on June 23, 1952, when the Toledo franchise was moved to Charleston. When Milwaukee entered the National League in 1953, the Brewers franchise was transferred to Toledo (where it remained until 1955).

[1] See page 323 for Key to Roster of League Teams.

From this point on, franchise shifts came frequently. The shifts were caused by realignments and expansion within the major leagues, as well as by realignments within the minor leagues themselves. The Kansas City franchise was transferred to Denver on November 29, 1954, when Kansas City entered the American League. The trend westward continued as the Columbus franchise was relocated in Omaha on December 1, 1954, while Wichita replaced Toledo beginning in 1956.

In a dramatic move three old-line Texas League teams (Dallas, Fort Worth, and Houston) joined the AA in 1959, boosting the circuit to ten teams and requiring the formation of Eastern and Western divisions composed of five teams each.

The awkward ten-team, two-division setup lasted for only one year, with the league going back to a more orthodox eight-team arrangement in 1960. Franchise shifting continued to be a way of life in the AA, with the loop down to only six teams for 1961 and 1962. Then league officials reluctantly agreed to completely suspend operations.

Attendance was down (only 759,358 total for the six teams in 1962), and the majors (now up to twenty teams) occupied some of the choicest AA territory: Kansas City, Milwaukee, St. Paul–Minneapolis, and Houston. This important territorial factor and the ever-present competition from televised major league games for the baseball dollar were just too much for the AA to swallow.

Denver, Dallas–Fort Worth, and Oklahoma City (the latter town was an AA member in 1962 only) joined the newly-expanded ten-team Pacific Coast League; Indianapolis went to the International League (also a newly expanded ten-team circuit); while Louisville and Omaha temporarily dropped out of Organized Baseball altogether. For Louisville Colonels' baseball fans, this was a particularly hard blow because it marked the first time in over sixty years that the city had been without a professional team. Old-timers down in Kentucky deplored the Colonels closing up shop as being the worst baseball disaster Louisville experienced since the town gave up its longstanding National League franchise to Pittsburgh after the 1899 season.

When franchises were shifted around in the 1950s and 1960s, tradition sometimes was the last thing club owners thought of.

In respect to the American Association's going out of business after the 1962 season, we ought to emphasize that there were only twenty Class AAA teams left at that time. Since there were not enough teams to make up three leagues, one of the leagues had to fold up its tent, at least temporarily.

After its six-year hiatus, the AA pulled itself back together again, and in 1969, it reentered the rough-and-tumble world of Organized Baseball, fielding teams in Denver, Indianapolis, Des Moines, Oklahoma City, Omaha, and Tulsa. Four of the six teams (Denver, Indianapolis, Oklahoma City, and Tulsa) came from the octopuslike twelve-team Pacific Coast League (now reduced to a more manageable eight), which had spread itself almost over the entire country except for the East. In fact, the league's westernmost outpost was Honolulu. Thus, the Pacific Coast League was not unhappy to unload four cities situated well within the country's interior.[2]

Both Des Moines and Omaha were reentering Organized Baseball, since they had no teams in town at the time they joined the AA in 1969.

With the addition of Evansville and Wichita in 1970, the league went back up to a healthy eight teams for the first time since 1960. The teams were conveniently grouped into Eastern and Western divisions of four units each. Both Evansville and Wichita were also reentering Organized Baseball, since they had not fielded teams in 1969. Evansville had dropped out of the Southern League after the 1968 season, while Wichita had dropped out of the American Association way back in 1958.

At present U.S. Organized Baseball has three Class AAA leagues consisting of a total of twenty-four teams. (This does not include the Class AAA Mexican League.) The majors soon realized that three Class AAA circuits were necessary to serve as a source of high-grade talent, and there is no question that the major league subsidy plan for player salaries had much to do with the reemergence of the American Association.

THE AMERICAN ASSOCIATION: THE EARLY YEARS

Though Thomas Jefferson Hickey, the founder and first president of the American Association, laid definite organizational plans for the circuit in 1901, the league's origins go as far back as 1878. In that year the AA's ancestor, an obscure little professional circuit called the Northwestern League and consisting of just four towns (Davenport, Iowa; Dubuque, Iowa; Omaha, Nebraska; and Rockford, Illinois) was organized. Regularly scheduled play began the next year. The Northwestern League is enormously important in the history of baseball since it developed into the Western League, out of which grew both the American Association and the American League.

According to baseball pioneer Albert Goodwill Spalding in his book *Historic Facts Concerning the Beginning, Evolution, Development and Popularity of Base Ball With Personal Reminiscences of its Vicissitudes,*

[2] See Pacific Coast League Highlights: 1964-69, on page 157.

Its Victories and its Votaries, this was the first exclusively Western minor league. (Dubuque won the pennant in the league's first season. Among the star players for the champion Dubuque team were Charles "The Old Roman" Comiskey, who was one of the founders of the American League, and Charles "Old Hoss" Radbourne, who won 308 games in a twelve-year big league career. Comiskey, whose major league career spanned thirteen seasons, also played for Dubuque when it was in an independent league in 1878. Both Comiskey and Radbourne have been elected to baseball's Hall of Fame.)

We must hasten to indicate at this point that Thomas J. Hickey's American Association should not be confused with the first American Association, which operated as a major league between 1882 and 1891.

The Northwestern League changed its name to the Western League in 1880, and then in 1882, the circuit was reorganized into a new North-western League. At a series of meetings in Chicago, teams were established in eight cities: Peoria, Springfield, and Quincy, Illinois; Bay City, East Saginaw, and Grand Rapids, Michigan; Fort Wayne, Indiana; and Toledo, Ohio.

The Northwestern League continually shuffled its membership, and when in 1888, its name was changed to the Western Association, it had teams in eight cities: Chicago, Des Moines, Kansas City, Milwaukee, Minneapolis, Omaha, St. Paul, and Sioux City.

A complete record of the Northwestern League and its offshoots, reasons for franchise shifts, and changes in league names would require a hefty doctoral dissertation. Suffice it to say that the Western Association was reorganized at Indianapolis in 1893 as the Western League with teams at Detroit, Grand Rapids, Kansas City, Milwaukee, Minneapolis, Sioux City, Iowa, and Toledo. (During this same period in the 1890s, there was an entirely different league named the "Western Association," which had franchises in Des Moines, Iowa; Omaha and Lincoln, Nebraska; St. Joseph, Missouri; and Peoria, Quincy, Rock Island, and Jacksonville, Illinois.)

All this intense organizational activity came to a climax when both the American League, as a major circuit, and the American Association came into being at about the same time (1901 and 1902, respectively). For years baseball men had tried to form a second major league that could compete on even terms with the National League, but all these attempts, including the old American Association that chugged on for a decade, ended in failure. Two other attempts at establishing major leagues, the Union Association of 1884 and the Players' League of 1890, ended in failure. Both circuits were forced to get out of business after only a single season.

In a bold move, Ban Johnson, the hard-driving president of the Western League, announced a new organizational plan at an October 11, 1899, Chicago meeting. He called for teams to be located at Chicago, Detroit, Cleveland, Minneapolis, Milwaukee, Indianapolis, Kansas City, and Buffalo. Moreover, the revamped circuit's new name was to be the "American League." In 1901, Johnson achieved his long-sought objective when he declared his circuit a major league, on a par with the National. In his drive for major league status, he pointed his circuit eastward and located teams at Baltimore, Boston, Chicago, Cleveland, Detroit, Milwaukee, Philadelphia, and Washington. In fact, as Johnson proceeded with his eastward thrust, he abandoned every city of his old Western League.

Meanwhile, Tom Hickey, forty years of age and recognized as a resourceful minor league organizer, became president of the rebuilt Western League in 1900. The circuit embraced six cities: Kansas City, St. Paul, Omaha, St. Joseph, Des Moines, and Sioux City. Since Ban Johnson had pointed the American League primarily in an easterly direction, some good midwestern baseball cities were left temporarily without good caliber teams. This is where Hickey stepped in and filled the breach by taking his Western League and using it as a base for the creation of the new American Association, which was ready to start play in 1902.

Hickey managed to pull eight good, solid, and sizable baseball teams into his AA: Columbus, Indianapolis, Kansas City, Louisville, Milwaukee, Minneapolis, St. Paul, and Toledo. And, as we said at the outset, the same eight teams stayed together for fifty years, except for the brief period when Toledo strayed from the flock.

A second Western League was reorganized for the 1902 season under a new president, James Whitfield, with teams in eight cities: Colorado Springs, Denver, Des Moines, Kansas City, Milwaukee, Omaha, Peoria, and St. Joseph. The league proved to be a bellweather of the National Association, continuing play until 1957. (See "Western League" in Part III.)

To a great degree Tom Hickey and Ban Johnson worked together in the business of carving out territories for their new leagues. This was a time of great confusion and rapid change in the structure of professional baseball, and it is to the credit of both Hickey and Johnson that they oversaw the founding of two leagues that proved to be astoundingly stable. Moreover, it was during this period that the National Association of Professional Baseball Leagues was formed, an organization that made possible the orderly development and operation of the minor leagues. It was Tom Hickey, of course, who led the drive for the formation of the National Association.

Territorial problems concerned Hickey in the early years. As we have seen already, James Whitfield's Western League also had teams in Kansas City and Milwaukee, and any baseball executive knows that it is almost impossible for one town to support two teams in the high minors for too long. The impasse continued for two seasons until the end of the 1903 campaign, when the AA succeeded in pressuring the Western League to give up their Kansas City and Milwaukee franchises. The Western League went down to six teams in the process. Whitfield had died prematurely during the 1902 season and was succeeded as WL president by Mike Sexton, who had to concede the loss of those two key cities in the territorial dispute. It goes almost without saying that the AA became a much stronger circuit after it won sole rights to Kansas City and Milwaukee.

Because of the territorial dispute with the Western League, the American Association did not become a member of the National Association until 1904. The National Association took the view that the AA encroached into the Western League's territory, and for all intents and purposes, it labeled the AA as an "outlaw" league. Once these territorial disputes were resolved (at the end of the 1903 season), the AA gained membership in the National Association and became one of its bulwarks.

Tom Hickey is truly one of the great figures in professional baseball. Throughout his exceptionally long career he was always recognized as an innovator, a man with original ideas. In fact, in his first connection with baseball in 1885, he organized a crack team of black players in St. Louis and took them on tour to play against white teams. He stepped out as AA president two years after the league was launched, but he kept a watchful eye on AA affairs. He served as the circuit's president again from 1917 until 1935. Hickey maintained his passion for baseball after his retirement and died in 1956, just short of his ninety-fifth birthday. As a league director, this extremely vigorous man attended AA games, banquets, and all sorts of official functions until he was into his nineties.

The American Association has poured a steady stream of players, coaches, managers, and executives into the major leagues during the past three generations. At the same time, however, we ought not to consider the AA—or any other minor league for that matter—as a mere proving ground for the majors. The AA above all endeavored continuously to play good baseball and to entertain fans in its own cities, and in that regard, the league has succeeded magnificently. Since the league, as it was originally conceived, enjoyed such a long life, intense rivalries developed between teams in the same area or region (between St. Paul and Minneapolis, for example). This factor was extremely important to the league's development. Rivalries were always excellent attendance builders.

At first, the AA teams were fairly independent of the major leagues.

They were free to sell players to the highest bidder. Toledo became affiliated with the Cleveland Indians as early as 1907, and by 1912, the Mud Hens were owned outright by Charles W. Somers, president of the Cleveland Club. This was an exception, however, since all other AA teams at the time operated with no such affiliations.

Since Judge Kenesaw Mountain Landis, the iron-fisted baseball commissioner, was friendly to the minor leagues and wanted them to avoid close alliances with the big leagues, it was not until the 1930s that all AA teams established full-fledged working agreements with the majors. Even Landis came to realize that a topflight minor league club was the vital link in the chain that made it possible for a talented player to progress from sandlot ball to the majors.

Moreover, since the majors now heavily subsidize salaries of minor league players under their control, it is incumbent upon minor league operators to align themselves with parent clubs.

Going into the 1974 season the alliances that AA teams had with the majors were as follows: Evansville, Detroit; Denver, Houston; Indianapolis, Cincinnati; Iowa, Chicago White Sox; Omaha, Kansas City; Oklahoma City, Cleveland; Tulsa, St. Louis; Wichita, Chicago Cubs. However, alliances between major and minor league teams change frequently.

The number of big league managers who won their spurs in the AA either as players or managers is impressive. There are also plenty of cases, of course, where ex-big league managers came over to the association as pilots. AA managers collectively constitute an interesting and colorful lot of baseball men.

Joe Cantillon, one of the really outstanding figures in AA history, was named manager of Milwaukee in midseason 1902. He piloted the Brewers through 1906 and then took over the managerial reigns of the Washington Senators in the American League for the next three years. "Pongo Joe" finished last, seventh, and last during his tenure in Washington, but nonetheless, he distinguished himself. It was Cantillon who sent catcher Cliff Blankenship (who was recovering from a broken finger) on a June 1907 scouting trip out west to sign a nineteen-year-old pitcher whose smoking fastball was the talk of Idaho's semi-pro Snake River Valley League—that pitcher's name was Walter Johnson. The young fast-baller signed his Washington contract on June 29 and won 416 games for the Senators before he retired twenty-one years later.

Cantillon began a fourteen-year tenure as manager of Minneapolis in 1910. He won pennants in his first three years and added another in 1915. Joe's brother Mike, an owner of the Millers, managed Minneapolis himself in 1907–08.

Bill Armour, who managed Cleveland in 1902–04 and Detroit in 1905–06, came to Toledo as president and manager in 1907 and remained as the Mud Hens' chief executive until 1912 (he gave up the managerial reins after the 1908 season). It was during Armour's regime that Swayne Field, then considered one of the finest parks in all the minor leagues, was constructed and opened to the public in 1909.

When the Mud Hens returned to the AA in 1916, they were led by Roger "Duke" Bresnahan, who held the dual title of owner and manager. Bresnahan, a native of Toledo, managed the Mud Hens through 1920. He retained his ownership until 1923, when he returned to the majors, first as a coach with the New York Giants and later as a coach with Detroit. Bresnahan, a Hall of Fame catcher who achieved his greatest fame with John McGraw's New York Giants in the century's first decade, had been player–manager with both the St. Louis Cardinals and the Chicago Cubs. When he came to Toledo he occasionally served as a catcher during the first three years of his tenure in addition to all his other responsibilities. Bresnahan is also remembered as the catcher who introduced shin guards. When he first wore them in 1908 while playing with the Giants, everybody in the park laughed at him, but today no catcher or plate umpire would think of going into a game without them.

The Indianapolis manager during the 1905 season was a sharp thirty-seven-year-old tactician named Edward Grant Barrow, who was already a twenty-year veteran of the game in all its departments. Before coming to Indianapolis he managed Toronto in the Eastern (International) League and Detroit in the American League. Later in his career he managed Boston in the American League (where he converted ace Red Sox pitcher Babe Ruth into an outfielder), before gaining even greater fame as general manager and empire builder of the New York Yankees.

Mike Kelley, a good first baseman who played with the Louisville Colonels of the National League in 1899 (Hans Wagner was a teammate), took over as manager of the St. Paul Saints in the AA's inaugural year. He was then twenty-six years old and the youngest manager in the league. This marked the beginning of Kelley's American Association career, which spanned more than forty years. During that period he managed the Saints for two decades (with several breaks, including one in 1913, in which he managed Indianapolis for a year), and in 1924, he succeeded Joe Cantillon as manager at Minneapolis, a post he held through 1931, when he hung up his uniform in order to concentrate on his new duties as owner of the Millers!

Kelley long remembered the 1938 season, for that is when the Red Sox sent their young slugger, Ted Williams, to the Millers for a final year of seasoning under the watchful eye of veteran manager Owen "Donie" Bush (Minneapolis then was Boston's top farm team.) Kelley had to contend with the continuous scrapping between Bush and Williams, a twenty-year-old who was immature for his years. Early in his career Williams was notorious for not running out all grounders or chasing after balls hit in his general direction in the outfield. Bush became so infuriated with Williams' lackadaisical attitude one day that he went to Kelley with an ultimatum: "It's Williams or me, one of us has to go." "If it ever comes to that, Donie, it'll have to be you," Kelley is reported to have said. Anyway, that's the version Williams himself gives in *My Turn at Bat: The Story of My Life* (1969). Despite his shenanigans Williams did manage to hit .366 with 43 home runs and 142 runs batted in, all league-leading figures.

Kelley, who died at Minneapolis in 1955 at the age of eighty, has long been regarded as one of the most versatile and resourceful baseball men the AA has ever produced.

Donie Bush also enjoyed one of the longest and most successful tenures in Organized Baseball, with a significant part of his career being spent in the AA. Bush, a native of Indianapolis, broke into baseball as a shortstop with Dayton of the old Central League in 1906. He went to South Bend of the same circuit during the following year, and at the end of a brilliant season with the Indianapolis Indians in 1908, he was called up by the Detroit Tigers. He remained with Detroit until August 1921, when he was picked up by Washington on waivers. He finished his playing days in 1923 and his appointment as the Senators pilot in that year was the first entry on a long list of managerial assignments: Indianapolis, 1924–26; Pittsburgh 1927–29; Chicago, AL, 1930–31; Minneapolis, 1932; Cincinnati, 1933; Minneapolis, 1934–38; Louisville, 1939; Indianapolis, 1943–44.

Bush also became president of the Indianapolis Indians in 1942, and he retained his post as the club's full-time chief executive for many years after his retirement from managing. The local park was eventually named "Bush Stadium" in his honor. In addition to his administrative duties, he served as a Red Sox scout in the 1950s and then as a White Sox scout for most of the rest of his life. He died on March 28, 1972, at the age of eighty-four. In all, Bush was continuously active as a player, scout, and administrator for sixty-five years.

As a player Donie Bush was an exponent of the old school "inside baseball," always scrapping for that one precious run. In his fifteen years in the majors, Bush (a runt at 5 feet, 6 inches, and 145 pounds) batted only .250; but he drew 1,158 walks, stole 403 bases, and scored 1,280 runs. Always a fine fielder, he is rated as one of the best shortstops the Tigers ever had.

Bush could never get used to a player like Ted Williams, who was nonchalant about his fielding and base running but could turn a game around with one stroke of the bat. These two men were of entirely different temperaments, but nevertheless, they got to like and respect each other. In his biography Williams called Donie Bush "a little tiger, but a lovable little tiger."

Men with big baseball names who managed in the AA abound:

Napoleon Lajoie, a Hall of Fame second baseman, was player–manager for Indianapolis in 1918.

Clarence "Pants" Rowland, who led the Chicago White Sox to a world title in 1917, piloted the Milwaukee Brewers in 1919, and the Columbus Red Birds in 1921–22. Rowland later became president of the Pacific Coast League.

Joe McCarthy earned his reputation as a brilliant tactician while leading the Louisville Colonels from 1919 through 1925. From that point he successively managed the Chicago Cubs, the New York Yankees, and the Boston Red Sox.

Casey Stengel, who had just completed his big league playing days, led Toledo from 1926 through 1931. He occasionally still played the outfield in those days. He also managed Milwaukee in 1944 and Kansas City in 1945.

Burt Shotton, pennant-winning manager with the Brooklyn Dodgers in 1947 and 1949, led the Columbus Red Birds from 1936 through 1941.

Fred Haney, manager of the world champion Milwaukee Braves in 1957, skippered the Toledo Mud Hens in 1935–38 and 1941–42.

Charlie Grimm, who led the Chicago Cubs to three pennants in the 1930s, piloted Milwaukee in 1941–44 (he shared duties with Casey Stengel during the latter year) and again in 1951–52.

Al Lopez prepped for a long and successful big league managerial career at Indianapolis in 1948–50.

Walt Alston, long-time the Brooklyn and Los Angeles Dodgers pilot, led St. Paul in 1948–49.

Bill Rigney, pilot of several major league teams, broke into the managerial ranks with Minneapolis in 1954–55.

Ralph Houk, long the New York Yankees manager, piloted Denver in 1955–57 at the close of his playing-bullpen catching career with the Yankees.

Jack McKeon, who never played an inning of major league baseball, became manager of the Kansas City Royals in 1973 because he had piloted Omaha so skillfully in 1969–72.

The number of AA players who later became major league managers is considerable, and only a few examples can be cited here:

Miller Huggins, who played second base for St. Paul's first AA team in 1902, managed the St. Louis Cardinals in 1913–17. Then during his 1918–29 tenure with the New York Yankees, he brought home the first pennants to Gotham's American League entry (six of them). He was elected to the Hall of Fame in 1964.

Clifford "Cactus" Cravath, Philadelphia Phillies pilot in 1919–20, led the AA in batting in 1910–11 while playing for Minneapolis. He swatted .327 and .363 in those years.

Chuck Dressen, star third baseman for St. Paul in 1922–24, played in the majors for seven years. Later he managed at Cincinnati, Brooklyn, Washington, Milwaukee, and Detroit.

Leo Durocher, who gained a reputation as a battler while starring at shortstop for St. Paul in 1927, managed Brooklyn, New York, Chicago, and Houston in the National League. When he retired as the Astros' manager after the 1973 season, his career in Organized Baseball had spanned almost fifty years.

Joe Cronin, shortstop for Kansas City in 1928, was called up by Washington in midseason, and within five years, he led the Senators to a pennant as player–manager.

Eddie Stanky, voted the American Association's Most Valuable Player in 1942 while playing shortstop for Milwaukee, managed the St. Louis Cardinals and the Chicago White Sox in the 1950s and 1960s.

Phil Rizzuto and Joe Garagiola, two ex-big leaguers who went on to highly successful careers in radio and television at the conclusion of their playing careers, are also American Association graduates. Rizzuto has developed into a highly-polished and articulate play-by-play broadcaster on radio and TV for the Yankees during the past dozen years; while Garagiola began broadcasting the St. Louis Cardinals games in the late 1950s, did play-by-play work for the Yankees in the 1960s, and has since established himself as a bonafide network television star.

Rizzuto, an undersized shortstop (he stood only five feet, 6 inches) but tough and brainy in the Donie Bush tradition, had two spectacular years with the Kansas City Blues in 1939–40. During the 1940 campaign he slammed out 201 hits, batted .347, fielded sensationally, and was named by *The Sporting News* as the "Number 1 Minor League Player of the Year." After that season "Scooter" Rizzuto was called up by the New York Yankees, with whom he won the Most Valuable Player Award in 1950 and participated in nine World Series. He then turned to the microphones for a second and equally distinguished career in baseball.

Garagiola grew up with Yogi Berra in the same neighborhood in St. Louis' Italian section. He was such a good ball player in his youth that he signed a contract with the Cardinals' Springfield, Missouri, farm club in the Class C Western Association when he was only sixteen years old. That was in 1942. From Springfield, Garagiola, a catcher, went to the Columbus Red Birds of the American Association in 1943, where he batted .293 in 81 games. After almost three years of military service, he spent the entire 1946 season with the Cardinals and starred in the World Series victory against Boston, batting .316.

He saw service with Columbus again in 1948, where he spent most of the year getting back his batting eye. He accomplished his mission by swatting .356. Garagiola went back to the Cardinals in 1949, and he played for three other National League clubs (Pittsburgh, Chicago, and New York) before retiring after the 1954 season because of a combination of injuries sustained during more than a decade of catching.

As a play-by-play broadcaster, no one was quicker with a metaphor or simile than Joe Garagiola. And through his numerous appearances on television, he has done a great deal to popularize baseball. He is particularly adept at bringing out the purely human qualities of players, hardboiled managers, and hardheaded baseball executives.

BILL BURWELL

The name Bill Burwell rarely appears in histories of baseball, but this man spent some sixty years in the game. In respect to the American Association, he holds that league's record for most games won (lifetime), winning 189 (losing 166), a mark compiled from 1922 to 1936. Burwell spent most of his AA pitching years with Indianapolis, but he also hurled for Columbus and Minneapolis.

A right-hander, Burwell began his Organized Baseball career with Elgin, Illinois, of the Bi-State League in 1915, though it is not known how he fared there since no records were kept. In 1916, he had a 6–8 record with Topeka of the Western League. When we consider his pitching for all other minor leagues, including his final active year with Crookston, Minnesota, of the Northern League in 1938, his total minor league record comes to 239–199. Moreover, when we tack on his 9–8 record compiled for two major league teams (St. Louis Browns in 1920–21 and Pittsburgh in 1928), his total pitching record stands at a hefty 247–207.

That is a lot of pitching, of course, but it led to a much longer career in managing, coaching, and scouting. By the time he arrived in Crookston as player–manager, Burwell already had piloting experience (with Fort Wayne of the Central League for part of the 1934 season and with Rock Island of the Western League in 1937). In the AA he managed Louisville in 1940–43 and Indianapolis in 1945–46. Later on he managed Davenport of the Three-I League (1949), New Orleans of the Southern League (1950), and Lincoln of the Western League (1955).

Between managerial assignments Burwell coached for the Boston Red Sox and Pittsburgh. He even managed the Pirates to a victory in the last game of the 1947 campaign as he took over the reins from Billy Herman who had just been fired. In fact, Burwell has done just about everything in baseball—he was even a good hitting pitcher!

In later years Burwell filled all types of posts for the Pirates: scout (1952–54); managerial consultant, farm system (1956–57); pitching coach (1958–62); and from 1963 until his death in June 1973, he handled special assignments such as scouting and troubleshooting.

Bill Burwell's career in Organized Baseball may not have been spectacular in the sense that men like Babe Ruth, Ty Cobb, and John McGraw enjoyed spectacular careers, but he is the type of solid baseball man who has supplied a lot of the mortar to keep the works going. Few men can match his length of service to baseball.

AMERICAN ASSOCIATION HIGHLIGHTS

1902: The American Association's first schedule called for 140 games for each club, 10 at home and 10 on the road with each one of its seven rivals. (This was increased to 154 games in 1904 and to 168 games in 1909. The league went back to a 154 game schedule in 1933, to 150 games in 1961–62 with six teams, and to 140 games since 1969.)

On the final day of the 1902 season, Indianapolis led Louisville by two games for the league lead. Each of the teams had three games left, and the league allowed Indianapolis to play a tripleheader at St. Paul and Louisville to play a tripleheader at Minneapolis. Indianapolis swept its three games from the Saints in the remarkably quick total playing time of three hours and twelve minutes, while the Colonels won all three from Minneapolis, winning the first one on a forfeit because the Millers were late for the game. Pat Flaherty, who was a twenty-game winner for the Chicago White Sox in 1904, pitched both of the Louisville games that were played. Thus, Indianapolis was still two games ahead when the marathon was over.

1903: Bill Klem, a New York State League umpire, was hired by the AA. In his only full year in the AA (1904), Klem, who was responsible for many innovations in umpiring, introduced the technique of drawing a line on the field with his spiked shoe to ward off argumentative players and managers. Klem umpired in the National League from 1904 to 1940, and he, Tom Connolly, Billy Evans, and Jocko Conlon are the only four umpires to have won election to the Hall of Fame.

1904: The first Junior World Series was played between the champions of the American Association and the champions of the Eastern (International) League. George Stallings, renowned in baseball history for leading the "Miracle" Boston Braves to the 1914 National League pennant, piloted the Buffalo Bisons to the title over the AA's St. Paul Saints. (The Junior World Series did not become an annual event until 1920.)

1906: In the second Junior World Series, Buffalo under George Stallings defeated the Columbus Red Birds 3 games to 2.

1908: Rube Marquard, Indianapolis left-hander who compiled a 28–19 record, was sold by the Indians to the New York Giants in mid-September for $11,000, then a record price for a ball player.

1911: Toward the end of the season, the Pittsburgh Pirates purchased pitcher Marty O'Toole from St. Paul for $22,500, a record price for a minor league ball player. O'Toole never made it big in the majors. In his four years with the Pirates, his best year was in 1912, when he had a 15–17 log and a 2.71 ERA.

1912: On April 11, Kansas City and Columbus played the entire game with one ball. Club officials were apparently extremely cost conscious.

Late in the season catcher Ray "Cracker" Schalk of Milwaukee was sold to the Chicago White Sox for $15,000. Schalk remained with Chicago for seventeen years and came to be recognized as one of the finest defensive catchers in baseball's history. He was elected to the Hall of Fame in 1955, while years earlier Babe Ruth named him to his personal all-time team.

Infielder John "Red" Corriden of Kansas City went to Detroit for $15,000. While Corriden's big league playing career spanned only five seasons, he spent many years as a coach for the Chicago Cubs, the Brooklyn Dodgers, and the New York Yankees. And in 1950, he managed the Chicago White Sox.

1914: George H. "Tiny" Johnson was hired as an umpire and called plays through the 1942 season, a remarkable stretch of twenty-nine years. When he left the diamonds, he became supervisor of umpires for the

National Association. (Beginning with the 1910 season, the AA had given up single umpire ball games and regularly assigned two arbiters to all games.)

1914–15: With the Toledo Mud Hens in Cleveland during these two years, there was the unusual situation of having a minor league and big league team (the Indians) in the same town. Both clubs were owned by Charles W. Somers. The AA played their games in Cleveland's League Park whenever the Indians were on the road. Somers engineered this situation to prevent the Federal League from muscling into Cleveland. The new league could not very well move into the city when baseball was being played continuously at the town's only suitable park.

1918: The season was cut at midpoint because of World War I.

1921: Anthony "Bunny" Brief, the Kansas City first baseman–outfielder, slammed 42 homers and knocked in a record 191 runs, as pro baseball everywhere was revolutionized by the introduction of the lively ball. Brief, who led the AA in homers five times while he was with the Blues and Milwaukee Brewers, had played in the big leagues from 1912 to 1917 with three clubs (the St. Louis Browns, the Chicago White Sox, and the Pittsburgh Pirates).

1924: Chuck Dressen, a St. Paul third baseman, reached base safely 14 consecutive times from July 1 through July 4. In that string he had 11 consecutive hits, walked, reached first on an error, and had another hit.
Dressen batted .346 for the season, slamming out 212 hits with 151 RBI's. In 1925 he was promoted to the Cincinnati Reds.

1925: Joe McCarthy led Louisville to the AA pennant with a fat 13½ game margin over Donie Bush's second place Indianapolis Indians. The next season, after having spent twenty solid years in the minors, he served as manager of the Chicago Cubs.

1927: Fred Schulte, the hard-hitting Milwaukee outfielder, was sold by Otto Borchert, Milwaukee's club president, to the St. Louis Browns for a record sum variously put at from $110,000 to $125,000. Schulte performed well in the majors for eleven seasons, batting .292 lifetime.

1930: Nick "Tomato Face" Cullop, a Minneapolis outfielder, belted 54 home runs, a new league record. Cullop later managed both Columbus and Milwaukee.

1931: Indianapolis was the first team in the AA to install lights for night baseball. In the following years other teams in the circuit also took the big step. When Minneapolis got its floodlights in 1937, all AA teams had lighted parks. The impact of night baseball cannot be overestimated; for example, after Minneapolis began playing night games on weekdays, the season's attendance jumped by 50,000.

1933: Joe Hauser's 69 homers for Minneapolis were the talk of the baseball world. Only Joe Bauman has hit more homers in one season (72 for Roswell, New Mexico, in the Longhorn League) in 1954, but Bauman's record was accomplished in a Class C league.

In order to stimulate baseball interest during the Depression, a post-season playoff plan was introduced, but it was dropped after two years because of its unpopularity.

1936: The new Shaughnessy playoff plan was introduced.

1937: Total attendance in the AA reached 1,425,000, nearly double the anemic 1933 figure of 777,000.

1939: Vince DiMaggio, a Kansas City outfielder, led the league with 46 homers and 136 RBI's.

1940: During a four-game stretch on July 9–12, Stanley "Frenchy" Bordagaray, a Kansas City outfielder, hit safely 13 consecutive times. The major league record is 12.

1942: Bill Veeck, Milwaukee's president, was voted by *The Sporting News* as the Minor League Executive of the Year. Veeck (only twenty-eight years old at the time) later operated the Cleveland Indians, the St. Louis Browns, and the Chicago White Sox.

1942–45: The AA maintained full playing schedules throughout World War II.

1946–48: League attendance reached record highs during the immediate postwar period: 2,021,000 in 1946; 2,159,000 in 1947; and 2,236,000 in 1948.

1947: Carl DeRose of Kansas City pitched the first perfect game in association history with a 5–0 victory over Minneapolis on June 26 at Kansas City.

1948: Roy Campanella, St. Paul's burly heavy-hitting catcher, became the first black to play in the AA when he appeared in a game on May 22. Campanella, who entered Organized Baseball with the Nashua, New Hampshire, team of the New England League in 1946, finished up the 1948 season with the Brooklyn Dodgers.

1949: Ellis "Cot" Deal pitched a complete game of 20 innings for Columbus, defeating Louisville 4–3.

Louisville's left-hander Maurice McDermott struck out 20 St. Paul batters on May 24 in defeating the Saints 3–1. He fanned the side in the third, fifth, sixth, eighth, and ninth innings. He gave up three hits. After compiling a 6–4 record and striking out 116 men in 77 innings, the twenty-one-year-old fastballer was called up in midseason by the Boston Red Sox.

1950: Right-hander Marlin Stuart of Toledo pitched the second perfect game in AA annals on June 25 with a 1–0 conquest over Indianapolis at Mud Hens' Swayne Field. During Stuart's six-years in the big league, his record was 23–17.

1951: Willie Mays, a twenty-year-old Minneapolis outfielder, was called up by the New York Giants after hitting .477 in 35 games (71 for 149).

Minneapolis shortstop Davey Williams hit four consecutive home runs over a two-game span on June 26–27.

The first AA hit by Milwaukee third baseman Eddie Mathews was a grand slam home run.

1954: Herb Score, Indianapolis's left-hander, was named by *The Sporting News* as the Minor League Player of the Year. He chalked up a 22–5 record with 330 strikeouts (the latter figure is still a league high).

1956: Kerby Farrell, pilot of the champion Indianapolis Indians, was named by *The Sporting News* Minor League Manager of the Year for the second time (he also won the award in 1954). He became manager of the Cleveland Indians in 1957.

1959: Louisville left-hander Juan Pizarro pitched 16⅔ hitless innings against Charleston. The Puerto Rican fastballer threw a no-hitter against the Senators on June 16, and in his next start against them (June 20), he held them hitless for 7⅔ innings. Shortly thereafter he was called up by the parent Milwaukee Braves.

1963–68: The AA suspended play.

1969: Luis Alcaraz of Omaha broke the AA fielding record for second basemen when he posted a glittering .989 mark.

1971: The AA won a trophy from the National Association for having the greatest total paid attendance of the three Class AAA leagues. The AA drew 1,710,000; the International League drew 1,364,000; and the Pacific Coast League drew 1,316,000 (figures include playoff and all-star games).

1973: The Indianapolis Indians are the only AA team to have participated in each of the league's sixty-six seasons. Through 1973, Indianapolis had played 10,166 games where a decision was reached, winning 5,196 and losing 4,970 for a .511 percentage.

AMERICAN ASSOCIATION PRESIDENTS

Year	President
1902–03	Thomas J. Hickey
1904	J. Ed Grillo
1905–09	Joseph D. O'Brien
1910–16	Tom Chivington
1917–35	Thomas J. Hickey
1936–45	George Trautman
1946	Roy Hamey
1947–48	Frank Lane
1949–53	Bruce Dudley
1954–60	Edward S. Doherty
1961–62	James H. Burris
1963–68	(The AA suspended operations.)
1969–71	Allie P. Reynolds
1971—	Joe Ryan

AMERICAN ASSOCIATION CHAMPIONS

Year	Championship Team	Manager	Won	Lost	Pct.
1902	Indianapolis	W. H. Watkins	95	44	.681
1903	St. Paul	M. J. Kelley	88	46	.657
1904	St. Paul	M. J. Kelley	95	52	.646
1905	Columbus	William Clymer	100	52	.658
1906	Columbus	William Clymer	91	57	.615
1907	Columbus	William Clymer	90	64	.584
1908	Indianapolis	C. C. Carr	92	61	.601
1909	Louisville	Henry Peitz	93	75	.554
1910	Minneapolis	Joe Cantillon	107	61	.637
1911	Minneapolis	Joe Cantillon	99	66	.600
1912	Minneapolis	Joe Cantillon	105	60	.636
1913	Milwaukee	Harry Clark	100	67	.599
1914	Milwaukee	Harry Clark	98	68	.590
1915	Minneapolis	Joe Cantillon	92	62	.597
1916	Louisville	William Clymer	101	66	.605
1917	Indianapolis	J. C. Hendricks	90	63	.588
1918	Kansas City	John H. Ganzel	43	30	.589

(The league suspended operations in midseason because of the World War).

Year	Championship Team	Manager	Won	Lost	Pct.
1919	St. Paul	M. J. Kelley	94	60	.610
1920	St. Paul	M. J. Kelley	115	49	.701

Year	Championship Team	Manager	Won	Lost	Pct.
1921	Louisville	Joe McCarthy	98	70	.583
1922	St. Paul	M. J. Kelley	107	60	.641
1923	Kansas City	Wilbur Good	112	54	.675
1924	St. Paul	Nick Allen	96	70	.578
1925	Louisville	Joe McCarthy	106	61	.635
1926	Louisville	Bill Meyer	105	62	.629
1927	Toledo	Casey Stengel	101	67	.601
1928	Indianapolis	Bruno Betzel	99	68	.593
1929	Kansas City	E. H. "Dutch" Zwilling	111	56	.665
1930	Louisville	Allan Sothoron	93	60	.607
1931	St. Paul	Albert Leifeld	104	63	.623
1932	Minneapolis	Donie Bush	100	68	.595
1933	*Columbus	Ray Blades	101	51	.664
	Minneapolis	Dave Bancroft	86	67	.562

(Under the American Association playoff plan, the highest standing Eastern Division team, which was Columbus, met the highest standing Western Division team, which was Minneapolis. Columbus won the official AA Crown by defeating Minneapolis 4 games to 2.)

1934	Minneapolis	Donie Bush	85	64	.570
	*Columbus	Ray Blades	85	68	.556

(Columbus defeated Minneapolis in a playoff 4 games to 3 under the same rules used in 1933.)

1935	Minneapolis	Donie Bush	91	63	.591

* Asterisk indicates winning team.

Year	Championship Team	Manager	Won	Lost	Pct.
1936	*Milwaukee	Allan Sothoron	90	64	.584
	St. Paul	Charles Street	84	68	.553
	Kansas City	"Dutch" Zwilling	84	69	.549
	Indianapolis	Wade Killefer	79	75	.513

(Under the Shaughnessy playoff plan, adopted in 1936 and used continuously through the 1962 season, Milwaukee won the Governor's Cup by defeating Indianapolis. In the first two series, Milwaukee eliminated Kansas City and Indianapolis eliminated St. Paul.)

1937	*Columbus	Burt Shotton	90	64	.584
	Toledo	Fred Haney	89	65	.578
	Minneapolis	Donie Bush	87	67	.565
	Milwaukee	Allan Sothoron	80	73	.523

(Playoffs: Columbus defeated Minneapolis 4 games to 2; Milwaukee defeated Toledo 4 games to 2. Finals: Columbus defeated Milwaukee 4 games to 2.)

1938	St. Paul	Foster Ganzel	90	61	.596
	*Kansas City	Bill Meyer	84	67	.556
	Milwaukee	Allan Sothoron	81	70	.536
	Indianapolis	Ray Schalk	80	74	.519

(Playoffs: St. Paul defeated Milwaukee 4 games to 3; Kansas City defeated Indianapolis 4 games to 2. Finals: Kansas City defeated St. Paul 4 games to 3.)

1939	Kansas City	Bill Meyer	107	47	.695
	Minneapolis	Tom Sheehan	99	55	.643
	Indianapolis	Ray Schalk–Wes Griffin	82	72	.532
	*Louisville	Donie Bush–Bill Burwell	75	78	.490

(Playoffs: Louisville defeated Minneapolis 4 games to 1; Indianapolis defeated Kansas City 4 games to 1. Finals: Louisville defeated Indianapolis 4 games to 1.)

1940	Kansas City	Bill Meyer	95	57	.625
	Columbus	Burt Shotton	90	60	.600
	Minneapolis	Tom Sheehan	86	59	.593
	*Louisville	Bill Burwell	75	75	.500

(Playoffs: Louisville defeated Columbus 4 games to 2; Kansas City defeated Minneapolis 4 games to 2. Finals: Louisville defeated Kansas 4 games to 2.)

* Asterisk indicates winning team.

Year	Championship Team	Manager	Won	Lost	Pct.
1941	*Columbus	Burt Shotton	95	58	.621
	Louisville	Bill Burwell	87	66	.569
	Kansas City	Bill Meyer	85	69	.552
	Minneapolis	Tom Sheehan	83	70	.542

(Playoffs: Columbus defeated Kansas City 4 games to 2; Louisville defeated Minneapolis 4 games to 2. Finals: Columbus defeated Louisville 4 games to 1.)

1942	Kansas City	Johnny Neun	84	69	.549
	Milwaukee	Charlie Grimm	81	69	.540
	*Columbus	Eddie Dyer	82	72	.532
	Toledo	Fred Haney	78	73	.517

(Playoffs: Columbus defeated Kansas City 4 games to 3; Toledo defeated Milwaukee 4 games to 2. Finals: Columbus defeated Toledo 4 games to 0.)

1943	Milwaukee	Charlie Grimm	90	61	.596
	Indianapolis	Donie Bush	85	67	.559
	*Columbus	Nick Cullop	84	67	.556
	Toledo	Jacques Fornier	76	76	.500

(Playoffs: Columbus defeated Milwaukee 3 games to 1; Indianapolis defeated Toledo 3 games to 2. Finals: Columbus defeated Indianapolis 3 games to 0.)

1944	Milwaukee	Charlie Grimm– Casey Stengel	102	51	.667
	Toledo	Ollie Marquardt	95	58	.621
	*Louisville	Harry Leibold	85	63	.574
	St. Paul	Ray Blades	85	66	.563

(Playoffs: Louisville defeated Milwaukee 4 games to 2; St. Paul defeated Toledo 4 games to 3. Finals: Louisville defeated St. Paul 4 games to 0.)

1945	Milwaukee	Nick Cullop	93	61	.604
	Indianapolis	Bill Burwell	90	63	.592
	*Louisville	Harry Leibold	84	70	.545
	St. Paul	Ray Blades	75	76	.497

(Playoffs: Louisville defeated Milwaukee 4 games to 2; St. Paul defeated Indianapolis 4 games to 2. Finals: Louisville defeated St. Paul 4 games to 2.)

* Asterisk indicates winning team.

Year	Championship Team	Manager	Won	Lost	Pct.
1946	*Louisville	Harry Leibold– Fred Walters	92	61	.601
	Indianapolis	Bill Burwell	88	65	.575
	St. Paul	Ray Blades	80	71	.530
	Minneapolis	Zeke Bonura–Bill Ryan–Tom Sheehan	76	75	.503

(Playoffs: Louisville defeated St. Paul 4 games to 1; Indianapolis defeated Minneapolis 4 games to 3. Finals: Louisville defeated Indianapolis 4 games to 0.)

Year	Championship Team	Manager	Won	Lost	Pct.
1947	Kansas City	Bill Meyer	93	60	.608
	Louisville	Harry Leibold	85	68	.556
	*Milwaukee	Nick Cullop	79	75	.513
	Minneapolis	Tom Sheehan	77	77	.500

(Playoffs: Milwaukee defeated Kansas City 4 games to 2; Louisville defeated Minneapolis 4 games to 3. Finals: Milwaukee defeated Louisville 4 games to 3.)

Year	Championship Team	Manager	Won	Lost	Pct.
1948	Indianapolis	Al Lopez	100	54	.649
	Milwaukee	Nick Cullop	89	65	.578
	*St. Paul	Walt Alston	86	68	.558
	Columbus	Harold Anderson	81	73	.526

(Playoffs: St. Paul defeated Indianapolis 4 games to 2; Columbus defeated Milwaukee 4 games to 3. Finals: St. Paul defeated Columbus 4 games to 3.)

Year	Championship Team	Manager	Won	Lost	Pct.
1949	St. Paul	Walt Alston	93	60	.608
	*Indianapolis	Al Lopez	92	61	.601
	Milwaukee	Nick Cullop	76	76	.500
	Minneapolis	Tommy Heath	74	78	.487

(Playoffs: Milwaukee defeated St. Paul 4 games to 3; Indianapolis defeated Minneapolis 4 games to 3. Finals: Indianapolis defeated Milwaukee 4 games to 3.)

Year	Championship Team	Manager	Won	Lost	Pct.
1950	Minneapolis	Tommy Heath	90	64	.584
	Indianapolis	Al Lopez	85	67	.559
	*Columbus	Rollie Hemsley	84	69	.549
	St. Paul	Clay Hopper	83	69	.546

* Asterisk indicates winning team.

Year	Championship Team	Manager	Won	Lost	Pct.

(Playoffs: Columbus defeated Minneapolis 4 games to 2; Indianapolis defeated St. Paul 4 games to 0. Finals: Columbus defeated Indianapolis 4 games to 2.)

1951	*Milwaukee	Charlie Grimm	94	57	.623
	St. Paul	Clay Hopper	85	66	.563
	Kansas City	George Selkirk	81	70	.536
	Louisville	Mike Higgins	80	73	.523

(Playoffs: Milwaukee defeated Kansas City 4 games to 1; St. Paul defeated Louisville 4 games to 1. Finals: Milwaukee defeated St. Paul 4 games to 2.)

1952	Milwaukee	Charlie Grimm–Bucky Walters–Dick Smith	101	53	.656
	*Kansas City	George Selkirk	89	65	.578
	St. Paul	Clay Bryant	80	74	.519
	Minneapolis	Frank Genovese	79	75	.513

(Playoffs: Milwaukee defeated St. Paul 4 games to 0, Kansas City defeated Minneapolis 4 games to 1. Finals: Kansas City defeated Milwaukee 4 games to 3.)

1953	Toledo	Tommy Holmes– George Selkirk	90	64	.584
	*Kansas City	Harry Craft	88	66	.571
	Louisville	Mike Higgins	84	70	.545
	Indianapolis	George "Birdie" Tebbetts	82	72	.532

(Playoffs: Toledo defeated Louisville 4 games to 3, Kansas City defeated Indianapolis 4 games to 2. Finals: Kansas City defeated Toledo 4 games to 3.)

1954	Indianapolis	Kerby Farrell	95	57	.625
	*Louisville	Mike Higgins	85	68	.556
	Minneapolis	Bill Rigney	78	73	.517
	Columbus	Johnny Keane	77	76	.503

(Playoffs: Indianapolis defeated Minneapolis 4 games to 2; Louisville defeated Columbus 4 games to 3. Finals: Louisville defeated Indianapolis 4 games to 1.)

* Asterisk indicates winning team.

Year	Championship Team	Manager	Won	Lost	Pct.
1955	*Minneapolis	Bill Rigney	92	62	.597
	Omaha	Johnny Keane	84	70	.545
	Denver	Ralph Houk	83	71	.539
	Louisville	John Marion	83	71	.539

(Playoffs: Minneapolis defeated Denver 4 games to 0; Omaha defeated Louisville 4 games to 3. Finals: Minneapolis defeated Omaha 4 games to 0.)

Year	Championship Team	Manager	Won	Lost	Pct.
1956	*Indianapolis	Kerby Farrell	92	62	.597
	Denver	Ralph Houk	86	67	.562
	Omaha	Johnny Keane	82	71	.536
	Minneapolis	Eddie Stanky	78	74	.513

(Playoffs: Indianapolis defeated Minneapolis 4 games to 3; Denver defeated Omaha 4 games to 2. Finals: Indianapolis defeated Denver 4 games to 0).

Year	Championship Team	Manager	Won	Lost	Pct.
1957	Wichita	Ben Geraghty	93	61	.604
	*Denver	Ralph Houk	90	64	.584
	Minneapolis	John "Red" Davis	85	69	.552
	St. Paul	Max Macon	82	72	.532

(Playoffs: St. Paul defeated Wichita 4 games to 1; Denver defeated Minneapolis 4 games to 0. Finals: Denver defeated St. Paul 4 games to 2.)

Year	Championship Team	Manager	Won	Lost	Pct.
1958	Charleston	Bill Norman–Bill Adair	89	62	.589
	Wichita	Ben Geraghty	83	71	.539
	*Minneapolis	Gene Mauch	82	71	.536
	Denver	Andy Cohen	78	71	.523

(Playoffs: Denver defeated Charleston 4 games to 3; Minneapolis defeated Wichita 4 games to 2. Finals: Minneapolis defeated Denver 4 games to 0.)

Year	Championship Team	Manager	Won	Lost	Pct.
1959	Louisville (Eastern Division)	Ben Geraghty	97	65	.599
	*Minneapolis (Eastern Division)	Gene Mauch	95	67	.586
	Omaha (Western Division)	Joe Schultz	83	78	.516
	Fort Worth (Western Division)	Lou Klein	81	81	.500

* Asterisk indicates winning team.

Year	Championship Team	Manager	Won	Lost	Pct.

(Playoffs: Fort Worth defeated Louisville 4 games to 0; Minneapolis defeated Omaha 4 games to 2. Finals: Minneapolis defeated Fort Worth 4 games to 3.)

1960	Denver	Charlie Metro	88	66	.571
	*Louisville	Ben Geraghty–Bill Adair	85	68	.556
	Houston	Enos Slaughter	83	71	.539
	St. Paul	Danny Ozark	83	71	.539

(Playoffs: Denver defeated Houston 4 games to 3; Louisville defeated St. Paul 4 games to 2. Finals: Louisville defeated Denver 4 games to 2.)

1961	Indianapolis	Ellis "Cot" Deal	86	64	.573
	*Louisville	Ben Geraghty	80	70	.533
	Denver	Charlie Metro	75	73	.507
	Houston	Grady Hatton–Lou Klein–Harry Craft	73	77	.487

(Playoffs: Houston defeated Indianapolis 4 games to 1; Louisville defeated Denver 4 games to 3. Finals: Louisville defeated Houston 4 games to 2.)

1962	Indianapolis	Luke Appling	89	58	.605
	Omaha	Danny Ozark	79	68	.537
	Denver	Frank Skaff	79	71	.527
	*Louisville	Jack Tighe	71	75	.486

(Playoffs: Louisville defeated Indianapolis 3 games to 0; Denver defeated Omaha 3 games to 1. Finals: Louisville defeated Denver 4 games to 2.)

| 1963–68 | (The AA suspended operations.) | | | | |

| 1969 | Omaha | Jack McKeon | 85 | 55 | .607 |

(No playoffs.)

| 1970 | *Omaha (Eastern Division) | Jack McKeon | 73 | 65 | .529 |
| | Denver (Western Division) | Whitey Kurowski–Dick Gernert | 70 | 69 | .504 |

(Championship series: Omaha defeated Denver 4 games to 1.)

* Asterisk indicates winning team.

Year	Championship Team	Manager	Won	Lost	Pct.
1971	Indianapolis (Eastern Division)	Vern Rapp	84	55	.604
	*Denver (Western Division)	Del Wilber	73	67	.521

(Championship series: Denver defeated Indianapolis 4 games to 3.)

| 1972 | *Evansville (Eastern Division) | Del Crandall– Mike Roarke | 83 | 57 | .593 |
| | Wichita (Western Division) | Jim Marshall | 87 | 53 | .621 |

(Championship series: Evansville defeated Wichita 3 games to 0.)

| 1973 | Iowa (Eastern Division) | Joe Sparks | 83 | 53 | .610 |
| | *Tulsa (Western Division) | Jack Krol | 68 | 67 | .509 |

(Championship series: Tulsa defeated Iowa 4 games to 3.)

* Asterisk indicates winning team.

AMERICAN ASSOCIATION BATTING CHAMPIONS

Year	Player and Club	G	AB	Hits	Pct.
1902	John Ganzel, Louisville	123	521	194	.370
1903	Philip Geier, St. Paul	136	518	187	.362
1904	George Stone, Milwaukee	153	626	254	.405
1905	Charles Hemphill, St. Paul	145	560	204	.364
1906	Billy Hallman, Louisville	147	572	196	.342
1907	Jake Beckley, Kansas City	100	378	138	.365
1908	John Hayden, Indianapolis	154	588	186	.316
1909	Mike O'Neill, Minneapolis	144	548	162	.296
1910	Clifford "Cactus" Gravath, Minneapolis	164	612	200	.327
1911	Clifford "Cactus" Cravath, Minneapolis	167	608	221	.363
1912	Arthur Butler, St. Paul	125	513	169	.329
1913	Alex Chappelle, Milwaukee	85	350	122	.349
1914	Bill Hinchman, Columbus	163	620	227	.366
1915	Jack Lelivelt, Kansas City	152	575	199	.346
1916	Beals Becker, Kansas City	153	508	174	.343
1917	Beals Becker, Kansas City	151	551	178	.323
1918	Wheeler "Doc" Johnston, Milwaukee	31	115	43	.374
1919	Timothy Hendryx, Louisville	143	514	189	.368
1920	Joseph Rapp, St. Paul	155	558	187	.335
1921	Jay Kirke, Louisville	168	730	282	.386

Year	Player and Club	G	AB	Hits	Pct.
1922	Glenn Myatt, Milwaukee	121	370	137	.370
1923	Bill Lamar, Toledo	126	489	191	.391
1924	Lester Bell, Milwaukee	154	630	230	.365
1925	Ed Murphy, Columbus	100	390	155	.397
1926	Bevo Lebourveau, Toledo	149	584	220	.377
1927	Ewell "Reb" Russell, Indianapolis	128	431	166	.385
1928	Bobby Veach, Toledo	151	566	216	.382
1929	Art Ruble, Toledo	89	367	138	.376
1930	Bevo Lebourveau, Toledo	138	526	200	.380
1931	Art Shires, Milwaukee	157	623	240	.385
1932	Art Ruble, Minneapolis	141	561	211	.376
1933	Frank Sigafoos, Indianapolis	152	635	235	.370
1934	Earl Webb, Milwaukee	106	424	156	.368
1935	Johnny Cooney, Indianapolis	142	603	224	.371
1936	Vernon Washington, St. Paul	73	305	119	.390
1937	Enos Slaughter, Columbus	154	642	245	.382
1938	Ted Williams, Minneapolis	148	525	193	.366
1939	Gilbert English, St. Paul	139	501	172	.343
1940	Albert Wright, Minneapolis	146	578	213	.369
1941	Lou Novikoff, Milwaukee	90	365	135	.370
1942	Eddie Stanky, Milwaukee	145	527	180	.342
1943	Grey Clarke, Columbus	142	534	185	.346
1944	Johnny Wyrostek, Columbus	110	416	149	.358
1945	Lewis Flick, Milwaukee	142	575	215	.374
1946	Sebastian "Sibbi" Sisti, Indianapolis	149	592	203	.343
1947	Heinz "Dutch" Becker, Milwaukee	131	457	166	.363
1948	Glenn McQuillen, Toledo	147	538	177	.329
1949	Tom Wright, Louisville	151	549	202	.368
1950	Bob Addis, Milwaukee	136	529	171	.323
1951	Harry Walker, Columbus	110	298	117	.393
1952	Dave Pope, Indianapolis	126	475	167	.352
1953	Vic Power, Kansas City	149	622	217	.349
1954	Hal Smith, Columbus	110	386	135	.350
1955	Rance Pless, Minneapolis	156	593	200	.337
1956	Charles Peete, Omaha	116	417	146	.350
1957	Norman Siebern, Denver	144	548	191	.349
1958	Gordon Windhorn, Denver	141	509	167	.328
1959	Luis Marquez, Dallas	142	510	176	.345
1960	Larry Osborne, Denver	141	482	165	.342
1961	Don Wert, Denver	137	519	170	.328
1962	Tom McCraw, Indianapolis	140	525	171	.326

Year	Player and Club	G	AB	Hits	Pct.
1963–68	(The AA suspended operations.)				
1969	Bernie Carbo, Indianapolis	111	404	145	.359
1970	Chris Chambliss, Wichita	105	383	131	.342
1971	Richie Scheinblum, Denver	106	374	145	.388
1972	Gene Locklear, Indianapolis	134	467	152	.325
1973	Jim Dwyer, Tulsa	87	349	135	.387

AMERICAN ASSOCIATION RECORDS

Individual Batting Season Records

Highest Percentage
.405—George Stone, Milwaukee, 1904
Most Runs Scored
175—Joe Mowry, Minneapolis, 1932
Most Total Bases
439—Joe Hauser, Minneapolis, 1933
Most Hits
282—Jay Kirke, Louisville, 1921
Most Doubles
69—Bill Knickerbocker, Toledo, 1932
Most Triples
28—Lancelot Richbourg, Milwaukee, 1928
Most Home Runs
69—Joe Hauser, Minneapolis, 1933
Most Runs Batted In
191—Bunny Brief, Kansas City, 1921
Most Stolen Bases
72—Douglas Baird, Indianapolis, 1921
Most Bases on Balls
147—Nick Polly, Louisville, 1944
Most Times Struck Out
174—Jim McDaniel, Denver, 1961

Individual Pitching Season Records

Most Games Won
31—Tom Hughes, Minneapolis, 1910
31—Tom Sheehan, St. Paul, 1923
Most Games Lost
25—E. G. Erickson, Minneapolis, 1923

Most Innings Pitched
    446—U. S. "Stony" McGlynn, Milwaukee, 1909
Most Strikeouts
    330—Herb Score, Indianapolis, 1954
Most Bases on Balls
    173—Harry Weaver, Indianapolis, 1922
Most Hit Batsmen
    34—Frank Schneiberg, Milwaukee, 1907
Most Wild Pitches
    22—Leroy Parmelee, Minneapolis, 1938
    22—Wayne Simpson, Indianapolis, 1969

THE JUNIOR WORLD SERIES:
A WORD ON THE KODAK WORLD BASEBALL
CLASSIC OF 1972

The Junior World Series, a best of seven games match between the champions of the American Association and the International League, was first held in 1904, but it did not become a regular event until 1920.

The series was suspended in 1972 in favor of the Kodak World Baseball Classic, a combination round-robin, single elimination tournament made up of postseason playoff winners from the American Association, International League, and the Pacific Coast leagues, plus an all-star team of Latin players who participate regularly in the Caribbean winter leagues and a team from the host site (the Hawaii Islanders of the Coast League).

The idea of a five-team series looked great on paper, but the Classic ran into trouble from the beginning when the players threatened a boycott until better financial arrangements were made. When only 1,877 fans showed up for the first game involving the Islanders and the Caribbean All-Stars, it was apparent that the Classic was ill-conceived. Local interest declined even further when the Islanders were eliminated from the competition. Only 992 patrons turned out for the championship game in which the Caribbean All-Stars defeated the Albuquerque Dukes of the Pacific Coast League 6–2. Evansville of the American Association and Tidewater of the International League were the other participants.

Despite a great deal of talk about future series from Japan and Mexico and Class AAA all-stars and rotating the site, the classic was suspended indefinitely. The Eastman Kodak Company of Rochester, New York, sponsored the 1972 event along with the three Class AAA Leagues and the Caribbean circuit.

The Junior World Series was resumed in 1973.

RESULTS OF THE JUNIOR WORLD SERIES

1904	Buffalo, EL, 2 games; St. Paul, AA, 1 game
1905	(No series played.)
1906	Buffalo, EL, 3 games; Columbus, AA, 2 games
1907	Toronto, EL, 4 games; Columbus, AA, 1 game
1908–16	(No series played.)
1917	Indianapolis, AA, 4 games; Toronto, IL, 1 game
1918–19	(No series played.)
1920	Baltimore, IL, 5 games; St. Paul, AA, 1 game
1921	Louisville, AA, 5 games; Baltimore, IL, 3 games
1922	Baltimore, IL, 5 games; St. Paul, AA, 2 games
1923	Kansas City, AA, 5 games; Baltimore, IL, 4 games
1924	St. Paul, AA, 5 games; Baltimore, IL, 4 games (1 tie)
1925	Baltimore, IL, 5 games; Louisville, AA, 3 games
1926	Toronto, IL, 5 games; Louisville, AA, 0 games
1927	Toledo, AA, 5 games; Buffalo, IL, 1 game
1928	Indianapolis, AA, 5 games; Rochester, IL, 1 game (1 tie)
1929	Kansas City, AA, 5 games; Rochester, IL, 4 games
1930	Rochester, IL, 5 games; Louisville, AA, 3 games
1931	Rochester, IL, 5 games; St. Paul, AA, 3 games
1932	Newark, IL, 4 games; Minneapolis, AA, 2 games
1933	Columbus, AA, 5 games; Buffalo, IL, 3 games
1934	Columbus, AA, 5 games; Toronto, IL, 4 games
1935	(No series played.)
1936	Milwaukee, AA, 4 games; Buffalo, IL, 1 game
1937	Newark, IL, 4 games; Columbus, AA, 3 games
1938	Kansas City, AA, 4 games; Newark, IL, 3 games
1939	Louisville, AA, 4 games; Rochester, IL, 3 games
1940	Newark, IL, 4 games; Louisville, AA, 2 games
1941	Columbus, AA, 4 games; Montreal, IL, 2 games
1942	Columbus, AA, 4 games; Syracuse, IL, 1 game
1943	Columbus, AA, 4 games; Syracuse, IL, 1 game
1944	Baltimore, IL, 4 games; Louisville, AA, 2 games
1945	Louisville, AA, 4 games; Newark, IL, 2 games
1946	Montreal, IL, 4 games; Louisville, AA, 2 games
1947	Milwaukee, AA, 4 games; Syracuse, IL, 3 games
1948	Montreal, IL, 4 games; St. Paul, AA, 1 game
1949	Indianapolis, AA, 4 games; Montreal, IL, 2 games
1950	Columbus, AA, 4 games; Baltimore, IL, 2 games
1951	Milwaukee, AA, 4 games; Montreal, IL, 2 games
1952	Rochester, IL, 4 games; Kansas City, AA, 3 games
1953	Montreal, IL, 4 games; Kansas City, AA, 1 game

1954	Louisville, AA, 4 games; Syracuse, IL, 2 games
1955	Minneapolis, AA, 4 games; Rochester, IL, 3 games
1956	Indianapolis, AA, 4 games; Rochester, IL, 0 games
1957	Denver, AA, 4 games; Buffalo, IL, 1 game
1958	Minneapolis, AA, 4 games; Montreal, IL, 0 games
1959	Havana, IL, 4 games; Minneapolis, AA, 3 games
1960	Louisville, AA, 4 games; Toronto, IL, 2 games
1961	Buffalo, IL, 4 games; Louisville, AA, 0 games
1962	Atlanta, IL, 4 games; Louisville, AA, 3 games
1963–68	(American Association did not operate.)
1970	Syracuse, IL, 4 games; Omaha, AA, 1 game
1971	Rochester, IL, 4 games; Denver AA, 3 games
1972	(No series played.)
1973	Pawtucket, IL, 4 games; Tulsa, AA, 1 game

8

THE INTERNATIONAL LEAGUE:
The Senior Minor League

NAMES UNDER WHICH THE INTERNATIONAL LEAGUE HAS OPERATED
International League Titles

1884	Eastern League
1885	New York State League
1886–87	International League
1888–89	International Association
1890	International League
1891	Eastern Association
1892–1911	Eastern League
1912–17	International League
1918–19	New International League
1920	International League

ROSTER OF INTERNATIONAL LEAGUE TEAMS
(CLASS A, 1902–07; CLASS AA, 1908–45; CLASS AAA, 1946) [1]

Team	Years in Operation
Akron, Ohio	1920
Albany, New York	1885, 1888, 1891–93, 1933–36
Allentown, Pennsylvania	1884, 1894
Atlanta, Georgia	1962–65
Baltimore, Maryland	1884, 1903–14, 1916–53
Binghamton, New York	1885–87, 1892–94, 1918–19
Buffalo, New York	1886–98, 1901–70 (franchise shifted to Winnipeg on June 11)
Charleston, West Virginia	1961#, 1971—
Columbus, Ohio	1955–70
Detroit, Michigan	1889–90
Elmira, New York	1886, 1892
Erie, Pennsylvania	1893–94
Grand Rapids, Michigan	1890
Hamilton, Ontario, Canada	1886–90, 1918#
Harrisburg, Pennsylvania	1884, 1915#
Hartford, Connecticut	1899–1901
Havana, Cuba	1954–60 (franchise shifted to Jersey City on July 13)
Indianapolis, Indiana	1963
Jacksonville, Florida	1962–68
Jersey City, New Jersey	1887, 1902–15, 1918–33, 1937–50, 1960#, 1961
Lancaster, Pennsylvania	1884
Lebanon, Pennsylvania	1891
Little Rock, Arkansas	1963
London, Ontario, Canada	1888–90
Louisville, Kentucky	1968–72
Memphis, Tennessee	1974—
Miami, Florida	1956–60
Montreal, Quebec, Canada	1890, 1897#, 1898–1903#, 1914–17, 1928–60
Newark, New Jersey	1884, 1887, 1902–15 (franchise shifted to Harrisburg on July 2, 1915) 1916–19, 1921–25 (franchise shifted to Providence in mid-season, 1926–49

[1] See page 323 for Key to Roster of League Teams.

Team	Years in Operation
New Haven, Connecticut	1891–92
Oswego, New York	1885–87
Ottawa, Ontario, Canada	1886–87, 1898#, 1951–54
Pawtucket, Rhode Island	1973—
Peninsula (Hampton and Newport News), Virginia	1972–73
Philadelphia, Pennsylvania	1892
Providence, Rhode Island	1891–1917, 1925#
Reading, Pennsylvania	1884, 1919–31
Richmond, Virginia	1884, 1915–17, 1954–64, 1966—
Rochester, New York	1885–89, 1891–92, 1895–97 (home games shifted to Montreal because of park fire), 1898 (finished its schedule in Ottawa), 1899—
Saginaw–Bay City, Michigan	1890
San Juan, Puerto Rico	1961 (franchise shifted to Charleston on May 19)
Scranton, Pennsylvania	1887, 1894–97
Springfield, Massachusetts	1893-1900, 1950–53
Syracuse, New York	1885–89, 1891–92, 1894–1901, 1918 (franchise shifted to Hamilton in midseason), 1920–27, 1934–55, 1961—
Tidewater (Norfolk, Portsmouth, and Virginia Beach), Virginia	1969—
Toledo, Ohio	1889, 1965—
Toronto, Ontario, Canada	1886–90, 1895–1967
Trenton, New Jersey	1884
Troy, New York	1888, 1891–94
Utica, New York	1885–87, 1892
Wilkes-Barre, Pennsylvania	1887, 1893–98
Wilmington, Delaware	1884
Winnipeg, Manitoba, Canada	1970#, 1971
Worcester, Massachusetts	1899–1903 (franchise shifted to Montreal In May)
York, Pennsylvania	1884

The International League completed its ninetieth consecutive year of play in 1973. Thus, the IL clearly ranks as baseball's oldest continuously operating minor league. Neither internal reorganizations, nor wars, nor hard economic times forced this hardy circuit to suspend operations. Even in the climactic war year of 1918, the International alone of all the minors completed its season, continuing play through Labor Day. Both major leagues also declared their seasons complete at the close of the Labor Day weekend.

The circuit was organized as the Eastern League in 1884. It began play the same year. At an organizational meeting held at Philadelphia on January 4, 1884, the named agreed upon was the "Union Association," but in order to avoid confusion with the outlaw Union Association, which was striving to become a second major league at the time, the name was changed quickly to the Eastern League.

In its first year the league was composed of ten cities from five states: Baltimore, Maryland; Newark and Trenton, New Jersey; Wilmington, Delaware; Richmond, Virginia; and Allentown, Harrisburg, Lancaster, Reading, and York, Pennsylvania.

The story of the league's continual reorganizations from 1885 through the rest of the century becomes a bit complicated. According to the league's archives, the IL continued its life in 1885 under the name of the New York League, a six-team circuit based in Binghamton, Rochester, Utica, Albany, Syracuse and Oswego. Also in 1885, a league was formed in Ontario, Canada, with teams in Toronto, Hamilton and other cities. Then in 1886, the New York State and Ontario circuits were merged to form the International League, a title that held for two years. Toronto and Hamilton came into the IL to form an eight-team league, joining Binghamton, Buffalo, Oswego, Rochester, Syracuse, and another franchise that operated in both Elmira and Utica. (See page 94 for a complete listing of changes in league titles from 1884 to the present.)

It should also be indicated here that our Eastern League of 1884 should not be confused with the "new Eastern League" of 1885–86, which was originally organized to operate in eight cities: Jersey City, Newark, Trenton, Lancaster, Richmond, Norfolk, Wilmington, Delaware, and Washington, D.C. (Washington was a member of the circuit only in 1885, since it joined the National League during the following year.)

The new Eastern League passed out of the professional baseball scene at the end of the 1886 campaign, with Jersey City and Newark then going into the International League to make it a ten-team circuit. The ten-team venture for 1887 proved to be unworkable, and from this point until 1963, the IL never consisted of more than eight teams.

In 1888, the league (known for two years as the "International Association") had teams in three Ontario cities (Hamilton, London, and Toronto) and five in New York state (Albany, Buffalo, Rochester, Syracuse, and Troy). In 1889, Toledo and Detroit replaced Albany and Troy, with Toledo remaining in the circuit for a single season and Detroit two.

One of baseball's bitterest and most expensive wars broke out in

1890, when a large group of big league players organized their own Players' (Brotherhood) League in competition with the National League and the American Association (also a major league). Buffalo jumped to the Brotherhood; while Rochester, Syracuse, and Toledo accepted bids from the association. Bidding for players by three major leagues led to widespread contract jumping as salary offers skyrocketed.

The International League was reduced to six teams. An effort to sustain a club in Buffalo collapsed shortly after the start of the season. The Bisons shifted to Montreal, met little success, and then moved on to Grand Rapids, Michigan. Later the Hamilton franchise was brought to Montreal and hung on until the league folded on July 7, 1890. It was the only time the International disbanded before season's end. In addition to Detroit and the other aforementioned cities, Saginaw–Bay City, Michigan, and Toronto and London, Ontario, rounded out the IL during this tumultuous year.

The Players' League, whose chief driving force had been Charles Comiskey, failed after its single year of operation, while the American Association ended its ten-year life at the close of the 1891 season.

In 1891, the IL was reorganized as the Eastern Association with eight teams. Present-day clubs in the 1891 loop include only Buffalo and Rochester.

The circuit changed its name to the Eastern League in 1892, a name it retained for twenty years. Since 1892 was a bad year for the country economically, baseball attendance was down everywhere and only six of the eight teams in the IL (or EL) finished the season.

In 1893, the hard-driving Patrick T. Powers began his seventeen-year tenure as league president, serving until 1911. His administration was interrupted by Harry L. Taylor's one-year term in 1906. Pat Powers, one of the great figures in professional baseball, also served as first president of the National Association beginning in 1901. He did a great deal to solidify the league. After the mid-1890s especially, the circuit began to develop a large following of baseball fans throughout the U.S. and Canada. Early in Powers' presidency (1895), Rochester and Toronto rejoined the league and became its bellwethers. Rochester has held continuous membership since then, and Toronto remaining in the fold for seventy-three consecutive years (until it dropped out of Organized Baseball after the 1967 season).

In 1896, for the first time in the league's history, there was not a single change in the roster of teams . . . in addition to Rochester and Toronto, teams were fielded in Buffalo, Providence, Scranton, Springfield, Syracuse, and Wilkes-Barre.

The country was concerned with the Spanish–American War during the 1898 season and attendance nosedived around most of the professional baseball circuit. Rochester failed to draw enough fans to meet expenses and finished its season in Ottawa, but this was the last time Rochester did not complete its schedule on homegrounds.

Ban Johnson, president of the Western League and ambitious to form a major league (the Western League became the American League), annexed the Buffalo territory for his circuit for the 1899–1900 seasons. Buffalo, however, returned to the IL fold in 1901, and it remained a member for the next seventy years.

Jersey City and Newark replaced Syracuse and Hartford in 1902, and in the following year, Baltimore, which was ousted by the American League, succeeded Montreal. The 1903 campaign was barely a month old, however, when the Worcester franchise was shifted to Quebec.

For the next eleven years (through 1914), the International League enjoyed a tranquil and prosperous period, with membership remaining absolutely stable. Fans flocked to the games as never before, and new stadiums were built with the generous assistance of trolley car companies, which viewed baseball as an excellent way to promote business. Moreover, the climate for baseball during the twelve or fifteen years before World War I was so healthy that professional leagues sprang up all over the country.

Ed Barrow, former manager at Montreal and Toronto, became league president in 1911 and held the post until 1918, when he became manager of the Boston Red Sox (at Boston, Barrow converted left-handed pitcher Babe Ruth into an outfielder). During Barrow's first full year as president in 1912, the circuit's name finally was changed permanently to International League, though it was known as the "New International League" in 1918–19.

Baseball's prosperity eventually spelled trouble for the International. In 1913, the Federal League, which was organized by a group of wealthy sportsmen, operated as an outlaw minor circuit. But in 1914, these men decided the time was ripe for a third major league. Three IL cities were invaded (Baltimore and Buffalo in 1914 and Newark in 1915), earning the International the title of "The Belgium of Baseball." (The Federal League also invaded cities in both major circuits.) For a long and bitter year, Baltimore and Buffalo stood firm, holding their IL franchises despite the presence of the Feds in their backyards, but in 1915 Buffalo alone held out. Baltimore moved to Richmond before the start of the season and Newark shifted to Harrisburg on July 2.

Barrow was promised the presidency of the Federal League if it achieved recognized big league status, but this was not to be. "The Great Baseball War," ended as have all the others, fortunately, in compromise and consolidation. Only the Baltimore Feds were dissatisfied with the results of the settlement. They carried their grievances into the U.S. Supreme Court, where in 1922 the historic decision that baseball was not subject to the Sherman Anti-Trust Act was handed down by Justice Oliver Wendell Holmes.

The demise of the Federal League saw Newark return from Harrisburg in 1916. When Richmond elected to stay in the circuit, Jack Dunn had to buy up the Jersey City franchise in order to bring Baltimore back into the fold.

America's all-out effort in World War I brought fresh crises and challenges to the league. Attendance fell and all of the teams were operating in the red. By the beginning of 1918, the league finances had reached such straits that all administrative salaries were halved. President Ed Barrow did not particularly care for this move and promptly resigned.

Richmond, Providence, and Montreal dropped out of the league in favor of Jersey City, Binghamton, and Syracuse. Syracuse fans, however, did not support the Chiefs at the gate and the franchise was shifted to Hamilton in midseason. As indicated previously, the International was the only minor league circuit to complete its season in 1918, and it accomplished this feat through an adroit shifting of franchises.

Frequent franchise shifts continued during the immediate postwar period. In 1919, Reading succeeded Hamilton, and in 1920, Akron and Syracuse replaced Newark and Binghamton. In 1921, Newark reacquired the Akron franchise.

Finally, the league settled down again, and shifts were relatively infrequent during the next two decades. Among the few changes was a Newark–Providence–Newark shuffle in 1925–26. Syracuse moved out of the circuit again after the 1927 season and was replaced by Montreal.

Night baseball was introduced into the International on July 3, 1930, at Buffalo when the Bisons hosted Montreal (the Bisons lost to Montreal 5–4 in this milestone contest). Within a few years all IL clubs lighted their parks, and this was a key factor in keeping attendance up to survival levels—and better—during the depths of the Depression.

Then in 1933, Frank Shaughnessy, general manager at Montreal, introduced his playoff system to the International League, and the scheme was soon adopted by most of the other minor leagues. The Shaughnessy Playoffs are credited for "saving the minors" during the Depression, and baseball historians further emphasize that the widespread introduction of lights during the 1930s also gave the minors a vital "shot-in-the-arm" at this highly critical period (see Chapter 4.)

In 1937, Jersey City came back into the league, replacing Albany in a major franchise shift, and once again there was the resumption of the natural rivalry between Jersey City and Newark. And rivalries always resulted in good attendance figures.

For the next dozen years, including World War II and the immediate postwar era, the International League saw no further franchise changes. The circuit prospered and attendance hit record levels. Then the advent of television shook the very foundations of baseball's senior minor league. Both New Jersey clubs were the first to succumb: Newark was forced to fold its tent after the 1949 season, while Jersey City collapsed after 1950.

Newark and Jersey City, both a part of New York City's metropolitan area, simply could not compete with the veritable blizzard of televised big league games available free of charge to anyone who had access to a television set. Once loyal supporters of the Newark Bears and Jersey City Giants now found themselves switching on the TV to watch either the Brooklyn Dodgers, the New York Giants, or the New York Yankees. This was really a momentous and tragic event in baseball history since Newark and Jersey City, which had fielded professional teams since the 1880s, would probably never be permanently represented in Organized Baseball again. Jersey City did enter the IL later on an emergency basis for a brief period, while Newark has never seriously attempted to reenter Organized Baseball since the demise of the Bears a quarter of a century ago. Springfield replaced Newark in 1950, and Ottawa, making its first appearance in the league in over fifty years, succeeded Jersey City in 1951.

A new era began when Havana was admitted to the league in 1954. The league, now truly "international," embraced three countries: Canada, Cuba, and the United States. In 1954, Richmond returned to the circuit after a long absence when the American League tapped Baltimore, ending an association of a half century between the Orioles and the International. Realignments continued, with Columbus replacing Ottawa in 1955 and Miami supplanting Syracuse in 1956.

Four years passed without a change in the league roster, but then in 1960, Castro took over in Cuba. The resultant strained Cuban–American relations caused the IL to transfer the Havana franchise to Jersey City in midseason (July 13).

To further complicate matters, the agitation for major league expansion adversely affected the IL's attendance. In 1959, the league's eight teams drew 1,778,000 paid admissions, and in 1960, they drew only 1,369,000. Historically, minor league fans had worried about their star *players* being picked off by the majors. Now they were concerned about their best *towns* being carried off.

Montreal ended its association with the IL at the close of the 1960 season, after holding membership for thirty-three consecutive years. Attendance was down to 112,000; a decade earlier, in 1951, the Royals had drawn nearly four times that number. Syracuse replaced Montreal and has held down a spot on the league's roster ever since.

Jersey City left the league after the 1961 campaign, primarily because it finished dead last in attendance figures, with less than 62,000 paid. A shift to San Juan, Puerto Rico, in 1961 also proved to be unworkable, and on May 19, the team was moved north to Charleston.

In 1962, the league steadied itself by transferring the Jersey City and Charleston franchises to the new territories of Atlanta and Jacksonville. Then in the following year, the league expanded to ten clubs with the admission of Little Rock and Indianapolis. This second ten-team experiment in IL history proved no more successful than had the first one, seventy-six years earlier, and the new members were dropped before the beginning of the 1964 season.

Toledo returned to the circuit in 1965, having been away for seventy-six years, and the Mud Hens have been on the league roster ever since. The Mud Hens replaced Richmond, but the Virginians were out of the fold for only one season. In 1966, when the National League moved from Milwaukee to Atlanta, Richmond took over the Atlanta franchise.

League attendance figures improved in 1966, with 1,249,000 paid admissions (an improvement of more than 100,000 over the preceding season). In 1971–73, IL attendance averaged at about the 1,200,000 figure, with Rochester pacing the league in this all-important department.

Toronto dropped out of the league with the close of the 1967 campaign, having been on the IL roster for seventy-three consecutive years, since attendance had skidded all the way down to 67,000. Louisville replaced Toronto in 1968. Then after 1972 Louisville itself, long a stronghold for professional baseball, withdrew to be replaced by Pawtucket.

In 1969, the International League entered the Tidewater area of Virginia (Norfolk and Portsmouth) for the first time. The New York Mets shifted their Jacksonville franchise to Tidewater because of sparse attendance in the Florida City.

A new stadium was completed at Norfolk in 1970, and it immediately became the pride and showcase of the league. As one of the "Grand Opening" events at the new Norfolk facility, the IL All-Stars took on the Baltimore Orioles and beat them 4–3. Also in 1970, Syracuse won its first league pennant since 1897. The team then proceeded to take both the Governor's Cup and the Junior World Series.

Columbus, another of the old-line top minor league cities, withdrew from the league after 1970. The gap was filled by Charleston. Columbus' withdrawal from the professional baseball scene was particularly significant since the National Association's headquarters had been located there for many years. The demise of the Columbus Red Birds contributed to the decision to move the headquarters to St. Petersburg in 1973.

Sadly enough, the International League is not really "international" any longer. The IL had no Canadian team from 1968 through 1969 after Toronto had left the flock. And after Winnipeg, which joined the league in June 11, 1970, when it replaced Buffalo, withdrew following the 1971 campaign, the circuit has been composed of American cities only.

INTERNATIONAL LEAGUE HIGHLIGHTS

1909: Joe "Iron Man" McGinnity, a thirty-eight-year-old Newark right-hander freshly retired from a brilliant ten-year major league pitching career, set all-time IL marks by pitching 422 innings and recording 11 shutouts. He piled up a 29–16 log and occupied his spare moments by managing the Bears.

Actually, McGinnity began a second career in 1909, for he pitched in the minors until 1925 (he missed the 1919–21 and 1924 seasons). He won no less than 207 games against 180 losses during that period. In his final active season as player–manager of Dubuque in the Mississippi Valley League, at the age of fifty-four, he checked in with a 6–6 mark. He had remained with the Bears through 1912 and had turned in his winningest IL season in 1910 when he stood at 30–19. All told, his minor league won–lost record, counting his three seasons in the minors before he graduated to the majors with Brooklyn in 1899, comes to 235–212. When we include McGinnity's 247–145 big league figures, his total professional won–lost record amounts to a gigantic 482–357. He worked a total of 7,332 innings (3,455 in the majors and 3,877 in the minors), more than enough to justify his title, the "Iron Man."

An absolutely tireless worker, McGinnity's favorite pitch was a half-sidearm, half-underhand delivery he called "Old Sal." He won election to the Hall of Fame in 1946.

On July 13, 1909, Irving "Young Cy" Young, a Minneapolis fire-baller, slammed a homer in the tenth inning to win the second of two shutouts he pitched vs. Milwaukee.

1910: Chester Carmichael, a Buffalo right-hander, pitched a perfect nine-inning game against Jersey City, winning 1–0. This was the IL's only nine-inning perfect game until August 15, 1952, when Dick Marlowe (another Buffalo right-hander) defeated Baltimore 2–0.

1914: George Herman "Babe" Ruth, a nineteen-year-old left-handed pitcher, was signed to a Baltimore contract in February by Jack Dunn, the Orioles' president. Ruth, who had just left St. Mary's Industrial School in Baltimore (where he had spent most of his boyhood), received a $600 bonus for signing. Fame came quickly for Ruth, for he pitched a spring exhibition game in Baltimore against the World Champion Philadelphia Athletics and beat them. Then in his first regular season start, he hurled a shutout against Buffalo.

In July, Dunn sold Ruth to the Boston Red Sox for $2,900. The Sox farmed him to Providence, also in the International League. His total pitching record in the IL for 1914 came to 22–9, along with a league-leading .710 winning percentage. He never hit a single home run for Baltimore (except in exhibition games), but he did belt one out of the park for Providence, where he played a few games in the outfield and first base. Ruth's minor league career was short since he was called up by Boston in September and remained in the majors for twenty-two years.

1924: Robert "Lefty" Grove, ace of the Baltimore Orioles pitching staff, was sold to the Philadelphia Athletics at the conclusion of the 1924 campaign for a record $100,600. The extra $600 was added to make the price a record for a transaction involving one player. (The Boston Red Sox had sold Babe Ruth to the New York Yankees for an even $100,000.)

In his five years with the Orioles, Grove won 109 games and lost only 36, having amassed 27 victories in each of his final two seasons. Grove, one of the fastest pitchers who ever lived, clearly compiled the most brilliant record of any moundsman in IL history, and it should also be noted that his total professional statistical record is staggering. Counting his 3–3 log for Martinsburg, West Virginia, in the Blue Ridge League during the first weeks of the 1920 season, together with his IL and big league records (the latter stands at 300–140 over seventeen seasons), we find that he won 412 and lost 179 for a percentage of .696. No other pitcher in the history of Organized Baseball has maintained that high a winning percentage over so long a period—twenty-two years.

Baltimore, of course, was not controlled by a big league club at this time, and it could thus hold out for the best possible price for a star like Grove. If the Orioles had been operating under the aegis of a major league outfit, there is no question that Lefty would have "graduated" much earlier.

1926: The Reading team compiled one of the worst records in the history of professional baseball, 31–129, for a .194 percentage. It finished exactly 75 games behind the first place Toronto Maple Leafs, still an

Organized Baseball record for "most games finishing behind league leader." Reading's unhappy managerial chores were shared by Frank Shaughnessy and George "Hooks" Wiltse.

1929: The pennant-winning Rochester Red Wings reeled off 225 double plays, a mark that has never been eclipsed in Organized Baseball. The Red Wing infield, which was responsible for most of the twin killings, consisted of: "Rip" Collins, first base; "Specs" Toporcer, second base; Heinie Sand, shortstop; and Joe "Poison" Brown, third base.

1932: Russell "Buzz" Arlett, a Baltimore outfielder, hit four homers against Reading on June 1 at Reading, and then in a July 4 game, he hit another four homers against Reading at Baltimore. Four other IL players have hit four home runs in one game, but no other player has done it twice. Arlett, who led the league in homers for the 1932 season with 54, established the Pacific Coast League record for lifetime homers with 251 for Oakland from 1918 to 1930.

1937: The Newark Bears, managed by Oscar Vitt and then the New York Yankees' top farm club, rolled to a 109–43 .717 season, finishing 25½ games ahead of second-place Montreal. No other team in International League history had won a pennant by such a wide margin. Newark's postseason record for 1937 was even more impressive than its amazing showing in the regular season! The Bears took four straight games from both Syracuse and Baltimore in the semifinals and finals for the Governor's Cup. Then after losing three straight games at home to the Columbus Red Birds in the Junior World Series, they went on to win the next four straight at Columbus. Thus, with a 12–3 playoff record, their total season's log ran to 121–46.

The Bears roster included such future Yankee stars as second baseman Joe Gordon, first baseman Babe Dahlgren, outfielder Charley Keller, catcher Buddy Rosar, and pitchers Steve Sundra and Atley Donald. Many baseball experts said the 1937 Newark Bears could have made a respectable showing in either of the two big leagues at the time.

1938: Bob Seeds, a right-handed Buffalo outfielder, put on perhaps the greatest two-day batting exhibition in the history of professional baseball. On May 6, against the Newark Bears at Buffalo, Seeds hit four home runs in four consecutive innings (the 4th, 5th, 6th, and 7th). He had singled in his first trip, going 5 for 5, and driving in 12 runs, an IL record for one game. On the following day at the same park against Newark, he singled once more, slammed 3 more homers, walked, and then struck out in his final trip . . . he added another 5 RBI's to his totals. Thus, for the two games, he went 9 for 10, hit 7 home runs, and drove in 17 runs. In mid-June, after fifty-nine games, "Suitcase Bob," batting .335 with a league-leading 28 homers and 95 RBI's, was called up by the New York Giants and finished the season with them. Seeds played intermittently in the majors between 1930 and 1940 for three other teams besides the Giants (Cleveland, the Boston Red Sox, and the New York Yankees) and batted .277 in 615 games.

1943: Albert "Red" Schoendienst, a twenty-year-old Rochester short-stop, won both the batting title (.337) and MVP honors. Schoendienst switched to second base after he reached the majors.

1946: The International League moved up from Class AA to the newly-created Class AAA ranking. The Pacific Coast League and the American Association also moved from Class AA to Class AAA at this time.

Jackie Robinson was signed to a Montreal contract and became the first black to enter Organized Baseball. Robinson, personally selected by the Brooklyn Dodger's president–general manager Branch Rickey to break baseball's color line, came through magnificently. Robinson led the IL in batting with a .349 mark and topped all IL second basemen with a .985 fielding average (he committed only 10 errors in 656 chances). Robinson became one of the most popular players ever to wear a Royals' uniform.

1947: Hank Sauer, a Syracuse outfielder, was selected as the league's most valuable player on the strength of his 50 homers, 141 RBI's, and .336 batting average. *The Sporting News* also selected him as the "Minor League Player of the Year."

1949: Bobby Morgan, a Montreal shortstop–third baseman, took MVP honors. He hit a league-leading .337 and batted in 112 runs.

1952: James "Junior" Gilliam, a twenty-three-year-old Montreal second baseman in his second year with the Royals, won the MVP award. He hit .301, scored 111 runs, and batted in 112, while making only 9 errors and fielding .987. Gilliam acquired the name "Junior" because, as a member of the Nashville Black Vols and Baltimore Elite Giants in the black leagues from 1945 to 1950, he was often the youngest player on the field.

1953: Glenn "Rocky" Nelson, a Montreal first baseman, won the first of his three MVP awards and became the only man in IL history to be so honored more than once.

A left-handed line-drive hitter, he received his second MVP award while with Montreal in 1955 and his third while with Toronto in 1958.

In 1953, Nelson batted .308, hit 34 homers, and had 136 RBI's; in 1955, he batted .364, hit 37 homers, and knocked in 130 runs; while in 1958, his figures were .326, 43, and 120. Nelson was elected to the International League's Hall of Fame in 1960, the same year he batted .300 in 93 games for the world champion Pittsburgh Pirates. He remained with the Pirates in 1961 and closed his IL career with Toronto in 1962 at the age of thirty-eight.

Bob Trice, an Ottawa right-hander, was the first pitcher to receive the International League Baseball Writer's Association "Most Valuable Pitcher" award. He compiled a 21–10 record with a 3.10 ERA.

At the end of the season, the owners of the St. Louis Browns gained permission to shift their franchise to Baltimore, marking the first territorial shift in American League history. The owners of the "new Baltimore Orioles" paid Jack Dunn, Jr., owner of Baltimore's International League franchise, a reported $350,000 and nearly $50,000 as an indemnity to the IL.

Springfield also left the IL at the end of 1953.

1954: Elston Howard, Toronto catcher, won the MVP by batting .330, hitting 22 homers, and knocking in 109 runs. Howard began his professional career in the Negro leagues and starred for the Kansas City Monarchs in 1948–50.

Two new teams, Richmond and Havana, joined the circuit.

1958: Luke Easter, a Buffalo first baseman, hit .307, socked 38 homers and drove in 109 runs—not bad for a man of forty-six years. Big Luke, who stood 6 feet, 4½ inches and weighed 245, shifted to Rochester early in the 1959 season and remained there as an active player until 1964 when he was fifty-two years old. Easter never revealed his true age until after he retired. While with the Rochester Red Wings, he helped develop a number of future big league long-ball hitters, such as Boog Powell and Curt Blefary.

Easter had played with the Cleveland Indians from 1949 to 1954, and many of his 93 big league homers were titanic shots.

1958–59: Bob Lennon, the man who blasted 64 homers for Nashville in the Southern Association in 1954, was with the Montreal Royals and was still hitting homers—he hit 25 in 1958 and 28 in 1959.

1967: Tommie Aaron, an outfielder–first baseman for the pennant-winning Richmond Braves, was voted the league's MVP on the basis of his .309 batting average and solid all-around play. Tommie, the younger brother of celebrated home run hitter Henry Aaron, played intermittently for both the Milwaukee and Atlanta Braves from 1962 through 1971. He is now starting a new career as a minor league manager, and is currently at the helm of the Savannah Braves in the Southern League.

1968: Merv Rettenmund, a speedy power-hitting Rochester outfielder, won MVP honors and the batting title with a .331 average. He scored a league-leading 104 runs in only 114 games.

1969: Ron Klimkowski, a Syracuse right-hander, was voted the league's Most Valuable Pitcher on the strength of his 15–7 record and a 2.18 ERA, the lowest in the IL.

1970: George Kopacz (a Columbus first baseman) and Roger Freed (a Rochester outfielder) tied for MVP honors. Kopacz batted .310, hit 29 homers, and knocked in 115 runs; while Freed batted .334, hit 24 homers, and knocked in 130 runs.

1971: Bobby Grich, a Rochester shortstop, was named the International League's MVP and *The Sporting News* tapped him as "Minor League Player of the Year." He had batted .336, hit 32 homers, and knocked in 83 runs. He crossed the plate 124 times in 130 games.

1972: Rochester topped the league in paid admissions with 296,864 and ranked second only to the Hawaii Islanders of the Pacific Coast League, which led the U.S. minors with 305,878. (The Mexico City Reds of the Class AAA Mexican League paced the National Association with 349,684 paid admissions.)

INTERNATIONAL LEAGUE PRESIDENTS

Year	President
1884	Henry H. Diddlebock
1885	W. S. Arnold
1886	F. R. Winne
1887	Frank T. Gilbert
1888	E. Strachen Cox
1889	Riley V. Miller
1890–92	Charles D. White
1893–1905	Patrick T. Powers
1906	Harry L. Taylor
1907–10	Patrick T. Powers
1911–17	Edward G. Barrow
1918	John H. Farrell
1919	David L. Fultz
1920–28	John Conway Toole
1929–36	Charles H. Knapp
1936	Warren C. Giles
1937–60	Frank J. Shaughnessy
1961–65	Thomas H. Richardson
1966—	George H. Sisler, Jr.

INTERNATIONAL LEAGUE CHAMPIONS

Year	Championship Team	Manager	Won	Lost	Pct.
1884	Trenton	R. T. "Pat" Powers	46	38	.547
1885	Syracuse	Henry J. Ormsbee	45	32	.584
1886	Utica	Emory J. Hengle	62	34	.646
1887	Toronto	Charles Cushman	65	36	.644
1888	Syracuse	John Chapman	81	31	.723
1889	Detroit	Bob Leadley	72	39	.649
1890	Detroit	Bob Leadley	Not Available		.617

Year	Championship Team	Manager	Won	Lost	Pct.
1891	Buffalo (regular season)	R. T. "Pat" Powers	72	27	.727
	Buffalo (supplemental)	R. T. "Pat" Powers	17	8	.680
1892	Providence	W. W. Burnham	40	25	.616
	*Binghamton	Frank Leonard	32	16	.667
	(Binghamton won split-season playoff over Providence.)				
1893	Erie	Charles Morton	63	41	.606
1894	Providence	W. J. "Bill" Murray	78	37	.678
1895	Springfield	Tom Burns	88	37	.704
1896	Providence	W. J. "Bill" Murray	71	46	.607
1897	Syracuse	Al Buckenberger	86	50	.632
1898	Montreal	Charles Dooley	68	47	.591
1899	Rochester	Al Buckenberger	73	44	.624
1900	Providence	W. J. "Bill" Murray	85	53	.616
1901	Rochester	Al Buckenberger	88	49	.642
1902	Toronto	Arthur Irwin	85	42	.669
1903	Jersey City	W. J. "Bill" Murray	92	33	.736
1904	Buffalo	George Stallings	88	46	.657
1905	Providence	Jack Dunn	83	47	.638
1906	Buffalo	George Stallings	85	55	.607
1907	Toronto	Joe Kelley	83	51	.619
1908	Baltimore	Jack Dunn	83	57	.593

* Asterisk indicates winning team.

Year	Championship Team	Manager	Won	Lost	Pct.
1909	Rochester	John Ganzel	90	61	.596
1910	Rochester	John Ganzel	92	61	.601
1911	Rochester	John Ganzel	98	54	.645
1912	Toronto	Joe Kelley	91	62	.595
1913	Newark	H. T. Smith	95	57	.625
1914	Providence	Bill Donovan	95	59	.617
1915	Buffalo	P. J. Donovan	86	50	.632
1916	Buffalo	P. J. Donovan	82	58	.586
1917	Toronto	Larry Lajoie	93	61	.604
1918	Toronto	Dan Howley	88	39	.693
1919	Baltimore	Jack Dunn	100	49	.671
1920	Baltimore	Jack Dunn	110	43	.719
1921	Baltimore	Jack Dunn	119	47	.717
1922	Baltimore	Jack Dunn	115	52	.689
1923	Baltimore	Jack Dunn	111	53	.677
1924	Baltimore	Jack Dunn	117	48	.709
1925	Baltimore	Jack Dunn	105	61	.633
1926	Toronto	Dan Howley	109	57	.657
1927	Buffalo	Bill Clymer	112	56	.667
1928	Rochester	Billy Southworth	90	74	.549

* Asterisk indicates winning team.

Year	Championship Team	Manager	Won	Lost	Pct.
1929	Rochester	Bill McKechnie– Billy Southworth	103	65	.613
1930	Rochester	Billy Southworth	105	62	.629
1931	Rochester	Billy Southworth	101	67	.601
1932	Newark	Al Mamaux	109	59	.649
1933	Newark	Al Mamaux	102	62	.622
	Rochester	George "Specs" Toporcer	88	77	.533
	Baltimore	Frank McGowan	84	80	.512
	*Buffalo	Ray Schalk	83	85	.494

(Playoffs: Rochester defeated Newark 3 games to 1; Buffalo defeated Baltimore 3 games to 0. Finals: Buffalo defeated Rochester 4 games to 2.)

1934	Newark	Bob Shawkey	93	60	.608
	Rochester	George "Specs" Toporcer	88	63	.583
	*Toronto	Isaac "Ike" Boone	85	67	.559
	Albany	Bill McCorry	81	72	.529

(Playoffs: Toronto defeated Newark 4 games to 3; Rochester defeated Albany 4 games to 1. Finals: Toronto defeated Rochester 4 games to 1.)

1935	Montreal	Frank Shaughnessy	92	62	.597
	*Syracuse	Harry Leibold	87	67	.565
	Buffalo	Ray Schalk	86	67	.562
	Newark	Bob Shawkey	81	71	.533

(Playoffs: Montreal defeated Buffalo 4 games to 2; Syracuse defeated Newark 4 games to 0. Finals: Syracuse defeated Montreal 4 games to 3.)

1936	*Buffalo	Ray Schalk	94	60	.610
	Rochester	Ray Blades	89	66	.574
	Newark	Oscar Vitt	88	67	.568
	Baltimore	Guy Sturdy	81	72	.529

(Playoffs: Buffalo defeated Newark 4 games to 1; Baltimore defeated Rochester 4 games to 2. Finals: Buffalo defeated Baltimore 4 games to 2.)

* Asterisk indicates winning team.

Year	Championship Team	Manager	Won	Lost	Pct.
1937	*Newark	Oscar Vitt	109	43	.717
	Montreal	Walter "Rabbitt" Maranville	82	67	.550
	Syracuse	Mike Kelly	78	74	.513
	Baltimore	Guy Sturdy– Bucky Crouse	76	75	.503

(Playoffs: Newark defeated Syracuse 4 games to 0; Baltimore defeated Montreal 4 games to 1. Finals: Newark defeated Baltimore 4 to 0.)

1938	*Newark	Johnny Neun	104	48	.684
	Syracuse	Dick Porter	87	67	.565
	Rochester	Ray Blades	80	74	.519
	Buffalo	Steve O'Neill	79	74	.516

(Playoffs: Newark defeated Rochester 4 games to 3; Buffalo defeated Syracuse 4 games to 0. Finals: Newark defeated Buffalo 4 games to 1.)

1939	Jersey City	Bert Niehoff	89	64	.582
	*Rochester	Billy Southworth	84	67	.556
	Buffalo	Steve O'Neill	82	72	.532
	Newark	Johnny Neun	82	73	.529

(Playoffs: Newark defeated Jersey City 4 games to 2; Rochester defeated Buffalo 4 games to 1. Finals: Rochester defeated Newark 4 games to 3. Note: Newark and Syracuse were tied at the close of the regular season and the Bears defeated the Chiefs in a single game playoff for the fourth place standing.)

1940	Rochester	Billy Southworth– Estel Crabtree–Mike Ryba–Tony Kaufman	96	61	.611
	*Newark	Johnny Neun	95	65	.594
	Jersey City	Bert Niehoff	81	78	.509
	Baltimore	Tommy Thomas	81	79	.506

(Playoffs: Newark defeated Jersey City 4 games to 0; Baltimore defeated Rochester 4 games to 2. Finals: Newark defeated Baltimore 4 games to 3.)

1941	Newark	Johnny Neun	100	54	.649
	*Montreal	Clyde Sukeforth	90	64	.584
	Buffalo	Al Vincent	88	65	.575
	Rochester	Tony Kaufman	84	68	.553

* Asterisk indicates winning team.

Year	Championship Team	Manager	Won	Lost	Pct.

(Playoffs: Newark defeated Rochester 4 games to 1; Montreal defeated Buffalo 4 games to 3. Finals: Montreal defeated Newark 4 games to 3.)

Year	Championship Team	Manager	Won	Lost	Pct.
1942	Newark	Bill Meyer	92	61	.601
	Montreal	Clyde Sukeforth	82	71	.536
	*Syracuse	Jewel Ens	78	74	.513
	Jersey City	Frank Snyder	77	75	.507

(Playoffs: Jersey City defeated Newark 4 games to 2; Syracuse defeated Montreal 4 games to 1. Finals: Syracuse defeated Jersey City 4 games to 0.)

Year	Championship Team	Manager	Won	Lost	Pct.
1943	Toronto	Burleigh Grimes	95	57	.625
	Newark	Bill Meyer	85	68	.556
	*Syracuse	Jewel Ens	82	71	.536
	Montreal	Fresco Thompson	76	76	.500

(Playoffs: Toronto defeated Montreal 4 games to 0; Syracuse defeated Newark 4 games to 2. Finals: Syracuse defeated Toronto 4 games to 2.)

Year	Championship Team	Manager	Won	Lost	Pct.
1944	*Baltimore	Tommy Thomas	84	68	.553
	Newark	Bill Meyer	85	69	.552
	Toronto	Burleigh Grimes	79	74	.516
	Buffalo	Stanley "Bucky" Harris	78	76	.506

(Playoffs: Baltimore defeated Buffalo 4 games to 3; Newark defeated Toronto 4 games to 0. Finals: Baltimore defeated Newark 4 games to 3.)

Year	Championship Team	Manager	Won	Lost	Pct.
1945	Montreal	Albert "Bruno" Betzel	95	58	.621
	*Newark	Bill Meyer	89	64	.582
	Toronto	Harry A. Davis, Jr.	85	67	.559
	Baltimore	Tommy Thomas	80	73	.523

(Playoffs: Montreal defeated Baltimore 4 games to 3; Newark defeated Toronto 4 games to 2. Finals: Newark defeated Montreal 4 games to 3.)

Year	Championship Team	Manager	Won	Lost	Pct.
1946	*Montreal	Clay Hopper	100	54	.649
	Syracuse	Jewel Ens	81	72	.529
	Baltimore	Tommy Thomas	81	73	.526
	Newark	George Selkirk	80	74	.519

(Playoffs: Montreal defeated Newark 4 games to 2; Syracuse defeated Baltimore 4 games to 2. Finals: Montreal defeated Syracuse 4 games to 1.)

* Asterisk indicates winning team.

Year	Championship Team	Manager	Won	Lost	Pct.
1947	Jersey City	Albert "Bruno" Betzel	94	60	.610
	Montreal	Clay Hopper	93	60	.608
	*Syracuse	Jewel Ens	88	65	.575
	Buffalo	Paul Richards	77	75	.507

(Playoffs: Buffalo defeated Jersey City 4 games to 0; Syracuse defeated Montreal 4 games to 0. Finals: Syracuse defeated Buffalo 4 games to 3.)

1948	*Montreal	Clay Hopper	94	59	.614
	Newark	Bill Skiff	80	72	.526
	Syracuse	Jewel Ens	77	73	.513
	Rochester	Cedric Durst	78	75	.510

(Playoffs: Montreal defeated Rochester 4 games to 3; Syracuse defeated Newark 4 games to 3. Finals: Montreal defeated Syracuse 4 games to 1.)

1949	Buffalo	Paul Richards	90	64	.584
	Rochester	Johnny Keane	85	67	.559
	*Montreal	Clay Hopper	84	70	.545
	Jersey City	Joe Becker	83	71	.539

(Playoffs: Buffalo defeated Jersey City 4 games to 1; Montreal defeated Rochester 4 games to 0. Finals; Montreal defeated Buffalo 4 games to 1.)

1950	Rochester	Johnny Keane	92	59	.609
	Montreal	Walter Alston	86	67	.562
	*Baltimore	Nick Cullop	85	68	.556
	Jersey City	Joe Becker	81	70	.536

(Playoffs: Rochester defeated Jersey City 4 games to 2; Baltimore defeated Montreal 4 games to 3. Finals: Baltimore defeated Rochester 4 games to 2.)

1951	*Montreal	Walter Alston	95	59	.617
	Rochester	Johnny Keane	83	69	.546
	Syracuse	Albert "Bruno" Betzel	82	71	.536
	Buffalo	George "Specs" Toporcer	79	75	.513

(Playoffs: Montreal defeated Buffalo 4 games to 0; Syracuse defeated Rochester 4 games to 1. Finals: Montreal defeated Syracuse 4 games to 1.)

* Asterisk indicates winning team.

Year	Championship Team	Manager	Won	Lost	Pct.
1952	Montreal	Walter Alston	95	56	.629
	Syracuse	Albert "Bruno" Betzel	88	66	.571
	*Rochester	Harry Walker	80	74	.519
	Toronto	Joe Becker	78	76	.506

(Playoffs: Montreal defeated Toronto 4 games to 3; Rochester defeated Syracuse 4 games to 0. Finals: Rochester defeated Montreal 4 games to 2.)

Year	Championship Team	Manager	Won	Lost	Pct.
1953	Rochester	Harry Walker	97	57	.630
	*Montreal	Walter Alston	89	63	.586
	Buffalo	Jack Tighe	87	65	.572
	Baltimore	Don Heffner	82	72	.532

(Playoffs: Rochester defeated Baltimore 4 games to 3; Montreal defeated Buffalo 4 games to 2. Finals: Montreal defeated Rochester 4 games to 0.)

Year	Championship Team	Manager	Won	Lost	Pct.
1954	Toronto	Luke Sewell	97	57	.630
	Montreal	Max Macon	88	66	.571
	Rochester	Harry Walker	86	68	.558
	*Syracuse	Lamar "Skeeter" Newsome	79	76	.510

(Playoffs: Syracuse defeated Toronto 4 games to 2; Montreal defeated Rochester 4 games to 2. Finals: Syracuse defeated Montreal 4 games to 3.)

Year	Championship Team	Manager	Won	Lost	Pct.
1955	Montreal	Greg Mulleavy	95	59	.617
	Toronto	Luke Sewell	94	59	.614
	Havana	Reggie Otero	87	66	.569
	*Rochester	Harry Walker	76	77	.497

(Playoffs: Rochester defeated Montreal 4 games to 1; Toronto defeated Havana 4 games to 1. Finals: Rochester defeated Toronto 4 games to 0.)

Year	Championship Team	Manager	Won	Lost	Pct.
1956	Toronto	Albert "Bruno" Betzel	86	66	.566
	*Rochester	Fred "Dixie" Walker	83	67	.553
	Miami	Don Osborn	80	71	.530
	Montreal	Greg Mulleavy	80	72	.526

(Playoffs: Toronto defeated Montreal 4 games to 1; Rochester defeated Miami 4 games to 1. Finals: Rochester defeated Toronto 4 games to 3.)

* Asterisk indicates winning team.

Year	Championship Team	Manager	Won	Lost	Pct.
1957	Toronto	Fred "Dixie" Walker	88	65	.575
	*Buffalo	Phil Cavaretta	88	66	.571
	Richmond	Ed Lopat	81	73	.526
	Miami	Don Osborn	75	78	.490

(Playoffs: Miami defeated Toronto 4 games to 2; Buffalo defeated Richmond 4 games to 2. Finals: Buffalo defeated Miami 4 to 1.)

1958	*Montreal	Clay Bryant	90	63	.588
	Toronto	Fred "Dixie" Walker	87	65	.572
	Rochester	Ellis "Cot" Deal	77	75	.507
	Columbus	Clyde King	77	77	.500

(Playoffs: Montreal defeated Columbus 4 games to 3; Toronto defeated Rochester 4 games to 1. Finals: Montreal defeated Toronto 4 games to 1.)

1959	Buffalo	Kerby Farrell	89	64	.582
	Columbus	Cal Ermer	84	70	.545
	*Havana	Preston Gomez	80	73	.523
	Richmond	Steve Souchock	76	78	.494

(Playoffs: Richmond defeated Buffalo 4 games to 1; Havana defeated Columbus 4 games to 0. Finals: Havana defeated Richmond 4 games to 2.)

1960	*Toronto	Mel McGaha	100	54	.649
	Richmond	Steve Souchock	82	70	.539
	Rochester	Clyde King	81	73	.526
	Buffalo	Kerby Farrell	78	75	.510

(Playoffs: Toronto defeated Buffalo 4 games to 0; Rochester defeated Richmond 4 games to 1. Finals: Toronto defeated Rochester 4 games to 1.)

1961	Columbus	Larry Shepard	92	62	.597
	Charleston	Joe Schultz	88	66	.571
	*Buffalo	Kerby Farrell	85	67	.559
	Rochester	Clyde King	77	78	.497

(Playoffs: Rochester defeated Columbus 4 games to 1; Buffalo defeated Charleston 4 games to 0. Finals: Buffalo defeated Rochester 4 games to 1.)

* Asterisk indicates winning team.

Year	Championship Team	Manager	Won	Lost	Pct.
1962	Jacksonville	Ben Geraghty	94	60	.610
	Toronto	Chuck Dressen	91	62	.595
	*Atlanta	Joe Schultz	83	71	.539
	Rochester	Clyde King	82	72	.532

(Playoffs: Jacksonville defeated Rochester 4 games to 3; Atlanta defeated Toronto 4 games to 2. Finals: Atlanta defeated Jacksonville 4 games to 3.)

1963	*Indianapolis (Southern Division)	Rollie Hemsley	86	67	.562
	Atlanta (Southern Division)	Harry Walker	85	68	.556
	Syracuse (Northern Division)	Bob Swift– Frank Carswell	80	70	.533
	Toronto (Northern Division)	Bill Adair	76	75	.503

(Playoffs: Indianapolis defeated Syracuse 4 games to 1; Atlanta defeated Toronto 4 games to 0. Finals: Indianapolis defeated Atlanta 4 games to 1.)

1964	Jacksonville	Harry Walker	89	62	.589
	Syracuse	Frank Carswell	88	66	.571
	Buffalo	George "Whitey" Kurowski	80	69	.537
	*Rochester	Darrell Johnson	82	72	.532

(Playoffs: Rochester defeated Jacksonville 4 games to 0; Syracuse defeated Buffalo 4 games to 3. Finals: Rochester defeated Syracuse 4 games to 2.)

1965	Columbus	Larry Shepard	85	61	.582
	Atlanta	Bill Adair	83	64	.565
	*Toronto	Dick Williams	81	64	.556
	Syracuse	Frank Carswell	74	73	.503

(Playoffs: Columbus defeated Syracuse 4 games to 2; Toronto defeated Atlanta 4 games to 0. Finals: Toronto defeated Columbus 4 games to 1.)

1966	Rochester	Earl Weaver	83	64	.565
	*Toronto	Dick Williams	82	65	.558
	Columbus	Larry Shepard	82	65	.558
	Richmond	Bill Adair	75	72	.510

* Asterisk indicates winning team.

Year	Championship Team	Manager	Won	Lost	Pct.

(Playoffs: Richmond defeated Rochester 3 games to 1; Toronto defeated Columbus 3 games to 2. Finals: Toronto defeated Richmond 4 games to 1.)

Year	Championship Team	Manager	Won	Lost	Pct.
1967	Richmond	Luman Harris	81	60	.574
	Rochester	Earl Weaver	80	61	.567
	*Toledo	Jack Tighe	73	66	.525
	Columbus	Harding "Pete" Peterson	69	71	.493

(Playoffs: Toledo defeated Richmond 3 games to 2; Columbus defeated Rochester 3 games to 1. Finals: Toledo defeated Columbus 4 games to 1.)

Year	Championship Team	Manager	Won	Lost	Pct.
1968	Toledo	Jack Tighe	83	64	.565
	Columbus	Johnny Pesky	82	64	.562
	Rochester	Billy DeMars	77	69	.527
	*Jacksonville	Clyde McCullough	75	71	.514

(Playoffs: Jacksonville defeated Toledo 3 games to 1; Columbus defeated Rochester 3 games to 2. Finals: Jacksonville defeated Columbus 4 games to 0.)

Year	Championship Team	Manager	Won	Lost	Pct.
1969	Tidewater	Clyde McCullough	76	59	.563
	Louisville	Eddie Kasko	77	63	.550
	*Syracuse	Frank Verdi	75	65	.536
	Columbus	Don Hoak	74	66	.529

(Playoffs: Columbus defeated Tidewater 3 games to 1; Syracuse defeated Louisville 3 games to 2. Finals: Syracuse defeated Columbus 4 games to 1.)

Year	Championship Team	Manager	Won	Lost	Pct.
1970	*Syracuse	Frank Verdi	84	56	.600
	Columbus	Joe Morgan	81	59	.579
	Rochester	Carl Ripken	76	64	.543
	Tidewater	Chuck Hiller	74	66	.529

(Playoffs: Syracuse defeated Tidewater 3 games to 0; Columbus defeated Rochester 3 games to 2. Finals: Syracuse defeated Columbus 3 games to 1.)

Year	Championship Team	Manager	Won	Lost	Pct.
1971	*Rochester	Joe Altobelll	86	54	.614
	Tidewater	Hank Bauer	79	61	.564
	Charleston	Joe Morgan	78	62	.557
	Syracuse	Loren Babe	73	67	.521

* Asterisk indicates winning team.

Year	Championship Team	Manager	Won	Lost	Pct.

(Playoffs: Rochester defeated Syracuse 3 games to 1; Tidewater defeated Charleston 3 games to 0. Finals: Rochester defeated Tidewater 3 games to 2.)

Year	Championship Team	Manager	Won	Lost	Pct.
1972	Louisville	Darrell Johnson	81	63	.563
	Charleston	John "Red" Davis	80	64	.556
	*Tidewater	Hank Bauer	78	65	.545
	Rochester	Joe Altobelli	76	68	.528

(Playoffs: Louisville defeated Rochester 2 games to 1; Tidewater defeated Charleston 2 games to 1. Finals: Tidewater defeated Louisville 3 games to 2.)

Year	Championship Team	Manager	Won	Lost	Pct.
1973	Rochester (American Division)	Joe Altobelli	79	67	.541
	*Pawtucket (American Division)	Darrell Johnson	78	68	.534
	Charleston (National Division)	Joe Morgan	85	60	.586
	Tidewater (National Division)	John Antonelli	75	70	.517

(Playoffs: Charleston defeated Rochester 3 games to 0; Pawtucket defeated Tidewater 3 games to 2. Finals: Pawtucket defeated Charleston 3 games to 2.)

* Asterisk indicates winning team.

INTERNATIONAL LEAGUE BATTING CHAMPIONS

Year	Player and Club	G	AB	Hits	Pct.
1884	J. W. Coogan, Newark	77	314	121	.380
1885	(Records are not available.)				
1886	Jon Morrison, Toronto	94	408	144	.353
1887	Frank Grant, Buffalo	105	459	168	.366
1888	Patsy Donovan, London	103	460	165	.359
1889	Perry Werden, Toledo	109	424	167	.394
1890	(Records are not available.)				
1891	Buck West, Syracuse	85	369	125	.336
1892	"Wee Willie" Keeler, Binghamton	93	410	153	.373
1893	Jack Drauby, Buffalo	105	414	157	.379
1894	Joe Knight, Wilkes-Barre–Providence	113	493	183	.371

Year	Player and Club	G	AB	Hits	Pct.
1895	Judson Smith, Toronto	113	466	174	.373
1896	Abel Lezotte, Wilkes-Barre	113	499	201	.404
1897	Dan Brouthers, Springfield	126	501	208	.415
1898	John "Buck" Freeman, Toronto	122	496	172	.347
1899	Jim Bannon, Toronto	111	454	155	.341
1900	Bill "Kitty" Bransfield, Worcester	122	501	186	.371
1901	Homer Smoot, Worcester	120	486	173	.356
1902	Bill "Jocko" Halligan, Jersey City	138	518	182	.351
1903	Harry "Moose" McCormick, Jersey City	122	447	172	.362
1904	Joe Yeager, Montreal	124	440	136	.332
1905	Frank LaPorte, Buffalo	120	447	148	.331
1906	Jack Thoney, Toronto	141	589	173	.294
1907	Jack Thoney, Toronto	102	413	136	.329
1908	Elijah Jones, Montreal	135	517	160	.309
1909	Myron Grimshaw, Toronto	124	482	149	.309
1910	Jack Slattery, Toronto	100	365	113	.310
1911	Hank Perry, Providence	140	539	185	.343
1912	Eddie Murphy, Baltimore	122	510	184	.361
1913	George Simmons, Rochester	150	545	185	.339
1914	Dave Shean, Providence	149	533	178	.334
1915	Chris Shorten, Providence	137	543	175	.322
1916	James "Red" Smyth, Montreal	114	436	150	.344
1917	Napoleon "Larry" Lajoie, Toronto	151	581	221	.380
1918	Howard McLarry, Binghamton	103	335	129	.385
1919	Otis Lawrey, Baltimore	133	494	180	.364
1920	Merwyn Jacobson, Baltimore	154	581	235	.404
1921	Jack Bentley, Baltimore	141	597	246	.412
1922	Bob Fothergill, Rochester	101	397	152	.383
1923	Clarence Pitt, Rochester–Baltimore	155	582	208	.357
1924	Dick Porter, Baltimore	129	509	185	.364
1925	James Walsh, Buffalo	154	544	194	.357
1926	James Walsh, Buffalo	147	526	204	.388
1927	Dick Porter, Baltimore	155	599	225	.376
1928	Dale Alexander, Toronto	169	621	236	.380
1929	Dan Taylor, Reading	125	426	158	.371
1930	James "Rip" Collins, Rochester	167	623	234	.376
1931	Isaac "Ike" Boone, Newark	124	469	167	.356
1932	George Puccinelli, Rochester	133	478	187	.391
1933	Julius "Moose" Solters, Baltimore	147	523	190	.363
1934	Isaac "Ike" Boone, Toronto	136	500	186	.372
1935	George Puccinelli, Baltimore	154	582	209	.359

Year	Player and Club	G	AB	Hits	Pct.
1936	Smead Jolley, Albany	155	592	221	.373
1937	Charley Keller, Newark	145	536	189	.353
1938	Charley Keller, Newark	150	578	211	.365
1939	Johnny Dickshot, Jersey City	153	557	198	.355
1940	Murray Howell, Baltimore	152	557	200	.359
1941	Gene Corbett, Baltimore–Newark	144	520	159	.306
1942	Hank Majeski, Newark	151	574	198	.345
1943	Albert "Red" Schoendienst, Rochester	136	555	187	.337
1944	Mayo Smith, Buffalo	150	500	170	.340
1945	Sherman Lollar, Baltimore	139	464	169	.364
1946	Jackie Robinson, Montreal	124	444	155	.349
1947	Vernal Jones, Rochester	118	445	150	.337
1948	Coaker Triplett, Buffalo	126	399	141	.353
1949	Bobby Morgan, Montreal	154	567	191	.337
1950	Don Richmond, Rochester	140	573	191	.333
1951	Don Richmond, Rochester	105	412	144	.350
1952	Frank Carswell, Buffalo	141	511	176	.344
1953	Sandy Amoros, Montreal	150	539	190	.353
1954	Bill Virdon, Rochester	139	505	168	.333
1955	Glenn "Rocky" Nelson, Montreal	154	506	184	.364
1956	Clyde Parris, Montreal	152	552	177	.321
1957	Joe Caffie, Buffalo	108	440	145	.330
1958	Glenn "Rocky" Nelson, Toronto	148	522	170	.326
1959	Frank Herrera, Buffalo	151	569	187	.329
1960	Jim Frey, Rochester	125	441	140	.317
1961	Ted Savage, Buffalo	149	547	178	.325
1962	Vic Davalillo, Jacksonville	150	578	200	.346
1963	Don Buford, Indianapolis	152	613	206	.336
1964	Hilario "Sandy" Valdespino, Atlanta	147	531	179	.337
1965	Joe Foy, Toronto	140	500	151	.302
1966	Reggie Smith, Toronto	143	506	162	.320
1967	Elvio Jimenez, Columbus	133	483	164	.340
1968	Merv Rettenmund, Rochester	114	393	130	.331
1969	Ralph Garr, Richmond	106	438	144	.329
1970	Ralph Garr, Richmond	98	391	151	.386
1971	Bobby Grich, Rochester	130	473	159	.336
1972	Alonza Bumbry, Rochester	108	435	150	.345
1973	Juan Beniquez, Pawtucket	131	440	131	.298

INTERNATIONAL LEAGUE RECORDS

Individual Batting Season Records

Highest Percentage
.415—Dan Brouthers, Springfield, 1897

Most Runs Scored
173—Joe Hauser, Baltimore, 1930

Most Total Bases
443—Joe Hauser, Baltimore, 1930

Most Hits
245—Jack Bentley, Baltimore, 1921

Most Doubles
57—Jim Holt, Jersey City, 1924

Most Triples
29—Guy Tutwiler, Providence, 1914

Most Home Runs
63—Joe Hauser, Baltimore, 1930

Most Runs Batted In
180—James "Rip" Collins, Rochester, 1930

Most Stolen Bases
112—Mike Slattery, Toronto, 1887

Most Consecutive Games Batting Safely
36—Bill Sweeney, Baltimore, 1935

Most Bases on Balls
167—Blas Monaco, Baltimore, 1944

Most Times Struck Out
199—Dave Nicholson, Richmond, 1968

Individual Pitching Season Records

Most Games Won
35—George Stovey, Newark, 1887

Most Games Lost
29—George Keefe, Troy, 1888
29—Frank Leary, Rochester, 1903
29—Charles Swaney, Reading, 1926

Most Innings Pitched
422—Joe McGinnity, Newark, 1909

Most Strikeouts
330—Robert "Lefty" Grove, Baltimore, 1923

Most Bases on Balls
186—Robert "Lefty" Grove, Baltimore, 1923

Most Hit Batsmen
34—Peter Wood, Hamilton, 1888
34—Frank Knauss, Detroit, 1889

Most Wild Pitches
47—Cornelius Murphy, Syracuse, 1888

Most Consecutive Victories
20—Jim Parnham, Baltimore, 1923

Most Consecutive Losses
20—George Haddock, Troy, 1888

Most Shutouts
11—Joe McGinnity, Newark, 1909

THE ROCHESTER RED WINGS

The Rochester Red Wings stand today as one of the strongest franchises, not only in the International League but in all of Organized Baseball as well. The Red Wings consistently rank near the top in paid admissions among all National Association teams, and in 1971, they led the minor leagues in paid attendance with 463,000 (including playoff and Junior World Series games).

One must go to Rochester's Silver Stadium, a truly attractive and extremely well-maintained park in order to see the intense local fan interest in the fortunes of the Red Wings. Sellout crowds of 13,000 to 14,000 are not uncommon for "crucial" games in the pennant race and for playoff contests. In 1966, the Red Wings recorded a net profit of $161,472 before taxes, a great financial showing for any baseball team, major or minor.

Rochester does well today both at the gate and on the field for a variety of reasons: they are the top farm club for the Baltimore Orioles and consistently have a cadre of fine young players headed for the majors; the town has no head-on competition from the majors since Rochester is located deep within the "hinterlands" of western New York State, hundreds of miles away from any big league city; and the team is largely owned by several thousand shareholding fans through Rochester Community Baseball, Inc. Thus, there is always a solid core of fans who will support the team through fair weather and foul.

The Red Wings promotional staff works continually at promoting special days and nights in order to attract large groups of fans for particular occasions; the main idea, of course, is to keep Silver Stadium packed. Special events include "Bat Nite," "Helmet Nite," "Pony Nite," "Camera Day," "T-Shirt Nite," "Knot Hole Gang Nite," "Little League Day," and "Stockholders Nite."

Since Rochester is so far off the big league track, its two newspapers, the *Times Union* and *Democrat & Chronicle,* are able to lavish their full attention on the Red Wings, while the town's three television stations and some half-dozen radio stations are also able to give the team full coverage. In fact, Joe Cullinane, who broadcasts all Red Wings games on radio, is thought to contribute so much to the success at the gate that he is usually included in the team picture.

The history of professional baseball in Rochester goes all the way back to 1877 when the city was represented in the International Association, the first of the minor leagues. Rochester's "Hop Bitters" remained in the International Association through 1878, and then the city was involved with pro ball only sporadically until 1885. In that year it joined the New York State League, which became known as the International League.

Rochester remained in the IL through 1889, and then in 1890 it went into the American Association, the only year in which the city had representation in a circuit considered as a major league. Rochester returned to the IL for the 1891 and 1892 campaigns and then was forced to drop out of the professional baseball picture completely for two years (the city's Culver Field was completely destroyed by fire in late 1892).

Rochester moved into new quarters at Riverside Park in 1895, and once again became a member of the IL. It has fielded an entry in the league ever since, or for eighty consecutive years, a record for longevity matched by few teams in either the majors or minors. Rochester's park burned down again about halfway through the 1897 season, and the team was forced to play its remaining home schedule in Montreal. The Montreal fans, however, took a strong liking to baseball and refused to give up their position in the league. Therefore, Rochester had to buy up the Scranton franchise early in 1898 in order to remain in the circuit.

For a time the team carried the nickname "Brownies," in honor of the Eastman Kodak camera that is manufactured in the city and which became enormously popular throughout the country during the 1890s.

Rochester, then known as the "Bronchos," captured its first pennant in 1899, winning 73 and losing 44 for a .626 percentage and finishing 9 full games ahead of second-place Montreal. Rochester clinched the title after winning the morning game of a Labor Day tripleheader. (In this era tripleheaders occasionally were staged in the minors on special holidays.) This was the first of fourteen Rochester pennants, the most recent coming in 1971. No other International League team has done as well.

Rochester had many outstanding stars at the turn of the century. On the 1901 championship team, for example, Billy Lush, a fleet-footed outfielder who had experience earlier with the Washington Nationals, scored 137 runs in 132 games, while stealing 54 bases; and "Reddy" Grey, brother of novelist Zane Grey, smashed 12 home runs in an era when the long ball was a rare occurrence.

John Ganzel came to Rochester as player–manager in 1909, after a decade-long career in the majors. He proceeded to lead the "Hustlers" (as the team was known then) to three straight league championships. Known as "Big Jawn" Ganzel, a first baseman, he paced Rochester's hitters in 1909 with a .305 average, good for second best in the league during that "dead ball" era.

Interest in the Hustlers remained at a fever pitch through the third consecutive championship campaign in 1911, as big right-hander George "Slats" McConnell paced the pitching staff with a brilliant 30–8 mark. Rochester's new Bay Street Park was often filled to capacity during the Ganzel pennant years, but interest declined sharply when star players were sold to various major league teams. (McConnell, for example, went to the New York Americans, while hard-hitting second baseman Hack Simmons also went to New York of the AL.)

Baseball in Rochester did not really recover until the 1920s. George Stallings, manager of Boston's "Miracle Braves" of 1914, became part owner and manager of Rochester's "Tribe" in 1921 and went on to achieve the city's first 100-plus victory seasons: 103 in 1921, 105 in 1922, and 101 in 1923. But Stallings kept finishing second to Jack Dunn's Baltimore Orioles, considered the finest minor league team of the era— or perhaps in history.

Maurice "Comet" Archdeacon, a fleet-footed outfielder, was the talk of the league in 1923 as he scored 162 runs; while Fred "Bone Head" Merkle, first baseman and a veteran of the majors, established the team's all-time two-base hit record of 54.

George Stallings resigned in midseason 1927 after six and one-half years at the helm. There were a variety of reasons for his resignation, but the principal reason was that Rochester was not heading for a pennant (despite the fact that it had such stars as Rabbit Maranville, Heinie Groh, and Wicky McAvoy. George Mogridge, a native Rochesterean and fifteen-year major league pitching veteran, managed the team for the rest of the campaign.

Rochester's baseball fortunes rose dramatically in 1928. In that year the St. Louis Cardinals bought the team, renamed it the "Red Wings" (a nickname that has been used ever since), and made it into the Cardinals' top farm club. St. Louis had been operating the Syracuse franchise in the International League, but Sam Breadon and Branch Rickey felt that the city on the banks of the Genesee River presented a more promising baseball future.

The Cardinals assigned Warren Giles (later National League president) as the Red Wings' president–general manager, and Billy Southworth (a veteran National League outfielder) as player–manager. Rochester proceeded to capture the International League pennant by one percentage point over the second-place Buffalo Bisons, but it dropped the Junior World Series to Indianapolis of the American Association 5 games to 1. Charley Gelbert (a young shortstop bound for the Cardinals) and George "Specs" Toporcer (a second baseman just down from the Cardinals) made a fine double play combination, while Southworth himself paced the Red Wing hitters with a .361 average during this championship season.

In 1929, the Cardinals sponsored the construction of a new park for the Red Wings at 500 Norton Street, a park which is still in use today after more than forty-five years.

Rochester went on to win flags in 1929, 1930, and 1931 and climaxed the 1930 and 1931 seasons with victories in the Junior World Series over Louisville and St. Paul, respectively.

Billy "The Kid" Southworth was promoted to manage the parent Cardinals in July 1929, as he switched jobs with Bill McKechnie who came over to Rochester from his St. Louis pilot's post. (Cardinal fans never forgave McKechnie for ordering his mound corps to pitch to Babe Ruth in the 1928 World Series. The Cardinals lost four straight to the Yankees as Ruth personally destroyed St. Louis with 10 hits, including 3 homers and 3 doubles.) In 1930, however, Southworth came back to the Red Wings for another tour of duty, as McKechnie took over the helm of the Boston Braves.

The 1930 aggregation, which ran up a 105–62 record and finished 8 full games over second-place Baltimore, is often called "the greatest team in Red Wing history." Specs Toporcer won the IL Most Valuable Player Award for the second year in a row; James "Rip" Collins drove in 180 runs for the all-time league record; Southworth batted a fat .370 in 92 games; and John Leonard "Pepper" Martin, just a step away from stardom with the Cardinals, established himself as one of the most colorful players in Red Wing annals and hit .363 as a regular outfielder. Big right-hander Paul Derringer led the pitching staff with a 23–11 record.

Southworth led the Red Wings to their fourth straight title in 1931 despite the fact that many of the previous year's stars had graduated to the Cardinals, were shifted around to other minor league teams, or were sold to various major league clubs by Branch Rickey. Rickey and Giles were able to get George Sisler to replace Rip Collins at first base, since Collins was moved up to St. Louis. Sisler (thirty-eight years old and fresh from fifteen brilliant years in the majors) played 159 games, delivered many key hits, and batted .303. Through acquisitions of this nature Rickey and Giles managed to retain the loyalty of the fans.

Rochester went nine years without a pennant before it entered the winner's circle again in 1940. The Red Wings had solid teams throughout the 1930s, but they received tough competition from the powerful Newark Bears, the New York Yankees' top farm club (which notched five flags during the decade).

In July 1932, Billy Southworth was transferred to Columbus. He was succeeded at the Red Wings' helm by Specs Toporcer, with Eddie Dyer, Burt Shotton, and Ray Blades following. (Except for Toporcer, all of these Rochester managers led major league clubs at one time or another.)

The Red Wings continued to supply the Cardinals with an array of fine players who went on to star in the majors; for example, Johnny Mize, Jimmy Brown, Marty Marion, Johnny Hopp, and Howie Krist. A fellow named Walter Alston played first base for Rochester for half of the 1937 season, and although he never achieved distinction as a player, he went on to become one of baseball's most successful and durable big league managers.

Slingin' Sammy Baugh played shortstop for the Red Wings in 1938, but he is better known as the long-time Washington Redskins' quarterback and is now in the Football Hall of Fame in Canton, Ohio.

Southworth came back to Rochester as manager in 1939 after having experienced a combination of personal difficulties. In the mid-1930s, Billy the Kid was down managing Asheville, North Carolina, in the Class B Piedmont League, but after he convinced Branch Rickey that he had gotten over the psychological hump he once again became one of the key men in the Cardinal organization.

Southworth did so well with the Red Wings that on July 7, 1940, he began a second tour of duty with St. Louis as manager, a post he held through 1945 when he was appointed manager of the Boston Braves (he held the latter post through 1951). During those twelve years he won a total of four National League pennants and became recognized as one of the really fine pilots in the major leagues. Stan Musial, who broke in with the Cardinals in late 1941, often said that Southworth had no peer when it came to working with younger players. Southworth scouted for the Braves (later based in Milwaukee) through 1958, when he retired after spending nearly a half-century in the game.

Rochester went on to grab the IL flag in 1940, but they required three more managers to do it. Estel Crabtree, long a Red Wings star outfielder, took command after Southworth left, but he had to step down after a week because of illness. Star pitcher Mike Ryba handled the post for another week before the arrival of Tony Kaufmann (manager of Decatur, Illinois, in the Three-I League and ex-big leaguer), who took the post on a permanent basis. Ryba, a crafty right-hander and a veteran of eighteen years in both the majors and minors, chalked up a 24–8 record and won the league's MVP award.

Ray Mueller and Bob Scheffing divided the catching chores and gave Red Wings' fans some of the best defensive work behind the plate that they had ever seen. Scheffing, twenty-five years old at the time, had already managed in the minors (Washington, Pennsylvania, in the Pennsylvania State Association in 1939) went on to manage the Detroit Tigers and serve as general manager of the New York Mets.

The Red Wings limped through the World War II years with makeshift lineups since their best players either went to the Cardinals or into the military service. Pepper Martin, manager in 1943, quit in disgust at the end of the season, because he did not like the howling of the third base "grandstand wolves" as he stood in the coacher's box.

Managers were changed frequently in succeeding years, as Ken Penner directed the club in 1944, Burleigh Grimes in 1945–46, and Cedric Durst in 1947–48. All were old-time ball players, and Grimes, a 270-game winner in the majors, eventually was elected to the Hall of Fame. Grimes, unfortunately, could not impart his winning ways to the struggling Red Wings.

Johnny Keane took the helm in 1949, and he led Rochester to a strong second-place finish behind Paul Richards' Buffalo Bisons, as the Red Wings enjoyed their greatest year at the gate up to that point (443,533 paid). The biggest crowd of the year was an 18,000-plus turnout for Opening Day. Keane's 1950 edition of the Red Wings won the IL flag in a breeze by finishing 7 games ahead of second-place Montreal. Russ Derry, slugging outfielder and a big league veteran, set the all-time Rochester mark of 42 homers in a season. Derry, a left-handed swinger, blasted 133 homers during the five-year span from 1947 through 1951.

Keane who never played an inning of big league baseball, but who had toiled in the Cardinals' farm system as a player and manager since 1930, went on to pilot the Cardinals to a world title (in 1964) and also managed the New York Yankees.

Harry Walker succeeded Keane as manager in 1952, and although the Wings wound up in third place for the regular season, they went on to win the playoffs and the Junior World Series. Walker put himself into 115 games, mostly as an outfielder and pinch hitter, and batted .365.

Walker's 1953 team brought Red Wings' fans plenty of excitement with a tremendous stretch drive that resulted in Rochester's capturing the league pennant. Rochester won 27 of its final 29 games, including 19 straight, which is still the club record.

On May 27, 1955, Harry Walker was summoned to take over the St. Louis Cardinals' helm, and his replacement was none other than his older brother Fred "Dixie" Walker, the noted star of the Brooklyn Dodgers and then a Cardinals' coach. Dixie's 1955 and 1956 teams finished fourth and second in the regular pennant races, but they got hot in September of both years and captured the Governor's Cup.

After the 1956 season, the Cardinals made overtures to pull out of Rochester (attendance had declined to about 180,000 and the Cardinals claimed the operation was costing them too much money), but the franchise was saved through the organization of Rochester Community Baseball, Inc. The Cardinals transferred the ownership of the Red Wings to a total of more than 8,000 local fans who purchased shares in the newly-organized public corporation. The entire transaction was completed in early 1957. No shareholder ever expected to receive a cash dividend or capital gain, since the only thing he was really interested in was seeing a continuation of professional baseball at 500 Norton Street.

Morrie Silver, local businessman and long-time Red Wings fan, invested heavily in the new corporation, induced others to buy stock, and was a natural choice to become the first president of Rochester Community Baseball, Inc. He retained an active interest in the fortunes of the team, and in 1968, Red Wing Stadium was renamed "Silver Stadium" in his honor.

The Cardinals retained a strong working agreement with the new Red Wings organization and continued its program of developing its top talent at Rochester. The agreement held through 1960 when a dispute ended the St. Louis–Rochester Association of thirty-two years.

Clyde King, a former Brooklyn Dodger pitcher and manager of the Wings since 1959, believed in trying to win with his best nine men on the field, certainly not an unpopular notion with the fans. King went with his veterans during most of the 1960 campaign as his charges finished third in the regular season race and went to the final round of the playoffs before losing to Toronto.

Attendance for regular season and playoff games passed the 250,000 mark and all seemed well in Wingville, but storm clouds were brewing in St. Louis. The Cardinals' front office believed that a farm team's main function should be to develop young talent. John L. Remington, a Rochester baseball writer, said of this situation:

> The Cardinals were obviously displeased at King's decision to bench the youngsters and win with the veterans. The Red Wing's management, to its everlasting credit, was just as adamant. King would remain as field boss even if it meant the end of the Cardinal reign. The final blow came when the Cardinals sold several of the better Red Wing players to Buffalo and Toronto just after the season closed. Without them, chances of success in 1961 seemed dim.

When Red Wing general manager George H. Sisler, Jr., formally rehired King, with the assent of Morrie Silver, the Cardinals abruptly ended the working agreement. The Wings immediately began negotiating with the Baltimore Orioles and a new agreement was signed in plenty of time to take effect for the 1961 campaign, a pact that has remained in effect to this day.

The Orioles management under the direction of Lee MacPhail, Jr. (president–general manager) and Harry Dalton (farm director) pledged to honor Clyde King's contract and promised to send their best available talent to Rochester. Their word was good. Moreover, they permitted the Red Wing manager to use veterans effectively as the Cardinals had not.

The Rochester–Baltimore relationship has flourished for more than a dozen years now. Future Baltimore stars who performed well at Rochester include John "Boog" Powell, Merv Rettenmund, Eddie Watt, Mark Belanger, Don Baylor, Bobby Grich, Alonza Bumbry, and others. Earl Weaver, who has managed Baltimore to a series of pennants in recent years, prepped at Rochester for two years (1966–67) before moving up to the Orioles.

Rochester, now the senior member of the International League, is already making plans to celebrate the centennial of its first professional baseball team in 1977.

GENERAL MANAGER CHARLIE SENGER AND THE TOLEDO MUD HENS

Toledo, an old-line minor league city, suddenly found itself without a pro team for the first time in over forty years when the Mud Hens pulled out of the American Association after the 1955 season. Toledo fielded its first professional teams in the early 1880s, and with the exception of a few brief interruptions, the "Glass City" was almost continuously represented in the game until the end of 1955.

Many sports experts around the country thought that Toledo had vanished from the Organized Baseball scene completely, because the town remained out of action for nine long years before the Mud Hens surfaced in 1965 as an entry in the International League. Toledo had been a member of the International League for one season way back in 1889, but in 1965 the city came to stay. It has remained as one of the league's most stable members during the past decade.

When the Mud Hens returned to the baseball wars in 1965, they abandoned their old park, Swayne Field, near downtown Toledo, and moved into a refurbished park in the Lucas County Recreation Center in suburban Maumee just southwest of town. The ninety-acre recreation complex includes a large all-purpose entertainment hall, a running track, swimming pools and softball diamonds in addition to the Mud Hens park having a seating capacity of 8,000.

The Mud Hens came back into the International League as a New York Yankees' affiliate, and then from 1967 through 1973 served as the chief farm club for the Detroit Tigers, and in 1974 they became the chief farm team for the Philadelphia Phillies. Charles G. "Charlie" Senger, who has proven to be one of the minor league's most capable and dynamic young executives, came on the scene in 1966 and has directed the fortunes of the Mud Hens ever since.

When I walked into Senger's office one late Saturday afternoon before a scheduled night game with the Louisville Colonels, I asked if I could not talk to the Mud Hens public relations man rather than taking up too much of the general manager's time. "What do you mean 'public relations man'?" snapped Senger. "We can't afford such frills around here. If you want photos, statistics, or any other kind of data, you'll just have to ask me," he said.

Senger proceeded to give me a graphic picture of the problems a general manager faces in running a Class AAA baseball team. "It's really a struggle," he explained. "We're in direct competition with the major league's for the fan's attention in this area because Detroit is only sixty miles north of us, and with expressways running from Toledo almost to the door of Tiger Stadium, we've got to go all out in order to attract a few people into our park. Of course, there are always those fans who would rather stay in their living rooms and watch the Tigers on television instead of driving a few blocks to Lucas County Recreation Center to root for the Mud Hens," he declared.

Charlie Senger, however, is a resourceful baseball entrepreneur, and he does not allow problems like direct competition to deter him from his primary mission of providing the fans of the Greater Toledo area with good competitive Class AAA baseball.

Senger does well these days to have his outfit break the 100,000 mark in paid attendance for the season. In 1972, the Mud Hens drew exactly 100,171 fans for seventy-two home games. That is just about enough to get into the black since minor league players' salaries are subsidized by the major leagues—in the case of the Mud Hens by the Philadelphia Phillies. And then, of course, the Mud Hens have ancillary income from concessions, the sale of souvenirs, the sale of scorecards, outfield fence advertising, etc.

The energetic Senger is primarily responsible for organizing the all-important "Diamond Club" in cooperation with Toledo's civic and business leaders, who share a common interest in promoting local baseball. In order to qualify for Diamond Club membership, an individual must sell at least ten season tickets valued at a total of $1,000. In 1971, 713 season tickets were sold, and in 1972, 722 were sold. "With the Diamond Club raising over $70,000 a year for us through the sale of season tickets, we're assured of a place in Organized Baseball," Senger emphasized. "I'd hate to think where we would be without them."

Senger is not aware of a similar plan in all of Organized Baseball. "Other cities have clubs for season ticket holders, but I don't know of any other organization quite like ours or one as successful," he explained.

Members of the Diamond Club, about seventy strong now, have

access to the air-conditioned and heated clubhouse, located high in the third base grandstand, where they may in plush comfort watch the Mud Hens play.

While the Mud Hens are affiliated with the Philadelphia Phillies on a "Player Development Contract" basis, the Toledo Baseball Club, Inc., is actually a nonprofit corporation that rents the baseball facilities at Lucas County Recreation Center for $10,000 annually. The officers and directors of the Corporation receive no remuneration for their services, and all revenues in excess of the cost of the operation of the club become the property of Lucas County. It should also be emphasized that the Phillies spend something like $200,000 annually on the Mud Hens franchise, with a substantial part of that sum going for player salaries.

For his efforts at promoting baseball in Toledo, Charlie Senger has been the recipient of all types of awards, including being named the International League's General Manager of the Year in 1968. He has amply proven that top-flight minor league baseball can survive in a medium-sized city in the face of enormous competition from the majors.

THE TOLEDO MUD HENS: THE TALE OF
A SOBRIQUET

Of all the nicknames given to baseball teams during the past century and a quarter, Toledo's "Mud Hens" has been of particular delight to fanciers of sobriquets.

Toledo was a hot bed of baseball long before it became a charter member of the American Association in 1902. Numerous amateur leagues operated there in the 1860s and 1870s. The city had its first taste of pro ball in 1882 when Toledo became a member of the Northwestern League, and for one year (1884), it had a taste of big league ball when it was a member of the twelve-team American Association. The team's nickname then was simply the "Toledos," or the "Blue Stockings." From that point on Toledo's professional teams were variously called the "Maumees" (from the Maumee River on which it is situated) and the "Black Pirates."

The term "Mud Hens" was probably first used in 1895 when Toledo, then a member of the Western League, played its games in Bay View Park, a ball field surrounded by marshes. Wild ducks—visible to the players and fans—continually flew around the marshland area and it was inevitable that a sportswriter would in time tag the local team as the "Mud Hens." Sometime in the late 1890s, the team was briefly called the "Swamp Angels," but "Mud Hens" had a peculiar sticking quality, and that is the name Toledo used when it entered the AA. Even today the Toledo entry in the International League is known as the Mud Hens.

THE DESIGNATED HITTER RULE

The minor leagues have historically served as a kind of experimental laboratory for the majors, and among the recent important innovations has been the designated hitter rule, so far adopted only by the American League. Before the DH rule was instituted in the American League in 1973, however, it was tested in a number of minor circuits, including in the International League during the 1969 campaign.

"We were interested in two things primarily when we instituted the designated hitter rule," said George H. Sisler, Jr., International League president, "we wanted more hitting and speedier games. Most pitchers are notoriously weak hitters, and since they aren't taken out for pinch-hitters under the DH rule, the games have to be quicker," Sisler added.

The experiment did work since IL team batting averages increased by approximately 10 to 12 points in 1969, run scoring increased by 6 percent, and games took an average of 6 minutes less to play.

The International League reinstituted the designated hitter rule in 1973 after a three-year lapse.

A scattering of other minor leagues have experimented with the designated hitter rule, including the Class A New York–Pennsylvania League. From a personal standpoint I had never seen a game with the DH in force until the summer of 1972, when I saw the Williamsport Red Sox play the Batavia Trojans at the Trojan's MacArthur Stadium in a New York–Pennsylvania League game. Frankly, the DH rule seemed highly unusual at the time, but after following American League play throughout the 1973 season, the entire DH syndrome just grew on me —and I am sure that it had the same effect on millions of other fans. A radical departure from tradition like this just takes a while before one gets used to it.

Anyone who examines the batting averages of majors league pitchers down through the years in Macmillan's *The Baseball Encyclopedia* will have to admit that the designated hitter rule removes a real weak spot from the game's makeup.

George Sisler also indicated that minor league officials have been discussing other possible changes in order to place more emphasis on the offensive part of the game, like flared-out foul lines. "We'd see a lot of extra base hits that normally would have been foul balls, if this change were made," Sisler explained. Sisler said, however, that most responsible men in Organized Baseball regard the flared-out foul lines proposal as being too radical a departure from tradition ever to be put into practice.

THE PACIFIC COAST LEAGUE:
The Long Season and
Giantlike Statistics

ROSTER OF PACIFIC COAST LEAGUE TEAMS
(CLASS A, 1903–07; CLASS AA, 1908–45; CLASS AAA, 1946–51;
OPEN CLASSIFICATION, 1952–57; CLASS AAA, 1958–) [1]

Team	Years in Operation
Albuquerque, New Mexico	1972—
Dallas, Texas	1964
Dallas–Fort Worth, Texas	1963
Denver, Colorado	1963–68
Eugene, Oregon	1969–73
Fresno, California	1906
Hollywood, California	1926–35, 1938–57
Honolulu, Hawaii	1961—
Indianapolis, Indiana	1964–68
Little Rock, Arkansas	1964–65
Los Angeles, California	1903–57
Mission (San Francisco), California	1914# [1] (Sacramento franchise shifted to San Francisco's Mission district on September 7), 1926–37
Oakland, California	1903–55
Oklahoma City, Oklahoma	1963–68
Phoenix, Arizona	1958–59, 1966—
Portland, Oregon	1903–17, 1918–72

[1] See page 323 for Key to Roster of League Teams.

Team	*Years in Operation*
Sacramento, California	1903, 1905# (Tacoma franchise moved back to Sacramento late in season), 1909–14 (shifted to San Francisco's Mission district; see notation under Mission, 1918–60), 1974—
Salt Lake City, Utah	1915–25, 1958–65, 1970—
San Diego, California	1936–1968
San Francisco, California	1903–57
Seattle, Washington	1903–6, 1919–68
Spokane, Washington	1958–71, 1973—
Tacoma, Washington	1904–05 (see note under Sacramento), 1960—
Tucson, Arizona	1969—
Tulsa, Oklahoma	1966–68
Vancouver, British Columbia	1956–62, 1965–69
Venice, California	1913–14
Vernon, California	1909–12, 1915–25

The Pacific Coast League perennially has been the premier minor league baseball circuit for innumerable reasons. Paramount among these reasons is that during the years immediately following World War II the quality of play and fan interest reached such high levels that club owners and league officials strove hard to gain major league status for the PCL. With the start of the 1952 season, the league achieved "Open Classification" in preparation for its eventual entry into the majors. The Open Classification was a breakthrough measure in Organized Baseball. Through this multifaceted plan the PCL voted to bar the use of players on option from the majors, to ban working agreements with the majors, and to require waivers to sell a player back to a major league organization from which he was acquired. However, when the National League moved into San Francisco and Los Angeles in 1958, the Coast League went back to Class AAA from Open Classification, and for all practical purposes, its chances of ever becoming a major league were killed. Despite the loss of San Francisco and Los Angeles, the league's two key cities, new cities were added in a full-scale realignment and the PCL has continued to prosper.

The Pacific Coast League has been the singular minor league circuit since most of the minor league's season batting, pitching, and fielding records are held by its performers. This is largely because, from the league's foundation in 1903 through 1957, the PCL played the longest schedule in Organized Baseball, as many as 225-odd games per season.

Pacific Coast League records are a statistician's delight. In fact, any baseball fan who loves big numbers would revel in paging through a PCL record book. Statistics piled up during a season some 70 games longer than major league campaigns of that time were almost monstrously delightful. Some teams won or lost over 130 games in one season; batters went to the plate officially over 900 times; and sluggers got well over 300 hits, scored and drove in more than 200 runs, and slammed 75 doubles all in a single campaign. Championship play started in late March and wound up in early November—and surely any regular who played the full schedule must have been so tired at the end that he chose to skip winter ball down in the Caribbean.

The mild weather of the Pacific Coast region, of course, permitted these marathon seasons, and any baseball historian will tell you that numerous players of bonafide big league caliber preferred to perform in the PCL's balmy climes rather than to chance the often disagreeable weather of the big league cities back East, especially in the early spring. Moreover, PCL players received extra compensation for those long drawn out seasons, which ran six to eight weeks longer than a normal 154-game schedule.

The Pacific Coast League became a haven for an entire coterie of career professionals. In fact, the PCL is one of the few minor leagues that has kept and published "lifetime" records of its top performers. As indicated previously, Arnold "Jigger" Statz, who starred in the outfield for the Los Angeles Angels for eighteen years, holds most of the league's important service and batting records, including games played (2,790), times at bat (10,657), hits (3,356), doubles (595), triples (137), runs scored (1,996), and others. Statz, who also found time to play a total of 683 major league games over a period of eight years, did not hang up his spikes with the Angels until he was forty-five years old. He participated in more Class AA and major league games combined than any other professional player in history (3,473). In fact, the *Baseball Register* for 1952, published by *The Sporting News,* maintains that no player at any level ever took part in more professional games played under the aegis of Organized Baseball.

Statz's career is really an amazing one. He attended Holy Cross College for three years, starred on the baseball team there, and broke into the pro ranks with John McGraw's New York Giants midway through the 1919 season. He played briefly with the Giants in 1920, was traded to the Boston Red Sox in the same year, and then was sent to Los Angeles later in 1920. He remained with Los Angeles through 1921, had his best big league years with the Chicago Cubs from 1922 through 1924, went back to Los Angeles for part of 1925 and all of 1926, came back to the National League with Brooklyn for 1927–28, and then settled down to fourteen consecutive years with the Angels from 1929 through 1942, managing the team during his final three seasons.

While with the Angels he collected over 200 hits in ten different seasons. His best year came in 1926 when he batted .354, slammed out 291 hits (including 68 doubles, 18 triples, and 4 homers), and scored 150 runs. Long recognized as one of the best golfers among all professional baseball players, he received his nickname from his frequent use of an iron known as a "jigger."

Russell "Buzz" Arlett holds the Pacific Coast League record for lifetime home runs. He achieved a total of 251 while playing for the Oakland Oaks for thirteen years (1918–30). Oddly enough, Arlett, a big switch-hitting outfielder–first baseman, batted over .300 in his only season in the majors. For the Philadelphia Phillies in 1931, he hit .313 in 121 games. His slugging average that year was a lofty .538 as he cracked 51 extra base hits, including 18 homers, but he never played in the majors again.

There is a small army of pitchers who spent a dozen or more years toiling in the Pacific Coast League vineyards. In fact, there are no less than twelve pitchers who won more than 200 games in PCL competition. Frank Shellenback, who hurled for four of the league's teams during the nineteen-year period between 1920 and 1938, leads the parade with 295 victories against 178 losses for a winning percentage of .624. (Actually, Shellenback is a 300-game winner in the high minors, for he also chalked up a 20–14 record from 1917 through 1919 while he was with Providence of the International League and Milwaukee and Minneapolis of the American Association. Moreover, he was 11–15 with the Chicago White Sox in 1918 and 1919, giving him a 326–207 career record. While with San Diego during his final three playing years in the PCL, Shellenback also doubled as field manager where he had the distinction of being Ted Williams' first manager in pro ball. Williams has always spoken highly of Shellenback both as a smart baseball tactician and as a man. And after he left the league, Shellenback enjoyed a long career as a coach and scout for St. Louis, Boston, and Detroit in the American League and for the New York Giants in the National League.)

Herman Pillette, a right-hander with twenty-three years of active service with seven teams between 1920 and 1945, holds the PCL record for longevity for a player at any position. When he retired from active mound duty with the Sacramento Sacts after the 1945 season, he was just a few months shy of his forty-eighth birthday, having some years earlier earned the title "Old Folks." His PCL log shows him just below .500 with 226 wins and 235 losses, but in his three years with the Detroit

Tigers (1922–24), he managed to break above .500 with a 34–32 mark.

Pillette spent a total of thirty years as an active player in professional baseball. Starting in 1916 he hurled for teams in Butte, Tacoma, Aberdeen, Des Moines, and Regina before joining Portland of the PCL after the beginning of the 1920 season. Ironically enough, his son Duane carried on the family name in baseball immediately after he retired. Duane entered the pro ranks with the Newark Bears of the International League in 1946 and went out to Portland of the Coast League for 1947–48. He went back to Newark in 1949, joined the New York Yankees late in the season, and then remained in the majors until 1956. For more than forty consecutive years father and son played professional baseball— that's got to be a record!

When it comes to individual records, either seasonal or lifetime, no minor league circuit has ever approached the Pacific Coast League.

EDDIE MULLIGAN

Any history of the Pacific Coast League must also prominently mention Eddie Mulligan, the man who played for a record number of eight teams in the circuit. Mulligan, an infielder born on August 27, 1894, in St. Louis, began his career in Organized Baseball in 1914 with Ottumwa, Iowa, in the Class C Central Association. After a stop at Davenport of the Three-I League, he found himself with the Chicago Cubs near the end of the 1915 season.

He also stopped at Kansas City, Mobile, and Chattanooga before he landed in the Pacific Coast League with Salt Lake City in 1919. He was to remain in the PCL through 1938 except for the three years he spent in the majors (with the Chicago White Sox in 1921–22 and with Pittsburgh in 1928—his major league log shows him batting .232 in 351 games). His PCL travels took him to San Francisco, Mission, Seattle, Portland, Oakland, Hollywood, and San Diego in addition to Salt Lake City.

Standing only 5-feet, 9-inches and weighing barely 155 pounds, Mulligan is one of the smartest and scrappiest infielders in the PCL's annals, although he did not break any batting records.

And Eddie Mulligan's twenty-five years as an active player really marked only the beginning of his career in Organized Baseball, for after he hung up his uniform he went into the executive ranks as owner or part-owner of several PCL teams, including Salt Lake City and Sacramento. Since 1956 he has held the important post of president of the Class A California League, and by all odds, it appears that this service will extend over a longer period than his service as a PCL player. As a league president Mulligan still takes the time to answer a great deal of his own correspondence in a clear and sharp hand. In fact, when interviewed in the late summer of 1973, he said that he has the same enthusiasm for baseball at the age of eighty—after sixty years in the game—as he did as a nineteen-year-old rookie at Ottumwa.

THE PACIFIC COAST LEAGUE IS BORN

The Pacific Coast League was formed as a top minor league circuit in 1903 as a result of intense interest in baseball at all levels in that region of the country. The balmy weather in California and environs made it possible for real baseball buffs to play the game almost the whole year around, and virtually every town of any size had its own team, either a full-fledged pro outfit or at least a semi-pro team.

We ought to indicate here that we have drawn liberally upon the late Fred W. Lange's *History of Baseball in California and Pacific Coast Leagues, 1847–1938* for material on the early history of the PCL. This is now a very rare volume, and we are indebted to William B. McKechnie, Jr., recently retired president of the Pacific Coast League, for loaning us his personal copy, which seems to be one of the very few still extant. Fred Lange, who subtitles his book "The Musings and Memories of an Old Time Baseball Player," played pro and semi-pro ball as a young man in the late 1880s and early 1890s, and although he is not a professional writer by any means, one can smell the dust of the diamond throughout his book. He gives us the impression that while he was a boy in Oakland there was a perpetual game of ball being fiercely contested on virtually every vacant lot in town from spring through late fall.

Thus, when any type of organized team was formed, there was keen competition for all positions, since there were eager ball players everywhere. Fred Lange recalls those days when baseball was a primary diversion for the nation's youth, since there were no automobiles or television sets to distract youngsters from the pursuit of glory on the diamonds.

Lange documents the fact that the first enclosed ball park on the Pacific Coast was constructed in Oakland (at 25th and Folsom Streets) in 1868. In the first game played at that park, on November 26, 1868, the Eagles of San Francisco defeated the Wide Awakes of Oakland 37–23.

Not enough space is available to relate in any detail the complex early history of professional baseball in California. Suffice it to say, there were plenty of teams on the semi-pro level active throughout the state in the 1870s and 1880s. Two professional leagues were formed in the 1885–86 period: the California League and the California State League.

The California League originally had one team in Sacramento (the Atlases) and three in San Francisco (the Haverlys, the Pioneers, and the Stars), while the California State League began with one team in Oakland (the G & M's), and three in San Francisco (the Californians, Damianias, and the K's). Thus, a lot of the young men walking around the streets of San Francisco were pro ball players—the town had an even half-dozen teams!

In the late 1880s and 1890s, both the California and California State leagues established franchises in other cities, since no one town obviously could support a proliferation of professional teams for very long. As the leagues branched out geographically, they laid a much stronger foundation for the future.

The brand of baseball in California during the mid-1880s apparently was good, since a number of players jumped right from these two leagues into the majors; for example, George Van Haltren who played for the Oakland G & M's in 1885–86. Van Haltren, a left-hander all the way, was a star G & M's pitcher who played the outfield when he was not on the mound. He went to the Chicago Cubs in 1887 in this dual capacity, and he remained in the majors for seventeen years, spending most of his career with the New York Giants as an outfielder.

Many baseball experts still wonder why Van Haltren has not been elected to the Hall of Fame considering the fact that he rolled up a lifetime batting average of .322 and garnered 2,527 base hits. After his days in the majors were over, he played for Seattle and Oakland in the Coast League for six years (1904–09), and almost until the time of his death at Oakland on October 1, 1945 at the age of seventy-nine, he was a welcomed guest at numerous Old Timers affairs held throughout the league.

Van Haltren liked to recall that during his days with the G & M's many players were still not wearing fielders' gloves, though some were starting to use thin gloves with the fingers cut off at the knuckles for protection. Errors were numerous and fielding averages were awful in that era, commonly referred to as the "Stone Age" of baseball.

When Van Haltren established the PCL record for most times at bat, 941 with Seattle in 1904, he collected 253 hits for a .269 average. This is the only case where a player's hit total almost equaled his batting percentage!

The Pacific Coast League grew directly out of the California League, the latter circuit having been composed of four teams in its final season in 1902 (Los Angeles, San Francisco, Oakland, and Sacramento). When the PCL began play in 1903, Portland and Seattle were added to give the new league a total of six teams.

Interestingly enough, it was not until after World War I, in 1919, that the PCL finally became an eight-team loop. In fact, in 1907 and 1908 the league dropped to only four clubs. Four- and six-team leagues were quite common, however, in all minor league classifications during the first twenty years or so of this century.

The PCL was an "Outlaw League" during its first year of operation in 1903, but it became a member of the National Association of Professional Baseball Leagues for the following season. Eugene F. Bert, the league's first president, felt that if the PCL was to establish a firm foundation it could not follow an independent course. He deemed that becoming a part of Organized Baseball was necessary to insure prosperity.

Los Angeles captured the first Pacific Coast League pennant by piling up a massive total of 133 victories against 78 losses for a winning percentage of .630. That figure was to stand as a league record until 1934 when Los Angeles won the astounding total of 137 games.

Starring in the Angels' outfield was young Clifford "Cactus" Cravath, who was in his second year of pro ball. Cravath was to stay with the Angels for five years, and after he eventually joined the Philadelphia Phillies in 1912 (after stints with Boston, Chicago, and Washington in the American League and Minneapolis in the American Association), he won or shared six National League home run championships.

After the State League had a bad season in 1909 because of poor attendance, the league's officials requested the protection of the National Association, and at the association's annual meeting held at Memphis in November 1909, the California circuit was given full membership. (The State League began with six teams in 1909—Fresno, Stockton, Santa Cruz, Oakland, San Jose, San Francisco—but San Jose and San Francisco dropped out in midseason.)

The State League began its first year in Organized Baseball in 1910 with Stockton, Fresno, Merced, and San Jose; but when Fresno was forced to drop out on June 24 because of low attendance, the whole circuit had to fold because the National Association required that each league must have at least four teams.

Meanwhile, the California State League went through all sorts of reorganizations, but the name continued to remain the same. When the National Association was formed in 1902, the league refused to join and battled the PCL vigorously for public support. The California State League had teams operating smack in the middle of PCL territory, and at times it fielded as many as eight different teams in eight different cities. In 1907, for example, the California State League went with clubs in Alemada, Fresno, Oakland, Sacramento, San Francisco, San Jose, Santa Cruz, and Stockton. The players were mostly local boys. Thus, in many ways these were "town" teams having enthusiastic local followings.

In 1913, the Pacific Coast League, under its president Allan T. Baum, revived the California State League as a wholly new organization to serve primarily as a training ground for the development of young players. The new league, also headed by Baum, began with Stockton, Fresno, Watsonville, and San Jose in the fold. Alas, the PCL's "farm system" failed to produce enough young talent to make the venture worthwhile, and the operation was canceled after the 1915 season.

The California State League, which really has been harder to kill off than Rasputin, was revived periodically: in 1929, in 1941–42, and continuously since 1946. Now known as the "California League" the circuit has held an A classification since 1963 (see pages 00–00).

The PCL's inaugural season began in mid-March, with the final game being played on November 29. The final standings were as follows:

Club	Won	Lost	Pct.
Los Angeles	133	78	.630
Sacramento	105	105	.500
Seattle	98	100	.495
San Francisco	107	110	.493
Portland	95	108	.468
Oakland	89	126	.414

Tacoma replaced Sacramento in the league for the 1904 and part of the 1905 season. While Tacoma moved back to Sacramento late in the 1905 campaign, its name only is listed in all the official record books for that season.

In 1904–05, the Pacific Coast League experimented with a first- and second-half champion arrangement. It then went back to the system of having the percentage championship based upon the entire season.

Tacoma won the first half of the 1904 race by a clear margin, but was tied for the second-half title by Los Angeles (as both clubs reached an identical .571 figure). Tacoma took the league crown by whipping the Angels in a playoff series. Tacoma captured first-half honors again in the following year, with second-half titlist Los Angeles taking the championship with a victory in the playoffs.

San Francisco was just beginning to stir on the soft spring morning of Wednesday April 18, 1906, when suddenly the earth almost literally buckled under it. As shocked San Franciscans poured out into the streets, pavings gaped open, buildings collapsed into rubble, water mains snapped —and one of recorded history's most devastating fires swept the stricken city. The great San Francisco earthquake caused nearly 500 deaths and the devastation of more than four square miles in the center of the city with property damage totaling some $500,000,000.

The Seals ball park was completely leveled—and many league officials feared this calamity would finish off professional baseball in San Francisco, as well as seriously weaken the very foundations of the Pacific Coast League.

The season was well underway when the earthquake struck, and president Bert was anxious that play continue on schedule despite the fact that the Seals now had no park. Los Angeles seriously considered withdrawing from the league after the disaster, but Bert convinced them to stay in the fold. Moreover, he sent telegrams to all club owners urging them to carry on with all scheduled games. In his drive to maintain the league's stability, he arranged for the Seals to play their home games at Oakland's Idora Park, located at Telegraph Avenue and 56th Street. Happily, the Seals drew well in Oakland, with many of the team's most avid fans traveling regularly across the Bay to see their favorite players in action.

When the season ended on November 4, Portland was the pennant winner with a fat 19-½ game bulge over second-place Seattle.

H. L. Haggerly of San Francisco, writing in the 1907 *Spalding Baseball Guide,* said that 1906 was to have been a banner year for the Coast League. He concluded that despite the San Francisco quake four of the six clubs finished in the black; only San Francisco and Fresno showed splotches on red ink on their ledgers—not a bad performance.

Pacific Coast League
1906 Standings

Club	Won	Lost	Pct.
Portland	115	60	.657
Seattle	99	83	.544
Los Angeles	95	87	.522
San Francisco	91	84	.520
Oakland	77	110	.411
Fresno	64	117	.353

Citizens of San Francisco, long noted for their civic pride, immediately went to work in rebuilding their town, vowing to create an even greater city than the one that had been destroyed. Consequently, when the Seals began championship play in late March 1907, their new baseball grounds, called "Recreation Park" and located at 14th and Valencia Streets, were ready for them. San Francisco opened the season with a morning-afternoon doubleheader against Portland, with a record crowd of

10,000 fans jamming their way into Recreation Park. In fact, hundreds of fans had to be turned away at the gate since every seat and every bit of "standing room only" space were occupied.

As indicated previously, the PCL dropped to a four-team circuit in 1907–08. Seattle moved back into the Pacific Northwest League, while Fresno felt it could not compete on an equal basis with the larger cities in the league. With a big 200-game schedule, teams played each other sixty-five to seventy times per season! PCL players got to know each other quite well, doubtlessly.

PACIFIC COAST LEAGUE HIGHLIGHTS

1909: The league went back up to six teams with the readmission of Sacramento and the creation of a franchise for Vernon, then a town just outside the Los Angeles city limits. San Francisco won the league championship with a near-record 132 victories, while last place Vernon set the league record for defeats with 131. However, Vernon still managed to win eighty games.

On June 8, San Francisco defeated Oakland (at Oakland's Freeman Park) 1–0 in 24 innings. This is the longest game in Pacific Coast League history. The Seals' Clarence "Cack" Henley outlasted Jimmy Wiggs of Oakland in a brilliant mound duel that saw both pitchers go the distance. The Seals scored the game's lone run in the last half of the twenty-fourth on a double by third baseman Rollie Zeider, an error by second baseman Tyler Christian, a fielder's choice, and a single by left fielder Nick Williams. Henley walked only 1 batter and allowed 9 hits; Wiggs walked 6 and gave up 11 hits. The time of game was only 3 hours and 35 minutes.

1910: Five of the six teams in the Pacific Coast League won over 100 games, and only last-place Sacramento failed to reach three figures in victories. The final standings were:

Club	Won	Lost	Pct.
Portland	114	87	.567
Oakland	112	98	.555
San Francisco	114	106	.518
Vernon	113	87	.514
Los Angeles	101	121	.455

Hitting was down in the Pacific Coast League, as Roy Shaw of San Francisco won the batting crown with a skinny .281, the lowest championship average in the league's history. Jack Lively of Oakland had the league's best pitching record with 32 wins and 13 losses for a .705 percentage. "Cack" Henley also won 32, but he dropped 19.

1911: On September 24, 1911, Portland and Sacramento tangled in the league's second 24-inning game (at Sacramento). The game was called because of darkness with the score tied 1–1. Both pitchers, Elmer Koestner of Portland and Jack Fitzgerald of Sacramento, went the distance.

On July 19, 1911, Walter Carlisle, a center fielder for Vernon, executed one of the most remarkable unassisted triple plays in professional baseball's history. Carlisle's spectacular performance came in a game against Los Angeles.

With the score tied in the ninth inning, Charles Moore and George Metzger of Los Angeles walked. Pitcher Al Carson of Vernon was replaced by Harry Stewart. The Angels' third baseman, Roy Akin, hit Stewart's first pitch low over second base for what appeared to be a clean single. Moore and Metzger were off on a hit-and-run signal; but Carlisle, playing in close, rushed forward and caught the line drive with a somersault, landing on his feet (he had been a circus acrobat). He raced to second and touched the bag, while Moore was well on his way to the plate; then he trotted to first, touching the bag to retire Metzger, who was still well past second.

In recognition of his achievement, the Vernon and Los Angeles fans presented Carlisle with a diamond-studded gold medal.

1912: Oakland nosed out Vernon for the league title by a scant single game. Vernon had an 118–83 record, but Oakland played two more games and won them both, finishing at 120–83. Walter Carlisle led the league in runs scored (177), and his 76 stolen bases were second only to "Wild Bill" Leard's 77. (Leard, an infielder, played briefly with the Brooklyn Dodgers in 1917.)

1913: For the second time, five of the six clubs won 100 or more games. Portland (109–86) won the flag with a seven game bulge over second-place Sacramento. Oakland (90–120) finished in the cellar.

Doubleheaders in the PCL were sometimes a bit unusual. For example, on the morning of April 13, Oakland played Portland at home, and then right after the game with the Beavers, the Oaks traveled across the bay to play an afternoon tilt with San Francisco!

1914: Portland (113–84) won the league crown for the second year in a row, but second-place Los Angeles (116–94) and third-place San Francisco (115–96) won more games. The Portland Beavers played fewer games due to a large number of rainouts. On May 16, San Francisco inaugurated a new park, Ewing Field (named for J. Cal Ewing, former Pacific Coast League president and long-time promoter of professional baseball in the West) in the Richmond district. Built at a cost of $100,000 —a lot of money in those days—it was the show place of the league, even if only briefly. Fog became a tough problem at the park right from the outset, and in 1915, the Seals were forced to move back to their old grounds, Recreation Park, at 14th and Valencia.

1915: Frank "Ping" Bodie, whose real name was Pezzola, (.325 in 192 games) and Harry Heilmann (.364 in 98 games) helped lead San Francisco to a pennant. Both were San Francisco natives, and both went on to have distinguished careers in the majors.

When Venice moved back to Vernon at the beginning of the season, it brought its own park in sections transported on rollers!

1916: Frank Chance, known as the "Peerless Leader" while he was player–manager of the Chicago Cubs, got back into the game after a year's layoff as owner–manager of the Los Angeles Angels and led his charges to the league championship. (Chance retained his dual post through the next season.) The Angels drew a crowd of 16,212 for their season's opener. Opening day ceremonies throughout the league were always gala occasions. There were parades through the towns before the game, speeches given by mayors and governors at home plate, first balls thrown out by all manner of celebrities, etc. PCL games throughout the season often drew better than 10,000 fans.

1917: The Pacific Coast League was now so well established and prosperous that the club owners called the two major leagues the "Eastern Leagues." Nevertheless, the PCL was always happy to have its alumni like "Ping" Bodie, "Cactus" Cravath, and Harry Heilmann do well in the major leagues.

1918: The Pacific Coast League suspended operations in midseason on July 14 because of the war. Many of the circuit's top players were in military service and attendance had dropped sharply. Though he played in only 93 games, Earl Sheely, Salt Lake City's first baseman, still found time to steal 55 bases. Sheely, who batted exactly .300 in nine big league seasons (mostly with the Chicago White Sox), was long active in the PCL as a player and executive. He managed Sacramento in 1943–45, and then served as general manager from 1948 until his death in 1952.

1919: The Pacific Coast League expanded to eight teams for the first time in its history with the readmission of Portland and Seattle. Thirty-nine-year-old Sam Crawford, the old Detroit Tiger star, played the outfield for Los Angeles, hit .360 in 173 games, and missed the batting title by only 2 points.

1920: Vernon, under manager Bill Essick (who pitched briefly for the Cincinnati Reds in 1906–07), won its third title in a row.
League officials were concerned with large-scale betting on games. Several ball players were alleged to have been involved with gamblers.

1921: Manager Wade Killifer, a former major league infielder–outfielder led the Los Angeles Angels to the pennant. (Wade's brother "Reindeer Bill" Killifer was a major league catcher for thirteen years and then managed the Chicago Cubs and the St. Louis Browns.)

1922: John "Dots" Miller, who had just completed a twelve-year career as a National League infielder, led the San Francisco Seals to an excellent 127–72 record for the league crown in his debut as a manager.
Frank "Lefty" O'Doul, better known as a hitter (he batted .349 in eleven major league seasons), paced the Seals pitching staff with a 25–9 record. Willie Kamm, who went on to become a standout American League third baseman for thirteen years, led the Seals with a .342 batting mark on 222 hits. He was so popular with the fans that on October 15 a special "Willie Kamm Day" was held. Fans contributed over $1,000 toward the purchase of a diamond ring for Willie.

1923: Paul Waner made his pro debut with the Seals as he batted .369 and helped them toward their second title in a row.
"Dots" Miller became ill and died on September 5, four days before his thirty-seventh birthday. Miller was among the first to recognize Waner's great batting talents.
Vernon routed Salt Lake City 35–11 in the latter city on May 11, 1923. In this wild and woolly game, many Pacific Coast League batting and scoring records were set and many may remain on the books for all

time. The contest established records for the most runs scored in a game (46) and the most home runs in a game (11). The Vernon team set the following marks for a game: most runs scored (35), most total bases (67), most runs batted in (34), and most home runs (9). Vernon's right-fielder Pete Schneider set six league records in this game and tied another. The marks he established were: most times at bat for a nine-inning game (8), most runs scored (6), most home runs (5), most home runs with the bases filled (2), most total bases (22), most runs batted in (14). (The latter five records are standards for a game of any length.) He tied the record for the most home runs in an inning (2). According to the PCL's historian, William J. Weiss, Schneider in his last time at bat almost clubbed a sixth homer, but the ball missed clearing the fence by a matter of inches and he had to settle for a double.

Box Score

Vernon	AB	H	PO	A	E	Salt Lake City	AB	H	PO	A	E
Smith, 3b	5	3	3	2	1	Sheean, 2b–p	6	3	2	2	0
Chadbourne, cf	4	3	1	0	0	Vitt, 3b	2	0	0	2	0
O'Brien, cf	2	0	0	0	0	Kerns, 3b	3	0	0	3	0
Locker, 1b	7	5	11	0	0	Frederick, rf	3	2	1	0	0
Bodie, lf	6	4	1	0	1	Strand, cf	5	2	6	0	0
High, lf	1	1	2	0	0	Wilhoit, lf	4	1	3	0	0
Schneider, rf	8	6	4	0	0	Leslie, 1b	5	2	11	1	0
Rader, ss	5	0	0	5	0	Pearce, ss	4	0	1	3	1
Warner, ss	2	1	0	0	0	Peters, c	1	1	1	1	0
Sawyer, 2b	6	2	3	4	0	Anfinson, c–2b	4	3	2	2	0
D. Murphy, c	7	4	3	0	1	Coumbe, p	1	0	0	0	0
Dell, p	7	4	0	0	0	Kinney, p	1	1	0	0	0
Totals	60	33	28	11	3	Jenkins, c	2	0	0	1	1
						Totals	41	15	27	15	2

O'Brien batted for Chadbourne in seventh.
High hit home run for Bodie in seventh.
Warner grounded out for Rader in seventh.

Vernon	4 3 8	5 0 4	11 0 0—35
Salt Lake City	0 2 2	0 0 1	0 6 0—11

Pitching Summary

	IP	AB	R	ER	H	BB	HB	SO	WP
Dell (Winner)	9	41	11	9	15	5	0	2	0
Coumbe (Loser)	2+	14	12	12	10	1	1	0	0
Kinney	3-2/3	23	12	11	11	2	0	1	0
Sheehan	3-1/3	23	11	10	10	3	0	0	0

Two-base hits—Dell, Smith, Schneider, Sawyer, Warner, Frederick, Sheehan. Three-base hit—Chadbourne. Home runs—Schneider (5), Murphy, Bodie, Locker, High, Leslie, Strand. Sacrifice hit—Chadbourne. Stolen bases—Leslie (2). Runs batted in—Schneider (14), Locker (6), Bodie (6), Murphy (5), Smith, Chadbourne, High, Sheehan (2), Strand (3), Frederick (2), Wilhoit, Leslie, Peters. Hit by pitcher —Smith by Coumbe. Double play—Vitt to Peters to Leslie. Left on bases—Vernon (8), Salt Lake City (4). Umpires—Ward and Byron. Time—2:11. (Note that the game took only 2 hours and 11 minutes to play despite all the scoring.)

1924: Seattle under Wade Killifer edged out Los Angeles for the title by a game and a half. "Lefty" O'Doul, playing the outfield for Salt Lake City, batted .392 in 140 games, but he lost the batting crown to Duffy Lewis by a fraction of a point.

1925: Paul Waner, disappointed that he had not made the majors after the 1924 season—he swatted .356 that year—vowed he would hit .400 in 1925 so that no one could turn him down again because of his size (he only weighed 153 pounds). Waner proceeded to lead the league with a .401 mark, becoming the Pacific Coast League's first .400 hitter. "Big Poison" was called up by Pittsburgh and remained in the majors for twenty years.

Waner's nineteen-year-old brother, Lloyd ("Little Poison"), joined San Francisco in 1925 as the Seals won the pennant with a fat 12-½ game bulge over second-place Salt Lake. Tony Lazzeri, a Salt Lake City shortstop, smashed 60 home runs and drove in 222 runs, Pacific Coast League records that still stand.

1926: With the loss of several key players to the majors, notably Paul Waner, San Francisco plummeted from first place straight to the bottom, finishing with a 84–116 record.

1927: In the formal opening day ceremonies held at San Francisco on March 27, the Seals defeated Portland 5–2 before a crowd of more than 12,000. San Francisco's mayor, James Rolph, Jr., pitched the first ball with chief of police Dan O'Brien doing the catching.

1928: San Francisco boasted perhaps the greatest hitting outfield in minor league history with Smead Jolley, Earl Averill, and Roy Johnson patrolling the gardens. Jolley averaged .404 on 309 hits; Averill hit .354 on 270 hits; and Johnson swatted. 360 on 234 hits—a total of 813 hits for the three outfielders! Averill and Johnson went on to enjoy successful careers in the major leagues, but Jolley's comic fielding cut his service in the majors to four years. Still, Jolley hit a respectable .305 during that span.

The Seals lead the league with a 120–71 record. On July 15, 1928, the Hollywood Stars became the first professional baseball club to travel by air. Following a long doubleheader in Seattle that Sunday afternoon, the Stars' owner, Bill Lane, arranged for the team to be transported by airplane to Portland (about 150 miles distant) so that they would be in time to catch the southbound train, the *Cascade Limited,* for arrival in Los Angeles on Tuesday morning. With schedules calling for nearly 200 games per season, the PCL teams did an enormous amount of traveling.

1929: Pacific Coast League owners continued to maintain only loose ties with the majors, and they were able to sell their top stars for hefty sums. After the 1929 season, the New York Yankees bought Lefty Gomez (18–11) from the San Francisco Seals for $35,000. At about the same time, the Yankees parted with no less than $100,000 for Oakland infielders Lynn Lary and Jimmy Reese.

1930: Big league teams came out to the coast continually to test the strength of PCL competition, usually during spring training and postseason "barnstorming" trips. On October 25, the Oakland Oaks beat a team of major league all-stars, with Lefty Grove as the losing pitcher. Catcher Ernie Lombardi, an Oakland native, climaxed a brilliant five-year career with the Oaks by hitting .370. His contract was purchased by Brooklyn, and he went on to spend 17 seasons in the majors.

1931: On opening day, April 7, San Francisco opened a new park at 16th and Bryant Streets, at a cost of more than $1 million. A crowd of 25,000 filled the park, called "The Finest in the West," and saw the Seals beat Oakland 8–0. Ty Cobb came from his home in Georgia to participate in the inaugural ceremonies.

1932: In this Depression year, the Pacific Coast League's club owners agreed to reduce ticket prices in order to keep the turnstiles clicking. Most clubs now charged only 50¢ for general admission.

1933: Joe DiMaggio, an eighteen-year-old phenom, electrified the PCL by hitting safely in a record 61 consecutive games. He kept the streak going from May 28 through July 25 by pounding out 104 hits in 257 official at bats for a .405 average. The streak was halted on July 26 when Ed Walsh, Jr. (son of the Chicago White Sox Hall of Fame pitcher), held DiMaggio hitless in 5 at bats. Young Walsh himself had pitched for the White Sox before being sent to Oakland. DiMaggio finished the season at .340 with a league-leading 169 RBI's. Vince DiMaggio, Joe's older brother, broke in with the Seals in 1932 and divided the 1933 season with the Seals and Hollywood Stars, batting .333. Vince went on to play with several National League clubs, and when he was not hitting home runs he was breaking strikeout records.

1934: Jack Lelivelt, a former American League infielder, managed Los Angeles to an amazing 137–50 season record, the best in the Pacific Coast League's history. Outfielder Frank Demaree paced the Angels' attack with a league-leading .383 batting average, 45 homers, 173 RBI's, and 190 runs scored. (Demaree, who had been with the Chicago Cubs for all of 1933 as a regular outfielder, went back to the majors for a solid decade after that performance.)

1935: On opening day in Los Angeles on April 6, the Angels defeated the Hollywood Stars 10–8 before a crowd of more than 15,000 paid. PCL openers in all towns were always festive occasions: pregame banquets, speeches, parades—the works.

1936: The Tokyo Giants of the Japanese professional league came over during the PCL's spring training sessions in early March and played a couple of exhibition games with San Francisco. On March 1, Tokyo beat the Seals 5–0, and four days later they whipped the Seals again 11–7. (In October 1934, Lefty O'Doul, who had just finished his short but brilliant career as a slugging National League outfielder, took a team of big league stars to Japan and did a great deal to popularize the game in the Orient. The stars—including Babe Ruth, Lou Gehrig, Charlie Gehringer, Earl Averill, Lefty Gomez, and Bing Miller—coached aspiring Japanese players as well as giving exhibitions.)

1937: Emil Sick, the brewing magnate, bought the Seattle Rainiers for $115,000, and as part of the deal Sick promised to build a new park for the team. The agreement was kept and Sick Stadium was long regarded as one of the best baseball facilities in the West.

1938: Nineteen-year-old Fred Hutchinson, later a star major league pitcher and successful manager, had a remarkable 25–7 record with Seattle in his first year of pro ball.

1939: Gilmore Field was opened, and for the first time in their history, the Hollywood Stars actually played their games within the limits of that community.

1940: Los Angeles outfielder Lou Novikoff (the "Mad Russian") won most of the league's batting honors (hitting .363 with 45 homers), but Seattle's fancy fielding first baseman George Archie (hitting .324) copped the MVP award.

1941: The Pacific Coast League staged its first All-Star Game at San Francisco on July 29, with top players from the "South" defeating the "North" 3–1. The All-Star games (sometimes the championship team of the previous year faced the league's All-Stars) were held in most years until they were suspended after 1963.

1942–45: The Pacific Coast League continued a normal playing schedule through World War II. Government leaders and league officials determined that baseball on the Pacific Coast was as important a diversion for war workers as was big league baseball played in the East and Midwest.

In 1943, the pennant-winning Los Angeles Angels achieved the league's longest undefeated streak (21 games) from April 28 through May 19. They were tied by Hollywood (1–1) during the sixth game of that streak in the second game of a doubleheader.

1946–47: With the end of the war, the Pacific Coast League enjoyed great prosperity, and many attendance records were broken. Larry Jansen, a San Francisco right-hander, chalked up an amazing 30–6 (ERA .157) record in 1946. He was the last PCL 30-game winner.

1948: Charles Dillon "Casey" Stengel climaxed a three-year tenure as manager of the Oakland Oaks by winning the PCL pennant and playoffs. He was named "Minor League Manager of the Year" for his efforts. Stengel's star shortstop–second baseman on the Oaks was a twenty-year-old youngster named Billy Martin.

1949: Fred Haney, a veteran major and minor league manager, led Hollywood to the league's championship. (Haney led the Stars to a second title with Hollywood in 1952, and then went on to manage the Pittsburgh Pirates and Milwaukee Braves.)

1950: Frankie Baumholtz, a Los Angeles outfielder, became the last Pacific Coast League player to get more than 250 hits in a single season. (He had 254 safeties and won the batting crown with a .379 mark.)

1951: After completing a fine career in the big leagues, Joe "Flash" Gordon, a California native, became player–manager at Sacramento and swatted a league-leading 43 homers.

1952: The Pacific Coast League received an "Open Classification" status.

1953: The Pacific Coast League celebrated its fiftieth anniversary. Commemorative celebrations and "Old Timers" days were held throughout the circuit.

1954: Lefty O'Doul, the veteran PCL manager, led San Diego to league championship and then signed to manage Oakland for 1955. He went on to pilot Vancouver in 1956 and Seattle in 1957 before retiring. He had managed four teams within four years!

1955–57: Steve Bilko, a Los Angeles first baseman, paced the league in home runs three years running with 37, 55, and 56, respectively. He also copped the MVP award for three straight years, a PCL record. Bilko, who began his pro career at the age of fifteen as the regular first baseman for Salisbury in the Eastern Shore League, played in the major leagues before and after performing his heroics with the Angels.

1958: With the National League moving into Los Angeles and San Francisco, the following transfers were made: the Hollywood Stars shifted to Salt Lake City; the Los Angeles Angels moved to Spokane; and the San Francisco Seals went to Phoenix. The league returned to its AAA classification. A normal 154-game schedule was adopted for the first time in the league's history. (In 1956–57, the PCL had already reduced its schedule to 168 games.) A separate set of season records has been kept by the PCL since 1958. The schedule has varied from 144 to 154 games during the past sixteen or seventeen years.

1959: Pacific Coast League attendance did not drop as severely as some baseball experts predicted following the loss of the prime Los Angeles and San Francisco territories. League attendance totaled

1,708,000 in 1957, and then leveled off to a still respectable 1,500,000-plus in both 1958 and 1959.

1960: Willie Davis, a Spokane outfielder, won both the batting crown and the MVP award, and set the PCL record for triples in one season, 26 (for a season of any length). Davis needed only 147 games to do the trick!

1961: The Sacramento franchise shifted to Honolulu, and the team became known as the Hawaii Islanders.

1962: Jesse Gonder, a San Diego catcher, won the batting crown (.342) and the MVP award, the only catcher in PCL history to take both honors.

1963: The Pacific Coast League expanded to ten teams with the admission of Denver, Dallas–Fort Worth, and Oklahoma City and with the temporary withdrawal of Vancouver. The three new teams were absorbed from the American Association, which suspended operations from 1963 through 1968.

1964–68: Major changes continued as the PCL expanded to twelve teams with the admission of Indianapolis and Arkansas (the latter club was located in Little Rock). Indianapolis and Arkansas left the International League because the league did not wish to continue with ten teams. There were now twenty Class AAA teams in operation, twelve in the PCL and eight in the IL.

In 1964, Dallas–Forth Worth became two separate franchises with Dallas remaining in the Pacific Coast League and Fort Worth entering the Texas League.

The Pacific League formed two six-team divisions, the Eastern Division and the Western Division, but continued to operate as a twelve-club circuit through 1968.

1969: Expansion of the major leagues placed a National League franchise in San Diego and an American League franchise in Seattle, with those cities leaving the PCL.

The revival of the American Association made a realignment necessary in the Class AAA leagues: Denver, Indianapolis, Oklahoma City, and Tulsa withdrew from the PCL to join the AA. Eugene and Tucson entered the PCL, and its eight teams were divided into a "Northern Division" and "Southern Division."

1970: Hawaii led the National Association in attendance with 467,217 paid admissions.

1971: Hawaii's attendance dropped to 375,957, but the figure was still number one in the National Association.

1972: With Albuquerque entering the Pacific Coast League and Spokane leaving (to join the Class A Northwest League), the divisions were realigned and renamed "Eastern" and "Western."

1974: Sacramento rejoined the league as a replacement for Eugene which transfered to the Northwest League.

Perhaps we might close the narrative section of the Pacific Coast League history with a personal note. In 1953, while on a cross-country auto trip, I drove into Los Angeles and took in a game between the Angels and the San Francisco Seals, which was played at Wrigley Field. It was the first time I ever had seen a Pacific Coast League game.

I was in luck for this was a special "Old Timers Day" with former Angels and Seals players engaging in an informal three-inning exhibition game. Some of the players on the field were real old-timers, having been active in the league as far back as 1905–07, and the fans enjoyed every minute of the proceedings. We gained the impression that PCL fans have a special sense of tradition since Old Timers days have been held regularly for many years in all cities on the circuit, though the league's map has undergone great changes.

I cannot recall the score of the regular Angels–Seals game, but I do remember that the fans second-guessed every decision made by Los Angeles manager Stan Hack. Hack must have been doing something right that season, however, for at the end of the year he was promoted to the managership of the parent Chicago Cubs.

PACIFIC COAST LEAGUE PRESIDENTS

Years	President
1903–06	Eugene F. Bert
1907–09	J. Cal Ewing
1910–11	Judge Thomas F. Graham
1912–19	Allan T. Baum
1920–23	William H. McCarthy
1924–31	Harry A. Williams
1932–35	Hyland H. Baggerly
1936–43	William C. Tuttle
1944–54	Clarence H. Rowland
1955	Claire V. Goodwin
1956–59	Leslie M. O'Connor
1960–68	Dewey Soriano
1968–73	William B. McKechnie, Jr.
1973—	Roy Jackson

PACIFIC COAST LEAGUE CHAMPIONS

Year	Championship Team	Manager	Won	Lost	Pct.
1903	Los Angeles	James Morley	133	78	.630
1904	†Tacoma	Michael Fisher	66	46	.582
	†Tacoma	Michael Fisher	64	48	.571
1905	Tacoma	Michael Fisher	63	45	.583
	‡Los Angeles	Frank Dillon	60	39	.604
1906	Portland	Walter McCreedie	115	60	.657
1907	Los Angeles	Frank Dillon	115	74	.608
1908	Los Angeles	Frank Dillon	110	78	.585
1909	San Francisco	James Gleason	132	80	.622
1910	Portland	Walter McCreedie	114	87	.567

† Won both halves of a split season.
‡ Won playoff between winners of first half and second half of a split season.

Year	Championship Team	Manager	Won	Lost	Pct.
1911	Portland	Walter McCreedie	113	79	.589
1912	Oakland	Bayard "Bud" Sharpe	120	83	.591
1913	Portland	Walter McCreedie	109	86	.559
1914	Portland	Walter McCreedie	113	84	.573
1915	San Francisco	Harry Wolverton	118	89	.570
1916	Los Angeles	Frank Chance	119	79	.601
1917	San Francisco	Harry Wolverton– Jerome Downs	119	93	.561
1918	Vernon	William Essick	58	44	.548

(Though Vernon finished first, it lost a postseason playoff to second-place Los Angeles. The league suspended operations in mid-July because of World War I.)

Year	Championship Team	Manager	Won	Lost	Pct.
1919	Vernon	William Essick	111	70	.613
1920	Vernon	William Essick	110	88	.556
1921	Los Angeles	Wade Killefer	108	80	.574
1922	San Francisco	John "Dots" Miller	127	72	.638
1923	San Francisco	John "Dots" Miller– Herbert Ellison	124	77	.617
1924	Seattle	Wade Killefer	109	91	.545
1925	San Francisco	Herbert Ellison	128	71	.643
1926	Los Angeles	Martin Krug	121	81	.599
1927	Oakland	Ivan Howard	120	75	.615
1928	‡San Francisco	Nick Williams	58	34	.630

‡ Won playoff between winners of first half and second half of a split season.

Year	Championship Team	Manager	Won	Lost	Pct.
	San Francisco	Nick Williams	62	37	.626
	Sacramento	John Ryan	62	37	.626

(Sacramento and San Francisco finished the second half tied for first place. Sacramento proceeded to win a one-game playoff for the second-half title.)

Year	Championship Team	Manager	Won	Lost	Pct.
1929	Mission	Wade Killefer	63	35	.643
	‡Hollywood	Oscar Vitt	61	42	.592
1930	Los Angeles	Jack Lelivelt	57	42	.576
	‡Hollywood	Oscar Vitt	65	35	.650
1931	Hollywood	Oscar Vitt	57	34	.626
	‡San Francisco	Nick Williams	59	38	.608
1932	Portland	Spencer Abbott	111	78	.587
1933	Los Angeles	Jack Lelivelt	114	73	.609
1934	Los Angeles	Jack Lelivelt	137	50	.733
1935	Los Angeles	Jack Lelivelt	46	25	.648
	†San Francisco	Frank "Lefty" O'Doul	62	40	.608
1936	Portland	Max Bishop-Bill Sweeney	96	79	.549
1937	San Diego	Frank Shellenback	97	81	.545

(Sacramento finished first in the season standings, while San Diego finished third and won the postseason playoff. Under league rules followed that year, San Diego became the PCL champion.)

Year	Championship Team	Manager	Won	Lost	Pct.
1938	Los Angeles	J. Harrison Hannah	105	73	.590
1939	Seattle	Jack Lelivelt	101	73	.580
1940	Seattle	Jack Lelivelt	112	66	.629

‡ Won playoff between winners of first half and second half of a split season.

Year	Championship Team	Manager	Won	Lost	Pct.
1941	Seattle	Bill Skiff	104	70	.598
1942	Sacramento	John "Pepper" Martin	105	73	.590
1943	Los Angeles	Bill Sweeney	110	45	.710
1944	Los Angeles	Bill Sweeney	99	70	.586
1945	Portland	Marvin Owen	112	68	.622
1946	San Francisco	Frank "Lefty" O'Doul	115	68	.628
1947	Los Angeles	William Kelly	106	81	.567
1948	Oakland	Casey Stengel	114	74	.606
1949	Hollywood	Fred Haney	109	78	.583
1950	Oakland	Charles Dressen	118	82	.590
1951	Seattle	Rogers Hornsby	99	68	.593
1952	Hollywood	Fred Haney	109	71	.606
1953	Hollywood	Bobby Bragan	106	74	.589
1954	San Diego	Frank "Lefty" O'Doul	102	67	.604

(San Diego and Hollywood finished in a tie for first place, and San Diego took the PCL championship by winning the single-game playoff.)

Year	Championship Team	Manager	Won	Lost	Pct.
1955	Seattle	Fred Hutchinson	95	77	.552
1956	Los Angeles	Bob Scheffing	107	61	.637
1957	San Francisco	Joe Gordon	101	67	.601
1958	Phoenix	John "Red" Davis	89	65	.578
1959	Salt Lake City	Larry Shepard	85	69	.552

Year	Championship Team	Manager	Won	Lost	Pct.
1960	Spokane	Preston Gomez	92	61	.601
1961	Tacoma	John "Red" Davis	97	57	.630
1962	San Diego	Don Heffner	93	61	.604
1963	Spokane (North)	Danny Ozark	98	60	.620
	*Oklahoma City (South)	Grady Hatton	84	74	.532

(Oklahoma City defeated Spokane in playoff 4 games to 3 for the league's crown.)

1964	Arkansas (East)	Frank Lucchesi	95	61	.609
	*San Diego (West)	Dave Bristol	91	67	.576

(San Diego defeated Arkansas in playoff 4 games to 3 for the league's crown.)

1965	*Oklahoma City (East)	Grady Hatton	91	54	.628
	Portland (West)	Johnny Lipon	81	67	.547

(Oklahoma City defeated Portland in playoff 4 games to 1 for the league's crown.)

1966	Tulsa (East)	Charley Metro	85	62	.578
	*Seattle (West)	Bob Lemon	83	65	.561

(Seattle defeated Tulsa In playoff 4 games to 3 for the league's crown.)

1967	*San Diego (East)	Bob Skinner	85	63	.574
	Spokane (West)	Roy Hartsfield	80	68	.541

(Spokane and Portland finished the regular season in a tie for first place, and Spokane won the Western Division PCL title in a single-game playoff.
(San Diego defeated Spokane in playoff 4 games to 2 for the league's crown.)

* Asterisk indicates winning team.

Year	Championship Team	Manager	Won	Lost	Pct.
1968	*Tulsa (East)	Warren Spahn	95	53	.642
	Spokane (West)	Roy Hartsfield	85	60	.586

(Tulsa defeated Spokane In playoff 4 games to 1 for the league's crown.)

1969	*Tacoma (North)	Carroll "Whitey" Lockman	86	60	.589
	Eugene (South)	Frank Lucchesi	88	58	.603

(Tacoma defeated Eugene In playoff 3 games to 2 for the league's crown.)

1970	*Spokane (North)	Tom Lasorda	94	52	.644
	Hawaii (South)	Chuck Tanner	98	48	.671

(Spokane defeated Hawall In playoff 4 games to 0 for the league's crown.)

1971	Tacoma (North)	Jim Marshall	78	65	.545
	*Salt Lake City (South)	Del Rice	78	68	.534

(Salt Lake City defeated Tacoma in playoff 3 games to 1 for the league's crown.)

1972	*Albuquerque (East)	Tom Lasorda	92	56	.622
	Eugene (West)	Andy Seminick	79	69	.534

(Albuquerque defeated Eugene in playoff 3 games to 1 for the league's crown.)

1973	Tucson (East)	Sherman Lollar	84	60	.583
	*Spokane (West)	Del Wilber	81	63	.563

(Spokane defeated Tucson in playoff 3 games to 0 for the league's crown.)

* Asterisk indicates winning team.

PACIFIC COAST LEAGUE PLAYOFF CHAMPIONS

From 1936 through 1949, and also in 1951 and 1954, the Pacific Coast League held a four-team playoff. From 1938 through 1943, the playoff was known as the "President's Cup Series," and from 1944 on it was known as the "Governor's Cup Series." When a nonpennant winner took the playoff, the percentage champion remained listed as the league champion, according to PCL records. The PCL regarded these playoffs as a kind of afterthought.

Year	Playoff Winner	Manager
1936	Portland	Max Bishop–Bill Sweeney
1937	San Diego	Frank Shellenback
1938	Sacramento	Phil Bartelme
1939	Sacramento	Phil Bartelme
1940	Seattle	Jack Lelivelt
1941	Seattle	Bill Skiff
1942	Seattle	Bill Skiff
1943	San Francisco	Frank "Lefty" O'Doul
1944	San Francisco	Frank "Lefty" O'Doul
1945	San Francisco	Frank "Lefty" O'Doul
1946	San Francisco	Frank "Lefty" O'Doul
1947	Los Angeles	William Kelly
1948	Oakland	Casey Stengel
1949	Hollywood	Fred Haney
1951	Seattle	Rogers Hornsby
1954	Oakland	Chuck Dressen

PACIFIC COAST LEAGUE BATTING CHAMPIONS

Year	Player and Club	Bats	G	AB	Hits	Pct.
1903	Harry Lumley, Seattle	L	109	465	180	.387
1904	Emil Frisk, Seattle	L	. . .	808	272	.337
1905	Norman "Kitty" Brashear, Los Angeles	R	189	650	197	.303
1906	Michael Mitchell, Portland	R	164	578	203	.351
1907	Charles Egan, Oakland	R	194	708	237	.335
1908	Harold "Babe" Danzig, Portland	R	180	685	204	.298
1909	Henry Melchior, San Francisco	L	195	692	206	.298
1910	Royal "Hunky" Shaw, San Francisco	L	155	520	146	.281
1911	John "Buddy" Ryan, Portland	L	190	741	237	.333
1912	Henry Heitmuller, Los Angeles	L	151	556	186	.335

Year	Player and Club	Bats	G	AB	Hits	Pct.
1913	Henry Bayless, Vernon	L	195	709	230	.324
1914	Harry Wolter, Los Angeles	L	203	802	263	.328
1915	Harry Wolter, Los Angeles	L	150	518	186	.359
1916	William "Duke" Kenworthy, Oakland	R	200	735	231	.314
1917	Maurice Rath, Salt Lake City	L–R	197	721	246	.341
1918	Arthur Griggs, Sacramento	R	89	344	130	.378
1919	William Rumler, Salt Lake City	R	151	591	214	.362
1920	Earl Sheely, Salt Lake City	R	188	700	260	.371
1921	Lawrence "Hack" Miller, Oakland	R	184	726	252	.347
1922	Paul Strand, Salt Lake City	R	178	752	289	.384
1923	Paul Strand, Salt Lake City	R	194	825	325	.394
1924	George "Duffy" Lewis, Salt Lake City	R	154	528	207	.392
1925	Paul Waner, San Francisco	L	177	699	280	.401
1926	William Bagwell, Portland	L	156	450	176	.391
1927	Smead Jolley, San Francisco	L	168	625	248	.397
1928	Smead Jolley, San Francisco	L	191	765	309	.404
1929	Isaac "Ike" Boone, Mission	L	198	794	323	.407
1930	Earl Sheely, San Francisco	R	183	718	289	.403
1931	Oscar Eckhardt, Mission	L	185	745	275	.369
1932	Oscar Eckhardt, Mission	L	134	539	200	.371
1933	Oscar Eckhardt, Mission	L	189	760	315	.414
1934	Frank Demaree, Los Angeles	R	186	702	369	.383
1935	Oscar Eckhardt, Mission	L	172	710	283	.399
1936	Joe Marty, San Francisco	R	164	599	215	.359
1937	Harlan Pool, Seattle	R	136	458	153	.334
1938	Bernard "Frenchy' Uhalt, Hollywood	L	166	635	211	.332
1939	Dominic Dallessandro, San Diego	L	157	541	199	.368
1940	Lou Novikoff, Los Angeles	R	174	714	259	.363
1941	John Moore, Los Angeles	L	134	474	157	.331
1942	Ted Norbert, Portland	R	149	481	182	.378
1943	Andy Pafko, Los Angeles	R	157	604	215	.356
1944	Les Scarsella, Oakland	L	156	596	196	.328
1945	Joyner "Jo Jo" White, Sacramento	L	177	688	244	.355
1946	Harvey Storey, Los Angeles–Portland	R	157	556	181	.326
1947	Hillis Layne, Seattle	L	138	499	183	.367
1948	Gene Woodling, San Francisco	L	146	524	202	.385
1949	Art Wilson, San Diego–Oakland	L	165	607	211	.348
1950	Frank Baumholtz, Los Angeles	L	172	670	254	.379
1951	Manuel "Jim" Rivera, Seattle	L	166	657	231	.352
1952	Bob Boyd, Seattle	L	161	641	205	.320
1953	Bob Dillinger, Sacramento	R	171	645	236	.366

Year	Player and Club	Bats	G	AB	Hits	Pct.
1954	Harry Elliot, San Diego	R	168	640	224	.350
1955	George Metkovich, Oakland	L	151	532	178	.355
1956	Steve Bilko, Los Angeles	R	162	597	215	.360
1957	Ken Aspromonte, San Francisco	R	143	512	171	.334
1958	Andre Rodgers, Phoenix	R	122	427	151	.354
1959	Tommy Davis, Spokane	R	153	612	211	.345
1960	Willie Davis, Spokane	L	147	624	216	.346
1961	Carlos Bernier, Hawaii	R	127	433	152	.351
1962	Jesse Gonder, San Diego	L	136	491	168	.342
1963	Rutherford "Chico" Salmon, Denver	R	148	591	192	.325
1964	Lou Klimchock, Denver	L	153	569	190	.334
1965	Ted Uhlaender, Denver	L	136	518	176	.340
1966	Walter Williams, Tulsa	R	146	585	193	.330
1967	Cesar Gutierrez, Phoenix	R	116	494	159	.322
1968	Jim Hicks, Tulsa	R	117	407	149	.366
1969	Angel Bravo, Tucson	L	132	515	176	.342
1970	Bob Valentine, Spokane	R	146	621	211	.340
1971	Tom Hutton, Spokane	L	145	540	190	.352
1972	Von Joshua, Albuquerque	L	125	484	163	.337
1973	Steve Ontiveros, Phoenix	B	113	401	143	.357

PACIFIC COAST LEAGUE RECORDS

Individual Batting

Highest Percentage, Season
.414—Oscar Eckhardt, Mission, 1933

Lowest Percentage by Leader, Season
.281—Royal "Hunky" Shaw, San Francisco, 1910

Most Seasons Leading League in Percentage
4—Oscar Eckhardt, Mission, 1931–32–33, 1935

Service

Most Years Played in League
23—Herman Pillette: Portland, 1920–21; Vernon, 1925; Mission, 1926–33; Seattle, 1933–36; Hollywood, 1935; San Diego, 1936–42; Sacramento, 1943–45

Most Years With One Club
>18—Arnold "Jigger" Statz, Los Angeles, 1920–21, 1925–26, 1929–42

Most Clubs Played in League
>8—Edward Mulligan: Salt Lake City, 1919–20; San Francisco, 1923–27; Mission, 1929–32; Seattle, 1932; Portland, 1932–33; Oakland, 1934; Mission, 1935; Hollywood, 1936; San Diego, 1936–38

Most Games Played, Lifetime
>2,790—Arnold "Jigger" Statz, Los Angeles, 18 years

Most Games Played, Season
>227—William Dunleavy, Oakland, 1905

Most Consecutive Games Played
>866—Hugh Luby, Oakland: 1939, 176; 1940, 178; 1941, 178; 1942, 177; 1943, 157

Times at Bat

Most Times at Bat, Lifetime
>10,657—Arnold "Jigger" Statz, Los Angeles, 18 years

Most Times at Bat, Season
>941—George Van Haltren, Seattle, 1904

Runs

Most Runs Scored, Lifetime
>1,996—Arnold "Jigger" Statz, Los Angeles, 18 years

Most Runs Scored, Season
>202—Tony Lazzeri, Salt Lake City, 1925

Most Runs Scored, Game
>6—Pete Schneider, Vernon vs. Salt Lake City, May 11, 1923; Frank "Lefty" O'Doul, Salt Lake City vs. Portland, August 19, 1925; John Peters, Salt Lake City vs. Portland, August 19, 1925; Theodore Jennings, San Francisco vs. Portland, September 14, 1939

Hits

Most Hits, Lifetime
>3,356—Arnold "Jigger" Statz, Los Angeles, 18 years

Most Hits, Season
> 325—Paul Strand, Salt Lake City, 1923 (825 times at bat, .394 pct.)

Most Hits Series
> 25—Bert Ellison, San Francisco vs. Salt Lake City, May 20–25, 1924 (37 times at bat)

Most Hits, Four Consecutive Games
> 19—Frank "Lefty" O'Doul, Salt Lake City vs. Vernon, July 15–16–17–18, 1925 (21 at bats)

Most Hits, Three Consecutive Games
> 16—Frank "Lefty" O'Doul, Salt Lake City vs. Vernon, July 16–17–18, 1925 (17 at bats)

Most Consecutive Hits
> 12—Minor "Mickey" Heath, Hollywood vs. Mission, September 2–3–4, 1930 (13 at bats, 12 hits, 1 walk)

> 12—Ted Beard, Hollywood vs. Oakland, April 24–25–26, 1953; Hollywood vs. Portland, April 28, 1953 (13 at bats, 12 hits, 1 walk)

Most Consecutive Games Batted Safely, Season
> 61—Joe DiMaggio, San Francisco, May 28 (2nd game) through July 25, 1933

Most Consecutive Pinch-Hits
> 6—Dick Smith, Hollywood, July 20, 28, 31; August 25, 27, 30, 1937
> 6—Jack Littrell, Sacramento, May 30, 31; June 4, 6, 10, 11, 1960

Total Bases

Most Total Bases, Lifetime
> 4,405—Arnold "Jigger" Statz, Los Angeles, 18 years

Most Total Bases, Season
> 555—Isaac "Ike" Boone, Mission, 1929 (323 base hits, including 55 home runs)

Most Total Bases, Game
> 22—Pete Schneider, Vernon vs. Salt Lake City, May 11, 1923, (5 home runs, 1 double)

One-Base Hits

Most One-Base Hits, Lifetime
    2,564—Arnold "Jigger" Statz, Los Angeles, 18 years

Most One-Base Hits, Season
    231—Oscar Eckhardt, Mission, 1933 (315 total hits)

Most One-Base Hits, Game
    7—Emmett McCann, Portland vs. Salt Lake City, September 20, 1924

Two-Base Hits

Most Two-Base Hits, Lifetime
    595—Arnold "Jigger" Statz, Los Angeles, 18 years

Most Two-Base Hits, Season
    75—Paul Waner, San Francisco, 1925

Most Two-Base Hits, Game
    5—William "Bucky" Walters, Mission vs. San Francisco, July 2, 1933

Three-Base Hits

Most Three-Base Hits, Lifetime
    137—Arnold "Jigger" Statz, Los Angeles, 18 years

Most Three-Base Hits, Season
    26—Willie Davis, Spokane, 1960

Most Three-Base Hits, Game
    3—John Fenton, Oakland vs. San Francisco, October 1, 1927

Home Runs

Most Home Runs, Lifetime
    251—Russell "Buzz" Arlett, Oakland, 1918–30

Most Home Runs, Season
    60—Tony Lazzeri, Salt Lake City, 1925

Most Home Runs, Three Consecutive Games
    8—Bert Ellison, San Francisco vs. Salt Lake City, May 24–25–25, 1924

Most Home Runs, Doubleheader
    5—Bert Ellison, San Francisco vs. Salt Lake City, May 25, 1924

Most Home Runs, Game
    5—Pete Schneider, Vernon vs. Salt Lake City, May 11, 1923

Most Consecutive Games Hitting One or More Home Runs
    6—Gene Lillard, Los Angeles, April 18–19–20–21–22–22, 1935 (total of 8
    home runs)

Runs Batted In

Most Runs Batted In, Lifetime
    1,135—Russell "Buzz" Arlett, Oakland, 1918–30 (Records unavailable for
    146 games in 1918–20

Most Runs Batted In, Season
    222—Tony Lazzeri, Salt Lake City, 1925

Most Runs Batted In, Game
    14—Pete Schneider, Vernon vs. Salt Lake City, May 11, 1923

Most Runs Batted In, Inning
    7—Alex Kampouris, Sacramento vs. Portland, July 9, 1932

Stolen Bases

Most Stolen Bases, Lifetime
    468—Bill Lane, Oakland, 1916–17, 1919–20; Seattle, 1921–26

Most Stolen Bases, Season
    124—James Johnston, San Francisco, 1913

Most Stolen Bases, Game
    6—Walter "Watt" Powell, San Francisco vs. Oakland, July 26, 1911
    6—Arnold "Jigger" Statz, Los Angeles vs. Oakland, September 16, 1934

Sacrifice Hits

Most Sacrifice Hits, Lifetime
    390—Edward Mulligan: Salt Lake City, 1919–20; San Francisco, 1923–27;
    Mission, 1929–32; Seattle, 1932; Portland, 1932–33; Oakland, 1934; Mission,
    1935; Hollywood, 1935; San Diego, 1936–38

Most Sacrifice Hits, Season
74—Clyde "Buzzy" Wares, Oakland, 1910

Most Sacrifice Hits, Game
4—Ray Rohwer, Sacramento vs. Hollywood, August 20, 1927

Bases on Balls

Most Bases on Balls, Season (No records available prior to 1940)
201—Max West, San Diego, 1949

Most Bases on Balls, Game
5—Held by many players

Strikeouts

Most Strikeouts, Season (No records available prior to 1941)
164—Brant Alyea, Hawaii, 1965

Most Strikeouts, Game
5—Held by many players

Most Consecutive Strikeouts
12—Wilbur Wood, Seattle pitcher, August 19–September 1, 1964 (Struck out last 2 times at bat against Tacoma, August 19; 4 times against San Diego, August 23; 4 times against Hawaii, August 28; first 2 times at bat against San Diego, September 1)

Individual Pitching
Service

Most Years Pitched in League
23—Herman Pillette (For teams and years see p. 140)

Most Clubs Pitched For in League
7—Herman Pillette

Games Pitched

Most Games Pitched, Lifetime
708—Herman Pillette

Most Games Pitched, Season
88—Ken Rowe, Spokane, 1964

Most Games Pitched in Relief, Season
   88—Ken Rowe, Spokane, 1964

Most Games Finished in Relief, Season
   74—Ken Rowe, Spokane, 1964

Complete Games

Most Complete Games, Lifetime
   361—Frank Shellenback: Vernon, 1920–24; Sacramento, 1925; Hollywood,
   1926–35; San Diego, 1936–38

Most Complete Games, Season
   48—Clarence "Cack" Henley, San Francisco, 1910

Most Consecutive Complete Games, Season
   33—Clarence "Cack" Henley, San Francisco, March 30–August 23, 1910

Percentage

Highest Percentage, Games Won, Season (20 or More Decisions)
   .875—Fay Thomas, Los Angeles, 1934 (won 28, lost 4)

Highest Percentage, Games Won, Season (15 or More Decisions)
   .938—Luis Tiant, Portland, 1964 (won 15, lost 1)

Games Won

Most Games Won, Lifetime
   295—Frank Shellenback: Vernon, 1920–24; Sacramento, 1925; Hollywood,
   1926–35; San Diego, 1936–38

Most Games Won, Season
   39—Eustace "Doc" Newton, Los Angeles, 1904
   39—Harry "Rube" Vickers, Seattle, 1906

Most Consecutive Games Won, Lifetime
   22—Fay Thomas, Los Angeles, 1933–34 (last seven games of 1933 and first
   fifteen games of 1934)

Most Consecutive Games Won, One Season
   16—Frank Browning, San Francisco, June 10–August 12, 1909

Most Games Won in Relief, One Season
>   20—Leo Kiely, San Francisco, 1957

Most Consecutive Games Won in Relief, One Season
>   14—Leo Kiely, San Francisco, April 14–July 21, 1957

Games Lost

Most Games Lost, Lifetime
>   235—Charles "Spider" Baum: Los Angeles, 1903–05; Sacramento, 1909–11;
>   Vernon, 1912; Venice, 1913; San Francisco, 1914–19; Salt Lake City,
>   1919–20
>   235—Herman Pillette

Most Games Lost, Season
>   31—Isaac Butler, Portland, 1903
>   31—Isaac Butler, Portland, 1904

Most Consecutive Games Lost, Season
>   12—Marvin Breuer, Oakland, April 4–May 26, 1937

Shutouts

Most Shutouts, Season (No records available, 1903–05, 1907–09, 1911–13)
>   14—Sylveanus "Vean" Gregg, Portland, 1910

Innings Pitched

Most Innings Pitched, Lifetime
>   4,185—Frank Shellenback

Most Innings Pitched Season
>   526—Harry "Rube" Vickers, Seattle, 1906

Most Consecutive Innings Pitched Without Relief, Season
>   312—Clarence Cack" Henley, San Francisco, March 30–August 23, 1910

Strikeouts

Most Strikeouts, Lifetime
>   1866—Tracy "Dick" Barrett: Seattle, 1935–42; Portland, 1946; Seattle, 1947–
>   49; San Diego, 1949–50; Hollywood, 1950

Most Strikeouts, Season
>   408—Harry "Rube" Vickers, Seattle, 1906

Most Strikeouts, Game
>19—Charles Shields, Seattle vs. Portland, July 8, 1905

Most Consecutive Strikeouts, Game
>8—Sylveanus "Vean" Gregg, Portland vs. Los Angeles, September 2, 1910

Bases on Balls

Most Bases on Balls, Season
>234—Oscar Graham, Oakland, 1903

Most Bases on Balls, Game
>13—John Hickey, Seattle vs. San Francisco, April 7, 1903

Most Consecutive Bases on Balls, Game
>6—Franz Hosp, Los Angeles vs. San Francisco, July 26, 1908 (first inning)
>6—Dick Radatz, Tacoma vs. Portland, July 23, 1967 (second game, third inning)

Most Consecutive Innings, No Bases on Balls
>68-2/3—George Bamberger, Vancouver, July 10 (fourth inning, two out)—August 14 (seventh inning, two out), 1958

Hit Batsmen

Most Hit Batsmen Season
>49—Oscar Graham, Oakland, 1903

Most Hit Batsmen, Game
>4—Franz Hosp, Los Angeles vs. San Francisco, July 26, 1908
>4—Charles Gassaway, Oakland vs. San Francisco, May 14, 1950

Most Hit Batsmen, Inning
>3—Robert Keefe, Tacoma vs. Los Angeles, August 31, 1905

Wild Pitches

Most Wild Pitches, Season
>28—Edward Willett, Vernon, 1910

Most Wild Pitches, Game
>5—Ted Wieand, Seattle vs. Phoenix, May 24, 1958
>5—Gerald Nelson, Oklahoma City vs. Dallas, July 28, 1964
>5—Richard Robertson, Phoenix vs. Spokane, June 26, 1968

PITCHERS WITH 200 OR MORE VICTORIES

Name	Won	Lost	Pct.
Frank Shellenback	295	178	.624
Charles "Spider" Baum	261	235	.526
Harry Krause	249	220	.531
Tracy "Dick" Barrett	234	168	.582
Otis "Doc" Crandall	230	151	.604
Antonio Freitas	228	175	.566
Samuel Gibson	227	140	.619
Herman Pillette	226	235	.491
Clarence "Cack" Henley	215	171	.557
Rudolph Kallio	205	210	.496
Jack Salveson	204	166	.551
Harold Turpin	203	158	.562

PACIFIC COAST LEAGUE ATTENDANCE RECORDS

Highest Attendance, Season, League (8 teams)
4,068,432—1947 (National/Association Record)

Highest Attendance, Season, Club
670,563—1946, San Francisco (National Association Record)

Highest Attendance, Single Series
111,622—Oakland at San Francisco, July 30 through August 4, 1946

Highest Attendance, Single Game
23,603—Oakland at San Francisco, July 30, 1946

Highest Attendance, Doubleheader
23,090—San Diego at Los Angeles, May 15, 1949

Highest Attendance, Day–Night Doubleheader
34,450—Sacramento at Portland, April 27, 1956 (16,929 at the afternoon game; 17,521 at the night game)

Lowest Attendance, Single Game
1—Portland at Oakland, November 8, 1905

Branch Rickey (*center*), St. Louis Cardinals general manager, inspecting his top farm team at Rochester in 1940. With Rickey are Billy Southworth (*left*), Red Wings manager, and Oliver French (*right*), club president. Rickey is given credit for having introduced the "farm system" for player development. (*Photo courtesy of The National Baseball Hall of Fame and Museum, Cooperstown, N.Y.*)

Judge Kenesaw Mountain Landis, long-time high commissioner of baseball, strongly opposed Branch Rickey's establishment of the farm system. (*Photo courtesy of The National Baseball Hall of Fame and Museum, Cooperstown, N.Y.*)

Henry J. "Hank" Peters has been president of the National Association of Professional Baseball Leagues since 1971. Before his selection to this post, Peters was a vice-president and director of player personnel for the Cleveland Indians. (*Photo courtesy of the National Association of Professional Baseball Leagues.*)

Arnold "Jigger" Statz amassed 3,356 base hits in his eighteen years in the Pacific Coast League. He also recorded 737 hits in the majors, mostly with the Chicago Cubs. (*Photo courtesy of The National Baseball Hall of Fame and Museum, Cooperstown, N.Y.*)

Mid-March 1903—the Sacramento Sacts and the Oakland Oaks are seen leaving the State House Hotel for the ballpark, after special ceremonies marking the opening day of Pacific Coast League play in Sacramento. The Oaks won the game 7–4. (*Photo from the collection of Douglas M. McWilliams.*)

Paul Waner was the first player in Pacific Coast League history to reach the magic .400 figure in batting. On the strength of his 280 hits in 1925, he hit .401. (*Photo courtesy of The National Baseball Hall of Fame and Museum, Cooperstown, N.Y.*)

While with Salt Lake City in 1925, Tony Lazzeri set three all-time Pacific Coast League records for slugging: he hit 60 home runs, scored 202 runs, and batted in 222! He's shown here wearing the uniform of the New York Yankees. (*Photo courtesy of The National Baseball Hall of Fame and Museum, Cooperstown, N.Y.*)

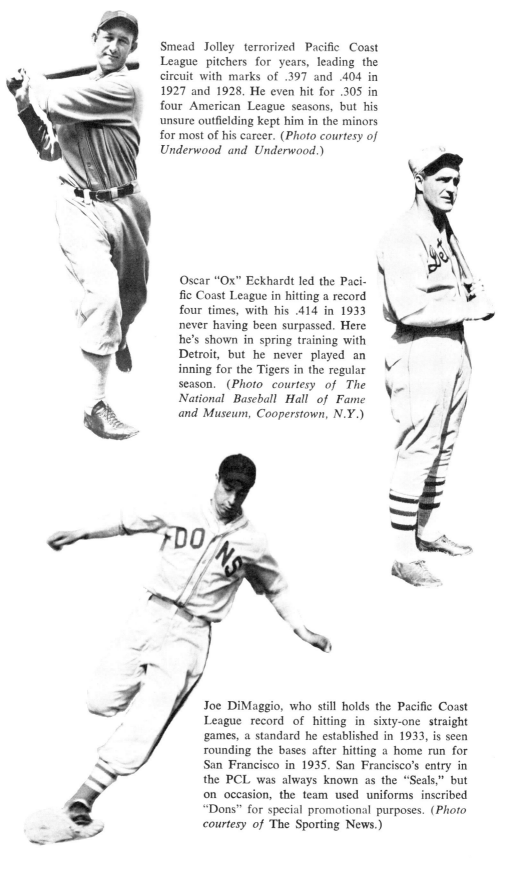

Smead Jolley terrorized Pacific Coast League pitchers for years, leading the circuit with marks of .397 and .404 in 1927 and 1928. He even hit for .305 in four American League seasons, but his unsure outfielding kept him in the minors for most of his career. (*Photo courtesy of Underwood and Underwood*.)

Oscar "Ox" Eckhardt led the Pacific Coast League in hitting a record four times, with his .414 in 1933 never having been surpassed. Here he's shown in spring training with Detroit, but he never played an inning for the Tigers in the regular season. (*Photo courtesy of The National Baseball Hall of Fame and Museum, Cooperstown, N.Y.*)

Joe DiMaggio, who still holds the Pacific Coast League record of hitting in sixty-one straight games, a standard he established in 1933, is seen rounding the bases after hitting a home run for San Francisco in 1935. San Francisco's entry in the PCL was always known as the "Seals," but on occasion, the team used uniforms inscribed "Dons" for special promotional purposes. (*Photo courtesy of* The Sporting News.)

Eddie Mulligan played for eight different Pacific Coast League clubs between 1919–38, a record. Mulligan, whose career in Organized Baseball stretches over a period of sixty years, has been president of the Class A California League since 1956. Here we see him in his office at League headquarters in Millbrae, California. (*Photo courtesy of The California League.*)

Frank Shellenback is the Pacific Coast League's winningest pitcher. In a nineteen-year career (1920–38), he posted 295 victories against 178 defeats. He later coached for the Boston Red Sox and the New York Giants. (*Photo courtesy of The National Baseball Hall of Fame and Museum, Cooperstown, N.Y.*)

Jack Salveson is one of the dozen Pacific Coast League pitchers to have chalked up more than 200 lifetime wins. He was 204–166 for twenty years in the PCL, with time out for brief stretches in the majors. (*Photo courtesy of the author.*)

Frank "Lefty" O'Doul, manager of the San Francisco Seals, giving a batting demonstration in 1941—he was forty-four at the time. As manager of the Vancouver Mounties in the PCL in 1956, O'Doul made his final appearance in a regularly scheduled game. He slammed a pinch-hit triple —at the age of fifty-nine! (*Photo courtesy of Acme Newspictures, Inc.*)

A record crowd of 23,090 came out to see San Diego battle Los Angeles in a doubleheader at the Angels' Wrigley Field on May 15, 1949. Los Angeles for many years was one of the key cities in the Pacific Coast League. (After the majors invaded the West Coast, Wrigley Field was torn down.) (*Photo by the author.*)

Albuquerque's Sports Stadium, completed on March 31, 1969, is the only "Drive-In Ballpark" in the country. Over 100 autos can be lined up behind the fence, and from this vantage point, fans can view the proceedings. Seating capacity is 10,510 (3,500 standees can also be accommodated), with the parking lots being able to handle 7,000 cars. Albuquerque is now in the Pacific Coast League. (*Photo courtesy of the Albuquerque Baseball Co.*)

Bill Burwell, whose career in Organized Baseball spanned almost sixty years, is the American Association's winningest pitcher, with 189 victories. He also spent many years in the Pittsburgh Pirates organization as a minor league manager, pitching coach, and scout. (*Photo courtesy of the Pittsburgh Pirates Baseball Co.*)

Joe McCarthy established himself as perhaps the first great manager who never played an inning in the majors. He became manager of the Chicago Cubs in 1926, after having been a highly successful pilot with Louisville in the American Association. (*Photo courtesy of The National Baseball Hall of Fame and Museum, Cooperstown, N.Y.*)

Dazzy Vance pitched in the minors for ten full years—with ten different teams in six leagues—before he made the grade with the Brooklyn Dodgers in 1922 at the age of thirty-one. From that point, Vance went on to win 197 games in 14 major league seasons and gained entry into the Hall of Fame. (*Photo courtesy of The National Baseball Hall of Fame and Museum, Cooperstown, N.Y.*)

Lefty Grove (*right*) with Connie Mack (*left*), early in Grove's career with the Philadelphia Athletics. Grove won 109 games and lost only 36 in five years with Baltimore, of the International League, before he finally went up to the majors. (*Photo courtesy of the author.*)

George Puccinelli, one of the International League's hitting standouts in the 1930s, starred for both Rochester and Baltimore in between short hitches in the majors. (*Photo couretsy of The National Baseball Hall of Fame and Museum, Cooperstown, N.Y.*)

Slingin' Sammy Baugh, best known as one of the National League's great quarterbacks, took a fling at professional baseball early in his career. He was a shortstop with the Rochester Red Wings in 1938. (*Photo courtesy of The National Baseball Hall of Fame and Museum, Cooperstown, N.Y.*)

Branch Rickey, with two of his proteges in baseball administration, in a 1936 photo. At *left* is Gabe Paul, assistant general manager of the Rochester Red Wings, and at *right* is Warren Giles, the Red Wings GM. Paul went on to become general manager of both the Cincinnati Reds and the Cleveland Indians, while Giles became president of the National League. Paul, who's now had more than forty years of experince as a baseball executive, is currently a part-owner and president of the New York Yankees. (*Photo courtesy of The National Baseball Hall of Fame and Museum, Cooperstown, N.Y.*)

Billy Southworth (*left*), Milwaukee Braves scout, and Johnny Keane (*right*), manager of the Rochester Red Wings in a 1953 photo. Southworth piloted the Red Wings on three different occasions. (*Photo courtesy of The National Baseball Hall of Fame and Museum, Cooperstown, N.Y.*)

Charlie Senger (*center*), one of the most imaginative and dynamic young minor-league executives, has been general manager of the Toledo Mud Hens of the International League since 1966. Stenger is shown with Loren Babe, manager of the 1966 Mud Hens (*left*), and coach Wilmer Shantz (*right*), both former major league players. (*Photo courtesy of the Toledo Mud Hens Baseball Co.*)

George H. Sisler, Jr., member of a famous baseball family, has been president of the International League since 1966. Prior to his election to that post, he had been general manager of the Rochester Red Wings for eleven years. (*Photo courtesy of the International League.*)

Local merchants obviously felt that the outfield wall at Chattanooga's Engel Stadium, circa 1950, was a good place to advertise. For years this was considered one of the finest facilities in all of minor league baseball. (*Photo courtesy of The National Baseball Hall of Fame and Museum, Cooperstown, N.Y.*)

Joe Hauser (*right*), one of the greatest of all home-run hitters in the high minors, hit 63 circuit clouts for Baltimore in the International League in 1930, and 69 for Minneapolis in the American Association in 1933—both still records for those leagues. As a member of the Philadelphia Athletics in 1924, he hit his highwater mark in the majors, with 27 homers. (*Photo courtsy of The National Baseball Hall of Fame and Museum, Cooperstown, N.Y.*)

Isaac "Ike" Boone, one of the greatest players in minor league history, won batting titles in both the Pacific Coast and International Leagues. In 355 major league games, Boone batted .319. (*Photo courtesy of* The Sporting News.)

10

THE TEXAS LEAGUE:
Baseball Deep in the
Heart of Texas

(CLASS D 1902–06; CLASS C, 1907–10; CLASS B, 1911–20; CLASS A, 1921–36; CLASS A1, 1936–42; CLASS AA, 1946—) *

ROSTER OF TEXAS LEAGUE TEAMS

Team	Years in Operation
Alexandria, Louisiana	1972—
Albuquerque, New Mexico	1962–71
Amarillo, Texas	1959–63, 1965—
Ardmore, Texas	1904# ¹ (see note for Paris), 1961# (see note for Victoria)
Austin, Texas	1888 (franchise shifted to San Antonio in mid-season), 1889–90, 1895–99, 1905X, 1907–08, 1911–14, 1956–57
Beaumont, Texas	1912–17X, 1919–55
Cleburne, Texas	1906
Corpus Christi, Texas	1958–59
Corsicana, Texas	1902–05X
Dallas, Texas	1888–90, 1892, 1895–98, 1902–42, 1946–58
Dallas–Fort Worth, Texas	1965–71

* See page 323 for Key to Roster of League Teams. None of the Texas League schedules from 1888 through 1899 was really completed, even in those years when playoffs were held. In order to simplify this listing, the symbol X, which indicates that an individual team dropped out before the season was completed, will not be indicated for the 1888–99 period. Technically, no team finished the complete schedule for those years.

177

Team	Years in Operation
Denison, Texas	1896 (Denison combined with neighboring Sherman for the 1897 and 1902 seasons; see entry under Sherman–Denison)
El Paso, Texas	1962–70, 1972—
Fort Worth, Texas	1888–90, 1892, 1895–98, 1902–42, 1946–58, 1964
Galveston, Texas	1888–90, 1892, 1895–99, 1907–15X, 1916–17, 1919–24, 1931–37
Greenville, Texas	1906X
Houston, Texas	1888–90, 1892, 1895–99, 1902–58
Little Rock, Arkansas	1966—
Longview, Texas	1932# (see note for Wichita Falls)
Memphis, Tennessee	1968–73
Midland, Texas	1972—
New Orleans, Louisiana	1888#
Oklahoma City, Oklahoma	1909–11, 1933–42, 1946–57
Paris, Texas	1896# (see note for Sherman), 1897, 1903 (franchise shifted to Waco on June 26), 1904 (franshise shifted to Ardmore late in season)
Rio Grande Valley (Harlingen), Texas	1960–61 (franchise shifted to Victoria; see note for Victoria)
San Antonio, Texas	1888# (see note for Austin), 1892#, 1895–99, 1907–42, 1946–64, 1967—
Sherman, Texas	1895–96 (franchise shifted to Paris on June 10)
Sherman–Denison, Texas	1897 (franchise shifted to Waco on July 11), 1902 (franchise shifted to Texarkana early in the season)
Shreveport, Louisiana	1895X, 1908–10, 1915–32 (franchise shifted to Tyler on May 4), 1938–42, 1946–57, 1968—
Temple, Texas	1905–06X, 1907
Texarkana, Texas	(1902#X (see note for Sherman–Denison)
Tulsa, Oklahoma	1933–42, 1946–65
Tyler, Texas	1932# (see note for Shreveport)
Victoria, Texas	1958–61 (there were some unusual franchise shifts in 1961: on May 27, the original Victoria club transferred to Ardmore; and on June 10, the Rio Grande Valley club, representing Harlingen, transferred to Victoria), 1974—
Waco, Texas	1889–90, 1892#, 1897# (see note for Sherman–Denison), 1902–03# (see note for Paris), 1905–19, 1925–30
Wichita Falls, Texas	1920–32 (franchise shifted to Longview on May 20)

SOUTH TEXAS LEAGUE (1903–06)

Austin, Texas	1906
Beaumont, Texas †	1903–06
Galveston, Texas	1903–06
Houston, Texas	1903–06
Lake Charles, Louisiana	1906
San Antonio, Texas	1903–06

† Beaumont played a few of its games in 1906 in Brenham, Texas.

Texas has the distinction of having had more towns represented in Organized Baseball than any other state, 101, surpassing North Carolina's 70 and Pennsylvania's 66. Professional baseball has been played across the length and breadth of this vast state, which has an area (267,339 square miles) greater than that of France and England combined. The greatest north–south distance, between Texhoma and Brownsville, is 770 miles; while the greatest east–west distance, between Orange and El Paso, is 760 miles. (Among these four towns, all have had pro teams at one time or another except Texhoma, which is too small.)

Boys who hooked on with lower classification teams in the smaller cities of the Great Plains, North Central Plains, Coastal Plains, the Panhandle, or other areas of the giant "Lone Star" state dreamed of the big leagues, of course. Nevertheless, many of them felt they had "arrived" if they could eventually make the team of one of the big towns (such as Dallas, Fort Worth, and Houston) of the fast Texas League. A star in the Texas League became a hero to youngsters over a wide region.

The Texas League, founded in 1888, is also the state's first true professional league. Amateur baseball caught hold in the state immediately following the Civil War, and by 1872, a loosely organized amateur league was formed with teams in cities like Austin, Dallas, and Waco. The clubs traveled from one town to another via stage coach, since this was the only means of transportation available at the time.

The Texas amateur league was more closely organized in 1884 when teams in six cities (Dallas, Fort Worth, Galveston, Houston, San Antonio, and Waco) played a definite schedule of some fifteen to twenty games. Each club had a few paid men on its roster (usually the pitcher, catcher, and shortstop), who were often imported from other towns. These paid players were for all intents and purposes "tramp professionals." Moreover, this Texas amateur circuit was carefully watched over by teams from the National League, and thus, it served as a farm system in a very rudimentary way.

Tough college baseball in Texas came into being at about the same time—in the mid-1880s—when Texas A & M and the University of Texas began a diamond rivalry that survives to this day. Many fine professional players have come out of the Texas colleges during the past ninety years.

Beginning in 1895, the Texas League began getting competition from other professional leagues that were being established within the state and its environs. Some of these circuits lasted for only a few months, while others stayed in business for many years. The long list of Texas-oriented B, C, and D leagues includes: the North Texas League, the Gulf Coast League, the Texas–Oklahoma League, the Middle Texas League, the Central Texas Trolley League, the East Texas League, the Texas Association, the Lone Star League, the Gulf Coast League, the Texas Valley League, the Rio Grande Valley League, the Longhorn League, and the Big State League. The Texas League has been the only one to survive.

JOHN J. McCLOSKEY: FOUNDER OF THE TEXAS LEAGUE

John J. McCloskey, who enjoyed a long and varied career in professional baseball, is generally considered to be the founder of the Texas League. Born in Louisville, Kentucky, on April 4, 1862, he began playing professionally around his hometown in 1882. Then in 1884, he came to Texas with a team of touring semi-pros. He continued organizing teams across the Midwest and Southwest, and in the fall of 1887, he returned to Texas with his barnstorming Joplin, Missouri, Independents. His Joplin team played other independents in such towns as Fort Worth, Waco, and Austin; and it was in Austin, the capital, that he finally realized great prospects for a professional league in Texas. The exhibition series had attracted wide attention throughout much of the state, especially in Austin.

McCloskey interested a group of businessmen (most of them young men) in the league proposal, and the first organizational meeting was held at Austin on December 15, 1887. Dallas, Austin, Houston, and New Orleans were represented. Letters favoring the league idea also were received from Fort Worth, Galveston, and Waco. Definite plans for the league were drawn up at this meeting, which was chaired by Fred W. Turner of Austin, who was elected as the circuit's first president. The moving force in getting the teams and schedule together, however, was McCloskey.

In subsequent organizational meetings the salary limit for players was set at $1,000, and a constitution and playing rules were adopted with the circuit's official name to be "The Texas League of Baseball Clubs." A standard admission price of 25¢ was set for all parks; umpires were to get $75 per month, plus railroad fares; and the league secretary's salary was set at $50 per month.

The league's first season commenced on April 8, 1888, with six teams on the roster: Dallas, Austin, San Antonio, Galveston, Houston, and Fort Worth. Player rosters consisted of former amateurs, semi-pros, and professionals who had been active in other minor leagues. McCloskey had moved his entire Joplin semi-pro club to Austin.

The 1888 season had a lot of rough edges. By July 1 every club except Dallas was experiencing serious financial difficulties, and shifts had to be made as teams dropped out of the circuit. Fort Worth had already thrown in the towel in late June, while early in July Austin moved into San Antonio after the original San Antonio team disbanded. Thus, the "Alamo City" had the unique Texas League experience of being represented in a single campaign by two completely different sets of ball players.

With Austin and Fort Worth vacant, the league went down to four teams temporarily. New Orleans, however, entered the circuit early in July, raising the number of clubs to an awkward five. With five teams scheduling became difficult, since one had to be idle on any given day. The idle team usually whiled away its off-day by playing a local amateur or semi-pro team.

The season was set to run well into October; but Houston, Galveston, and New Orleans all dropped out, leaving Dallas and San Antonio as the only teams intact. Continuing league play with only two teams was impossible, of course, and play had to be suspended on September 3. Dallas, with a 55–27 record, took the unofficial league title, while McCloskey argued unsuccessfully that his Austin–San Antonio team with a 38–29 record should be declared "co-champion" for being the only other entry to stay in the race.

Texas newspapers had a very difficult time publishing accurate standings, particularly because all games were not reported and reports issued under an "official" label were sometimes very dubious indeed. William B. Ruggles, a long-time Texas League officer and statistician, maintained that the 1888 standings now accepted "represent a coordination of newspaper reports of day to day games."

From these humble beginnings the Texas League began to grow in prestige, although it took another dozen years before the circuit really got itself on to a firm foundation. In 1889, the loop operated with six teams, a new entry, Waco, being added to go along with Austin, Dallas, Fort Worth, Galveston, and Houston.

McCloskey moved his team from San Antonio to Houston, and with a 54–44 record, he edged out Dallas (49–42) by 3½ games. The pennant was again disputed because Houston had not paid its dues to the league. League president Louis Newburg maintained that while Houston had won the most games, Austin had paid its dues in full and led the three clubs that had done so and therefore should take the flag. A spirited widely publicized controversy arose over this matter, and after Houston finally raised the cash for the dues payment, it was officially awarded the league title. The season again was cut short—this time by a month—because of generally poor attendance.

The Texas League's first doubleheader was played on July 4, 1889, at Austin between Houston and Austin; the homestanders won both games, 13–9 and 5–2. The 1889 season was also notable in that official statistics were compiled and released for the first time; the batting, pitching and fielding records, however, were far from complete according modern statistical standards.

The same six teams took the field for the 1890 season, although Austin was not ready for its March 30 opener, since it had neither a complete ball club nor a manager. It seems that Harry "Bird Eye" Truby signed one contract to manage Austin and another to play for Fort Worth. Truby, an infielder, was scheduled to play for Fort Worth in its season's opener against Dallas, but league president Joseph Sensheimer instructed the umpire not to permit him to appear. Fort Worth refused to take the field without him and forfeited the game. The league office resolved the affair by placing Truby on the blacklist. Nevertheless, Truby continued his career outside the Texas League and played second base briefly for the Chicago Cubs in 1895–96. Austin club president Joe A. Barbisch finally signed Ed Reeder as manager and rounded up enough qualified players to field a respectable team.

Galveston, one of the Texas League's strongest cities in the circuit's early days, won the pennant under manager Bill "Farmer" Works with a fine 31–13 season record. Unfortunately, the season was cut short for the third year in a row, since most of the clubs were in dire financial straits by early June. On June 10, President Sensheimer formally announced the dissolution of the League.

Houston manager John McCloskey finished the season playing semi-pro ball in Dallas, and since he saw no chance for the Texas League to operate in 1891, he took a group of TL players to Sacramento early in the year. There he formed his own semi-pro team.

McCloskey, nevertheless, still saw great possibilities for high-level pro ball in Texas, and he returned to the state early in 1892 and once again became the driving force in putting together the Texas League. McCloskey took the nucleus of his semi-pro club back to Houston with him, and with Houston club president Si Packard (who also held the Houston presidency in 1889–90), he began hustling around to get at least three more teams together to form a league.

Early in May, Galveston, Dallas, and Fort Worth had teams ready for action, but the teams were composed primarily of amateur players. On about July 7, Dallas and Fort Worth decided to disband because of poor attendance; as a result Houston was forced to play Galveston every afternoon! Houston and Galveston played their "long series" for some two weeks before league officials, led by Packard and McCloskey, succeeded in getting Waco and San Antonio to join the league in order to bring the circuit back up to a respectable four teams.

On July 22, 1892, in one of their many games together Houston and Galveston made baseball history at Houston when they played perhaps the first night game in the annals of professional baseball. The game was limited to 5 innings with Galveston taking a 9–8 decision. William B. Ruggles commented, "There was an epidemic of the exhibition night games in Texas at about this time." This is amazing when we consider that night baseball did not become an integral part of the pro game until nearly forty years later.

Houston's 59–26 (.694 pct.) record easily paced the league, but the championship was strictly unofficial, since the league had to be reorganized in midseason.

The Texas League went into limbo for two years after the 1892 season, but "Honest John" McCloskey, who did more than anyone else to keep the circuit together during its infancy, was still only on the threshold of a long career in pro ball. He became manager of the Montgomery, Alabama, team in the Southern League in 1893, where Fred C. Clarke and Joe "Iron Man" McGinnity were serving their professional apprenticeships. (Clarke became noted as the Pittsburgh Pirates longtime outfielder–manager, while McGinnity's pitching feats for John McGraw's New York Giants are legendary. Both men are now in the Hall of Fame.)

McCloskey's travels through the world of baseball, mostly as a manager, read almost like a gazetteer. He managed Savannah in the Southern League in 1894, Louisville in the National League in 1895–96, Dallas in the Texas League in 1897–98, and Montgomery again in 1899.

Other managerial stops included: Great Falls, Montana, in the Pacific Northwest League in 1900; Tacoma, Washington, also in the Pacific Northwest League in 1901; Butte, Montana, in the Pacific National League in 1902; San Francisco, California, in the Pacific Coast League in 1903; Boise, Idaho, in the Pacific National League in 1904; Vancouver, Washington, in the Puget Sound League in 1905; St. Louis

Cardinals, in the National League in 1906–08; Minneapolis, Minnesota in the American Association in 1909–10; Butte, Montana, in the Union Association in 1911; Ogden, Utah, in the Union Association in 1912; and Salt Lake City, Utah, also in the Union Association in 1913.

McCloskey scouted for the Cincinnati Reds in 1914, organized a Rio Grande League in 1915, and then for the next three seasons operated a semi-pro circuit composed mostly of U.S. Army service teams. "Honest John" then made his final appearance in the Texas League as Beaumont's manager in 1919. From then until 1930 he made managerial stops at Memphis in the Southern League; Bartlesville, Oklahoma, and Newton, Kansas, in the Southwestern League; Wilmington in the Atlantic League; and Akron, Ohio, in the Central League. While managing Akron in 1927 (he was sixty-five years old then), he was still able to circle the bases in 19 seconds! Basically an outdoor man, McCloskey always stayed in top condition and served as a good example of clean-living to the young ball players in his charge.

In 1931, McCloskey, basically the organizer at heart, came back to Texas where he tried to launch a new "Panhandle League," and with his base at Amarillo (where he expected to manage), he succeeded in lining up two other teams, Pampa and Lubbock, but he was forced to give up the effort when he failed to sign up a fourth team. He then retired to his Louisville home and spent his remaining years scouting for various major league teams and talking baseball with anyone who would listen to him. He died on November 17, 1940, at the age of seventy-eight.

John McCloskey never made the big money in baseball, but his contributions to the professional game over a span of more than fifty years were enormous—and no one in baseball earned more friendships than he did.

THE TEXAS LEAGUE RESUMES PLAY

The Texas League was revived in 1895, largely through the efforts of Ted Sullivan, who got the ball rolling by reorganizing the Dallas franchise. A native of County Clare, Ireland, and an organizer in the style of John McCloskey, Sullivan was an experienced baseball man. He had managed major league teams at St. Louis, Kansas City, and Washington in the 1880s. By the time the season began in mid-April, Sullivan and his associates succeeded in rounding up eight teams for the league (the TL never had more than six clubs previously). In addition to Dallas, Fort Worth, Austin, Galveston, Houston, San Antonio, Sherman, and Shreveport entered the fold. Austin, Houston, San Antonio, and Shreveport were forced to drop out at midseason, but this was still the first time the league as a whole had survived an entire campaign.

Moreover, league secretary James Nolan issued the first really comprehensive statistics for the Texas League. Algie McBride, an Austin outfielder, was awarded the batting crown after compiling a stratospheric .444 average in 94 games. No other TL batting champ ever exceeded that mark. (McBride went on to play for Chicago and Cincinnati in the National League.) Batting averages generally ran high with free scoring games being quite common during this era.

Again in 1896, eight teams started the season and only four finished. Teams that did finish, like Galveston and Houston, each played a record number of 130 games, not counting playoffs.

The league continued to show a good measure of stability through the 1897 season, despite various internal problems. On July 11, for example, Sherman–Denison decided to disband without notice; but John McCloskey (then Dallas manager) persuaded James M. Drake (the Waco businessman–politician) to back the team in Waco. Since Waco did not permit Sunday ball, Drake arranged to have his regularly scheduled games played in neighboring Hillsboro and Corsicana.

The 1898 season lasted little more than a month before it was suspended on May 13 because of the Spanish–American War. The United States had declared war on Spain shortly after the season opened on April 9, and the State of Texas had become much more interested in troop mobilization than in professional baseball. Moreover, a number of the Texas League's players enlisted in the armed services after hostilities broke out. Of the six teams which had started play (Austin, Dallas, Fort Worth, Galveston, Houston, and San Antonio), John McCloskey's Dallas club had the best winning percentage (13–7, .650 pct.), but it was only an unofficial pennant-winner since the season had ended so abruptly. Austin at 18–11 for a .621 pct. stood second.

The Texas League (now formally known as the "Texas Association," though still commonly referred to as the "Texas League") was reorganized for 1899 and was limited to only four teams in South Texas: Austin, Galveston, Houston, and San Antonio. League officials at this time felt that traveling expenses were too high and scheduling problems too complex when teams from the northern part of the state, namely Dallas and Fort Worth, were included.

Dallas had entered the Southern Association for the 1899 campaign, and during this period as well as in subsequent years, we often find teams switching from the Texas to the Southern League and vice versa. The histories of the Texas and Southern Leagues are, therefore, closely intertwined.

In order to spur interest in the 1899 season, Texas League officials arbitrarily split the campaign into two halves on June 13, but again the circuit could not survive for an entire season despite all the promotional efforts to lure fans into the parks. When Austin decided to pull out on July 5, the three remaining club owners had no other choice except to disband. The Galveston Sandcrabs won both halves conclusively and thus took clear title to the league championship.

John Holland, a star outfielder for the Sandcrabs, went on to a long career as a minor league executive and served for many years as president of Oklahoma City, both in the Western League and the Texas league.

THE TEXAS LEAGUE RESTORED

The Texas League went into complete hibernation for two years (1900–01), and when it was revived again in 1902, the circuit finally got on the road toward becoming a stable and permanent part of the professional baseball scene. The league has maintained full schedules ever since —except for World War I, when the season was cut in the middle, and for World War II when play had to be halted for three years. Individual teams did continue to drop out of the league from time to time, however, but "dropping out" is a part of the minor league story.

After the two-year lapse, Texas promoters and fans alike were hungry for baseball, and suddenly everyone seemed to forget the league's first dozen years of rough going. In fact, Bill Ruggles once said of those early days: "The Texas League had never been a financial success in its first years, and it is very doubtful if *any* club owner made any money out of baseball here from 1888 through 1899."

The 1902 circuit was made up of six teams: Corsicana, Dallas, Fort Worth, Paris, Waco, and the twin cities Sherman–Denison (which moved to Texarkana on May 6). In the standings compiled for the 1902 season (see page 00) Sherman–Denison and Texarkana are listed as one entry with a combined 20–47 record.) Only Corsicana, Dallas, Fort Worth, and Paris finished the campaign, which ran from April 26 through August 31. It is important to note that the revived league took a definite northward "tilt"; the old-line Texas League cities in the southern part of the state —namely Galveston, Houston, and San Antonio—were out of the picture at this time.

The Corsicana "Oil City" team led by "Big Mike" O'Connor, a

6-foot, 5-inch manager–first baseman, made a travesty of the pennant race by piling up a formidable 88–23 (.793) record and capturing the league crown by a fat 29 games over second-place Dallas, which came in at 60–53. In the long "first half," O'Connor's charges were almost invincible, taking 58 out of 67 games. At one point the team rolled up a winning streak of 27 games, which is still good for the league record.

Mike O'Connor is one of the legendary figures in the Texas League, having started his career in the circuit's inaugural year (1888) as manager at Fort Worth. He never reached the majors, but he spent eighteen years in the high minors, including thirteen seasons in the Texas League. From 1888 through 1905, he played with no less than nine Texas League clubs and managed eight of them: Austin, Sherman, Denison, San Antonio, Paris, Waco, Corsicana, and Fort Worth. He played for Dallas briefly in 1895 but did not manage there, and while with Denison and San Antonio in 1896, he led the league in batting with a lofty .401 mark in 114 games. Big Mike died prematurely at the Texas State Hospital in Austin in 1906.

CORSICANA 51, TEXARKANA 3

Corsicana's most memorable game under Big Mike O'Connor came on Sunday June 15, 1902, when it annihilated Texarkana by the incredible score of 51–3. Corsicana was forced to host Texarkana at neighboring Ennis, because local "blue laws" did not allow them to play Sunday games at home.

O'Connor's catcher Justin "Nig" Clarke, only nineteen years old and already a noted left-handed power hitter, immortalized his name in baseball when he blasted *8 home runs in 8 times at bat,* drove in 16 runs, scored 8 runs (naturally), and hit for a total of 32 bases. All are professional records. According to all available information, all 8 home runs went over the outfield fences, although reports also indicate that the home run barriers at the Ennis park were in close. No team in professional baseball has ever scored more than 51 runs in one game.

Also going "8 for 8" in this massacre were Corsicana's Bill Alexander and Ike Pendleton. Mike O'Connor himself went 7 for 8 and ripped 3 homers, and George Markley went 6 for 7. Both players scored 7 runs. Corsicana pounded out a total of 53 hits, including 21 home runs.

Interestingly enough, only one pitcher, Texarkana's C. B. DeWitt, absorbed all the pounding; yet he walked only 3 batters on this fateful Sunday. The game was only 2 hours and 10 minutes long. The box score was as follows:

Box Score

Texarkana	AB	R	H	PO	A	E	Corsicana	AB	R	H	PO	A	E
Deskin, cf	5	1	2	6	1	0	Maloney, cf	6	5	3	5	0	0
Mulkey, 2b	4	0	1	0	2	1	Alexander, 2b	8	5	8	4	5	0
Welter, 3b	4	0	1	2	2	2	Ripley, rf	8	6	5	0	0	0
Wolfe, c	4	1	1	2	2	0	Pendleton, lf	8	6	8	1	2	0
Murphy, lf	4	0	1	3	1	0	Markley, 3b	7	7	6	3	4	0
DeWitt, p	3	0	1	0	2	0	O'Connor, 1b	8	7	7	8	0	0
Tackaberry, 1b	4	1	1	9	0	0	Clarke, c	8	8	8	3	1	0
Gillon, rf	4	0	1	1	0	0	Morris, ss	8	6	6	3	4	0
Burns, ss	4	0	0	4	3	2	Wright, p	4	1	2	0	2	0
Totals	36	3	9	27	13	5	Totals	65	51	53	27	18	0

```
Texarkana      0 1 0  0 0 0  0 2 0—3
Corsicana      6 2 9  2 7 5  4 8 8—51
```

Two base hits—Morris, Alexander, Maloney, Pendleton, Deskin, Tackaberry. Home runs—Maloney, Alexander (3), Ripley (2), Pendleton (2), Markley, O'Connor (3), Clarke (8), Morris. Stolen bases—Maloney, Alexander, Morris, Ripley. Double plays—Morris to O'Connor; Markley to Alexander to O'Connor; Burns to Tackaberry. Left on bases—Corsicana (15), Texarkana (5). Bases on balls—Wright (1), DeWitt (3). Earned runs—Corsicana (26), Texarkana (1). Umpires—Method and Cavender. Time of game—2:10.

This game has been widely discussed over the years, and everyone who has looked into the matter agrees it was clearly a mismatch. As we have seen, Sherman–Denison switched over to Texarkana on May 6, and then the club changed ownership after it had been in Texarkana for three weeks or so. The team had been shaky to begin with, and the instability at the front office certainly did not help matters any. Texarkana dropped out of competition when the first half ended on July 8 and never re-entered the Texas League again, although it did join other pro loops from time to time. Bill Ruggles made this comment: "Texarkana simply did not have a club able to compete on even terms with other cities in the circuit, and its chief contribution to Texas League history was as the victim of Corsicana's 51–3 victory at Ennis."

Before we leave our 51–3 game and its aftermath altogether, we ought to say a word about Nig Clarke, who enjoyed that "perfect day" at bat. Clarke's professional playing career lasted twenty-five years, and from 1905 through 1920 he played intermittently in the major leagues: with Cleveland, Detroit, and St. Louis in the American League, and with Philadelphia and Pittsburgh in the National League. Always considered a fine catcher, his hitting in the majors was only fair, averaging .254 for 506 games and hoisting only 6 homers, or 2 less than he had on that single Sunday afternoon against C. B. DeWitt.

THE SOUTH TEXAS LEAGUE

Baseball was revived again in the southern part of the state with the creation of the South Texas League. James Nolan, who helped reorganize the Texas League in 1902, led the movement for the creation of the new circuit, which had four teams to start with: Beaumont, Galveston, Houston, and San Antonio. These four cities stuck together for the four-year life of the circuit, with Austin, Texas, and Lake Charles, Louisiana, being added in the final year to make it a six-team affair.

Farsighted club owners in both the Texas and South Texas circuits knew the only way to operate profitably was to merge the two in an all-state league. In 1906, the Texas League came down to four teams at the beginning of the second half (Cleburne, Dallas, Fort Worth, and Waco— Temple and Greenville dropped out). Club owners were all too familiar with the defects of a four-team circuit: too much competition was required between the same teams, and this killed fan interest more than anything else. All advantages of short mileage were thus offset.

Officials from both leagues met during the fall and winter of 1906–07, with negotiations for the merger being led by J. Doak Roberts (TL president) and Dr. W. R. Robbie (STL president). Roberts was more than happy to take a brief respite from baseball and allowed Dr. Robbie to be elected unanimously as TL chief executive. The STL's Austin, Galveston, Houston, and San Antonio franchises went into the new all-state league, where they were joined by Dallas, Fort Worth, Temple, and Waco. Bill Ruggles maintains that the modern history of the Texas League begins with this historic merger.

THE TEXAS LEAGUE HIGHLIGHTS

1904: Branch Rickey, a twenty-two-year-old graduate of Ohio Wesleyan University was signed as a catcher by Dallas Tigers' owner Joseph W. Gardner. Rickey already had a year of pro experience, having played for both Terre Haute in the Central League and LeMars in the Iowa–South Dakota League in 1903. He missed a chance to graduate to the Cincinnati Reds later in the 1904 season because of his refusal to play on Sunday, the most profitable day in the week for the owners. Rickey started the

1905 campaign with St. Louis in the American League, but spent most of the year at Dallas where he batted .295 in 37 games. Rickey's numerous accomplishments in baseball, including his development of the farm system, are legendary (see Chapter 3).

1905: The Fort Worth Cats captured the league percentage with a .545 percentage, the lowest winning figure in the Texas League's history. The Panthers edged out the Temple Boll Weevils by 2 points. On one fateful Sunday in Waco, Henry Fabian, president of the Waco Navigators, and all his players were arrested for violating State of Texas statutes forbidding "Sunday amusement." They were convicted; but the Court of Criminal Appeals reversed the decision maintaining the laws had been passed before baseball became a "professional amusement" and, therefore, did not apply to entertainment of this character. Under this ruling Sunday baseball has since been legal in Texas, except in those cities where municipal laws specifically forbid it.

1906–07: Tris Speaker, an eighteen-year-old center fielder and native of Hubbard, Texas, broke into pro ball with Cleburne and hit .268 in 84 games. Shifting to Houston for the following year, he led the league with a .314 mark.

Pitching was dominant in the Texas League at this time; for example, Houston won four straight games with 1–0 scores, while Waco pitcher Harry Guyn hurled 41 consecutive scoreless innings—that is still a league record.

1908: Shreveport, Louisiana replaced the Temple franchise, and in view the resultant increased mileage, Shreveport agreed to pay a $75 guarantee to the visiting club daily rather than the customary $50.

Going north on their first trip of the year, Houston Buffalo players found a baby boy abandoned on the train, and they immediately decided to make his welfare a team responsibility. Several times during the season Houston fans were asked to contribute to a small endowment fund raised for the infant's benefit. Subsequently, the child was legally adopted by Buffalo's third baseman Roy Akin, who raised him as his own son. Akin, who played in the Texas League for a dozen years, was the first player in the circuit to make an unassisted triple play and the only known player in organized baseball to do it at third base.

1909: Oklahoma City entered the league for the first time and was required to guarantee visiting clubs $100 per day because of the long mileage involved.

Everett "Pep" Hornsby, older brother of Rogers Hornsby, was one of the star pitchers for the champion Houston Buffalos. His favorite pitch was the spitball.

1910: The tightness of the pennant race, the intense rivalries between Houston and Galveston in the south and Dallas and Fort Worth in the north, and prejudice against the two out-of-state teams (Oklahoma City and Shreveport) combined to cause frequent fistfights between opposing players on the field.

1911: The continuing controversy over Oklahoma's obligation to pay the $100 daily guarantee caused the franchise to be shifted to Beaumont at the end of the season.

1912: Dallas president Joe Gardner saved San Antonio president Morris Block from drowning in a swimming pool. The circumstances of this case (near tragic though it was) caused much merriment at the next league meeting.

1913: The Houston Buffs, badly in need of a catcher, purchased Frank Kitchens from Fort Worth for the then unheard of intraleague price of $1,200.

1914: Austin wound up with the worst record of any one team in the league's history: 31 wins and 114 losses (.214 pct.). Moreover, there were 31 consecutive defeats in June–July. Austin players were hired and fired with astonishing rapidity, with no less than seventy players representing the city during that awful season. "We tell 'em hello in the morning and kiss 'em goodbye at night," commented pitcher Ross Helm who stuck it out for the whole year. Austin owner W. E. Quebbedeaux was charged by the league with "gross mismanagement."

1915: The Texas League was hurt by a series of natural disasters. In June the Trinity River flood and accompanying windstorms severely damaged the Fort Worth park, while a mid-August Gulf Coast hurricane demolished both the Galveston and Houston ball parks. Houston played the rest of its schedule on the road, while Galveston was given league permission to disband early, since there were only two weeks remaining in the season.

1916: The Galveston and Houston parks were rebuilt in time for the opening of the season, and the Texas League was able to maintain its strength at eight teams.

1917: Ralph Sharman, a Galveston–Fort Worth outfielder, became the first Texas Leaguer to get more than 200 hits (203) in a single season. A young player of great promise, he died a few months after the end of the season.

1918: Play was suspended on July 7 because of World War I, and Dallas was declared the league champion.

1919–25: The Fort Worth Panthers, under manager Jake Atz, dominated Texas League play for seven years by winning the percentage championship in 1919 (the Shreveport Gassers, the first-half winners, beat the Panthers in the playoffs that year), and then for the next six years winning both halves so that no playoffs were necessary. (In 1922, Wichita Falls put together a phenomenal string of 25 victories, but could finish no better than third place at 86–74.) Atz's powerhouse teams included such stars as first basemen Clarence "Big Boy" Kraft and "Big Ed" Konetchy and pitchers Paul Wachtel and Joe Pate. Kraft played first base for the Panthers for seven years (1918–24) and retired with honors after the 1924 campaign (at the age of thirty-eight). He slammed 55 home runs that year, then the minor league record for circuit clouts and the Texas League standard until 1956. His 196 RBI's that year still stands as a Texas League record. After Kraft's retirement, Ed Konetchy, a thirty-nine-year old and fifteen-year veteran of the National League, took over first base and led the Panthers attack with a .345 average, 213 hits, 41 homers, and 166 RBI's. Big Ed also played first base for the Panthers in 1926–27. Right-hander Paul Wachtel was a consistent 20-game winner for Fort Worth during this period, leading the league in victories with 26 in 1922 and 23 in 1925 and tying Wachtel in 1920. During his thirteen-year Texas League career, he won a record 232 games while losing 141. A spitball specialist, he was effectively barred from entering the big leagues, since the majors had abolished the spitball in 1920. He did pitch briefly for the Brooklyn Dodgers in 1917. Joe Pate, a left-hander, was also a consistent winner for the Panthers, leading the league in victories with 30 in 1921 and again in 1924, and tying Wachtel with 26 in 1920. During his thirteen-year pitching career in the TL (1914, 1918–28, 1931), he won 193 games and lost only 91. During the early 1920s, league president J. Doak Roberts had to deal with the serious problem of gambling and thrown games. In one case, a 1921 game won by Dallas from Wichita Falls was stricken from the records because of strong suspicion that it had been thrown.

1926: The Texas League recorded 1,160,000 paid admissions, with Dallas' 287,000 leading the league. Both figures remained as records until the post World War II period.

1927: The Texas League abolished the spitball. In general, Organized baseball had already moved against the spitball except the TL, which continued to permit its unregulated use. At a fall 1926 meeting, the league decided to permit one spitballer per team, but in January 1927, this rule was changed so that nine pitchers were certified as spitball hurlers and given authority to use the delivery as long as they should be active in the Texas League. No other spitballers were to be certified later—and the last of those certified retired in 1932.

The Waco Navigators led the Texas League in team batting with a record .316.

1928: Houston, a St. Louis Cardinals farm club since 1920, won the league championship with many players who were being groomed for the majors. Houston was the first Texas League club to be completely controlled by a major league team, a fact that at first was kept secret because most TL club owners and officials objected to "alien ownership."

1929: J. Doak Roberts, long-time Texas League president and club owner, who helped revive the circuit in 1902 while general manager at Corsicana, died on November 25 at the age of fifty-eight.

1930: Waco equipped Katy Park with floodlights for night baseball shortly before the end of the first half, while Houston San Antonio and Shreveport installed lights in time for the second half. All four teams drew more fans for night games than they did for day games.

1931: Jay Hanna "Dizzy" Dean, a Houston right-hander, won the Texas League's first "Most Valuable Player" award with a 26–10 record, 303 strikeouts, and an ERA of 1.57.

1932: With the country in a deep economic depression players' salaries were sharply cut as attendance took a nosedive.

The Shreveport park burned down after a May 4 game, and the franchise was shifted to Tyler, making the circuit an all-Texas league for the first time since 1914.

Hank Greenberg, the Beaumont Exporters' first baseman, was named MVP on the basis of his 39 homers and 131 RBI's.

1933: Overall attendance increased for two primary reasons: a heavy schedule of night games (all parks now had lights except Beaumont) and the great interest created by the introduction of the Shaughnessy playoffs.

1934: Paul Easterling, a Tulsa outfielder and one of the league's finest all-time players, led the home run derby with 29. In his thirteen-year Texas League career, Easterling established the following lifetime records: games, 1,777; runs, 1,134; hits, 1,922 (.296 pct.); RBI's, 1,136; home runs, 223; total bases, 3,081. Easterling played briefly for the Detroit Tigers and the Philadelphia Athletics. A scouting report on Easterling read: "A great right-hand hitter and fielder handicapped by inability to observe training."

1935: Rudy York, Beaumont's first baseman–catcher, took the MVP award (32 homers, 117 RBI's).

1936: Galveston's manager Jake Atz retired at the close of the season, after managing a record twenty-two years in the Texas League (eighteen of those years with Fort Worth).

1937: Hank Severeid, the forty-six-year-old Galveston manager, closed out his active playing career, which spanned twenty-eight seasons, by catching both games of a doubleheader on the last day of the season. He played a total of 2,603 games in Organized Baseball (half those games were in the majors). Severaid, who went on to scout for a number of major league teams until his death in 1968, also wrote several authoritative instructional books on baseball.

1938: The Texas League established a solid alignment of eight teams in three states (Beaumont, Dallas, Fort Worth, Houston, Oklahoma City, San Antonio, Shreveport, and Tulsa) that was to be maintained without a break through 1957.

1939: Broadcasts of Texas League games were extremely popular with the fans, but "bootleg" transcriptions continued to trouble club owners.

1940: Homer Peel, Galveston's manager and outfielder (he had also managed Fort Worth) concluded his fourteen-year Texas League playing career with a record .325 lifetime batting average in 1,430 games. His 1,549 hits rank second behind Paul Easterling's 1,922.

1941: Danny Murtaugh, the star second baseman for the champion Houston Buffs, was sold to the Philadelphia Phillies in midseason. Joe Greenberg, Hank's younger brother, led the Texas League's third basemen in fielding while playing with Fort Worth.

1942: Rogers Hornsby signed to manage the Fort Worth Cats shortly after he was elected to baseball's Hall of Fame.

1946: The Texas League enjoyed a banner year at the gate, with a record 1,592,567 paid admissions. The playing limit was fixed at 18 men (for years the limit had been 16).

1947: Al "Flip" Rosen, an Oklahoma City third baseman, was voted MVP. He led the league in batting (.349), total bases (330), and RBI's (141).

1948: Bobby Bragan, now the Texas League's president, paced the Fort Worth Cats to the league championship as player–manager. Bragan left the Brooklyn Dodgers early in the season and replaced Les Burge as manager.

1949: Bragan's Cats won the percentage title but lost the playoffs to the Tulsa Oilers, led by manager Al Vincent. Vincent, a veteran minor league catcher, put himself into the Tulsa lineup occasionally, even though he was forty-two years old.

1950: Dallas, in its season opener against Fort Worth, set a league attendance record of 53,578. The Dallas Rebels were given the opportunity to play this game at the big State Fair Park in Dallas rather than at their own stadium.

Gil McDougald, the Beaumont second baseman, won MVP honors. He batted .336 and drove in 115 runs.

1951: Wilmer "Vinegar Bend" Mizell, now a U.S. Congressman from the fifth district in North Carolina (Winston–Salem), led the Texas League in strikeouts with 257 while compiling a 16–14 record with Houston. Mizell, a left-hander, spent nine years in the National League.

1952: Gordon "Billy" Hunter, a Baltimore coach for the previous ten years, won the MVP award while starring at shortstop for Fort Worth.

1953: Harry Heslet, a Shreveport right fielder, paced the league in homers for the second year in a row with 41. He had 31 in 1952.

1954: Les Fleming, in professional baseball since 1935 and thirty-nine years old, led the league in batting with a resounding .358 average.

1955: John "Red" Davis, a veteran pilot who led Dallas to the league title, won the Texas League's first "Manager of the Year" award. He repeated in 1956.

1956: Ken Guettler, a Shreveport outfielder, hit a league record 62 home runs, breaking "Big Boy" Kraft's standard of 55 (which had stood since 1924). Guettler batted .293 in 140 games and drove in 143 runs.

1957: Willie McCovey, a nineteen-year-old Dallas first baseman, was perhaps the youngest player in history to be selected to the Texas League's All-Star Team. Bobby Winkles, a Tulsa shortstop, was also selected to this team. Winkles later scored a first in baseball when he jumped from college coaching to big league managing (from Arizona State to the California Angels).

1958: Though his Houston Buffs finished in second place, Harry "The Hat" Walker was still chosen "Manager of the Year." Walker later managed the Houston Astros in the National League.

1959–61: Beginning in 1959, the reorganized six-team Texas League (Amarillo, Austin, Corpus Christi, San Antonio, Tulsa, and Victoria) entered into an unusual arrangement with the Class AA Mexican League in forming the Pan-American Association. In 1959, the six-team Mexican League consisted of the Mexico City Reds, the Mexico City Tigers, Monterrey, Nuevo Laredo, Poza Rica, and Vera Cruz. In 1960–61, Puebla replaced Nuevo Laredo. In an interlocking schedule, each club visited the park of every team in the rival circuit for three games with all intra-league games counting in the standings. In midseason, the two leagues played a pair of Pan-Am all-star games (one in the United States and the other in Mexico), and the whole arrangement was climaxed at the season's end when the league champions met in the Pan-American Series, a best of seven affair. (For the Texas League, the Pan-Am Series replaced the Dixie Series.) The Texas League took all three series, winning 12 games and losing 4. In 1959, Austin defeated the Mexico City Reds 4 games to 1; in 1960, Tulsa defeated the Mexico City Tigers 4 games to 1; and in 1961, San Antonio defeated Vera Cruz 4 games to 2. At the end of 1961, both leagues mutually agreed to terminate the series.

1962: Charlie Dees, left-handed hitting El Paso first baseman, set a modern Texas League record when he slammed four consecutive homers to lead an 11–3 rout of Amarillo at El Paso's Dudley Field on August 30.

El Paso fans demonstrated their appreciation by throwing $79 on the field for Dees.

El Paso led the league in team batting with a fat .310 mark. No Texas League team has hit .300 since.

1963: Jim Beauchamp, a Tulsa outfielder, won MVP honors. He hit .337, smacked 31 homers, and drove in 105 runs.

1964: Joe Morgan, a San Antonio second baseman, took the MVP award. He swatted .323, scored 113 runs, and led the league in fielding.

1965: Ike Futch, a Tulsa second baseman, set a league record by striking out only 5 times in 594 plate appearances. He hit .290.

1966: Tom Hutton, an Albuquerque first baseman, won both the MVP award and the batting title with a .340 mark. While with Spokane in 1971, he captured the Pacific Coast League batting crown with a .352 average.

1967: Nate Colbert, an Amarillo first baseman–outfielder, won both the MVP award and home run crown with 28 circuit clouts. He also batted .293, despite an eye-popping figure of 143 strikeouts.

1968–69: There was a tie for the MVP award two years in a row: Jim Spencer (an El Paso first baseman) and Bill Sudakis (an Albuquerque third baseman) shared the award in 1968; while Larry Johnson, (first baseman) and Bobby Grich (shortstop), both of Dallas–Fort Worth, shared the honor in 1969.

1970: Albuquerque led the league in attendance with 177,747 paid admissions. Total attendance for the eight teams was 770,070.

1971: Enos Cabell, a Dallas–Fort Worth first baseman and a top Baltimore Oriole prospect, was chosen MVP. He led the league with a .311 batting average.

1972: The San Antonio Missions finished last in the Western Division and led the league in attendance with 253,139. Total attendance for the eight teams was 848,877.

TEXAS LEAGUE PRESIDENTS

Year	President
1887–88	Fred W. Turner
1888	Robert Adair
1889	Louis Newburg
1890	Joseph Sensheimer
1892	Si Packard
1894–95	J. C. McNealus
1895	C. P. Gregory
1895–96	John L. Ward
1896–97	Louis Heuermann
1897–98	John L. Ward
1899	George B. Dermody
1901–02	John L. Ward
1903	Newton D. Lassiter
1904	William A. Abey
1904–06	J. Doak Roberts
1907–08	William R. Robbie
1909–13	Wilbur P. Allen
1914–15	William R. Davidson
1916–20	J. Walter Morris
1921–29	J. Doak Roberts
1929	William B. Ruggles
1930–53	J. Alvin Gardner
1954	John L. Reeves
1955–63	Dick Butler
1964–65	James H. Burris
1965	Dick Butler
1965–69	Hugh J. Finnerty
1969	Dick Butler
1970-–	Robert R. "Bobby" Bragan

TEXAS LEAGUE CHAMPIONS

Year	Championship Team	Manager	Won	Lost	Pct.
1888	Dallas	Charles Levis	55	27	.671
1889	Houston	John J. McCloskey	54	44	.551
1890	Galveston	William L. Works	31	13	.705
1891	(League did not operate.)				
1892	Houston	John J. McCloskey	59	26	.694
1893–94	(League did not operate.)				
1895	Dallas	Ted Sullivan	82	33	.713
	Dallas (1st half)	Ted Sullivan	43	14	.754
	*Fort Worth (2nd half)	George Reilly	45	15	.750

(Fort Worth defeated Dallas in playoff 7 games to 6.)

1896	Fort Worth	George W. Carmen–	71	29	.710
		L. L. McAllister			
	*Houston	Charles A. Schaffer	81	49	.623
	Galveston	Jack Huston	69	61	.530

(Houston defeated Galveston in playoff 5 games to 2. Fort Worth did not participate in the playoff because it dropped out of the league In August.)

1897	Galveston	Jack Huston	72	44	.621
	San Antonio (1st half)	Mike O'Connor	46	24	.657
	Galveston (2nd half)	Jack Huston	33	13	.717

(No playoff for title.)

1898	Dallas	John J. McCloskey	13	7	.650

(Play was suspended on May 13 because of the Spanish–American War.)

* Asterisk indicates winning team.

Year	Championship Team	Manager	Won	Lost	Pct.
1899	Galveston	Frank Pequinney	52	26	.667

(Since Galveston won both halves, no playoff was necessary.)

1900–01	(League did not operate.)				
1902	Corsicana	Mike O'Connor	88	23	.793

(Since Corsicana won both halves, no playoff was necessary.)

1903	*Dallas	Charles B. Moran	61	47	.565
	Paris–Waco (1st half)	Ted Sullivan	32	20	.615
	Dallas (2nd half)	Charles B. Moran	35	19	.648

(Dallas defeated Paris–Waco in playoff 7 games to 3.)

1904	Fort Worth	Fred Wills	71	31	.696
	*Corsicana (1st half)	J. J. Maloney	32	20	.615
	Fort Worth (2nd half)	Fred Wills	40	10	.800

(Corsicana defeated Fort Worth in playoff 11 games to 8.)

1905	Fort Worth	Fred Wills	72	60	.545
1906	Fort Worth	Dred Cavender	78	46	.629
	Fort Worth (1st half)	Dred Cavender	42	20	.677
	*Cleburne (2nd half)	Ben Shelton	39	25	.609

(Playoff was conceded to Cleburne by default.)

1907	Austin	Brooks Gordon	88	52	.629
1908	San Antonio	George O. Leidy	95	48	.664
1909	Houston	Hunter B. Hill	86	57	.601
1910	Houston	Hunter B. Hill	82	58	.586
	Dallas	James J. Maloney	82	58	.586

(No playoff. Houston and Dallas were declared co-champions.)

1911	Austin	C. Dale Gear	84	62	.575
1912	Houston	John Fillman	87	62	.626

* Asterisk indicates winning team.

Year	Championship Team	Manager	Won	Lost	Pct.
1913	Houston	John Fillman	93	57	.620
1914	Houston	Pat Newman	102	50	.670
	Waco	Ellis Hardy	102	50	.670

(No playoff. Houston and Waco were declared co-champions.)

1915	Waco	Ellis Hardy	87	60	.592
1916	Waco	Ellis Hardy	84	59	.587
1917	Dallas	Hamilton Patterson	96	64	.600
1918	Dallas	Hamilton Patterson	52	37	.584

(Play was suspended on July 7 because of World War I.)

1919	Fort Worth	Jake Atz	94	60	.610
	*Shreveport (1st half)	Billy Smith	44	21	.677
	Fort Worth (2nd half)	Jake Atz	56	30	.651

(Shreveport defeated Fort Worth in playoff 4 games to 2 with 1 tie.)

1920	Fort Worth	Jake Atz	108	40	.730

(Since Fort Worth won both halves, no playoff was necessary.)

1921	Fort Worth	Jake Atz	107	51	.677

(Since Fort Worth won both halves, no playoff was necessary.)

1922	Fort Worth	Jake Atz	109	46	.703

(Since Fort Worth won both halves, no playoff was necessary.)

1923	Fort Worth	Jake Atz	96	56	.632
1924	Fort Worth	Jake Atz	109	41	.727

(Since Fort Worth won both halves, no playoff was necessary.)

1925	Fort Worth	Jake Atz	103	48	.682

(Since Fort Worth won both halves, no playoff was necessary.)

* Asterisk indicates winning team.

Year	Championship Team	Manager	Won	Lost	Pct.
1926	Dallas	J. P. Conley	89	66	.574
1927	Wichita Falls	W. C. Williams	102	54	.654
1928	*Houston	Frank Snyder	104	54	.658
	Houston (1st half)	Frank Snyder	55	26	.679
	Wichita Falls (2nd half)	W. C. Williams	57	21	.731

(Houston defeated Wichita Falls in playoff 3 games to 1.)

Year	Championship Team	Manager	Won	Lost	Pct.
1929	Wichita Falls	J. C. Galloway	94	65	.591
	*Dallas (1st half)	Milton Stock	47	33	.588
	Wichita Falls (2nd half)	J. C. Galloway	49	30	.620

(Dallas defeated Wichita Falls in playoff 3 games to 1.)

Year	Championship Team	Manager	Won	Lost	Pct.
1930	Wichita Falls	W. C. Williams	95	58	.621
	Wichita Falls (1st half)	W. C. Williams	53	23	.697
	*Fort Worth (2nd half)	Frank Snyder	48	28	.632

(Fort Worth defeated Wichita Falls in playoff 3 games to 2.)

Year	Championship Team	Manager	Won	Lost	Pct.
1931	Houston	Joe Schultz	108	51	.679

(Since Houston won both halves, no playoff was necessary.)

Year	Championship Team	Manager	Won	Lost	Pct.
1932	*Beaumont	Del Baker	100	51	.662
	Beaumont (1st half)	Del Baker	48	27	.640
	Dallas (2nd half)	Harry "Hap" Morse	56	21	.727

(Beaumont defeated Dallas in playoff 3 games to 0.)

Year	Championship Team	Manager	Won	Lost	Pct.
1933	Houston	Carey Selph	94	57	.623
	Galveston	Billy Webb	88	64	.579
	Dallas	Harry "Hap" Morse–Fred Brainard	82	70	.539
	*San Antonio	Hank Severeid	79	72	.523

(Playoffs: Galveston defeated Dallas 3 games to 0; San Antonio defeated Houston 3 games to 0. Finals: San Antonio defeated Galveston 4 games to 2.)

* Asterisk indicates winning team.

Year	Championship Team	Manager	Won	Lost	Pct.
1934	*Galveston	Billy Webb	88	64	.579
	San Antonio	Hank Severeid	89	65	.578
	Beaumont	Ernest Lorbeer	81	69	.540
	Dallas	Fred Brainard	80	73	.523

(Playoffs: Galveston defeated Dallas 3 games to 1; San Antonio defeated Beaumont 3 games to 2. Finals: Galveston defeated San Antonio 4 games to 2.)

1935	*Oklahoma City	Bert Niehoff	95	66	.590
	Beaumont	Ernest Lorbeer	90	69	.566
	Galveston	Jack Mealey	86	75	.534
	Tulsa	Arthur Griggs	82	79	.509

(Playoffs: Beaumont defeated Galveston 3 games to 2; Oklahoma City defeated Tulsa 3 games to 1. Finals: Oklahoma City defeated Beaumont 4 games to 1.)

1936	Dallas	Alex Gaston	93	61	.604
	Houston	Ira D. Smith	83	69	.547
	*Tulsa	Marty McManus	80	74	.519
	Oklahoma City	Bert Niehoff	79	75	.513

(Playoffs: Dallas defeated Oklahoma City 3 games to 1; Tulsa defeated Houston 3 games to 1. Finals: Tulsa defeated Dallas 4 games to 3.)

1937	Oklahoma City	James Keesey	101	58	.635
	Tulsa	Bruce Connatser	89	69	.563
	*Fort Worth	Homer Peel	85	74	.535
	San Antonio	Zack Taylor	85	76	.528

(Playoffs: Oklahoma City defeated San Antonio 3 games to 2; Fort Worth defeated Tulsa 3 games to 2. Finals: Fort Worth defeated Oklahoma City 4 games to 2.)

1938	*Beaumont	Al Vincent	99	57	.635
	San Antonio	Zack Taylor	93	67	.581
	Oklahoma City	James Keesey– John Fitzpatrick	89	70	.560
	Tulsa	Bruce Connatser	86	75	.534

(Playoffs: Beaumont defeated Tulsa 3 games to 0; San Antonio defeated Oklahoma City 3 games to 0. Finals: Beaumont defeated San Antonio 4 games to 3.)

* Asterisk indicates winning team.

Year	Championship Team	Manager	Won	Lost	Pct.
1939	Houston	Eddie Dyer	97	63	.606
	Dallas	Harry "Hap" Morse	89	72	.553
	San Antonio	Zack Taylor	89	72	.553
	*Fort Worth	Claud Linton	87	74	.540

(Playoffs: Fort Worth defeated Houston 3 games to 2; Dallas defeated San Antonio 3 games to 2. Finals: Fort Worth defeated Dallas 4 games to 1.)

Year	Championship Team	Manager	Won	Lost	Pct.
1940	*Houston	Eddie Dyer	105	56	.652
	San Antonio	Marty McManus	89	72	.553
	Beaumont	Al Vincent	88	72	.550
	Oklahoma City	James Keesey– Rogers Hornsby	82	78	.513

(Playoffs: Houston defeated Oklahoma City 3 games to 1; Beaumont defeated San Antonio 3 games to 1. Finals: Houston defeated Beaumont 4 games to 1.)

Year	Championship Team	Manager	Won	Lost	Pct.
1941	Houston	Eddie Dyer	103	50	.673
	Tulsa	Roy Johnson	86	66	.566
	Shreveport	Francis "Salty" Parker	80	71	.530
	*Dallas	Wallace Dashiell	80	74	.519

(Playoffs: Dallas defeated Houston 3 games to 1; Tulsa defeated Shreveport 3 games to 0. Finals: Dallas defeated Tulsa 4 games to 2.)

Year	Championship Team	Manager	Won	Lost	Pct.
1942	Beaumont	Steve O'Neill	89	58	.615
	*Shreveport	Francis "Salty" Parker	83	61	.576
	Fort Worth	Rogers Hornsby	84	68	.559
	San Antonio	Ralph Winegarner	80	68	.546

(Playoffs: Beaumont defeated San Antonio 4 games to 2; Shreveport defeated Forth Worth 4 games to 3. Finals: Shreveport defeated Beaumont 4 games to 3.)

1943–45 (League suspended operations because of World War II.)

Year	Championship Team	Manager	Won	Lost	Pct.
1946	Fort Worth	Ray Hayworth	101	53	.656
	*Dallas	Al Vincent	91	63	.591
	San Antonio	Jimmy Adair	87	65	.572
	Tulsa	Gus Mancuso	84	69	.549

* Asterisk indicates winning team.

Year	Championship Team	Manager	Won	Lost	Pct.

(Playoffs: Fort Worth defeated Tulsa 4 games to 0; Dallas defeated San Antonio 4 games to 1. Finals: Dallas defeated Fort Worth 4 games to 1.)

1947	*Houston	Johnny Keane–Art Nelson	96	58	.623
	Fort Worth	Lester Burge	95	58	.621
	Dallas	Al Vincent	79	74	.516
	Tulsa	Gus Mancuso	79	75	.513

(Playoffs: Houston defeated Tulsa 4 games to 0; Dallas defeated Fort Worth 4 games to 3. Finals: Houston defeated Dallas 4 games to 2.)

1948	*Fort Worth	Lester Burge–Bobby Bragan	92	61	.601
	Tulsa	Al Vincent	91	63	.591
	Houston	Johnny Keane	82	71	.536
	Shreveport	Francis "Salty" Parker	76	77	.497

(Playoffs: Fort Worth defeated Shreveport 4 games to 2; Tulsa defeated Houston 4 games to 2. Finals: Fort Worth defeated Tulsa 4 games to 2.)

1949	Fort Worth	Bobby Bragan	100	54	.649
	*Tulsa	Al Vincent	90	64	.584
	Oklahoma City	Joe Vosmik	81	72	.529
	Shreveport	Francis "Salty" Parker	80	74	.519

(Playoffs: Fort Worth defeated Shreveport 4 games to 1; Tulsa defeated Oklahoma City 4 games to 2. Finals: Tulsa defeated Fort Worth 4 games to 3.)

1950	Beaumont	Rogers Hornsby	91	62	.595
	Fort Worth	Bobby Bragan	88	64	.579
	Tulsa	Al Vincent	83	69	.546
	*San Antonio	Don Heffner	79	75	.513

(Playoffs: Tulsa defeated Fort Worth 4 games to 1; San Antonio defeated Beaumont 4 games to 0. Finals: San Antonio defeated Tulsa 4 games to 2.)

1951	*Houston	All Hollingsworth	99	61	.619
	San Antonio	Joyner "Jo Jo" White	86	75	.534
	Dallas	L. D. "Dutch" Meyer	85	75	.531
	Beaumont	Harry Craft	84	77	.522

* Asterisk indicates winning team.

Year	*Championship Team*	*Manager*	*Won*	*Lost*	*Pct.*

(Note: Beaumont defeated Fort Worth in single game playoff to decide fourth place. Playoffs: Houston defeated Beaumont 4 games to 2; San Antonio defeated Dallas 4 games to 3. Finals: Houston defeated San Antonio 4 games to 0.)

1952	*Dallas	L. D. "Dutch" Meyer	92	69	.571
	Fort Worth	Bobby Bragan	86	75	.534
	*Shreveport	Mickey Livingston	84	77	.522
	Oklahoma City	Tom Tatum	82	79	.509

(Note: From 1952 through 1964, the percentage-winning team and the playoff-winning team, if they were not the same, were declared Texas League co-champions and were entitled to compete in the Dixie Series. Playoffs: Oklahoma defeated Dallas 4 games to 2; Shreveport defeated Fort Worth 4 games to 0. Finals: Shreveport defeated Oklahoma City 4 games to 1.)

1953	*Dallas	L. D. "Dutch" Meyer	88	66	.571
	Tulsa	Joe Schultz	83	71	.539
	Fort Worth	Max Macon	82	72	.532
	Oklahoma City	Tom Tatum	80	74	.519

(Playoffs: Dallas defeated Oklahoma City 4 games to 3; Tulsa defeated Fort Worth 4 games to 2. Finals: Dallas defeated Tulsa 4 games to 1.)

1954	*Shreveport	Mel McGaha	90	71	.559
	*Houston	Fred "Dixie" Walker	89	72	.553
	Oklahoma City	Tom Tatum	87	74	.540
	Fort Worth	Al Vincent	81	80	.503

(Playoffs: Fort Worth defeated Shreveport 4 games to 1; Houston defeated Oklahoma City 4 games to 1. Houston defeated Fort Worth 4 games to 1.)

1955	*Dallas	John "Red" Davis	93	67	.581
	San Antonio	Don Heffner	93	68	.578
	*Shreveport	Mel McGaha	87	74	.540
	Houston	Dominic "Mike" Ryba	86	75	.534

(Playoffs: Houston defeated Dallas 4 games to 2; Shreveport defeated San Antonio 4 games to 2. Finals: Shreveport defeated Houston 4 games to 3.)

* Asterisk indicates winning team.

Year	Championship Team	Manager	Won	Lost	Pct.
1956	*Houston	Harry Walker	96	58	.623
	Dallas	John "Red" Davis	94	60	.610
	Fort Worth	Clay Bryant	84	70	.545
	Tulsa	Al Widmar	77	77	.500

(Playoffs: Houston defeated Tulsa 4 games to 1; Dallas defeated Fort Worth 4 games to 0. Finals: Houston defeated Dallas 4 games to 1.)

1957	*Dallas	Francis "Salty" Parker	102	52	.662
	*Houston	Harry Walker	97	57	.630
	San Antonio	Joe Schultz	76	78	.494
	Tulsa	Al Widmar	75	79	.487

(Playoffs: Dallas defeated Tulsa 4 games to 2; Houston defeated San Antonio 4 games to 3. Finals: Houston defeated Dallas 4 games to 3.)

1958	*Fort Worth	Lou Klein	89	64	.582
	Houston	Harry Walker	79	74	.516
	*Corpus Christi	Ray Murray	77	75	.507
	Austin	Harry "Peanuts" Lowrey	77	76	.503

(Playoffs: Austin defeated Fort Worth 4 games to 0; Corpus Christi defeated Houston 4 games to 1. Finals: Corpus Christi defeated Austin 4 games to 3.)

1959	*Victoria	Pete Reiser	86	60	.569
	*Austin	Ernie White	80	66	.548
	Tulsa	Vern Benson	77	67	.535
	San Antonio	Grady Hatton	75	70	.517

(Playoffs: San Antonio defeated Victoria 2 games to 0; Austin defeated Tulsa 2 games to 1. Finals: Austin defeated San Antonio 3 games to 0.)

1960	*Rio Grande Valley	Ray Murray	85	59	.590
	San Antonio	Grady Hatton-Lou Klein	77	68	.531
	*Tulsa	Vern Benson	76	68	.528
	Victoria	Johnny Pesky	77	69	.527

(Playoffs: Victoria defeated Rio Grande Valley 3 games to 0; Tulsa defeated San Antonio 3 games to 1. Finals: Tulsa defeated Victoria 3 games to 0.)

* Asterisk indicates winning team.

Year	Championship Team	Manager	Won	Lost	Pct.
1961	*Amarillo	Warren "Sheriff" Robinson	90	53	.643
	Tulsa	George "Whitey" Kurowski	83	55	.601
	*San Antonio	James "Rip" Collins– Harry Craft-Bobby Adams	74	65	.532
	Austin	Bill Adair	69	71	.543

(Note: Austin defeated Victoria in single game playoff to decide fourth place. Playoffs: Austin defeated Amarillo 3 games to 2; San Antonio defeated Tulsa 3 games to 1. Finals: San Antonio defeated Austin 3 games to 0.)

Year	Championship Team	Manager	Won	Lost	Pct.
1962	*El Paso	George Genovese	80	60	.571
	*Tulsa	George "Whitey" Kurowski	77	63	.550
	Albuquerque	Bob Hofman	70	70	.500
	Austin	James Brown	69	71	.493

(Playoffs: Austin defeated El Paso 3 games to 2; Tulsa defeated Albuquerque 3 games to 0. Finals: Tulsa defeated Austin 4 games to 1.)

Year	Championship Team	Manager	Won	Lost	Pct.
1963	*San Antonio	Lou Fitzgerald	79	61	.564
	Austin	James Brown	75	65	.536
	*Tulsa	Grover Resinger	74	66	.529
	El Paso	George Genovese	68	72	.486

(Playoffs: San Antonio defeated El Paso 3 games to 2; Tulsa defeated Austin 3 games to 0. Finals: Tulsa defeated San Antonio 3 games to 1.)

Year	Championship Team	Manager	Won	Lost	Pct.
1964	*San Antonio	Lou Fitzgerald	85	55	.607
	Tulsa	Grover Resinger	79	61	.564
	Albuquerque	Clay Bryant	75	65	.536
	El Paso	David Garcia	67	73	.479

(Playoffs: San Antonio defeated El Paso 3 games to 1; Tulsa defeated Albuquerque 3 games to 2. Finals: San Antonio defeated Tulsa 3 games to 1.)

Year	Championship Team	Manager	Won	Lost	Pct.
1965	Tulsa (Eastern Division)	Vern Rapp	81	60	.574
	*Albuquerque (Western Division)	Roy Hartsfield	77	63	.550

* Asterisk indicates winning team.

Year	Championship Team	Manager	Won	Lost	Pct.

(Note: Tulsa defeated Fort Worth in single game playoff to decide the Eastern Division championship. Playoff: Albuquerque defeated Tulsa 3 games to 1.)

1966	Arkansas	Vern Rapp	81	59	.579
	Amarillo	Morris "Buddy" Hancken	77	63	.550
	Albuquerque	Bob Kennedy	74	66	.529
	*Austin	Hub Kittle	67	73	.479

(Playoffs: Austin defeated Arkansas 2 games to 1; Albuquerque defeated Amarillo 2 games to 1. Finals: Austin defeated Albuquerque 1 game to 0 in a series cut short because of rainouts.)

1967	Albuquerque	Edwin "Duke" Snider	78	62	.557
	(No playoff.)				

1968	Arkansas (Eastern Division)	Vern Rapp	82	58	.586
	*El Paso (Western Division)	Chuck Tanner	77	60	.562

(Playoff: El Paso defeated Arkansas 3 games to 1.)

1969	*Memphis (Eastern Division)	Pete Pavlick–John Antonelli–Roy McMillan	66	65	.504
	Amarillo (Western Division)	Andy Gilbert	80	55	.593

(Playoff: Memphis defeated Amarillo 3 games to 0.)

1970	Memphis (Eastern Division)	John Antonelli	69	67	.507
	*Albuquerque (Western Division)	Del Crandall	83	52	.615

(Playoff: Albuquerque defeated Memphis 3 games to 1.)

1971	Arkansas (Central Division)	Jack Krol	75	64	.540
	Amarillo (Western Division)	Andy Gilbert	88	54	.620
	*Charlotte (Eastern Division)	Harry Warner	92	50	.648

(Note: Because the Texas League and Southern League could field only seven teams each in 1971, they merged into the "Dixie Association" for this one year. Ashville, a second-place finisher in the Eastern Division, was declared the "wild card" team so that four teams could participate in the playoffs for the Dixie Association title. Playoffs: Charlotte defeated Ashville 2 games to 1; Arkansas defeated Amarillo 2 games to 0. Finals: Charlotte defeated Arkansas 3 games to 0.)

* Asterisk indicates winning team.

Year	Championship Team	Manager	Won	Lost	Pct.
1972	Alexandria (Eastern Division)	Edwin "Duke" Snider	84	56	.600
	*El Paso (Western Division)	Monty Basgall– Stan Wasiak	78	62	.557

(Playoff: El Paso defeated Alexandria 3 games to 0.)

Year	Championship Team	Manager	Won	Lost	Pct.
1973	*Memphis (Eastern Division)	Joe Frazier	77	61	.558
	San Antonio (Western Division)	Tony Pachecho	82	57	.590

(Playoff: Memphis defeated San Antonio 3 games to 2.)

* Asterisk indicates winning team.

TEXAS LEAGUE BATTING CHAMPIONS

Year	Player and Club	G	AB	Hits	Pct.
1888	(No records issued.)	...	...	...	...
1889	Pierce Works, Galveston	84	366	136	.372
1890	(No records issued.)	...	...	...	...
1891	(League did not operate.)	...	...	...	...
1892	(No records issued.)	...	...	...	...
1893–94	(League did not operate.)	...	...	...	...
1895	Algie McBride, Austin	94	419	186	.444
1896	Mike O'Connor, Denison–San Antonio	30	96	39	.401
1897	Bill Nance, Galveston	73	304	123	.405
1898	(League disbanded on May 1.)	...	...	...	...
1899	(No records issued.)	...	...	...	...
1900–01	(League did not operate.)	...	...	...	...
1902	Allen Nickel, Dallas	31	121	48	.397
1903	Harry Clark, Dallas	59	238	82	.344
1904	Trapper Longley, Corsicana	70	285	106	.372
1905	Scott Ragsdale, Waco	106	425	124	.292
1906	George Whiteman, Cleburne	120	466	131	.281
1907	Tris Speaker, Houston	118	468	147	.314
1908	F. W. Salm, Fort Worth	103	375	114	.304
1909	A. C. "Red" Downey, Oklahoma City	134	471	163	.346
1910	Hank Gowdy, Dallas	139	493	154	.312
1911	Bill Yohe, Oklahoma City	139	550	181	.329
1912	Frank Metz, San Antonio	142	530	171	.323

Year	Player and Club	G	AB	Hits	Pct.
1913	Dennis Wilie, Beaumont	102	352	114	.324
1914	Bob Clemens, Waco	155	599	196	.327
1915	Al Walters, Waco	108	274	89	.325
1916	Clarence "Little Bit" Bittle	138	556	185	.333
1917	Ralph Sharman, Galveston–Fort Worth	156	595	203	.341
1918	Olen Nokes, Dallas	55	192	64	.333
1919	Al Nixon, Beaumont	150	594	215	.362
1920	Godfrey "Red" Josefson, Wichita Falls	142	565	195	.345
1921	Clarence Kraft, Fort Worth	154	602	212	.352
1922	Homer Summa, Wichita Falls	156	621	225	.362
1923	Isaac "Ike" Boone, San Antonio	148	600	241	.402
1924	Art Weis, Wichita Falls	126	499	188	.377
1925	Danny Clark, San Antonio	144	564	225	.399
1926	Tom Jenkins, Wichita Falls	116	473	177	.374
1927	Derrill "Del" Pratt, Waco	155	562	217	.386
1928	George Blackerby, Waco	118	443	163	.368
1929	Randolph "Randy" Moore, Dallas	168	664	245	.369
1930	Oscar "Ox" Eckhardt, Beaumont	147	573	217	.379
1931	Raymond "Rip" Radcliff, Shreveport	155	596	215	.361
1932	Ervin "Pete" Fox, Beaumont	115	446	159	.357
1933	Everett Purdy, San Antonio	114	427	153	.358
1934	Chester Morgan, Beaumont–San Antonio	154	631	216	.342
1935	Art Weis, Fort Worth	159	556	184	.331
1936	Les Mallon, Dallas	131	483	166	.344
1937	Homer Peel, Fort Worth	147	525	194	.370
1938	Harlin Pool, Dallas	154	566	187	.330
1939	Lou Novikoff, Tulsa	110	419	154	.368
1940	Gordon Donaldson, Tulsa	136	502	160	.319
1941	Grey Clarke, Dallas	128	446	161	.361
1942	Dick Wakefield, Beaumont	149	556	192	.345
1943–45	(Play was suspended.)	. . .	. . .	. . .	. . .
1946	Dale Mitchell, Oklahoma City	108	415	140	.337
1947	Al Rosen, Oklahoma City	146	533	186	.349
1948	Tom Tatum, Tulsa	148	532	177	.333
1949	Herb Conyers, Oklahoma City	147	603	214	.355
1950	Frank Saucier, San Antonio	125	440	151	.343
1951	Bob Nieman, Oklahoma City	144	497	161	.324
1952	Grant Dunlap, Shreveport	134	462	154	.333
1953	Joe Frazier, Oklahoma City	152	548	182	.332
1954	Les Fleming, Dallas	158	523	187	.358
1955	Ed Knoblauch, Dallas	157	588	192	.327

Year	Player and Club	G	AB	Hits	Pct.
1956	Albie Pearson, Oklahoma City	122	480	178	.371
1957	Jim Frey, Tulsa	155	589	198	.336
1958	Eric Rodin, Corpus Christi	146	534	171	.320
1959	Al Nagel, Amarillo	135	482	166	.344
1960	Chuck Hiller, Rio Grande Valley	144	560	187	.334
1961	Phil Linz, Amarillo	105	433	151	.349
1962	Charley Dees, El Paso	141	515	179	.348
1963	Dick Dietz, El Paso	134	469	166	.354
1964	Mel Corbo, Albuquerque	121	443	150	.339
1965	Dave Pavlesic, Tulsa	112	389	134	.344
1966	Tom Hutton, Albuquerque	103	385	131	.340
1967	Luis Alcaraz, Albuquerque	137	475	156	.328
1968	Bob Taylor, Amarillo	126	442	142	.321
1969	Larry Johnson, Dallas–Fort Worth	131	483	163	.337
1970	Johnny Rivers, El Paso	114	449	154	.343
1971	Enos Cabell, Dallas–Fort Worth	140	521	162	.311
1972	Randy Elliot, Alexandria	138	474	159	.335
1973	Morris Nettles, El Paso	126	470	156	.332

TEXAS LEAGUE RECORDS

Individual Batting, Season Records

Highest Percentage
.402—Isaac Morgan "Ike" Boone, San Antonio, 1923

Most Runs Scored
171—Jimmy Single, Houston, 1896

Most Total Bases
414—Clarence "Big Boy" Kraft, Fort Worth, 1924

Most Hits
245—Randolph Moore, Dallas, 1929

Most Doubles
70—Rinaldo "Rhino" Williams, Dallas, 1925

Most Triples
30—J. Eddie Moore, Fort Worth, 1929

Most Home Runs
62—Kenneth Guettler, Shreveport, 1962

Most Runs Batted In
196—Clarence "Big Boy" Kraft, Fort Worth, 1924

Most Stolen Bases
116—Will Blakey, Galveston, 1895 (accomplished in 115 games)

Most Bases on Balls
153—Eddie Lake, Houston, 1939

Most Times Struck Out
186—Willie Crawford, Albuquerque, 1966

Individual Pitching, Season Records

Most Games Won
34—Al McFarland, Fort Worth, 1895

Most Games Lost
28—William Doyle, Temple, 1907

Most Innings Pitched
378—Bill Bailey, Beaumont, 1919

Most Strikeouts
325—Harry Ables, San Antonio, 1910

Most Bases on Balls
185—Bill Bailey, Beaumont, 1919

Most Hit Batsmen
32—George Crabble, Galveston, 1909

Most Shutouts
11—Jay Hannah "Dizzy" Dean, Houston, 1931

11

THE SOUTHERN ASSOCIATION AND THE SOUTHERN LEAGUE:
Baseball Way Down South in Dixie

ROSTER OF SOUTHERN ASSOCIATION TEAMS
(CLASS A 1901–18X—LEAGUE SUSPENDED OPERATIONS
JUNE 28; CLASS A, 1919–35; CLASS A–1, 1936–45;
CLASS AA, 1946–61) [1]

Team	*Years in Operation*
Atlanta, Georgia	1902–18X, 1919–61
Birmingham, Alabama	1901–18X, 1919–61
Chattanooga, Tennessee	1901–02, 1910–18X, 1919–61
Knoxville, Tennessee	1932–43
Little Rock, Arkansas	1901–10, 1915–18X, 1919–56 (franchise transferred temporarily to Montgomery July 14), 1957–58, 1960–61
Macon, Georgia	1961
Memphis, Tennessee	1901–18X, 1919–60
Mobile, Alabama	1908–18X, 1919–31, 1944–61
Montgomery, Alabama	1903–14, 1943, 1956 #
Nashville, Tennessee	1901–18X, 1919–61
New Orleans, Louisiana	1901–18X, 1919–59
Selma, Alabama	1901
Shreveport, Louisiana	1901–07, 1959–61

[1] See page 323 for Key to Roster of League Teams.

ROSTER OF SOUTH ATLANTIC LEAGUE TEAMS
(CLASS C, 1904–17X—LEAGUE SUSPENDED OPERATIONS
JULY 20, 1917); SOUTH ATLANTIC ASSOCIATION
(CLASS C 1919–20); AND SOUTH ATLANTIC LEAGUE
(CLASS B, 1936–41; CLASS A, 1946–62; CLASS AA, 1963)

Albany, Georgia	1911–15X, 1916X
Asheville, North Carolina	1924–30, 1959–63
Augusta, Georgia	·1904–11, 1914–15X, 1916–17X, 1919–30, 1936–42, 1946–63
Charleston, South Carolina	1904–09#, 1911X, 1913–15X, 1916–17X, 1919–23X, 1940#, 1941–42, 1946–53, 1959–61
Charlotte, North Carolina	1919–30, 1954–63
Chattanooga, Tennessee	1909, 1963
Columbia, South Carolina	1904–12, 1914–15X, 1916–17X, 1919–23, 1925–30, 1936–42, 1946–57, 1960–61
Columbus, Georgia	1909–15X, 1916–17X, 1936–42, 1946–57, 1959 (franchise shifted to Gastonia July 6)
Gastonia, North Carolina	1923#, 1959#
Greenville, South Carolina	1919–30, 1938–42, 1946–50, 1961–62
Jacksonville, Florida	1904–15X, 1916–17X, 1936–42, 1946–61
Knoxville, Tennessee	1909 (franchise shifted to Charleston in mid-season), 1924, 1956#, 1957–63
Lynchburg, Virginia	1963
Macon, Georgia	1904–15X, 1916–17X, 1923 (franchise shifted to Gastonia on June 5), 1924–30, 1936–42, 1946–1960, 1962–63
Montgomery, Alabama	1916X, 1951–56 (franchise shifted to Knoxville on June 11)
Nashville, Tennessee	1963
Norfolk-Portsmouth, Virginia	1961–62
Savannah, Georgia	1904–15X, 1936–42, 1946–60, 1962
Spartanburg, South Carolina	1919–29, 1938–40 (franchise shifted to Charleston in midseason)

ROSTER OF SOUTHERN LEAGUE TEAMS
(CLASS AA 1964—)

Asheville, North Carolina	1964–66, 1969—
Birmingham, Alabama	1964—
Charlotte, North Carolina	1964–72
Chattanooga, Tennessee	1964–65

Columbus, Georgia	1964–66, 1969—
Evansville, Indiana	1966–68
Jacksonville, Florida	1970—
Knoxville, Tennessee	1964–67, 1972—
Lynchburg, Virginia	1964–65
Macon, Georgia	1964, 1966–67
Mobile, Alabama	1966, 1970
Montgomery, Alabama	1965—
Orlando, Florida	1973—
Savannah, Georgia	1968—

Professional baseball has been played as extensively and with as much zeal down South as in any other place in the country—and perhaps more so. As we make this statement, we bear in mind fully the rich history of the professional game in areas like California and Texas.

The South's mild climate has, of course, been a major factor in making baseball so popular in Dixie. In Georgia, Louisiana, Mississippi, Florida, and other states of the Deep South, baseball could be virtually a year-round proposition. When the seasons ended for the myriad of Southern pro leagues, big league barnstorming outfits invaded the region, and they had scarcely left before the major league teams came down to start spring training and their spring exhibition tours. (Years ago spring training sites were scattered through the Deep South; they were not confined strictly to Florida and Arizona as they are today.) And the fans always came out to see the games because their appetite for baseball was insatiable.

Professional baseball teams, from the humblest Class D outfits to the tough Class AA clubs in the major Southern cities, once covered Dixie like the dew. Mississippi had teams in 19 cities at one time or another; Louisiana had 21; Arkansas had 23; Tennessee had 25; Alabama had 32; Florida and Georgia had almost 40 each; while baseball-mad North Carolina found places for the professionals in 70 cities in every nook and cranny of the state. Farther north, Virginia, the "Old Dominion" state, fielded teams in no less than 42 towns.

During the current era when the number of minor leagues has been drastically reduced, the South still has an impressive number of active circuits. The Southern Association did cease operations after the 1961 season, but of the sixteen U.S. leagues in Organized Baseball operating in 1973, five were based in the South: the Class AA Southern League, the Class A Carolina League, the Class A Western Carolinas League, the Class A Florida State League, and the Rookie Gulf Coast League. Moreover, the Class AA Texas League and the Rookie Appalachian League each maintain several teams in the South.

The Southern Association dates its early beginnings to 1885, but the modern eight-team circuit we are dealing with was formally organized in 1901. Any connections with the league of the 1880s and 1890s are loose.

The original 1885 Southern League was comprised of six teams: Atlanta, Augusta, Columbus, and Macon, Georgia; Birmingham, Alabama; and Chattanooga, Tennessee. Other cities represented in the Southern League at one time or another were: Charleston, South Carolina; Charlotte, North Carolina; Memphis, Tennessee; Montgomery and Mobile, Alabama; New Orleans, Louisiana; and Savannah, Georgia. In its final two years (1898–99) the old Southern was based in these six towns: Atlanta, Augusta, Birmingham, Chattanooga, Macon, and Savannah.

Like the Texas League in its early years, however, the old Southern League suffered from sparse attendance on too many occasions, and there was a good deal of franchise switching as well. Although records for some years are sketchy, the league appears to have remained at six teams throughout the bulk of its life. And since the Southern could not always get six teams together, it did not operate in 1890–91 or 1897 and then folded altogether after the 1899 season.

CHARLES ABNER POWELL "INVENTS" LADIES' DAY

Charles Abner Powell unquestionably ranks as one of the most innovative and colorful baseball men of the old Southern League. While a player–manager at New Orleans in 1887, Powell introduced both Ladies' Day and the rain check. He convinced the club owners that on a certain day of the week ladies should be admitted into the park free, and eventually Ladies' Day became a featured event at all Southern League ball parks. The majors adopted the idea as well, and over the years, Ladies' Day has made countless legions of women avid baseball fans. Moreover, Ladies' Day was an important factor in helping to clean up the language used around the ball parks, both on the field and in the grandstands. And with the rain check, a fan did not have to worry about losing the price of his ticket if rain or wet grounds caused a postponement. He simply retained his ticket stub and used it to see any other game of his choice.

Powell, a pitcher–outfielder, played two years in the majors (with Washington in the Union Association and with Baltimore and Cincinnati in the American Association in 1884 and 1886) before he came to New Orleans. He also became New Orleans' first manager in the new Southern

Association in 1901, a post he held for two years. Early in the 1901 season, with his team doing badly, he released every single player and recruited an entire new club within a couple of days! This is without precedent in baseball history. Powell must have known what he was doing for his team finished the season in fourth place with a respectable 68–55 record.

Charley "The Count" Campau, who stole 115 bases for Powell's championship 1887 New Orleans team, succeeded his old mentor as field manager in 1903, but he failed to finish the season as the team skidded badly again.

Powell in his later years became the Southern League's "Grand Old Man," as he kept a keen interest in the circuit up to the time of his death in August 1953 at the age of ninety-two.

THE NEW SOUTHERN ASSOCIATION

The Southern Association, as established in 1901, developed into one of professional baseball's most stable and efficiently administered minor league operations. Six of the league's eight charter members (Birmingham, Chattanooga, Little Rock, Memphis, Nashville, and New Orleans) stayed in the league for fifty years or more.

Shreveport, the seventh charter member, dropped out of the circuit after seven years, but came in again and hosted a team in the Southern Association's last years; while Selma, the last charter member, exited after the initial campaign and never came back. However, Atlanta took Selma's place, became a Southern Association stalwart, and remained in the circuit for sixty consecutive years. Mobile, which first entered the Association in 1908, spent a total of forty-two years in the league during three separate tenures of membership.

The league experienced serious difficulties during the middle of the 1905 season when a yellow fever epidemic struck New Orleans. The Crescent City was prone to yellow fever epidemics because of its low elevation (one or two feet above the mean level of the Gulf of Mexico), the surrounding marshes, and extremely high humidity during the summer months. Moreover, preventive measures against yellow fever were still being developed.

New Orleans' Pelicans agreed to play the rest of their games on the road, and the league held together. The Pelicans, under manager Charley Frank (who played the outfield for the St. Louis Cardinals in the mid-1890s), went on to roll up a record of 84–45, good enough for the league championship.

The Southern League's stability was due in no small part to its presidents (see page 233), who for the most part administered the league in an even-handed way, especially in trying to find a middle ground in disputes between players and management. Judge William Kavanaugh of Little Rock, who served as chief executive for twelve years (1903–15), did much to shape the destiny of the league; and under Judge John D. Martin of Memphis (1919–38) the Southern Association solidified its reputation as one of the strongest minor leagues in the National Association.

The Southern Association continued to operate a full schedule throughout World War II. Both Baseball Commissioner Kenesaw Mountain Landis and the Roosevelt Administration agreed that baseball constituted an important part of the life on the "home front," and the league was given the go-ahead "green light." Landis was firm in his faith that the game could be continued with over-age, under-age, and 4-F players, both in the majors and minors. "Unless some sort of rule is passed making it impossible to put nine men on the field, baseball is not dead," he declared.

PETE GRAY: THE ONE-ARMED OUTFIELDER

The most famous 4-F of them all was one-armed outfielder Pete Gray, who batted a solid .333 and stole 68 bases for the Memphis Chicks in 1944, achievements that won him election as the association's Most Valuable Player. Gray became the talk of the baseball world and his play in the SA was so impressive that the St. Louis Browns eagerly signed him for the 1945 campaign.

Gray had lost his right arm at the bicep in a boyhood accident, but he developed his left arm to such a degree and compensated for his handicap with such quickness that he became a really fine ball player. The author saw Gray play several times in 1945 and recalls vividly his performance against the Cleveland Indians at Cleveland's Municipal Stadium in one particular four-game series. Gray cracked out 7 hits, including 2 long line drive triples to center field, in 16 at bats, and he fielded his left field post flawlessly. When he caught a fly ball, he flipped his glove under the stump of his right arm in a rapid-fire motion so that he could throw the ball with his bare left hand.

Gray batted only .218 in the much tougher American League competition. Amazingly enough, however, he struck out only 11 times in 234 official at bats. When Gray took the field either in a Southern Association or American League park, no one ever did him any favors—he got along on his own grit. As a result, he became an inspiration to the multitude of disabled U.S. war veterans.

THE POSTWAR ERA

With the end of the war, the Southern Association enjoyed a boom period, as did most of professional baseball. In 1946, the Southern Association established its banner year at the gate up to that point by drawing 1,831,236 fans, far surpassing the previous high mark of 1,351,570 reached in 1925. Atlanta, the 1946 pennant winner, rolled up the highest attendance of any SA team in history by drawing 395,699 fans, breaking its own season's record of 330,795 set in 1935.

Southern Association watchers predicted that the high attendance levels of 1946 would drop off in 1947, but the reverse happened: attendance records went right through the ceiling as the total reached 2,180,344. Two clubs reached the 400,000 figure: the Atlanta Crackers (with a league-leading 404,584 despite a fifth-place finish) and the New Orleans Pelicans (with 400,036).

The euphoria of the postwar boom subsided by 1950, and Southern Association attendance began declining, with the downward trend being almost inexorable. In 1951, the total attendance figure was still a healthy 1,534,000, and in 1952, it was 1,464,000. But the downward trend became a fact of life. In 1957, the SA barely managed to clear a million (1,012,000), while the figure had slid all the way down to 614,000 in 1959. Attendance recovered somewhat, jumping to 780,000 in 1960; and then it plopped down to 647,000 in 1961, the final season for the grand but tired old league.

Attendance at Atlanta, a stronghold of the Southern Association, tailed off to a dismal 71,000, 154,000, and 59,000 in 1959–60–61, respectively. In 1959, paid admissions to cities like Chattanooga, Memphis, and Shreveport skidded to 60,000, 50,000, and 48,000, respectively —these are dangerously low levels. Memphis pulled out of the SA before the start of the 1961 season, and the other team's in the league's final campaign (Birmingham, Little Rock, Macon, Mobile, and Nashville) did not have strong gates either.

Thus, for sheer economic reasons the Southern Association disbanded after an existence of sixty continuous years. Southern Association cities did not stay out of baseball, however. Atlanta, for example, went into the International League in 1962 and then in 1966 gained entry in the National League, marking the first time the South was represented in the big leagues. (If you want to consider Houston a part of the South, then this Texas city holds the honor rather than Atlanta, since it joined the National League in 1962.)

Little Rock stayed out of baseball in 1962, joined the International

League in 1963, switched to the Pacific Coast League for 1964–65, and then found a permanent home in the Texas League (where it has been a member since 1966). The team is now known as "Arkansas" rather than simply as "Little Rock," since it is supposed to represent the whole state. In fact, Arkansas' only entry in Organized Baseball today is Little Rock.

Shreveport is also currently a member of the Texas League.

THE NEW SOUTHERN LEAGUE

The Class A South Atlantic League (popularly called the "Sally League") graduated to Class AA in 1963 and changed its name to the Southern League in 1964. Since then it has been the South's most important professional loop. Moreover, during the past dozen years the new Southern League has taken in some of the old Southern Association cities, including Birmingham (which is a current member).

Nashville entered a team in the Class AA South Atlantic League in 1963, but it has been out of Organized Baseball entirely since that time; while Charlotte, Macon, and Mobile all fielded teams in the new Southern League for stretches of several years each. Charlotte, Macon, and Mobile were not represented in any league in 1973. Interestingly enough, though, Charlotte fielded teams in both the Southern League and the Class A Western Carolinas League in 1972.

The Southern League of today is composed of cities that are generally smaller than those of the Southern Association during its heyday, with the 1974 roster of teams including Asheville, Birmingham, Columbus, Jacksonville, Knoxville, Montgomery, Orlando, and Savannah. Total attendance in 1973 reached only 454,000 (the highwater mark came in 1964, the SL's first year, when paid admissions were registered at 484,000). But the league has serious competition for fan interest, from televised big league games, particularly Atlanta Braves games (which are beamed over a wide area of the South) and the "Big League Game of the Week" (which is now being produced for nationwide consumption twice a week, on Saturday afternoons and Monday nights). In 1967–68–69, the league slid down to six teams, but it now appears that the present healthier eight-team setup will be retained indefinitely.

Billy Hitchcock, a former American League infielder and ex-manager of the Baltimore Orioles and Atlanta Braves, took over as the Southern League's president in 1971 and has been both a dynamic and intelligent administrator. Hitchcock, a true son of the South, is a native of Inverness, Alabama, and a graduate of Auburn University.

LARRY GILBERT: THE SOUTHERN ASSOCIATION'S
MOST DURABLE MANAGER

Few managers in the history of professional baseball can offer a record that compares with the one established by Larry Gilbert, who played a major role in the history of the Southern Association. Gilbert, a utility outfielder with the "miracle" Boston Braves of 1914, took over as manager of the New Orleans Pelicans at the beginning of the 1923 season. He was then thirty-one years old, and with the exception of one season, he managed from that time through 1948 in either New Orleans or Nashville. In 1932 he acted as president of the New Orleans club and hired the veteran Jake Atz to serve as field manager. When the Pelicans finished sixth that year, Gilbert resumed his managerial duties.

Gilbert won a record nine championships, five with the New Orleans Pelicans and four with the Nashville Vols. In addition, he finished second five times; third, six times; and fourth, twice (in split seasons where New Orleans won the playoff, only first place is figured as the standing for that year). He finished out of the first division only four times in his twenty-five years of managing.

Gilbert had two sons who played in the majors: Charlie (an outfielder who saw service with Brooklyn, Chicago, and Philadelphia in the National League from 1940 to 1947) and Harold "Tookie" (who played first base for the New York Giants in 1950 and 1953). All three Gilberts were born in New Orleans.

Larry Gilbert's Record as a
Southern Association Manager

Club	Year	Finish	Won	Lost	Pct.
New Orleans	1923	First	89	57	.610
New Orleans	1924	Third	93	60	.608
New Orleans	1925	Second	85	68	.556
New Orleans	1926	First	101	53	.656
New Orleans	1927	First	96	57	.627
New Orleans	1928*	Third	40	33	.548
New Orleans	1928*	Sixth	33	41	.446
New Orleans	1929	Third	89	64	.582
New Orleans	1930	Second	91	61	.599

* Asterisk denotes split season.

Club	Year	Finish	Won	Lost	Pct.
New Orleans	1931	Fifth	78	75	.510
New Orleans	1933*	Second	41	34	.547
New Orleans	1933*	First	47	31	.603
New Orleans	1934*	Second	40	32	.556
New Orleans	1934*	First	54	28	.659
New Orleans	1935	Second	86	67	.562
New Orleans	1936	Fourth	81	71	.533
New Orleans	1937	Fourth	84	65	.560
New Orleans	1938	Third	79	70	.530
Nashville	1939	Third	85	68	.556
Nashville	1940	First	101	47	.682
Nashville	1941	Second	83	70	.542
Nashville	1942	Second	85	66	.563
Nashville	1943*	First	49	26	.653
Nashville	1943*	Third	34	29	.540
Nashville	1944*	Fifth	32	36	.471
Nashville	1944*	First	47	25	.653
Nashville	1945	Seventh	55	84	.396
Nashville	1946	Fifth	75	78	.490
Nashville	1947	Third	80	73	.523
Nashville	1948	First	95	58	.621
	25 Years		2128	1627	.566

* Asterisk denotes split season.

JOHNNY DOBBS

Johnny Dobbs, a native of Chattanooga, ranks second to Larry Gilbert in longevity among Southern Association managers. Dobbs, a speedy little outfielder, played regularly with Cincinnati, Chicago, and Brooklyn in the National League from 1901 through 1905. His managerial assignments were: Nashville, 1907; Chattanooga, 1910; Montgomery, 1911–13; New Orleans, 1914–22; Memphis, 1923–24; Birmingham, 1925–29; and Atlanta, 1930–31. He compiled a record of 1,841 victories against 1,452 losses for a winning percentage of .559 as he led his teams to five pennants: two with New Orleans, one with Memphis, and two with Birmingham.

JOE ENGEL: CHAMPION IVORY HUNTER AND
IRREPRESSIBLE PRESIDENT OF THE
CHATTANOOGA LOOKOUTS

The Southern Association had many colorful club owners during its long history, but perhaps none matched the Chattanooga Lookouts' Joe Engel for versatility and resourcefulness. Engel served as president and chief stockholder of the Lookouts from 1929 through 1965, and early in his executive career he earned the title of "Barnum of Baseball."

When Engel became president of the Lookouts in 1929, at the age of thirty-six, he did so with the full support of his old friend Clark C. Griffith. Griffith, owner of the Washington Senators, had decided to make Chattanooga his top farm club.

Engel's association with the Senators ran deep, for he was a native of the nation's capital and as a boy he hustled off to the ball park every chance he had. His good fortunes began in 1907, when he was hired as the team's mascot and batboy (a post he held for three years). He idolized Walter Johnson, Washington's big strong right-hander from the Kansas prairies, who also had joined the team in 1907. Engel, an excellent natural athlete in his own right, wanted to become a star fireballer, just like the "Humboldt Thunderbolt," and he went on to distinguish himself as a member of Mount St. Mary's College (Emmitsburg, Maryland) varsity pitching staff by hurling a perfect game against Susquehanna College, striking out 19. The perfect game was part of a string of three consecutive shutouts in college competition.

In the fall of 1911, the Senators signed Engel to a contract, and during the following season, he was no longer a batboy and mascot, but a teammate of the great Walter Johnson himself. Engel never quite lived up to expectations as a world-beater on the mound. Yet he still managed to log 3–5, 9–9, and 6–5 records in 1912, 1913, and 1914, respectively before losing 3 decisions early in 1915 and being sent to Minneapolis. Troubled by wildness, he saw brief service with Cincinnati and Cleveland, and he pitched a couple of innings for the Senators again in 1920. He then retired from active play and went into the business side of baseball, for which he was now well-prepared. (We should add that in-between his sojourns back to the majors, Engel pitched effectively for both Buffalo in the International League and Atlanta in the Southern Association.)

Almost immediately after hanging up his uniform, Engel was hired by Clark Griffith as a "super-scout," which meant in effect that the former pitcher was to act as a one-man scouting staff for the Senators.

(In 1920, Griffith was preparing to relinquish his duties as field manager in order to concentrate on his new responsibilities as club president.)

Even before Engel formally took up his scouting post, he recommended that Griffith sign a young second baseman named Stanley "Bucky" Harris. The scouting job which Engel looked back on with the greatest pleasure, however, was the landing of Joe Cronin in midseason 1928. He bought the twenty-one-year-old shortstop from the Kansas City Blues of the American Association for $7,500 without Griffith's okay. When Engel telephoned the "Old Fox" about the purchase, the conversation was congenial until he mentioned the price and the fact that Cronin was batting a puny .245. Then Griffith hit the ceiling and raged: "He's not my ball player—he's yours. You keep him and don't either you or Cronin show up at the Washington ball park."

Griffith relented the next day: "Well, as long as he's mine and I have to pay for him, let me at least have a look at him," he growled. Cronin, of course, became a hard-hitting, sure-handed shortstop for the Senators. He won the MVP award in 1930 and managed Washington to the American League pennant in 1933 (he also married Griffith's adopted daughter). The Old Fox turned in a nice profit on Cronin when he sold him to the Boston Red Sox in October 1934 for $250,000 and shortstop Lyn Lary.

After Engel became the major domo at Chattanooga, he continued in his search for talent to send to Washington, with some of the players of big league caliber going to other clubs besides the Senators. Other players either scouted or developed by Engel at Chattanooga include: Jimmy Bloodworth, Lloyd Brown, Dick Coffman, Gil Coan, Alvin Crowder, Charlie Dressen, Goose Goslin, Jackie Hayes, Sid Hudson, Joe Judge, Joe Kuhel, Buddy Lewis, Mickey Livingston, Earl McNeely, Fred Marberry, Bing Miller, Bill Nicholson, Lance Richbourg, Ray Scarborough, Cecil Travis, and Early Wynn.

For many years Joe Engel had the reputation of being one of the shrewdest judges of player talent in all of baseball. As a professional "ivory hunter," he scarcely had a peer.

One of Engel's first acts upon becoming president of the Lookouts in 1929 was to have a new ball park constructed which was named, appropriately enough, "Engel Stadium." Called the "Finest in the South," it seated 12,000 and was for years considered the best baseball facility of its size in the country. When Branch Rickey visited Engel Stadium in 1953, twenty-four years after it was built, he declared that it ranked as one of the best maintained parks in either the majors or minors.

Soon after the stadium was completed, Engel put in a pressroom, the first in the Southern Association. Engel, a great believer in the power of the press, always made it his business to win the friendship of sports-writers and other newspapermen. "Without them, where would we be?" he asked.

A thoroughly uninhibited character, Engel traded shortstop Johnny Jones to Charlotte in the Sally League, also a Washington affiliate, for a twenty-five-pound turkey. Joe then invited some twenty-five Southern Association sportswriters to a turkey dinner. "I still think I got the worst of that deal," Joe recalled. "That was a mighty tough turkey."

Engel guided the fortunes of the Lookouts through 1965 when Chattanooga, unfortunately, dropped out of Organized Baseball. After the Southern Association folded in 1961, Engel took the Lookouts briefly into the Sally League and then into the new Southern League. He died at Chattanooga on June 12, 1969, at the age of seventy-six.

SOUTHERN ASSOCIATION HIGHLIGHTS

1902: Hugh Hill, a Nashville outfielder, hit .416, the all-time high batting average in the Southern Association. Hill went on to play briefly in the majors. His older brother, "Still Bill" Hill, was a prominent National League pitcher in the 1890s.

1904: Frank Smith rolled up a 31–10 record for Atlanta and became the first SA pitcher to win 30 or more games.

1905: Carleton Molesworth, a Montgomery outfielder, won the batting crown with a .312 mark. Molesworth is better known in SA history as manager of Birmingham for fourteen years (1909–22).

1906: Glenn Liebhardt, a Memphis right-hander, established the all-time SA record by winning 35 games. He lost 11 for a winning percentage of .761. Liebhardt started 46 games and finished 45 of them. In the only game he did not complete (May 5), he was thrown out by the umpire in the seventh inning for protesting a call. After the SA season ended, Liebhardt was called up by Cleveland and won two games for the Indians; thus, he actually chalked up 37 victories for the entire season. (Liebhardt's major league log with Cleveland from 1906 through 1909 reads 37–36.) While Liebhardt had a good fastball and a fair curve, his money pitch was the elusive spitball.

1908: Tris Speaker, a Little Rock outfielder, took the SA batting crown with a .350 mark, his second hitting title in two years (he had led

Texas League batters during the previous year). When the SA season ended early in September, Speaker was recalled by the Boston Red Sox. He remained in the majors for the next twenty years.

1909: Franchises were still relatively cheap at this period in the Southern Association's history. At the end of the 1909 campaign, a syndicate purchased the Little Rock franchise and all of the players on its roster for $12,000. The team was moved to Chattanooga in time for the 1910 season.

1910: "Shoeless Joe" Jackson, a New Orleans outfielder, paced the league in hitting with .354, marking the third year in a row that he captured a minor league batting crown. With Greenville in the Carolina Association in 1908, he swatted .346; and with Savannah in the Sally League in 1909, he registered .358. He finished the 1910 season with Cleveland and rapped the ball at a .387 clip for 20 games. Called one of greatest "natural" hitters in baseball history, "Shoeless Joe" batted .408 for Cleveland in 1911 but lost the hitting crown to Ty Cobb, who posted .420. Joe Jackson may have signed his contracts with an "X," but in the batter's box, he was a genius.

The shortest regulation nine-inning game in the history of professional baseball is credited to the Southern Association. In this game, which was played at Atlanta on September 19, Mobile edged the Atlanta Crackers 2–1. The contest required only 32 minutes to complete. With the score tied 1–1 in the first half of the ninth, Mobile pushed across the decisive run. Apparently, the game was conducted as an experiment by the league and the players to demonstrate how quickly a game could be played. Both teams hustled every minute of the way. Batters did not wait out the pitchers, but rather swung at every good pitch. There was only one walk; not a single player struck out; and Mobile even reeled off a triple play. Mobile made 6 hits against 4 for Atlanta. On the same afternoon, the Chattanooga at Nashville game required only 42 minutes to complete.

1910–11: Otto Hess, a native of Berne, Switzerland, and star of the pennant-winning New Orleans Pelicans pitching staff, led SA pitchers with 25–9 and 23–8 marks during these two years. Hess was a 20-game winner for the Cleveland Indians in 1906.

1913: Harry Coveleski, a Chattanooga Lookouts left-hander, paced the league's hurlers with a 28–9 record. From this time on no SA pitcher has won that many games in one season. Harry, brother of Hall of Fame pitcher Stan Coveleski, went on to become a 20-game winner for Detroit in 1914, 1915, and 1916.

1916: Dickie Kerr, a Memphis left-hander, led SA pitchers with a 24–12 record. Kerr, who won two World Series games for the Chicago White Sox against the Cincinnati Reds in 1919 while his teammates were trying to throw the games, is also remembered for converting Stan Musial from a pitcher to an outfielder while he managed Daytona Beach in the Florida State League in 1940.

1919: In the SA's longest game, on June 23, Atlanta and Chattanooga played 23 innings to a 2–2 tie (at Chattanooga's Andrews Field) before the contest was called because of darkness. Jimmy Dykes, an Atlanta third baseman, handled a record 22 chances without an error, 11 putouts and 11 assists. The marathon was played in the surprisingly fast time of 3 hours and 40 minutes, because plate umpire Harry "Steamboat Johnson kept both teams hustling as he continuously chattered "Hurry it up, boys."

Steamboat Johnson, an umpire in Organized Baseball since 1909, began his long and colorful career as a Southern Association arbiter. Except for 1921 when he plied his trade in the Sally League, Johnson remained in the SA continuously until his retirement after the 1949 season. Johnson umpired one year (1914) in the National League, but for mysterious reasons his contract was not renewed. Once he reconciled himself to a career of minor league umpiring, he became a beloved figure in the SA, and on July 28, 1949, in New Orleans, players and fans alike paid him an extraordinary compliment when they held a "night" for him. In his 1935 autobiography, *Standing the Gaff,* Johnson said, "I have rendered one million decisions since I began umpiring in 1909. Something like 4,000 bottles have been thrown at me in my day, but only about twenty ever hit me. That does not speak very well for the accuracy of the fans' throwing."

1921: Arthur "Dazzy" Vance, a New Orleans right-handed fireballer, chalked up a 21–11 record and then moved up to Brooklyn where he achieved fame. Vance pitched almost ten solid years in the minor leagues before he established himself in the majors at the age of thirty-one. Vance won 197 National League games after he passed his thirty-first birthday.

"Ike" Boone, a New Orleans outfielder, led the SA with a .389 batting mark and won the first of his five minor league hitting championships.

1923: Larry Gilbert signed as manager of New Orleans and began a record twenty-five-year tenure as an SA pilot. He managed New Orleans for fifteen years and Nashville for ten years.

1925: Wilbur Good, a thirty-nine-year-old Atlanta outfielder, led the SA in hitting with a .379 mark and set the all-time league record of 236 base hits. Good, a speedy 5-foot, 6-inch left-handed swinger, spent eleven years in the majors between 1905–18, playing for six different clubs in both leagues.

1927: The Birmingham Barons, under manager Johnny Dobbs, established the SA team record by winning 19 games in succession. With a 91–63 season log, they finished 5-½ games behind the champion New Orleans Pelicans.

1928: The Memphis Chicks, the second-half champions, won 18 games in a row under manager Doc Prothro.

1930: A record 40 SA regulars batted .300 or better. In 1909 no regular in the league had hit .300.

Colonel Bob Allen, president of the Little Rock Travelers, introduced the Southern League to night baseball on June 21 in a game against Birmingham. By the mid-1930s all SA parks were equipped with lights.

Jim Poole, a thirty-five-year-old Nashville first baseman, led the SA in homers with 50, in total bases with 403, and in RBI's with 167. Poole, who also won the home run title in 1929 with 33, played for the Philadelphia Athletics in 1925–27 and batted .288 for his 283 games in the American League.

Jay Partridge, Nashville's second baseman and Poole's teammate, set the SA record for runs scored with 155. He also slammed 40 homers. Poole and Partridge, both left-handed hitters, found the short right field wall at Nashville very inviting. Partridge played second base for the Brooklyn Dodgers in 1927–28, his only experience in the big leagues.

1932: Walter "Boom Boom" Beck, a Memphis right-hander, topped the SA in pitching with a 27–6 record. In an active pitching career that spanned twenty-seven years (1924–50), Beck worked for twenty-three teams in thirteen different leagues, including both major leagues. In addition to his American and National League experience, Beck toiled in the following circuits: Three-I League, Texas Association, Western League, American Association, International League, Southern Association, Pacific Coast League, Inter-State League, Southeast League, Central League and Middle Atlantic League. In the latter three leagues he was a player–manager.

1934: Phil Weintraub, a Nashville outfielder–first baseman, won the SA batting crown with a .401 mark. Weintraub also played in thirty-one games for the New York Giants in 1934 and hit .351. While he spent the bulk of his career in the minors, he did play first base for the Giants in 1944–45, when he was nearing forty.

Eddie Rose, a New Orleans infielder, in a July 9 game against Knoxville, fouled off 19 successive pitches delivered by pitcher Hank Hulvey of the Smokies before finally grounding out.

1935: Catcher Lee Head of Knoxville struck out only once during the entire 1935 season, playing in 122 games and batting officially 402 times. He was not a power hitter, but his timing was uncanny.

1936: Joe Dwyer, a stocky little left-handed hitting Nashville outfielder, set the all-time SA record for doubles in one season by cracking out 65. By the time he reached the Cincinnati Reds in 1937 as a pinch-hitting specialist, he was known as "Double Joe."

1940: Fred Tauby, a Birmingham outfielder, threatened Dwyer's two-base hit record but finished the season with 61. Tauby had played briefly with the Chicago White Sox in 1935 and the Philadelphia Phillies in 1937.

1941: Les Fleming, a Nashville first baseman, became the third Vol to reach the .400 mark in batting. He socked for a .414 average, 2 points below Hugh Hill's all-time SA record. Fleming, who won the Texas League batting title in 1954 with a .358 figure at the age of thirty-nine, played for Detroit, Cleveland, and Pittsburgh in the majors.

Les Burge, an Atlanta outfielder–first baseman, won the SA MVP award as he hit 38 homers and drove in 146 runs. Burge, who managed Fort Worth in the Texas League in 1947–48, never played an inning in the majors.

1942: Willis Hudlin, a fifteen-year big league pitching veteran, led Little Rock to the SA pennant as player–manager. Hudlin, who contributed a 11–9 record on the mound, continued his dual role for the Travelers through the 1946 season.

1943: In his seventh year in the minor leagues, Eddie Lopat, a

Little Rock left-hander, chalked up a 19–10 record and then moved on to a brilliant twelve-year major league career, spent mostly with the Chicago White Sox and the New York Yankees.

1944: This was Pete Gray's year in the Southern Association.

1945: Gil Coan, a speedy Chattanooga outfielder, won the batting crown with a fat .372 and set the SA record for triples with 28 (three players had previously held the record with 27 three-baggers: Ike Boone of New Orleans in 1921, Elliott Bigelow of Chattanooga in 1925, and Danny Taylor of Memphis in 1927).

Mobile catcher Harry Chozen established a new Southern Association record when he hit safely in 49 consecutive games. In setting this standard, Chozen broke a record that had stood for 20 years. In 1925, Nashville outfielder Johnny Bates had hit safely in 46 straight games.

When Chozen surpassed Bates' streak, it was necessary, however, that Southern Association President Billy Evans be called upon to rule on a technicality on which the record hinged. On July 6, after having hit safely in 33 games, Chozen in his first time at bat in a game against Memphis drew a base on balls. In the fourth inning of this game, while kneeling in the on deck circle, he was hit on the head and knocked unconscious by a flying bat that slipped out of the hands of teammate Pete Thomassie as he followed through on a vicious swing. Chozen was forced to retire from the game. After this episode, Chozen proceeded to hit safely in 16 additional games before being stopped. Evans ruled that Chozen's failure to get a hit in the July 6 game where he walked in his only time at bat did not break the hitting streak.

Chozen's record is interesting in several other ways. Twice during the streak he was used as a pinch hitter and delivered. On two other occasions he entered the game in late innings, batting only once in each game, but he managed to get his base hit. He broke Bates' record in a truly dramatic manner by smashing a long home run in his first time at bat in his forty-seventh game. (Chozen's only big league experience came in 1937 at the age of twenty-two, when he caught one game for the Cincinnati Reds.)

1946: Lew Flick, a Little Rock outfielder, hit safely 9 straight times in a 19-inning game against Memphis on July 21, 1946. Kerby Farrell, a Little Rock first baseman, collected 8 base hits in the same game.

Don Lund, a Mobile outfielder, went to bat 10 times in a 21-inning game at Atlanta on August 8, 1946, without getting a hit or getting on base. He flied out to the outfield 6 times, struck out once, hit into a double play, and popped to the infield twice. Despite this dismal performance, Lund, a good ball player, went on to play in the majors for several years.

1947: Gil Coan, back in Chattanooga after a year with Washington, led the SA in triples a second time with 17, while batting .340. Coan, a great minor leaguer, was only fair in the majors.

1948: Larry Gilbert, the Nashville manager, concluded twenty-five years as an SA pilot by winning the pennant.

Charley Workman, a Nashville outfielder, slammed 52 homers and drove in a record-breaking total of 182 runs.

1951: Jimmy Piersall, the future Boston Red Sox star outfielder, hit .346 and fielded sensationally for Birmingham.

1952: Chuck Tanner, an Atlanta outfielder, hit a lusty .345 in 117 games. Tanner, a successful pilot at the conclusion of his playing days, was later named "Manager of the Year" in the Texas League while with El Paso and "Major League Manager of the Year" while with the Chicago White Sox.

1954: Bob Lennon, a Nashville outfielder, smashed all SA records for home runs (with 64) and total bases (with 447). He led the league with a .345 average, and he batted in 161 runs for good measure. Lennon, a 6-foot, 200-pound left-handed hitter, played in a total of 38 major league games for the New York Giants and the Chicago Cubs in 1954–57, but he batted only .165 and hit exactly 1 homer.

1955: Jack Cassini, a Memphis second baseman–manager, was beaned on August 2 and was forced to sit out the rest of the season. Ted Lyons, who had been recently named to the Hall of Fame for winning 260 games with the Chicago White Sox, took over the Chicks and led them to the SA pennant.

1957: This is the last year that the SA drew over a million paid admissions.

1958: On May 21 at Birmingham, Chuck Coles a Nashville first baseman–outfielder, became the thirty-first SA player and the nineteenth Vol to hit 3 homers in one game. He singled on his fourth trip. Coles, who slammed 29 homers for the season, played five games for Cincinnati at the end of the season and then went back to Nashville in 1959. Like too many other long ball hitters he struck out too much.

Cal Ermer, who began his managing career in 1950 at the age of twenty-six with Orlando in the Florida State League, piloted Birmingham to the league title. He later managed Minnesota in the majors.

1959–61: Mel McGaha and Frank Lucchesi, who managed top SA teams at this time, both eventually became big league managers without the benefit of big league playing experience. Their promotions to the majors were based almost entirely on solid minor league managing experience. McGaha and Lucchesi began their careers as pilots while still in their twenties.

The Southern Association disbanded at the end of the 1961 season.

1964: The South Atlantic ("Sally") League was renamed the Southern League and for all intents and purposes replaced the Southern Association as the top minor league circuit south of the Mason–Dixon line.

SOUTHERN ASSOCIATION PRESIDENTS

Year	President
1901	Reed W. Kent, W. J. Boles, J. B. Nicklin
1902	J. B. Nicklin
1903–15	Judge William B. Kavanaugh
1915–18	Robert H. Baugh
1919–38	Judge John D. Martin
1938–42	Major Trammell Scott
1943–46	William G. "Billy" Evans
1947–60	Charles A. Hurth
1960–61	Hal Totten

SOUTHERN LEAGUE PRESIDENTS

1964–71	Sam C. Smith
1971—	Billy Hitchcock

SOUTHERN ASSOCIATION LEAGUE CHAMPIONS

Year	Championship Team	Manager	Won	Lost	Pct.
1885	Atlanta	Gus Schmelz	60	31	.659
1886	Atlanta	Bill Purcell	64	28	.696
1887	New Orleans	Abner Powell	75	40	.652
1888	Birmingham	Waldon Goldsby	32	19	.627
1889	New Orleans (1st half)	Abner Powell	9	2	.818
	New Orleans (2nd half)	Abner Powell	34	5	.871
1890–91	(League did not operate.)				
1892	Chattanooga (1st half)	T. P. Sullivan	52	30	.634
	Birmingham (2nd half)	Jim Manning	30	11	.732
1893	Augusta (1st half)	George Stallings	44	17	.721
	Macon (2nd half)	Dan Shannon	..	..	.750
1894	Memphis	Frank Graves	40	17	.702
1895	Atlanta	James Knowles	70	37	.654
1896	New Orleans	Abner Powell	68	31	.686
1897	(League did not operate.)				
1898	Augusta	Frank Leonard	..	..	.741
1899	Mobile	Jack Huston	24	16	.600
1900	(League did not operate.)				
1901	Nashville	Newt Fisher	78	45	.634
1902	Nashville	Newt Fisher	80	40	.667
1903	Memphis	Charley Frank	73	51	.589

Year	Championship Team	Manager	Won	Lost	Pct.
1904	Memphis	Lew Whistler	81	54	.600
1905	New Orleans	Charley Frank	84	45	.651
1906	Birmingham	Harry Vaughan	85	47	.644
1907	Atlanta	William Smith	78	54	.591
1908	Nashville	William Bernhard	75	56	.573
1909	Atlanta	William Smith	87	49	.640
1910	New Orleans	Charley Frank	87	53	.621
1911	New Orleans	Charley Frank	78	54	.591
1912	Birmingham	Carlton Molesworth	85	51	.625
1913	Atlanta	William Smith	81	56	.591
1914	Birmingham	Carlton Molesworth	88	62	.591
1915	New Orleans	Johnny Dobbs	91	63	.591
1916	Nashville	Roy Ellam	84	54	.609
1917	Atlanta	Charley Frank	98	56	.637
1918	New Orleans	Johnny Dobbs	49	21	.700

(The league suspended operations in midseason because of World War I.)

Year	Championship Team	Manager	Won	Lost	Pct.
1919	Atlanta	Charley Frank	85	53	.616
1920	Little Rock	Norman Elberfeld	88	59	.599
1921	Memphis	Spencer Abbott	104	49	.680
1922	Mobile	Bert Niehoff	97	55	.638
1923	New Orleans	Larry Gilbert	89	57	.610

Year	Championship Team	Manager	Won	Lost	Pct.
1924	Memphis	Johnny Dobbs	104	48	.684
1925	Atlanta	Bert Niehoff	87	67	.565
1926	New Orleans	Larry Gilbert	101	53	.656
1927	New Orleans	Larry Gilbert	96	57	.627
1928	Birmingham	Johnny Dobbs	99	54	.647
	Birmingham (1st half)	Johnny Dobbs	50	26	.658
	Memphis (2nd half)	James T. "Doc" Prothro	51	26	.662

(Birmingham defeated Memphis in playoff 4 games to 0.)

Year	Championship Team	Manager	Won	Lost	Pct.
1929	Birmingham	Johnny Dobbs	93	60	.608
1930	Memphis	James T. "Doc" Prothro	98	55	.641
1931	Birmingham	Clyde Milan	97	55	.638
1932	Chattanooga	Bert Niehoff	98	51	.658
1933	New Orleans	Larry Gilbert	88	65	.575
	Memphis (1st half)	James T. "Doc" Prothro	50	27	.649
	New Orleans (2nd half)	Larry Gilbert	47	31	.605

(New Orleans defeated Memphis in playoff 3 games to 2.)

Year	Championship Team	Manager	Won	Lost	Pct.
1934	New Orleans	Larry Gilbert	94	60	.638
	Nashville (1st half)	Charles Dressen–Lance Richbourg	46	26	.639
	New Orleans (2nd half)	Larry Gilbert	54	28	.659

(New Orleans defeated Nashville in playoff 3 games to 2.)

Year	Championship Team	Manager	Won	Lost	Pct.
1935	*Atlanta	Eddie Moore	91	60	.605
	New Orleans	Larry Gilbert	86	67	.562
	Memphis	Fred Hofmann	84	70	.545
	Nashville	Lance Richbourg	82	69	.543

* Asterisk indicates winning team.

Year	Championship Team	Manager	Won	Lost	Pct.

(Playoffs: Atlanta defeated Nashville 3 games to 0; New Orleans defeated Memphis 3 games to 0. Finals: Atlanta defeated New Orleans 3 games to 0.)

1936	Atlanta	Eddie Moore	94	59	.614
	Nashville	Lance Richbourg	86	65	.570
	*Birmingham	Riggs Stephenson	82	70	.539
	New Orleans	Larry Gilbert	81	71	.533

(Playoffs: Birmingham defeated Nashville 3 games to 2; New Orleans defeated Atlanta 3 games to 2. Finals: Birmingham defeated New Orleans 3 games to 0 with 1 tie.)

1937	*Little Rock	James T. "Doc" Prothro	97	55	.638
	Memphis	Billy Southworth	88	64	.579
	Atlanta	Eddie Moore	84	66	.560
	New Orleans	Larry Gilbert	84	66	.560

(Playoffs: Atlanta defeated Memphis 3 games to 1; Little Rock defeated New Orleans 3 games to 1. Finals: Little Rock defeated Atlanta 4 games to 3.)

1938	*Atlanta	Paul Richards	91	62	.595
	Nashville	Charles Dressen	84	66	.560
	New Orleans	Larry Gilbert	79	70	.530
	Memphis	Billy Southworth	77	75	.507

(Playoffs: Atlanta defeated Memphis 3 games to 2; Nashville defeated New Orleans 3 games to 2. Finals: Atlanta defeated Nashville 4 games to 1 with 1 tie.)

1939	Chattanooga	Hazen "Kiki" Cuyler	85	65	.567
	Memphis	Frank Brazill	84	67	.556
	*Nashville	Larry Gilbert	85	68	.555
	Atlanta	Paul Richards	83	67	.553

(Playoffs: Atlanta defeated Chattanooga 3 games to 0; Nashville defeated Memphis 3 games to 0. Finals: Nashville defeated Atlanta 4 games to 3.)

*Asterisk indicates winning team.

Year	Championship Team	Manager	Won	Lost	Pct.
1940	*Nashville	Larry Gilbert	101	47	.682
	Atlanta	Paul Richards	93	58	.616
	Memphis	Truck Hannah	79	72	.523
	Chattanooga	Hazen "Kiki" Cuyler	73	79	.480

(Playoffs: Nashville defeated Chattanooga 3 games to 0; Atlanta defeated Memphis 3 games to 2. Finals: Nashville defeated Atlanta 4 games to 2.)

1941	Atlanta	Paul Richards	99	55	.643
	*Nashville	Larry Gilbert	83	70	.542
	New Orleans	Ray Blades	78	75	.510
	Chattanooga	Hazen "Kiki" Cuyler	78	76	.506

(Playoffs: Nashville defeated New Orleans 3 games to 1; Atlanta defeated Chattanooga 3 games to 1. Finals: Nashville defeated Atlanta 4 games to 3.)

1942	Little Rock	Willis Hudlin	87	59	.596
	*Nashville	Larry Gilbert	85	66	.563
	Birmingham	Johnny Riddle	79	73	.520
	New Orleans	Pat Ankenman	77	73	.513

(Playoffs: Nashville defeated Birmingham 3 games to 1; Little Rock defeated New Orleans 3 games to 1. Finals: Nashville defeated Little Rock 4 games to 0.)

1943	*Nashville	Larry Gilbert	83	55	.601
	Nashville (1st half)	Larry Gilbert	49	26	.653
	New Orleans (2nd half)	Ray Blades	40	22	.645

(Nashville defeated New Orleans in playoff 4 games to 1.)

1944	*Nashville	Larry Gilbert	79	61	.564
	Memphis (1st half)	James T. "Doc" Prothro	41	26	.612
	Nashville (2nd half)	Larry Gilbert	47	25	.653

(Nashville defeated Memphis in playoff 4 games to 3.)

1945	Atlanta	Hazen "Kiki" Cuyler	94	46	.671
	Chattanooga	Bert Niehoff	85	55	.607
	*Mobile	Clay Hopper	74	65	.532
	New Orleans	Fresco Thompson	73	67	.521

*Asterisk indicates winning team.

Year	Championship Team	Manager	Won	Lost	Pct.

(Playoffs: New Orleans defeated Atlanta 4 games to 1; Mobile defeated Chattanooga 4 games to 2. Finals: Mobile defeated New Orleans 4 games to 1.)

1946	*Atlanta	Hazen "Kiki" Cuyler	96	58	.623
	Memphis	James T. "Doc" Prothro	90	63	.588
	Chattanooga	Bert Niehoff	79	73	.523
	New Orleans	Johnny Peacock	75	77	.493

(Playoffs: Atlanta defeated New Orleans 4 games to 3; Memphis defeated Chattanooga 4 games to 2. Finals: Atlanta defeated Memphis 4 games to 3.)

1947	*Mobile	Al Todd	94	59	.614
	New Orleans	Fred Walters	93	59	.612
	Nashville	Larry Gilbert	80	73	.523
	Chattanooga	Bert Niehoff	79	75	.513

(Playoffs: Moblle defeated Chattanooga 4 games to 0; Nashville defeated New Orleans 4 games to 1. Finals: Mobile defeated Nashville 4 games to 3.)

1948	Nashville	Larry Gilbert	95	58	.621
	Memphis	Jack Onslow	92	61	.601
	*Birmingham	Fred Walters	84	69	.549
	Mobile	Al Todd	75	75	.500

(Playoffs: Nashville defeated Mobile 4 games to 3; Birmingham defeated Memphis 4 games to 2. Finals: Birmingham defeated Nashville 4 games to 2.)

1949	*Nashville	Rollie Hemsley	95	57	.625
	Birmingham	Frank Higgins	91	62	.595
	Mobile	Paul Chervinko	82	69	.543
	New Orleans	Hugh Luby	77	75	.507

(Playoffs: Nashville defeated New Orleans 4 games to 2; Moblle defeated Birmingham 4 games to 1. Finals: Nashville defeated Mobile 4 games to 2.)

*Asterisk indicates winning team.

Year	Championship Team	Manager	Won	Lost	Pct.
1950	Atlanta	Fred "Dixie" Walker	92	59	.609
	Birmingham	Frank Higgins	87	62	.584
	*Nashville	Don Osborn	86	64	.573
	Memphis	Al Todd	81	70	.536

(Playoffs: Atlanta defeated Memphis 4 games to 0; Nashville defeated Birmingham 4 games to 1. Finals: Nashville defeated Atlanta 4 games to 1.)

1951	Little Rock	Gene Desautels	93	60	.608
	*Birmingham	John "Red" Marion	83	71	.539
	Moblle	Paul Chervinko	80	74	.519
	Memphis	Luke Appling	79	75	.513

(Playoffs: Little Rock defeated Memphis 4 games to 2; Birmingham defeated Mobile 4 games to 0. Finals: Birmingham defeated Little Rock 4 games to 0.)

1952	Chattanooga	Cal Ermer	86	66	.566
	Atlanta	Fred "Dixie" Walker	82	72	.532
	Mobile	Ed Head	80	73	.523
	*Memphis	Luke Appling	81	74	.523
	New Orleans	Danny Murtaugh	80	75	.516

(Note: Memphis defeated New Orleans in a one-game playoff to determine fourth place. Playoffs: Memphis defeated Chattanooga 4 games to 0; Mobile defeated Atlanta 4 games to 2. Finals: Memphis defeated Moblle 4 games to 2 with 1 tie.)

1953	Memphis	Luke Appling	87	67	.565
	*Nashville	Hugh Poland	85	69	.552
	Atlanta	Gene Mauch	84	70	.545
	Birmingham	Mayo Smith	78	76	.506

(Playoffs: Birmingham defeated Memphis 4 games to 1; Nashville defeated Atlanta 4 games to 2. Finals: Nashville defeated Birmingham 4 games to 1.)

1954	*Atlanta	Whitlow Wyatt	94	60	.610
	New Orleans	Danny Murtaugh	92	62	.597
	Birmingham	Mayo Smith	81	70	.536
	Memphis	Don Gutteridge	80	74	.519

(Playoffs: Atlanta defeated Memphis 4 games to 2; New Orleans defeated Birmingham 4 games to 2. Finals: Atlanta defeated New Orleans 4 games to 1.)

*Asterisk indicates winning team.

Year	Championship Team	Manager	Won	Lost	Pct.
1955	Memphis	Jack Cassini–Ted Lyons	90	63	.588
	Birmingham	Phil Page	88	65	.575
	Chattanooga	Cal Ermer	80	74	.519
	*Mobile	Clay Bryant	79	75	.513

(Playoffs: Mobile defeated Memphis 4 games to 3; Birmingham defeated Chattanooga 4 games to 2. Finals: Mobile defeated Birmingham 4 games to 2.)

Year	Championship Team	Manager	Won	Lost	Pct.
1956	*Atlanta	Clyde King	89	65	.578
	Memphis	Jack Cassini–Don Griffiin	82	72	.532
	Mobile	Joyner "Jo Jo" White	82	73	.529
	Birmingham	Phil Page	81	74	.523

(Note: Mobile defeated Birmingham in a one-game playoff to determine third place. Playoffs: Atlanta defeated Birmingham 4 games to 0; Memphis defeated Mobile 4 games to 3. Finals: Atlanta defeated Memphis 4 games to 3.)

Year	Championship Team	Manager	Won	Lost	Pct.
1957	*Atlanta	Buddy Bates	87	67	.565
	Memphis	Lou Klein	86	67	.562
	Nashville	Dick Sisler	83	69	.546
	Chattanooga	Cal Ermer	83	70	.542

(Playoffs: Atlanta defeated Chattanooga 4 games to 2; Nashville defeated Memphis 4 games to 2. Finals: Atlanta defeated Nashville 4 games to 0.)

Year	Championship Team	Manager	Won	Lost	Pct.
1958	*Birmingham	Cal Ermer	91	62	.595
	Mobile	Mel McGaha	84	68	.553
	Atlanta	Buddy Bates	84	70	.545
	Chattanooga	John "Red" Marion	77	76	.503

(Playoffs: Birmingham defeated Chattanooga 4 games to 1; Mobile defeated Atlanta 4 games to 0. Finals: Birmingham defeated Mobile 4 games to 1.)

Year	Championship Team	Manager	Won	Lost	Pct.
1959	Birmingham	Lamar "Skeeter" Newsome	92	61	.601
	Birmingham (1st half)	Lamar "Skeeter" Newsome	38	20	.655
	*Mobile (2nd half)	Mel McGaha	61	34	.642

(Mobile defeated Birmingham in playoff 4 games to 1.)

*Asterisk indicates winning team.

Year	Championship Team	Manager	Won	Lost	Pct.
1960	Atlanta	Albert "Rube" Walker	87	67	.565
	Shreveport	Les Peden	86	67	.562
	*Little Rock	Fred Hatfield	82	69	.543
	Birmingham	Lamar "Skeeter" Newsome	83	70	.542

(Playoffs: Birmingham defeated Atlanta 3 games to 2; Little Rock defeated Shreveport 3 games to 1. Finals: Little Rock defeated Birmingham 3 games to 2.)

Year	Championship Team	Manager	Won	Lost	Pct.
1961	Chattanooga	Frank Lucchesi	90	62	.592

(No playoff.)

SOUTHERN LEAGUE CHAMPIONS

Year	Championship Team	Manager	Won	Lost	Pct.
1964	Lynchburg	George Noga	81	59	.579
1965	Columbus	Loren Babe	79	59	.572
1966	Mobile	John McNamara	88	52	.629
1967	Birmingham	John McNamara	84	55	.604
1968	Asheville	George "Sparky" Anderson	86	54	.614
1969	Charlotte	Ralph Rowe	81	59	.579
1970	Columbus	Jim Williams	78	59	.569
1971					

(The Texas League and Southern League merged in 1971 to form the "Dixie Association." See page 208 for 1971 standings.)

Year	Championship Team	Manager	Won	Lost	Pct.
1972	Asheville (Eastern Division)	Carl Ripken	81	58	.583
	*Montgomery (Western Division)	Fred Hatfield	78	61	.561

(Montgomery defeated Asheville in playoff 3 games to 0.)

*Asterisk indicates winning team.

Year	Championship Team	Manager	Won	Lost	Pct.
1973	Jacksonville (Eastern Division)	Billy Gardner	76	60	.559
	*Montgomery (Western Division)	Fred Hatfield	80	58	.580

(Montgomery defeated Jacksonville in playoff 3 games to 1.)

*Asterisk indicates winning team.

SOUTHERN ASSOCIATION BATTING CHAMPIONS

Year	Player and Club	G	AB	Hits	Pct.
1901	Jack Hulseman, Shreveport	121	487	191	.392
1902	Hugh Hill, Nashville	91	358	149	.416
1903	James Smith, New Orleans–Shreveport	127	361	128	.354
1904	John Gilbert, Little Rock	132	482	158	.327
1905	Carleton Molesworth, Montgomery	129	448	140	.312
1906	Sid Smith, Atlanta	134	420	137	.326
1907	"Buttermilk" Meek, Birmingham	120	441	150	.340
1908	Tris Speaker, Little Rock	127	471	165	.350
1909	Bill McGilvray, Birmingham	143	478	139	.291
1910	Joe Jackson, New Orleans	136	466	165	.354
1911	Derrill Pratt, Montgomery	139	528	167	.316
1912	Harry Welchonce, Atlanta	123	471	157	.325
1913	Harry Welchonce, Atlanta	144	574	194	.338
1914	Harry "Moose" McCormick, Chattanooga	113	404	134	.332
1915	Elmer Miller, Mobile	129	470	153	.326
1916	Bill "Baby Doll" Jacobson, Little Rock	139	508	176	.346
1917	Sam Hyatt, Chattanooga	149	506	169	.334
1918	Ira Flagstead, Chattanooga	49	182	69	.381
1919	Larry Gilbert, New Orleans	136	490	171	.349
1920	Harry Harper, Little Rock	151	567	196	.346
1921	Isaac "Ike" Boone, New Orleans	156	574	223	.389
1922	Dutch Schleibner, Little Rock	150	548	194	.354
1923	Emil Huhn, Mobile	153	531	183	.345
1924	Carlyle Smith, Atlanta	131	475	183	.385
1925	Wilbur Good, Atlanta	152	622	236	.379
1926	Tommy Taylor, Memphis	155	553	212	.383
1927	Wilbur Davis, New Orleans	152	591	222	.376
1928	Elliot Bigelow, Birmingham	134	489	193	.395
1929	Art Weis, Birmingham	148	510	176	.345
1930	Joe Hutcheson, Memphis	121	403	153	.380

Year	Player and Club	G	AB	Hits	Pct.
1931	John "Moose" Clabaugh, Nashville	116	439	166	.378
1932	John "Moose" Clabaugh, Nashville	124	445	170	.382
1933	Frank Waddey, Knoxville	143	562	203	.361
1934	Phil Weintraub, Nashville	101	372	149	.401
1935	Doug Taitt, Nashville	142	546	194	.355
1936	Fred Sington, Chattanooga	142	526	202	.384
1937	Coaker Triplett, Memphis	152	582	207	.356
1938	Johnny Hill, Atlanta	146	544	184	.338
1939	Bert Haas, Nashville	118	460	168	.365
1940	Mike Dejan, Chattanooga–Birmingham	104	304	126	.371
1941	Les Fleming, Nashville	106	374	155	.414
1942	Charles English, Nashville	150	590	201	.341
1943	Ed Sauer, Nashville	136	543	200	.368
1944	Rene Monteagudo, Chattanooga	116	419	155	.370
1945	Gil Coan, Chattanooga	140	540	201	.372
1946	Tom Neill, Birmingham	139	554	207	.374
1947	Ted Kluszewski, Memphis	115	427	161	.377
1948	Forrest "Smokey" Burgess, Nashville	116	433	167	.386
1949	Bob Borkowski, Nashville	140	471	177	.376
1950	Pat Haggerty, Little Rock	142	482	167	.346
1951	Herb Barna, Nashville	131	438	157	.358
1952	Rance Pless, Nashville	135	538	196	.364
1953	Bill Taylor, Nashville	107	406	142	.350
1954	Bob Lennon, Nashville	153	609	210	.345
1955	Charles Williams, Nashville	141	573	211	.368
1956	Stanley Roseboro, Chattanooga	126	473	161	.340
1957	Stan Palys, Nashville	134	493	177	.359
1958	Jim Fridley, Nashville	142	515	179	.348
1959	Gordon Coleman, Mobile	137	507	179	.353
1960	Stan Palys, Birmingham	147	540	200	.370
1961	Don Saner, Little Rock	119	404	141	.349

SOUTHERN LEAGUE BATTING CHAMPIONS

Year	Player and Club	G	AB	Hits	Pct.
1964	Len Boehmer, Macon	140	511	168	.329
1965	Gerry Reimer, Knoxville	132	506	157	.310
1966	John Fenderson, Knoxville	115	429	139	.324
1967	Minnie Mendoza, Charlotte	134	528	157	.297
1968	Arlie Burge, Asheville	123	438	139	.317
1969	Don Anderson, Asheville	133	472	153	.324

Year	Player and Club	G	AB	Hits	Pct.
1970	Steve Brye, Charlotte	106	374	115	.307
1971	Minnie Mendoza, Charlotte	131	516	163	.316
1972	Mike Reinbach, Asheville	136	488	169	.346
1973	Rob Andrews, Asheville	138	541	167	.309

THE DIXIE SERIES

The Dixie Series, inaugurated in 1920, pitted the champions of the Southern Association against the champions of the Texas League. The series was launched only when it was felt that the Texas League had attained equal stature with the Southern.

Almost immediately the Dixie Series became the leading baseball event in America's Southland, but it was suspended after 1958, when the Texas League abandoned the postseason classic in favor of the Pan-American Championships played in conjunction with the Mexican League. The SA passed out of the picture after 1961, but the Dixie Series was revived for one season, in 1967, when the new Southern League champions took on the Texas League champs.

The revival proved short-lived, since the seasons of the two leagues ended at different times (the Southern League had no playoffs, while the Texas League continued to have its regular divisional playoffs, giving it a longer season).

In the thirty-seven years that the Dixie Series was played, the Texas League won 19 times, while the Southern Association/Southern League won 18 times.

RESULTS OF THE DIXIE SERIES

1920   Fort Worth, TL, 4 games; Little Rock, SA, 2 games (1 tie)

1921   Fort Worth, TL, 4 games; Memphis, SA, 2 games

1922   Mobile, SA, 4 games; Fort Worth, TL, 2 games (1 tie)

1923   Fort Worth, TL, 4 games; New Orleans, SA, 2 games (1 tie)

1924   Fort Worth, TL, 4 games, Memphis, SA, 3 games (1 tie)

1925   Fort Worth, TL, 4 games; Atlanta, SA, 2 games

1926   Dallas, TL, 4 games, New Orleans, SA, 2 games (1 tie)

1927   Wichita Falls, TL, 4 games straight; New Orleans, SA, 0

1928   Houston, TL, 4 games; Birmingham, SA, 2 games

1929   Birmingham, SA, 4 games; Dallas, TL, 2 games

1930   Fort Worth, TL, 4 games; Memphis, SA, 1 game

1931   Birmingham, SA, 4 games; Houston, TL, 2 games

1932   Chattanooga, SA, 4 games; Beaumont, TL, 1 game

1933   New Orleans, SA, 4 games; San Antonio, TL, 2 games

1934   New Orleans, SA, 4 games; Galveston, TL, 2 games

1935   Oklahoma City, TL, 4 games; Atlanta, SA, 2 games

1936   Tulsa, TL, 4 games straight; Birmingham, SA, 0

1937   Fort Worth, TL, 4 games; Little Rock, SA, 1 game

1938   Atlanta, SA, 4 games straight (with 1 tie); Beaumont, TL, 0

1939   Fort Worth, TL, 4 games; Nashville, SA, 3 games

1940   Nashville, SA, 4 games; Houston, TL, 1 game

1941   Nashville, SA, defeated Dallas, TL, 4 straight

1942   Nashville, SA, 4 games; Shreveport, TL, 2 games

1943–45 No series.

1946   Dallas, TL, 4 games straight; Atlanta, SA

1947   Houston, TL, 4 games; Mobile, SA, 2 games

1948   Birmingham, SA, 4 games; Fort Worth, TL, 1 game

1949   Nashville, SA, 4 games; Tulsa, TL, 3 games

1950   San Antonio, TL, 4 games; Nashville, SA, 3 games

1951   Birmingham, SA, 4 games; Houston, TL, 2 games

1952   Memphis, SA, 4 games; Shreveport, TL, 2 games

1953   Dallas, TL, 4 games; Nashville, SA, 2 games

1954   Atlanta, SA, 4 games; Houston, TL, 3 games

1955   Mobile, SA, 4 games straight; Shreveport, TL, 0

1956   Houston, TL, 4 games; Atlanta, SA, 2 games

1957   Houston, TL, 4 games; Atlanta, SA, 2 games

1958   Birmingham, SA, 4 games; Corpus Christi, TL, 2 games

1959–66 (No series.)

1967   Birmingham, SL, 4 games; Albuquerque, TL, 2 games

12

THE EASTERN LEAGUE:
Fifty Years of Professional Baseball

EASTERN LEAGUE (CLASS B, 1923–32; CLASS A,
1933–62; CLASS AA, 1963—)
(KNOWN AS THE NEW YORK–PENNSYLVANIA LEAGUE,
1923–37) [1]

Team	Years in Operation
Albany, New York	1937–59
Allentown, Pennsylvania	1935–36, 1954–56, 1957#, 1958–60
Binghamton, New York	1923–37, 1940–63, 1966–68
Bristol, Connecticut	1973—
Charleston, West Virginia	1962–64
Elmira, New York	1923–55, 1961–72
Harrisburg, Pennsylvania	1924–35
Hartford, Connecticut	1938–52
Hazleton, Pennsylvania	1929–32, 1934–37
Johnstown, Pennsylvania	1955#, 1956, 1961
Lancaster, Pennsylvania	1958–61
Manchester, New Hampshire	1969–71
Pawtucket, Rhode Island	1966–67, 1972
Pittsfield, Massachusetts	1965—
Quebec City, Quebec	1971—

[1] See page 323 for Key to Roster of League Teams.

Team	Years in Operation
Reading, Pennsylvania	1933–34, 1952–61, 1963–65, 1967
Schenectady, New York	1951–57
Scranton, Pennsylvania	1923–37, 1939–53
Shamokin, Pennsylvania	1925–27
Sherbrooke, Quebec	1972–73
Springfield, Massachusetts	1939–43, 1957–65
Syracuse, New York	1956–57 (franchise shifted to Allentown on July 13)
Thetford Mines, Quebec	1974—
Three Rivers, Quebec	1971—
Trenton, New Jersey	1936#, 1937–38
Utica, New York	1943–50
Utica–Oneonta, New York	1924
Waterbury, Connecticut	1966–71, 1973—
West Haven, Connecticut	1972—
Wilkes-Barre, Pennsylvania	1923–51, 1953–55 (franchise shifted to Johnstown on July 1)
Williamsport, Pennsylvania	1923–42, 1944–62, 1964–67
York, Pennsylvania	1923–33, 1936, 1958–59, 1962–69

In 1972, the Eastern League celebrated its fiftieth anniversary by having one of its most prosperous years ever. Total attendance for the eight teams reached 678,000, a big improvement over past seasons; for example, 1971 league attendance totaled 567,000, and when the circuit had six teams in 1969 attendance was only 388,000.

Much of the credit for the Eastern League's success must go to Roy Jackson, the dynamic young baseball man who became the league's chief executive in early 1971 following the death of Thomas H. "Tommy" Richardson, one of the great names in Organized Baseball. When Jackson took the reins, he was only thirty-four and was the youngest head of a professional league in the United States. Because of his success in the Eastern League post, Jackson was named as president of the Class AAA Pacific Coast League at the end of 1973.

As one of the country's three Class AA leagues, the Eastern League plays a vital role in the development of talent for the majors. Sometimes it is very difficult to assess the value of one farm club to a parent team. However, it is easy to see that a team like the West Haven Yankees proved its worth in 1972, the first year that Connecticut city ever had a professional team. (After the 1971 campaign the New York Yankees Manchester, New Hampshire, farm in the Eastern League had to find a new home with West Haven being chosen.)

West Haven, loaded with talent, breezed to the pennant, and a number of its stars either crashed the major leagues in 1973 or were being tabbed for promotion in the immediate future. George "Doc" Medich, West Haven's ace pitcher, did very well for New York after his promotion; while Charlie Spikes, a slugging outfielder who led the club with 26 home runs and 111 RBI's, ranked close to the American League leaders in both those departments after he was traded to the Cleveland Indians for 1973.

In this chapter, we are considering the present Eastern League apart from two other circuits which carried that name, specifically the International League (which bore the name as well as several others from its founding in 1884 through 1911) and the Class A Eastern League (which operated from 1916 to June 17, 1932, when it permanently suspended play because of unstable economic conditions caused by the Depression). The current Eastern League does, however, have some direct relationships to the 1916–32 circuit, since it included some of the same towns at one time or another, namely: Albany, Allentown, Hartford, Pittsfield, Springfield, and Waterbury. Moreover, four of the choicest cities of the old EL (Albany, Allentown, Hartford, and Springfield) joined the new EL during the mid to late 1930s. This factor gave the new circuit more strength and viability.

The new Eastern League developed more directly out of the old New York State League, which operated from 1897 through 1917 and then suspended play. The Eastern League picked up the pieces of the New York State League in 1923 and resumed its operations with teams in six cities: Binghamton, Elmira, Scranton, Wilkes-Barre, Williamsport, and York. Bear in mind, though, that the circuit used the name "New York–Pennsylvania League" until 1938, when it was renamed "Eastern League," a more all-inclusive term (since teams from outside the two-state area were being taken in). In taking this action, league officials adopted the name of the defunct 1916–32 organization. (Some baseball historians like to lump all three "Eastern Leagues" into one category for listing purposes, but in the author's estimation, that is not logical).

The new Eastern League began with a B classification in 1923, went up to Class A in 1933, and advanced to its present Class AA rating in 1963.

JOHN H. FARRELL: FOUNDER AND FIRST
PRESIDENT OF THE NEW EASTERN LEAGUE

John H. Farrell, one of the most important figures in minor league history, was the founder and first president of the new Eastern League. From Auburn, New York, he came onto the national scene as one of the founders of the National Association in 1901 and served as its secretary–treasurer continuously from that time until 1931.

Farrell, who enjoyed an extraordinarily long career in Organized Baseball, was also founding president of the old New York State League in 1897, and after that league disbanded (1917), baseball interest remained high in most of the league's cities. (Farrell served as the NYS league's president for its entire twenty-one-year existence.) Four of the six towns that had teams in the NYS League (Binghamton, Elmira, Scranton, and Wilkes-Barre) became charter members of the new New York–Pennsylvania League (or new EL). In 1924, Harrisburg, another old-line NYS team, joined the new circuit.

Eastern League club owners sought out Farrell, a domineering personality and a baseball man respected everywhere, to put together the new league and serve as its president. Farrell accepted the new post and continued on with his important responsibilities with the National Association.

Under John Farrell's guidance all of the Eastern League teams were able to establish some sort of alliance with major league clubs, for he never lost sight of the fact that the minors' most important single function was to develop players. The Elmira Red Jackets franchise, however, was already owned by the Buffalo Bisons of the International League in its inaugural season of 1923. Ownership of the Red Jackets then passed into the hands of a local group (who dealt off star Elmira players to a variety of big league teams), and then in 1931, the franchise was taken over by the St. Louis Cardinals. Over the years Elmira has been affiliated with an assortment of major league teams, as have other clubs in the EL. Affiliations are often switched from one year to another.

Farrell's administrative abilities were of vital importance to the league during its formative years, and when he retired from the presidency in 1929, he was succeeded by his son Perry, who was also an experienced baseball man.

THE EASTERN LEAGUE DURING
THE ROARING TWENTIES

The Eastern League was born during the Roaring Twenties (just like the Middle Atlantic League), when the popularity of pro baseball at all levels reached new highs.

The circuit's inaugural game (on May 9, 1923) had Wilkes-Barre at Williamsport, with the home team winning 10–4. George "Mule" Haas, a nineteen-year-old Williamsport centerfielder, playing in his first pro game, singled and homered in three official trips. Haas went on to the majors and starred on Connie Mack's pennant-winning Philadelphia Athletics in 1929, 1930, and 1931. He was traded to the Chicago White Sox in 1933, and ironically enough, he closed out his playing career with Williamsport during the first part of the 1939 season. He then went on to manage Oklahoma City in the Texas League for the remainder of the season. He spent the entire decade of the 1940s as a Chicago White Sox coach. For Mule Haas it had all began with that 2 for 3 in the Eastern League's first game.

The Williamsport Grays won the pennant in both 1923 and 1924, largely on their robust hitting. The Grays led the league in team batting in 1923, with a fat .318 average (still a league record) and in 1924, with a .306. The game today *is* different. For comparison, Sherbrooke led the EL in team hitting in 1972 with a paltry .268 mark, while Elmira ranked last with a horrendous .218. Too many of the kids in the minors today are trying to hit home runs with those long skinny bats, and they wind up striking out like crazy. That is why the averages are so low.

The Grays were edged out for the 1925 pennant by York in a playoff, but they still managed to punish enemy pitching with a league-leading team batting average of .304. Harry Hinchman, Williamsport's manager during these free-hitting days spent most of his playing career in the minors, but he did get into fifteen games as a second baseman with the Cleveland Indians in 1907. His younger brother Bill, an outfielder–infielder, became the better known ball player, since he logged ten years' service in the majors.

Scranton won the first of its El pennants in 1926, and over the years, it developed into one of the most solid baseball towns in the circuit, often setting attendance records.

PERRY B. FARRELL: A CHIP OFF THE OLD BLOCK

The Eastern League was a pillar of stability during the 1920s, as compared with other leagues of the same classification; but trouble struck in 1929, when Perry Farrell was in his first year in the driver's seat.

It was Perry Farrell who guided the league through the tough Depression years and kept it going when other circuits around the country were falling like tenpins. The younger Farrell, as shrewd an executive as his father, kept the league membership at its full complement of eight teams during the entire lean period. In fact, the league's stature increased when the National Association raised it to an A classification for 1933.

And as indicated earlier, the new Eastern League gained strength when it brought in four of the top cities from the old EL in the years immediately following that circuit's collapse in midseason 1932. When the newer circuit took in Hartford, Connecticut, in 1938 and Springfield, Massachusetts, in 1939 (they had been with the old EL for its entire seventeen-year life), this marked the first time it had moved into New England. Since then the league has almost continuously had at least one team in New England.

THE RICHARDSON YEARS

Thomas H. "Tommy" Richardson (a successful Williamsport auto dealer, sportsman, and a director of the local Grays) was elected league president in November 1937, succeeding Perry Farrell who wanted to devote all his time to his private business. Richardson, now forty-two years old, was already widely known in baseball circles. The Williamsport Grays had become an important farm team for the Philadelphia Athletics, and Richardson became intimately acquainted with Connie Mack, the A's owner–manager, as well as with pro baseball executives at every level around the country.

Richardson guided the Eastern League for twenty-five years: from 1937 to 1960, and again from 1968 to September 1970 (when illness forced his resignation). During most of the intervening years in the 1960s, he took on the demanding post of International League president.

Tommy Richardson was the ideal man to be a league president. He was outgoing, always in demand as a banquet speaker, witty, energetic, imaginative, shrewd, and tough when he had to be.

Shortly after taking office, Richardson, together with the club owners, changed the circuit's name to "Eastern League," and with the new name he began a serious drive to increase attendance in all eight cities. In 1938, the league attracted 718,000 paid admissions (an increase of nearly 180,000 over the previous record), and in 1939, Richardson realized his goal when the EL broke the magic million figure for the first time in its history by drawing 1,075,000 fans. (All figures include attendance during playoffs.)

In 1939, Scranton shattered all single club attendance records when it recorded 317,000 paid admissions. Moreover, in that same year Scranton set a new one-day mark, when 12,630 persons came to see a crucial game with Albany. The EL did not crack the million figure again until 1946, when combined attendance hit 1,055,000.

Richardson, the club owners, and the National Association officials, (together with the blessing of the Roosevelt administration) decided to keep the league operating throughout World War II. War workers in the various EL towns depended upon baseball as a major form of relaxation, and the major leagues (which had President Roosevelt's personal sanction—or "green light"—to continue play) badly needed the few minor leagues still functioning from which to draw players.

During the grimmest days of the war in 1943–44, the Eastern League was one of only ten minor leagues still active. The caliber of ball playing dropped, of course, during this period (as it did from the majors on down), but the EL always had eight teams playing a full 140-game schedule.

Servicemen and servicewomen were admitted without charge to all EL games throughout the war. "This was a small contribution the league made to boost the morale of our men and women in uniform," Richardson commented at the time.

The Eastern League had survived both the severest economic depression the country ever experienced and the most disastrous global conflict experienced by man, and in 1947, it celebrated its twenty-fifth anniversary. The league continued to prosper during the postwar boom, and then survived the decades of the 1950s and 1960s, as the impact of television and a combination of other factors cut the number of pro circuits from a high of fifty-nine in 1949 down to the nineteen or so of recent years.

Charles Darwin always talked about "the survival of the fittest," and there is no questioning the fact that the Eastern League always survived because it was fit. Tommy Richardson died little more than a year before the Eastern League celebrated its fiftieth anniversary in 1972 (commemorative ceremonies were held throughout the circuit to mark the occasion), but he would be glad to know the league is in good hands today and shows every sign of being around to celebrate another milestone anniversary in 1996–97.

In recent years, membership in the Eastern League has been marked by the entrance of cities from Canada. In fact, in 1974, three of the eight cities in the EL were Canadian: Quebec City, Thetford Mines, and Three Rivers (Trois Rivieres), all in Quebec Province. Interestingly enough, these were the only three Canadian cities holding membership in the National Association for 1973. (Montreal, of course, represents Canada in the major leagues.) In past years, these three Canadian cities, along with others, were represented in either or both of the Class C Border and Canadian–American leagues.

THE WEST HAVEN, CONNECTICUT, YANKEES

The New York Yankees switched their Eastern League farm club from Binghamton, New York, to Manchester, New Hampshire, at the beginning of the 1969 season. The switch was possible because a group of Boston businessmen agreed to maintain the working agreement with the Yankees when they bought the franchise. (The Yankees had to leave Binghamton, their long-time EL affiliate, because a highway construction project forced the demolition of the local ball park.) In Manchester, however, the team floundered both on the field and at the box office; and in midseason 1970, Ron Duke of Hanover, Massachusetts, in association with his family and a business friend or two, bought the team.

Duke suffered through the rest of the 1970 season and all of the 1971 campaign at Manchester. In 1971, the paltry paid attendance of 29,000 was by far the lowest in the league.

In 1972, Duke made his big switch to West Haven, keeping in mind that the New Haven metropolitan area had not had a professional team in years. The working agreement with the Yankees was to be maintained.

Somehow, Duke got everything together for 1972. The Yankees named Bobby Cox, one of their former infielders, as manager and sent him some of their best prospects (including Medich and Spikes) and the fans responded as West Haven rolled on to win both the EL pennant and the playoff. In August, for example, West Haven merchants sponsored a "Kid Night," and the city fire marshal forced the event to become a two-night affair when he closed the gates after 7,200 persons had been admitted to the 4,000-seat Quigley Stadium.

Paid attendance for the season's fifty-five home dates reached a very respectable 103,000, the highest figure of any American team in the circuit and a total surpassed only by Quebec City and Three Rivers.

Ron Duke just had one of those natural desires to get into baseball on the executive side. He played a lot of semi-pro ball as an outfielder while a young man in the 1940s, but he could not quite make the big jump to the high classification professional leagues. He then went into the electronics business, where he remained for almost two decades before taking over the Manchester franchise.

His wife Audrey has helped him mightily in both the Manchester and West Haven ventures, and now she is the club's vice president and secretary. Among her many duties are making sure that the scorecards are printed on time, advising the West Haven players with their personal problems, and handling sales at the ticket booth.

Ron Duke is not a middle-aged conservative averse to new ideas. He will try anything within reason to make his operation more attractive. For example, he does not use ushers—rather he has employed usherettes who sport white boots and hot pants! As he sat in the stands at Quigley Field observing his West Haven Yankees going through a pregame drill before an encounter with Three Rivers, he reflected, "I've received the greatest satisfaction in my life through running a professional baseball team."

EASTERN LEAGUE HIGHLIGHTS

1924–25: Tom "Lefty" George, a York pitching ace, chalked up a 25–8 mark in 1924 and a 27–7 mark in 1925. The 27 victories still stands as an Eastern League record. George remained on the York pitching staff until 1933 when he was forty-seven, and then shifted over to Wilkes-Barre in the Inter-State League, where he pitched until he was past fifty. (He had a 7–21 record with four major league clubs between 1911–18.)

1927: Jim Conley of Elmira and John Burke of Harrisburg tied for the league lead in strikeouts. They both whiffed 59 times each, very low for the high mark.

1930: Ken Strong, a Hazleton outfielder, hit 41 home runs and drove in 130 runs; the 41 homers still stand as an Eastern League record. Strong, however, is best remembered as one of the greatest running backs and placekickers in National Football League history. Hazleton led the league with a potent .313 team batting mark, but finished seventh in the standings.

1933: George McQuinn, a Binghamton first baseman and a minor league veteran at twenty-four (he had already played for both New Haven and Albany in the old EL, with Wheeling in the Middle Atlantic League, as well as with Scranton in 1931), led the league with a .357 batting mark. McQuinn went on to perform in the majors for a dozen years, but only after stops with Toronto and Newark in the International League.

1934: The Eastern League adopted the split season plan. (It adopted the Shaughnessy Playoffs Plan in 1937.)

1934–36: Scranton left-hander Joe Shaute, a veteran of thirteen years in the majors, won the pitching percentage title for three years in a row: 1934 (16–3, .842), 1935 (21–7, .750), 1936 (20–7, .741).

1936: Walter "Rabbitt" Maranville, a veteran of twenty-three years in the National League, paced Elmira to the pennant as player–manager. Maranville, then forty-four years old, hit .323 in 123 games and fielded sensationally at both shortstop and second base. Maranville later managed two other EL teams: Albany in 1939 and Springfield in 1941. With Albany he even put himself into six games as a second baseman.

1937: Joe Cicero, a Scranton outfielder, led the league in base stealing for the fifth year in a row, with 40 pilfered sacks. (He stole 190 bases in those five years.) Cicero played briefly for the Boston Red Sox in 1929–30, and did not reach the majors again until he caught on briefly with the Philadelphia A's in 1945.

1941: Charles "Red" Embree, a Wilkes-Barre right-hander, compiled a brilliant 21–5 record, with a 1.69 ERA and 213 strikeouts. The latter figure was then an EL record.

1942: Ralph Kiner, a nineteen-year-old outfielder in his second year of pro ball with Albany, led the EL in homers with 14. After World War II service, Kiner won or shared seven straight National League home run titles.
Allie Reynolds, a Wilkes-Barre fireballer, established an EL record by throwing 11 shutouts in one season. Reynolds had an 18–7 record, with a league leading 1.56 ERA and 193 strikeouts.

1943: Chet Covington, a Scranton left-hander, led all EL pitchers, with a 21–7 mark and a 1.51 ERA. On May 23, he hurled the only nine-inning perfect game in the league's history.

1946: Right-hander Tommy Fine of Scranton established a league record by winning 17 games in succession (a record later broken). On May 13, he was defeated by Hartford 2–1 in a seven-inning game, but he gave up only 2 hits. He won his next 17 outings, and then on August 13 he lasted only 4⅔ innings when Wilkes-Barre routed the Red Sox 15–1. His season record was a glittering 23–3. Fine had a 1–2 record with the parent Boston Red Sox in 1947—this was his only victory in the majors.

Mel Parnell, a Scranton left-hander and Fine's teammate, established the Eastern League ERA record, with a low 1.30 based on a 13–4 log. He went on to become a standout Boston Red Sox moundsman for a decade.

1949: Orie "Old Folks" Arntzen, a forty-year-old Albany right-hander, was named by *The Sporting News* as the Minor League Player of the Year on the strength of his 25–2 record. Arntzen pitched in Organized Baseball from 1931 through 1952, and had one year in the majors, with the Philadelphia A's in 1943.

1953: Rocky Colavito, a twenty-year-old Reading outfielder, won the EL home run crown with 28 circuit clouts. Rocky hit 150 four basers in six different minor leagues before he collected the first of his 374 major league home runs.

1959: In his second year of pro ball, Juan Marichal, a right-hander from the Dominican Republic, led the league with 208 strikeouts, while posting an 18–13 record. After spending half the 1960 season with Tacoma in the Pacific Coast League, he went on to a sensational career with the San Francisco Giants.

1962: Ken "Hawk" Harrelson, a twenty-year-old Binghamton first baseman–outfielder already in his fourth year of pro ball, hit 38 home runs and drove in 138 runs, the latter an EL record. While with the Boston Red Sox in 1968, Harrelson was named by *The Sporting News* as the American League Player of the Year. Within three years after receiving this award, however, Harrelson gave up baseball altogether to become a professional golfer.

1965: Bill MacLeod, a Pittsfield left-hander, broke Tommy Fine's record winning streak of 17 games by taking 18 decisions in a row. MacLeod's 1965 log was 18–0. Though the only pitcher in EL history to finish with a 1.000 percentage, MacLeod stood only fifth in the ERA ratings with a 2.73.

1967: Eastern League pitchers threw a record total of eight no-hitters.

1968: Tony Torchia, a Pittfield outfielder, became the first man in EL history to win the batting title with a sub-.300 average, hitting .294. (This is the same year that Carl Yastrzemski of the Boston Red Sox led the American League in batting with a skinny .301.) Carmen Fanzone, a Pittsfield third baseman, finished second with a low .270; while Gene Clines, a York outfielder, finished in the top ten in batting with a miserable .241.

1971: Quebec City and Three Rivers became the first Canadian cities to join the Eastern League, with Sherbrooke following in 1972. The EL really became an "International League."

1972: Quebec City led the EL in paid admissions with 148,818.

EASTERN LEAGUE PRESIDENTS

Years	President
1923–29	John H. Farrell
1929–37	Perry B. Farrell
1937–60	Thomas H. Richardson
1960–68	A. Rankin Johnson
1968–70	Thomas H. Richardson
1971–73	Roy Jackson

EASTERN LEAGUE CHAMPIONS

Year	Championship Team	Manager	Won	Lost	Pct.
1923	Williamsport	Harry Hinchman	82	42	.661
1924	Williamsport	Harry Hinchman	87	46	.654
1925	*York	Frank Dessau	77	55	.583
	Williamsport	Harry Hinchman	77	55	.583

(Since York and Williamsport finished the regular season in a tie a best of 5 playoff was held. York won the playoff 3 games to 1.)

* Asterisk indicates winning team.

Year	Championship Team	Manager	Won	Lost	Pct.
1926	Scranton	Jim Egan	84	50	.627
1927	Harrisburg	Win Clark	87	51	.630
1928	Harrisburg	Glenn Killinger	82	54	.603
1929	Binghamton	Mike McNally	83	56	.597
1930	Wilkes-Barre	Mike McNally	79	59	.572
1931	Harrisburg	Eddle Onslow	83	56	.597
1932	Wilkes-Barre	Mike McNally	78	61	.561
1933	Binghamton	Bill Meyer	79	55	.590
1934	*Williamsport	Mike McNally	78	60	.565
	Binghamton (1st half)	Bill Meyer	41	28	.594
	Williamsport (2nd half)	Mike McNally	41	27	.603

(Williamsport defeated Binghamton in playoff 4 games to 2.)

1935	Scranton	Joe Shaute	81	54	.600
	Scranton (1st half)	Joe Shaute	44	23	.657
	*Binghamton (2nd half)	Bill Meyer	40	29	.580

(Binghamton defeated Scranton in playoff 4 games to 3.)

1936	Elmira	Walter "Rabbit" Maranville	79	58	.577
	*Scranton (1st half)	Eimer Yoter	42	27	.609
	Elmira (2nd half)	Walter "Rabbit" Maranville	44	26	.629

(Scranton defeated Elmira in playoff 4 games to 0 with 1 tie, but Binghamton, which finished second in each of the split seasons, actually won the season's percentage championship, winning 81 and losing 58 for .583.)

1937	Elmira	Albert Betzel	84	51	622
1938	Binghamton	Albert Betzel	84	51	.622

* Asterisk indicates winning team.

Year	Championship Team	Manager	Won	Lost	Pct.
1939	Scranton	Nemo Leibold	80	60	.571
1940	Scranton	Nemo Leibold	79	60	.568
1941	Wilkes-Barre	Earl Wolgamot	87	51	.630
1942	Albany	James "Rip" Collins	84	56	.600
1943	Scranton	Nemo Leibold	87	51	.630
1944	Hartford	Del Bissonette	99	38	.723
1945	Utica	Eddie Sawyer	83	52	.615
1946	Scranton	Elmer Yoter	96	43	.691
1947	Utica	Eddie Sawyer	90	48	.652
1948	*Scranton	Mike Ryba	89	51	.636
	Albany	Merrill May	86	54	.614
	Utica	Dick Porter	83	56	.597
	Hartford	Earle Browne	74	67	.525

(Playoffs: Scranton defeated Utica 4 games to 1; Albany defeated Hartford 4 games to 3. Finals: Scranton defeated Albany 4 games to 0.)

1949	Albany	Merrill May	93	47	.664
	Scranton	Mike Ryba–Jack Burns	79	61	.564
	Wilkes-Barre	Bill Norman	77	63	.550
	*Binghamton	George Selkirk	70	70	.500

(Playoffs: Wilkes-Barre defeated Albany 4 games to 0; Binghamton defeated Scranton 4 games to 0. Finals: Binghamton defeated Wilkes-Barre 4 games to 3.)

1950	*Wilkes-Barre	Bill Norman	90	48	.652
	Binghamton	George Selkirk	81	58	.583
	Hartford	James "Rip" Collins	80	59	.576
	Albany	Merrill May	66	73	.475

(Playoffs: Wilkes-Barre defeated Hartford 4 games to 2; Binghamton defeated Albany 4 games to 1. Finals: Wilkes-Barre defeated Binghamton 4 games to 1.)

* Asterisk indicates winning team.

Year	Championship Team	Manager	Won	Lost	Pct.
1951	Wilkes-Barre	Bill Norman	85	54	.612
	*Scranton	Jack Burns	77	60	.562
	Elmira	George Fallon	74	64	.536
	Hartford	Tommy Holmes– Travis Jackson	75	65	.536

(Playoffs: Elmira defeated Wilkes-Barre 4 games to 3; Scranton defeated Hartford 4 games to 0. Finals: Scranton defeated Elmira 4 games to 0.)

1952	Albany	Jack Burns	82	54	.603
	*Binghamton	James Gleeson	77	60	.562
	Reading	Kerby Farrell	75	63	.543
	Schenectady	Dan Carnevale	73	65	.529

(Playoffs: Reading defeated Albany 4 games to 1; Binghamton defeated Schenectady 4 games to 3. Finals: Binghamton defeated Reading 4 games to 1.)

1953	Reading	Kerby Farrell	101	47	.682
	*Binghamton	Phil Page	96	55	.636
	Schenectady	Lamar "Skeeter" Newsome	86	65	.570
	Albany	Jack Burns	78	74	.513

(Playoffs: Reading defeated Schenectady 4 games to 2; Binghamton defeated Albany 4 games to 1. Finals: Binghamton defeated Reading 4 games to 2.)

1954	Wilkes-Barre	Dan Carnevale	80	59	.576
	Elmira	Tommy Holmes	77	63	.550
	*Albany	Jack Burns	75	64	.540
	Reading	Merrill May	71	69	.507

(Playoffs: Albany defeated Wilkes-Barre 4 games to 2; Reading defeated Elmira 4 games to 0. Finals: Albany defeated Reading 4 games to 1.)

1955	Reading	Joyner "Jo Jo" White	84	53	.613
	*Allentown	Harold Olt	78	60	.565
	Binghamton	George "Snuffy" Stirnweiss	75	62	.547
	Schenectady	Don Osborn	74	64	.536

* Asterisk indicates winning team.

Year	Championship Team	Manager	Won	Lost	Pct.

(Playoffs: Schenectady defeated Reading 3 games to 1; Allentown defeated Binghamton 3 games to 1. Finals: Allentown defeated Schenectady 3 games to 2.)

Year	Championship Team	Manager	Won	Lost	Pct.
1956	*Schenectady	Richard Carter	84	54	.609
	Binghamton	Freddie Fitzsimmons	81	58	.583
	Reading	Don Heffner	80	59	.576
	Allentown	Nat LeBlan	70	67	.511

(Playoffs: Schenectady defeated Allentown 3 games to 0; Reading defeated Binghamton 3 games to 0. Finals: Schenectady defeated Reading 3 games to 0.)

Year	Championship Team	Manager	Won	Lost	Pct.
1957	Binghamton	Steve Souchock	85	55	.607
	Schenectady	Richard Carter	83	57	.593
	*Reading	Joyner "Jo Jo" White	74	66	.529
	Albany	Eddie Popowski	66	73	.475

(Playoffs: Albany defeated Binghamton 3 games to 2; Reading defeated Schenectady 3 games to 0. Finals: Reading defeated Albany 3 games to 1.)

Year	Championship Team	Manager	Won	Lost	Pct.
1958	*Binghamton (Northern Division, 1st half)	Steve Souchock	45	27	.625
	York (Southern Division, 1st half)	Joe Schultz	40	28	.588
	Williamsport (Northern Division, 2nd half)	Richard Carter	34	27	.557
	Lancaster (Southern Division, 2nd half)	Johnny Pesky	38	24	.613

(Playoffs: Lancaster defeated York 3 games to 1; Binghamton defeated Williamsport 3 games to 0. Finals: Binghamton defeated Lancaster 3 games to 2.)

Year	Championship Team	Manager	Won	Lost	Pct.
1959	*Springfield	Andy Gilbert	85	55	.607
	Allentown	Warren "Sheriff" Robinson	82	59	.582
	Williamsport	Frank Lucchesi	81	60	.574
	Binghamton	Charley Silvera	71	68	.511

(Playoffs: Springfield defeated Binghamton 3 games to 0; Williamsport defeated Allentown 3 games to 0. Finals: Springfield defeated Williamsport 3 games to 1.)

* Asterisk indicates winning team.

Year	Championship Team	Manager	Won	Lost	Pct.
1960	*Williamsport	Frank Lucchesi	76	62	.551
	Binghamton	Damon Phillips	70	69	.504
	*Springfield	Andy Gilbert	69	70	.496
	Reading	Ray Mueller	69	71	.493

(Playoffs: Williamsport defeated Reading 2 games to 0; Springfield defeated Binghamton 2 games to 1. Finals: Williamsport led Springfield 1 game to 0 in the best-of-5 finals when the series was cancelled because of heavy rains. The two clubs were declared playoff co-champions.)

1961	Springfield	Andy Gilbert	85	54	.612

(No playoffs.)

1962	Williamsport	Frank Lucchesi	83	57	.593
	*Elmira	Earl Weaver	72	68	.514
	York	Mel Parnell	70	70	.500
	Springfield	Andy Gilbert	68	72	.486

(Playoffs: Williamsport defeated Springfield 2 games to 1; Elmira defeated York 2 games to 1. Finals: Elmira defeated Williamsport 3 games to 1.)

1963	Charleston	Johnny Lipon	83	57	.593

(No playoffs.)

1964	Elmira	Earl Weaver	82	58	.586

(No playoffs.)

1965	Pittsfield	Eddie Popowski	85	55	.607

(No playoffs.)

1966	Elmira	Darrell Johnson	88	51	.633

(No playoffs.)

1967	*Binghamton (Eastern Division)	Jack Reed	82	58	.586
	Elmira (Western Division)	Billy DeMars	74	65	.532

(Binghamton defeated Elmira In playoff 3 games to 1.)

* Asterisk indicates winning team.

Year	Championship Team	Manager	Won	Lost	Pct.
1968	Pittsfield	Billy Gardner	84	55	.604
	*Reading	Frank Lucchesi	81	59	.579
	Elmira	Carl Ripken	77	63	.550
	Binghamton	Frank Verdi–Cloyd Boyer– James Gleeson	67	72	.482

(Playoffs: Pittsfield defeated Elmira 2 games to 0; Reading defeated Binghamton 2 games to 0. Finals: Reading defeated Pittsfield 3 games to 1.)

1969	York	Joe Morgan	89	50	.640
	Reading	Bob Wellman	81	59	.579
	Elmira	Harry Bright	70	71	.496
	Pittsfield	Billy Gardner	68	72	.486

Playoffs were cancelled after 2 games with Elmira leading Reading 1 game to 0 and Pittsfield leading York 1 game to 0.)

1970	*Waterbury	John "Red" Davis	79	62	.560
	Reading	Andy Seminick	78	63	.553

(Waterbury and Reading finished the regular season in a tie. Waterbury defeated Reading in a one-game playoff 3–2.)

1971	*Elmira (American Division)	Harry Malmberg	78	61	.561
	Three Rivers (National Division)	Jim Snyder	78	59	.569

(Elmira defeated Three Rivers in playoff 3 games to 1.)

1972	*West Haven (American Division)	Bobby Cox	84	56	.600
	Three Rivers (National Division)	Jim Snyder	76	60	.559

(West Haven defeated Three Rivers in playoff 3 games to 0.)

1973	Pittsfield (American Division)	Joe Klein	75	61	.551
	*Reading (National Division)	Cal Emery	76	62	.551

(Reading defeated Pittsfield in playoff 3 games to 1.)

* Asterisk indicates winning team.

EASTERN LEAGUE BATTING CHAMPIONS

Year	Player and Club	G	AB	Hits	Pct.
1923	Walt French, Williamsport	112	465	169	.363
1924	Dewey Steffens, York	130	508	191	.376
1925	Joe Munson, Harrisburg	131	470	188	.400
1926	Red Shilling, York	112	354	125	.353
1927	Mike Martineck, Harrisburg	139	508	186	.366
1928	Dave Robertson, York	123	431	155	.360
1929	Cy Anderson, Williamsport	130	469	179	.382
1930	Horace McBride, Harrisburg	136	524	198	.378
1931	Bill Steinecke, Binghamton	137	496	179	.361
1932	Babe Fischer, Harrisburg	138	530	191	.360
1933	George McQuinn, Binghamton	129	507	181	.357
1934	John Rizzo, Elmira	106	438	166	.379
1935	Mike Martineck, Scranton	136	512	189	.369
1936	Paul Dunlap, Binghamton	126	480	183	.381
1937	Como Cotelle, Albany	122	479	162	.338
1938	Tommy Holmes, Binghamton	135	543	200	.368
1939	George Staller, Elmira	137	557	187	.336
1940	Kermit Lewis, Albany	114	388	126	.325
1941	Frank Madura, Elmira	139	502	161	.321
1942	Steve Souchock, Binghamton	129	476	150	.315
1943	Gene Woodling, Wilkes-Barre	128	453	156	.344
1944	James "Rip" Collins, Albany	100	323	128	.396
1945	John Mayhew, Albany	132	457	147	.322
1946	Sam Mele, Scranton	119	450	154	.342
1947	Joe Tipton, Wilkes-Barre	108	371	139	.375
1948	Bruce Blanchard, Williamsport	135	493	161	.327
1949	Bill Reed, Hartford	114	461	156	.338
1950	George Crowe, Hartford	139	524	185	.353
1951	Bob Verrier, Hartford	117	430	139	.323
1952	Mike Lutz, Reading	116	390	125	.321
1953	Danny Schell, Schenectady	149	556	185	.333
1954	Clyde Parris, Elmira	133	504	158	.313
1955	Zeke Bella, Binghamton	109	372	138	.371
1956	Tony Bartirome, Williamsport	115	442	135	.305
1957	Dick McCarthy, Albany	106	376	123	.327
1958	John Easton, Williamsport	118	473	152	.321
1959	Lou Jackson, Lancaster	132	522	177	.339
1960	Pedro Gonzalez, Binghamton	131	547	179	.327

Year	Player and Club	G	AB	Hits	Pct.
1961	Charles Keller, Binghamton	139	464	162	.349
1962	Jim Ray Hart, Springfield	140	540	182	.337
1963	Bob Chance, Charleston	130	464	159	.343
1964	Paul Blair, Elmira	108	415	129	.311
1965	George Scott, Pittsfield	140	523	167	.319
1966	Howie Bedell, York	107	397	128	.322
1967	Bernie Smith, Williamsport	108	402	123	.306
1968	Tony Torchia, Pittsfield	106	381	112	.294
1969	Robert Kelly, Reading	118	477	154	.323
1970	Greg Luzinski, Reading	141	471	153	.325
1971	Gene Locklear, Three Rivers	124	403	130	.323
1972	Fernando Gonzalez, Sherbrooke	140	517	172	.333
1973	Jim Rice, Bristol	119	423	134	.317

EASTERN LEAGUE RECORDS

Individual Batting Season Records

Highest Percentage
.400—Joe Munson, Harrisburg, 1925

Most Runs Scored
134—Babe Fischer, Harrisburg, 1932

Most Total Bases
355—Joe Munson, Harrisburg, 1925

Most Hits
214—Don Brown, York, 1930

Most Doubles
54—Dewey Steffens, York, 1924

Most Triples
28—Al Gionfriddo, Albany, 1944

Most Home Runs
41—Ken Strong, Hazleton, 1930

Most Runs Batted In
    138—Ken Harrelson, Binghamton, 1962

Most Stolen Bases
    96—Larry Lintz, Quebec City, 1972

Most Bases on Balls
    151—Merrill May, Albany, 1947
    151—Herschel Held, Albany, 1949

Most Times Struck Out
    163—Ed Gagle, Manchester, 1969

Individual Pitching Season Records

Most Games Won
    27—Tom George, York, 1925

Most Games Lost
    24—Ernie Walters, Elmira, 1923

Most Innings Pitched
    325—Hugh Mulcahy, Hazleton, 1936

Most Strikeouts
    258—Fred Norman, Binghamton, 1963

Most Bases on Balls
    180—Dick Rozek, Wilkes-Barre, 1948

Most Hit Batsmen
    21—Dudley Foulk, Williamsport, 1923
    21—Ted Pritchard, Elmira, 1928

13

THE MIDDLE ATLANTIC LEAGUE:
The Toughest Class C Circuit
in the History of Organized Baseball

ROSTER OF MIDDLE ATLANTIC LEAGUE TEAMS
(CLASS C, 1925–42, 1946–51) [1]

Team	Years in Operation
Akron, Ohio	1935–41
Altoona, Pennsylvania	1931 # (franchise shifted to Beaver Falls. See note for Jeannette)
Beaver Falls, Pennsylvania	1931 # (See note for Jeannette)
Beckley, West Virginia	1931–35
Butler, Pennsylvania	1946–51
Canton, Ohio	1936–42
Charleroi, Pennsylvania	1927–31
Charleston, West Virginia	1931–42
Clarksburg, West Virginia	1925–32
Cumberland, Maryland	1925–32
Dayton, Ohio	1933–42
Erie, Pennsylvania	1938–39, 1941–42, 1946–51
Fairmont, West Virginia	1925–31

[1] See page 323 for Key to Roster of League Teams.

Team	Years in Operation
Hagerstown, Maryland	1931 (two months after the season started, Hagerstown moved first to Parkersburg and then to Youngstown)
Huntington, West Virginia	1931–36
Jeannette, Pennsylvania	1926–31 (midway through the 1931 season, Jeannette first moved to Altoona and then to Beaver Falls)
Johnstown, Pennsylvania	1925–38, 1946–50
Lockport, New York	1951
New Castle, Pennsylvania	1948–51
Niagara Falls, New York	1946–47, 1950–51
Oil City, Pennsylvania	1946–51#X (Youngstown franchise shifted to Oil City on June 2 and the Oil City club disbanded on August 6)
Portsmouth, Ohio	1935–40
Scottdale, Pennsylvania	1925–31
Springfield, Ohio	1933–34, 1937–39, 1941–42
Uniontown, Pennsylvania	1926, 1947–49
Vandergrift, Pennsylvania	1947–50X
Wheeling, West Virginia	1925–31, 1933–34
Youngstown, Ohio	1939–41, 1946–51 (see note for Oil City)
Zanesville, Ohio	1933–37, 1941–42

The Middle Atlantic League ranks as one of the most successful of all lower classification leagues in the entire history of the National Association, primarily because it helped to develop some 400 major league players and dozens of big league coaches and executives during its quarter century of operations from 1925 through 1951. The league operated continuously except from 1943 through 1945 when play was temporarily suspended because of World War II. Founded during the height of baseball's "Golden Twenties," the Middle Atlantic League survived and prospered despite emergency franchise shifts, economic depression, floods, and assorted other disasters. Ultimately, the MAL passed from the scene, when blanket television coverage of big league games sounded the death knell for numerous minor league circuits, even those that had hitherto enjoyed good health.

The Middle Atlantic League owes its birth to an out-of-work Pittsburgh sportswriter, Dick Guy. On February 14, 1923, two of Pittsburgh's daily newspapers, the *Leader* (of which Dick Guy was the sports editor) and the *Dispatch* (of which Bill Pete was the sports editor), folded, and two of the city's ablest and most resourceful sportswriters suddenly had nothing to do. Guy and Pete got together almost immediately for a strategy session concerning possible employment opportunities outside Pittsburgh. Guy suggested that they get into professional baseball as proprietors, considering their combined backgrounds; but Pete accepted the post of sports editor offered by a newspaper in Honolulu, and he forgot about the possibilities of life in baseball's executive suite.

Undaunted, Dick Guy pushed on alone. At first he had to be content with an interest in operating the Pittsburgh franchise of the United States Hockey League. He failed at an attempt to gain control of the Syracuse Chiefs in the International League and was thwarted in his efforts to revive the Class B Central League, which was disbanded in 1922. (However, the Central League, which had a spotty history, did resume operations in 1928.)

Finally, in late 1924, Guy received a phone call from Jimmy McGuire, an effervescent Cumberland, Maryland, sports promotor, concerning the possibility of setting up a new baseball circuit for the tri-state area of Maryland, West Virginia, and Pennsylvania. Because of his earlier setbacks in attempting to get established in organized baseball, Guy was wary at first. McGuire, however, had him tabbed as a go-getter, and the two men met to pursue the league idea further. They invited potential franchise holders to a formal meeting, which was held at Pittsburgh's Hotel Henry shortly after New Year's Day, January 1925. The principals in attendance were all eager to get down to business as soon as possible, and the new league was officially launched at the Hotel Henry meeting, with teams being definitely set in five cities: Clarksburg, Fairmont, and Wheeling, West Virginia; Cumberland, Maryland; and Johnstown, Pennsylvania. Though the cities in the circuit were located in three states, they were still grouped fairly close together, with Pittsburgh acting as a kind of focal point.

Of all the key issues discussed at the Pittsburgh organizational session, the most controversial concerned the adoption of a name for the new loop. The wrangling over the name issue dragged on until the wee hours of the following morning, with Dick Guy's proposal of "Middle Atlantic League" finally being adopted unanimously. Middle Atlantic League was an appropriate name for a number of reasons. For example, it fitted the league's general location, and cities could be added later without the necessity of changing the name.

Dick Guy was elected as the league's first president at this meeting. By the middle of March, however, Ray Archibald, a Pittsburgh oil man and president of the Wheeling Stogies, told Guy that he was too busy to operate the club. Guy immediately suggested that they ought to trade jobs. Thus, with the consent of the other owners, Dick Guy took over the management of the Stogies, while Archibald became MAL president.

All of the owners were deeply concerned that an awkward five-team setup could kill the league before it got started. For one thing, scheduling was a problem since one team was forced into idleness each day.

Despite all their trepidations, however, play began in late April. Luck was with the new league as the weather in the early part of the season was ideal for baseball. More importantly, fans in the tri-state area were immediately attracted to the spirited fighting type of baseball offered by the embryonic MAL.

The MAL finally became a six-team league on July 4, when an entry for Scottdale was added for the second half. Scottdale, located some forty miles southeast of Pittsburgh, had a population of about 6,000 at the time and thus became the smallest town in the new league.

Quay King, owner of the Scottdale franchise, had operated a successful semi-pro team in that town for several years. He had wavered in joining the MAL because he felt that the new pro circuit would cause the caliber of the baseball played in his town to drop. With King's semi-pro club kept intact, Scottdale finished a dead last in the MAL for the second half of the 1925 season, winning 18 and losing 41.

Since most of the MAL teams had no firm major league affiliations at this time, Dick Guy's methods of recruiting players were typical for operators of lower classification minor league teams. He signed several of the tri-state area's top sandlotters, as well as experienced semi-pros and outstanding collegians. Among his recruits were the Rooney brothers, Art and Dan, of Pittsburgh. Art gained fame later as the long-time owner and operator of the Pittsburgh Steelers in the National Football League, while Dan entered the Catholic priesthood and eventually became athletic director at St. Bonaventure College at Olean, New York.

During their one year at Wheeling, the brothers were the talk of the league. Art, an outfielder, finished second in the batting race with a .369 mark; while Dan, a catcher, finished third at .359. Art led the MAL in runs, hits, and stolen bases; while Dan led in doubles. Following are their complete batting marks:

	G	AB	R	H	2B	3B	HR	SB	Pct.
Art Rooney	106	388	109	143	26	5	8	58	.369
Dan Rooney	99	374	77	134	35	9	13	8	.359

Johnstown, however, had its own collection of outstanding players, including infielder Mike Martineck who won the batting crown (.372);

and the Johnnies went on to win both halves, eliminating the necessity for a playoff. Johnstown remained as one of the strongest teams in the MAL's early years.

The Johnnies shortstop was a square-jawed eighteen-year-old native of San Francisco who was in his first year of pro ball. His name was Joe Cronin, and he batted a potent .313. Cronin, of course, went on to manage both Washington and Boston in the American League and to earn a niche in baseball's Hall of Fame. He served as American League president from 1959 to 1974.

James "Rip" Collins (then an outfielder) and Eddie Montague (an infielder) were two of the other Johnstown stars who began their pro careers in the MAL's inaugural year. Collins is best remembered as the hard-hitting first baseman on the St. Louis Cardinals "Gashouse Gang" of the 1930s, while Montague went on to become a shortstop for the Cleveland Indians for several years.

While the MAL to a large extent operated independently of the majors at this time, the Pittsburgh Pirates worked fairly closely with Johnstown, since they optioned a number of their promising young players to the Johnnies (including Martineck, Cronin, and Montague). This was a major factor accounting for Johnstown's early success in the league. The balance of the team's players, including Rip Collins, came from semi-pro circuits.

As the Middle Atlantic League developed and prospered, all sixteen of the major league organizations established working agreements with teams in this fast Class C circuit at one time or another. Because the major leagues sent some of their hottest prospects here for instruction and seasoning, the MAL was able to compile a long list of alumni who reached the "big show" (see pages 279–81).

At the conclusion of the 1925 season, Ray Archibald resigned the MAL presidency because of the increasing personal responsibilities connected with his oil business. Club owners met in special session in order to fill the post. Dozens of names were suggested but no one of them could satisfy all the owners. Finally, after hours of bickering and shouting, Dick Guy took the floor and announced, "I have a man in mind whom I've never mentioned before and whom I know can do a great job for the Middle Atlantic League."

The man was Elmer M. Daily, an all-around athlete in his student days at Bethany College, a pitcher in the old New York–Pennsylvania League, and an athletic coach at Waynesburg and West Virginia Wesleyan colleges. Daily was contacted at his home in Windber, Pennsylvania, and the post was formally offered to him. At first Daily was reluctant to take on the job, but upon being assured that his nomination had the unanimous support of the club owners, he accepted the MAL presidency. He continued in that position until the MAL passed from the professional baseball scene twenty-six years later. Thus, he held one of the longest tenures among league presidents in the history of Organized Baseball.

It was Elmer Daily more than anyone else who kept the Middle Atlantic League operating as a viable enterprise for a quarter of a century. He was particularly adept at helping to rejuvenate an ailing franchise— but when a franchise was too far gone to benefit from even his skilled doctoring, he was just as adept in finding a new town to "take in" a homeless team.

When the 1926 season began, Dick Guy was still at the helm of the Wheeling Stogies as president, but before the campaign ended, he sold his interest in the club and bowed out of the MAL altogether. By this time he had already succeeded in making a permanent contribution to professional baseball.

Under Daily's leadership, the MAL expanded to an eight-club circuit in 1926, adding Uniontown and Jeannette. (Uniontown, however, failed to attract sufficient patronage and dropped out of the league at season's end; Charleroi was brought in to fill the gap the next year. The Uniontown "Coal Barons" were to reenter the loop twenty years later.)

Johnstown won the league championship again in 1926, despite the loss of most of its stars (who went on to teams in higher classifications). The Johnnies were managed for a second year by Norman McNeill, who saw long service as a catcher in the minors and who played briefly with the Boston Red Sox. While Fairmont did win second-half honors, the Johnnies defeated the West Virginians in the playoffs 4 games to 2.

The Cumberland Colts broke Johnstown's hold on the MAL championship in 1927 by beating the Johnnies in the playoffs 4 games to 2. The Colts under catcher–manager Gus Thompson easily won first-half honors, while the Johnnies, directed by Charles "Babe" Adams (who had just completed a twenty-year career as a National League pitcher with 194 victories and 140 defeats, floundered to a 22–34 mark. Harry Meehan, Johnstown's president, bought out Adams' contract at midseason for a reported $5,000—a great deal of money for a minor league manager's contract in those days—and promptly hired another old big league pitcher to run the Johnnies, Charles "Chief" Bender. Bender, who won 208 games for the Philadelphia Athletics, and was now forty-three years of age, led Johnstown to second-half honors not only through his managing but also by taking the mound and chalking up a 7–3 record with a glittering 1.33 ERA. Although the Johnnies could not continue their momentum into the playoffs against the Colts, they had, nevertheless, satisfied Meehan; they drew record crowds both at home and on the road whenever Chief Bender took the mound.

Bender's stay at Johnstown was brief, for he signed to coach the U.S. Naval Academy baseball team for the 1928 season and then went on to manage a succession of minor league teams around the country before rejoining the Philadelphia Athletics as a scout in 1947. He was elected to the Hall of Fame in 1953, one year before his death.

Teams of the Middle Atlantic League continued to supply baseball fans with plenty of solid action down through the years, and from this point on we will survey the highlights.

MIDDLE ATLANTIC LEAGUE HIGHLIGHTS

1928: Joe Drugmond, pitching ace for the Charleroi Governors, was awarded the league prize of $100 for being voted the Most Valuable Player. He chalked up a 23–12 record, and his 307 innings pitched is the all-time MAL high.

1929: The MAL was now considered a great hitting league, since 58 players on the 8 teams in 1929 batted .300 or better. Fred Lucas, a Charleroi outfielder, became the first man in the circuit to crack the .400 barrier swatting .407 in 113 games.

The league had an excellent year financially with good attendance.

1930: Joe Medwick, a husky eighteen-year-old Scottdale outfielder from Carteret, New Jersey, in his first year of pro ball, won the batting title with a .419 mark, the highest in MAL history. The future Hall of Famer rapped 139 hits and drove in 100 runs in only 75 games. Some MAL historians felt that Frank Doljack, a Wheeling outfielder (officially ranked second with a .386 average in 116 games), should have been awarded the batting crown because he played in more than 100 games. According to the rules at that time, however, a player needed to get into just over half of his team's contests to qualify. Later the rules were changed so that a player had to take part in three-quarters of the regularly scheduled games to qualify for the batting championship.

Frank Doljack finished the 1930 season with the Detroit Tigers and remained in the big leagues through 1934. He also played a few games with the Cleveland Indians in 1943.

1931: Gordon "Babe" Phelps, a Hagerstown–Youngstown catcher, won the batting title with a .408 average and finished the season with

Washington. Phelps remained in the majors for eleven years and compiled a lifetime batting mark of .310, one of the highest in history for a catcher.

The MAL operated as a twelve-club circuit and had the distinction of being the minor league with the greatest number of teams up to that point.

1932: During this season, the deepest of all Depression years, the MAL dropped from twelve to six teams. Charleroi, Fairmont, Jeannette, Hagerstown, Scottdale, and Wheeling—all active in 1931—withdrew because of financial difficulties.

1933: The MAL got back up to the eight-club level, a really unusual occurrence since membership in the National Association fell to a low of fourteen leagues. Cumberland and Clarksburg dropped out of the loop; but Wheeling came back in after a lapse of one year, and Dayton, Springfield, and Zanesville (all in Ohio) were added to the league membership.

The majors continued to show great interest in the MAL. For example, Wheeling became a New York Yankee farm club with George Weiss acting as president.

1934: Howard "Ducky" Holmes, Dayton's colorful owner–manager (he was a catcher for the St. Louis Cardinals in 1906), attracted nearly 120,000 paid admissions into his newly completed park, appropriately called "Ducks Park."

1935: With Wheeling and Springfield dropping out of the league and being replaced by two new cities, Akron and Portsmouth, Johnstown was the only surviving MAL charter member. Jimmy Wasdell, a Zanesville first baseman in his first year of pro ball, won the batting crown with a .357 mark and set the all-time league mark in two-base hits with 54. Wasdell went on to have a successful ten-year career in the majors.

Tommy Henrich, Wasdell's teammate on the Zanesville Greys and a future New York Yankees star outfielder, batted a healthy .337 and rapped out 56 extra base hits, including 43 doubles. Henrich had spent the 1934 season, his first year in pro ball, with Monessen, Pennsylvania, of the Class D Penn State League, a circuit that served as a kind of "farm system" for the MAL. That is how tough the Middle Atlantic League was with only a Class C status. (The Penn State Association operated from 1934 through 1942.) Zanesville, one of the most powerful teams in the league, enjoyed an excellent working agreement with the Cleveland Indians.

1936: Jeff Heath, a husky twenty-year-old outfielder for the champion Zanesville Greys, drove in 187 runs (in only 124 games) for the all-time MAL record. Heath's .383 average was second only to Charleston out-fielder Barney McCosky's .407. "Jolly Jeff," as he was called during his 14-year big league career, was called up by the Cleveland Indians late in the season and batted .341 in 12 games, knocking in 8 more runs. When Heath's big league career ended because of injuries, he signed a playing contract with Scattle of the Pacific Coast League for the 1950 season for a reported $25,000, making him one of the highest salaried minor leaguers in history up to that time.

Walter Alston, a twenty-four-year-old Huntington first baseman–outfielder in his second year of pro ball, led the league with 35 homers. Alston was called up by the St. Louis Cardinals at the end of the season and got into one game, the only action he ever saw as a big league player.

1937: Floyd "Pat" Patterson, the Canton Terrier's player–manager led his teams to a photo-finish percentage championship over Springfield by defeating Portsmouth in a doubleheader on the last day of the season. Patterson, a fine outfielder, swatted .358, the third best average in the league. Canton served as a Boston Red Sox farm club.

1938: George "Whitey" Kurowski, a twenty-year-old Portsmouth third baseman, paced his team to the league title with a championship .386 average. First baseman Walt Alston contributed 28 homers and 106 RBI's to the Portsmouth cause. Portsmouth had a working agreement with the Pittsburgh Pirates when it entered the league in 1935, but it switched its affiliation to the St. Louis Cardinals for the 1938 season.

1939: Youngstown replaced Johnstown, as the Johnnies, the last charter member of the MAL, dropped out of the league. The Johnnies, however, reentered the league in 1946.

1940: Walter Alston, one of the most durable and successful man-agers in big league history, began his managing career with Portsmouth. He switched over to Springfield of the MAL for the 1941–42 season, where he continued playing as a home run-hitting first baseman.

1941: The league dropped back to a six-team loop, with Erie and Springfield leaving the fold.

The MAL went back up to eight teams as Portsmouth dropped out and Zanesville and Springfield rejoined.

Lou Lucier, a Canton right-hander, led the league in pitching with a 23–5 record and a remarkable 1.51 ERA. Lucier pitched briefly with the Boston Red Sox in 1943–45.

Springfield manager Walt Alston was named first baseman on the MAL all-star team.

1942: Akron and Youngstown strayed from the MAL flock, as the league again fielded only six teams.

Pitchers seemed to be dominant, as only eleven hitters entered the charmed .300 circle. Six pitchers finished with ERA's of less than 2.00, a league record.

1943–45: Wartime conditions caused the suspension of play. MAL officials sent Judge W. G. Bramham, the National Association's president, a letter on February 21, 1943, which read in part:

> . . . The action concerning suspension of operations becomes effective as of February 25, 1943. This was deemed necessary because of the World War emergency, and its attendant circumstances such as transportation difficulties, lack of manpower, and local conditions in our league cities. . . ."

1946: A league reorganization meeting was held at Erie in January. Six teams made up the postwar league: Erie, Johnstown, and Youngstown, previous league members; and Butler, Oil City, and Niagara Falls, first-time members.

Erie became the dominant team in the MAL's final six years, winning 3 percentage championships and 3 playoff championships.

1947: The league expanded to eight teams again with the reentry of Uniontown (after an absence of twenty-one years) and the addition of Vandergrift. Pat Patterson, a veteran MAL manager, led Vandergrift to the percentage and playoff championships in the Pioneers' baptismal year in the circuit.

1948: On August 17, the Vandergrift Pioneers, en route toward their second straight pennant, annihilated the Oil City Refiners 30–4, scoring the most runs in a single game of any MAL team in history. The rout took place at Vandergrift's Davis Field. Manager Lew Krausse's charges scored 4 runs in the second, 7 in the fourth, 11 in the fifth, 3 in the eighth, and 5 in the ninth (for some strange reason, the Pioneers batted in the last half of the ninth even though they were the home club). Vandergrift had "only" 22 hits, but Oil City pitchers gave up 17 walks along the way. Hitting stars for the Pioneers were right-fielder Herman Kiel and third baseman Rocky Tedesco. Kiel smashed 3 home runs (2 of them in the big fifth inning) and drove in 5 runs, while Tedesco whacked 4 doubles and a single in 5 official trips to the plate; his 9 RBI's established a new league record.

1949: The Erie Sailors under manager Pete Pavich, veteran of many years service in the high minors as an infielder, continued their dominance of the MAL by winning the pennant and their second straight playoff title.

1950: Butler, formerly a member of the Penn State Association, won its only playoff title in the MAL. Marvin Olson, the Butler's manager and veteran of many years in professional baseball, saw service as a Boston Red Sox second baseman in the 1930s.

1951: Niagara Falls achieved its only playoff championship (against pennant-winning Erie in the final Middle Atlantic League season). Rudy York, a thirty-eight year old long-time American league slugger, was in his last year of pro ball as a player. He led the MAL in home runs, with 34, while serving as the first-string catcher for Youngstown–Oil City.

League attendance fell 202,255 (for six teams). MAL officials, including President Elmer M. Daily and Secretary–Treasurer Russell Hockenbury, along with team owners, reluctantly decided to suspend operations permanently. With televised major league baseball covering the area, the league was no longer economically viable.

MAJOR LEAGUE PLAYERS FROM THE MIDDLE ATLANTIC LEAGUE

Player and Position	Team Entered Majors With	Middle Atlantic League Team
Hegan, Jim, C	Cleveland, AL	Springfield
Lemon, Bob, P	Cleveland, AL	Springfield
Milnar, Al, P	Cleveland, AL	Zanesville
Reynolds, Allie, P	Cleveland, AL	Springfield
Donald, Atley, P	New York, AL	Wheeling
Murphy, Johnny, P	New York, AL	Scottdale
Rosar, Buddy, C	New York, AL	Wheeling
Sundra, Steve, P	New York, AL	Zanesville
Tamulis, Vito, P	New York, AL	Beckley

Player and Position	Team Entered Majors With	Middle Atlantic League Team
Dorish, Harry, P	Boston, AL	Canton
Hughson, Tex, P	Boston, AL	Canton
Ostermueller, Fritz, P	Boston, AL	Wheeling
Parnell, Mel, P	Boston, AL	Canton
Ryba, Mike, P	Boston, AL	Scottdale
Solters, Julius, OF	Boston, AL	Fairmont
Baker, Floyd, Inf	Chicago, AL	Youngstown
Rigney, John, P	Chicago, AL	Portsmouth
Bridges, Tommy, P	Detroit, AL	Wheeling
Fox, Pete, OF	Detroit, AL	Wheeling
Hogsett, Elon, P	Detroit, AL	Wheeling
Mayo, Eddie, Inf	Detroit, AL	Johnstown
Outlaw, Jimmy, OF	Detroit, AL	Beckley
Walker, Gerald, OF	Detroit, AL	Wheeling
Berardino, John, Inf	St. Louis, AL	Johnstown
Dillinger, Bob, Inf	St. Louis, AL	Youngstown
Galehouse, Denny, P	St. Louis, AL	Johnstown
Judnich, Walt, OF	St. Louis, AL	Akron
McQuinn, George, 1B	St. Louis, AL	Wheeling
Stephens, Vern, Inf.	St. Louis, AL	Johnstown
Swift, Bob, C	St. Louis, AL	Charleston
Siebert, Dick, 1B	Philadelphia, AL	Dayton
Suder, Pete, Inf	Philadelphia, AL	Akron
Wolff, Roger, P	Philadelphia, AL	Dayton
Powell, Jake, OF	Washington, AL	Dayton
Masi, Phil, C	Boston, NL	Springfield
Ross, Chet, OF	Boston, NL	Zanesville
Workman, Charley, OF	Boston, NL	Springfield
Hassett, Buddy, 1B	Brooklyn, NL	Wheeling
Rojek, Stan, Inf	Brooklyn, NL	Dayton
Chiozza, Lou, Inf	Philadelphia, NL	Beckley
Litwhiler, Danny, OF	Philadelphia, NL	Charleston
May, Merrill, 3B	Philadelphia, NL	Cumberland
Passeau, Claude, P	Philadelphia, NL	Charleston
Gumbert, Harry, P	New York, NL	Charleroi
Parmelee, Roy, P	New York, NL	Charleroi
Ripple, Jimmy, OF	New York, NL	Jeannette
Voiselle, Bill, P	New York, NL	Canton
Dyer, Eddie, Inf	St. Louis, NL	Scottdale
Marion, Marty, SS	St. Louis, NL	Huntington
Sauer, Ed, OF	St. Louis, NL	Zanesville

Player and Position	Team Entered Majors With	Middle Atlantic League Team
White, Ernie, P	St. Louis, NL	Portsmouth
Tobin, Jim, P	Pittsburgh, NL	Wheeling
Westlake, Wally, OF	Pittsburgh, NL	Dayton
Bryant, Clay, P	Chicago, NL	Zanesville
Gleeson, Jimmy, OF	Chicago, NL	Zanesville
Lee, Bill, P	Chicago, NL	Scottdale
McCullough, Clyde, C	Chicago, NL	Akron
Gamble, Lee, OF	Cincinnati, NL	Beckley
Lakeman, Al, C	Cincinnati, NL	Beckley
McCormick, Frank 1B	Cincinnati, NL	Beckley
McCormick, Mike, OF	Cincinnati, NL	Zanesville
Miller, Eddie, Inf	Cincinnati, NL	Springfield
Vander Meer, Johnny, P	Cincinnati, NL	Dayton

(Note: A few of the players cited here had Class D experience before they saw service with the Middle Atlantic League. Only players who have not been mentioned previously in this chapter are included.)

MIDDLE ATLANTIC LEAGUE
CHAMPIONS

Year	Championship Team	Manager	Won	Lost	Pct.
1925	Johnstown	Norman McNeill	64	31	.674
	Johnstown (1st half)	Norman McNeill	25	14	.641
	Johnstown (2nd half)	Norman McNeill	39	17	.696
1926	*Johnstown	Norman McNeill	63	43	.594
	Johnstown (1st half)	Norman McNeill	39	20	.661
	Fairmont (2nd half)	Joe Phillips	32	19	.627

(Johnstown defeated Fairmont in playoff 4 games to 2.)

1927	*Cumberland	Guy Thompson	66	47	.584
	Cumberland (1st half)	Guy Thompson	37	19	.661
	Johnstown (2nd half)	Chief Bender	35	21	.625

(Cumberland defeated Johnstown in playoff 4 games to 2.)

1928	*Fairmont	Joe Phillips	70	51	.581
	Wheeling (1st half)	Bob Prysock	36	20	.643
	Fairmont (2nd half)	Joe Phillips	39	24	.619

(Fairmont defeated Wheeling in playoff 4 games to 2.)

* Asterisk indicates winning team.

Year	Championship Team	Manager	Won	Lost	Pct.
1929	*Charleroi	Bob Rice	67	47	.587
	Charleroi (1st half)	Bob Rice	37	23	.617
	Wheeling (2nd half)	Pat Haley	37	22	.627

(Charleroi defeated Wheeling in playoff 4 games to 1.)

1930	*Johnstown	Wilbur Good	64	63	.504
	Johnstown (1st half)	Wilbur Good	36	20	.643
	Clarksburg (2nd half)	Earl "Greasy" Neale	37	24	.607

(Johnstown defeated Clarksburg in playoff 4 games to 3.)

1931	*Cumberland	Leo Mackey	82	46	.640
	Cumberland (1st half)	Leo Mackey	42	19	.689
	Charleston (2nd half)	Dick Hoblitzell	39	21	.650

(Cumberland defeated Charleston in playoff 4 games to 2.)

1932	*Charleston	Dan Boone	70	54	.564
	Beckley (1st half)	Frank Welch	34	25	.576
	Charleston (2nd half)	Dan Boone	39	26	.600

(Charleston defeated Beckley in playoff 4 games to 2.)

1933	*Zanesville	"Buzz" Wetzel	76	59	.563
	Zanesville (1st half)	"Buzz" Wetzel	38	29	.567
	Wheeling (2nd half)	John T. Sheehan	45	26	.634

(Zanesville defeated Wheeling in playoff 4 games to 1.)

1934	*Zanesville	Harry Lane	72	51	.585
	Dayton (1st half)	"Ducky" Holmes	37	25	.597
	Zanesville (2nd half)	Harry Lane	42	19	.689

(Zanesville defeated Dayton in playoff 4 games to 3.)

1935	*Huntington	Benny Borgmann	60	58	.508
	Huntington (1st half)	Benny Borgmann	39	22	.639
	Dayton (2nd half)	Riley Parker	40	23	.635

(Huntington defeated Dayton in playoff 4 games to 2.)

* Asterisk indicates winning team.

Year	Championship Team	Manager	Won	Lost	Pct.
1936	*Zanesville	Earl Wolgamot	81	48	.628
	Zanesville (1st half)	Earl Wolgamot	41	25	.621
	Dayton (2nd half)	"Ducky" Holmes	40	23	.635
	Zanesville (2nd half)	Earl Wolgamot	40	23	.635

(Zanesville defeated Dayton 2 games to 1 for the second-half and league championships.)

1937	*Canton	"Pat" Patterson	81	46	.638
	Springfield	Earl Wolgamot	81	47	.633
	Portsmouth	Benny Borgmann	72	57	.558
	Akron	Leo Mackey	64	61	.512

(Playoffs: Canton defeated Portsmouth 3 games to 1; Akron defeated Springfield 3 games to 1. Finals: Canton defeated Akron 3 games to 2.)

1938	*Portsmouth	Benny Borgmann	79	50	.612
	Canton	"Pat" Patterson	79	51	.608
	Springfield	Earl Wolgamot	71	59	.546
	Akron	"Pip" Koehler	66	62	.516

(Playoffs: Portsmouth defeated Springfield 3 games to 1; Akron defeated Canton 3 games to 0. Finals: Portsmouth defeated Akron 4 games to 3.)

1939	*Canton	"Pat" Patterson	77	52	.597
	Charleston	Ed Hall	70	60	.538
	Akron	"Pip" Koehler	69	61	.531
	Springfield	Earl Wolgamot	66	64	.508

(Playoffs: Canton defeated Akron 3 games to 1; Springfield defeated Charleston 3 games to 1. Finals: Canton defeated Springfield 4 games to 1.)

1940	*Akron	"Pip" Koehler	73	54	.575
	Charleston	Ed Hall	64	62	.508
	Youngstown	Rodney Whitney	62	62	.500
	Dayton	Andy Cohen	60	65	.480

(Playoffs: Akron defeated Youngstown 3 games to 2; Dayton defeated Charleston 3 games to 1. Finals: Akron defeated Dayton 3 games to 2.)

* Asterisk indicates winning team.

Year	Championship Team	Manager	Won	Lost	Pct.
1941	Akron	Ralph Boyle	77	48	.616
	*Erie	Kerby Farrell	75	51	.595
	Canton	"Pat" Patterson	71	54	.568
	Springfield	Walter Alston	69	57	.548

(Playoffs: Erie defeated Springfield 3 games to 0; Canton defeated Akron 3 games to 2. Finals: Erie defeated Canton 4 games to 1.)

1942	Charleston	Jack Knight	75	51	.595
	Dayton	Paul Chervinko– "Ducky" Holmes	74	53	.583
	Canton	"Pat" Patterson	68	61	.527
	*Erie	Kerby Farrell	63	.65	.492

(Playoffs: Canton defeated Charleston 3 games to 0; Erie defeated Dayton 3 games to 2. Finals: Erie defeated Canton 4 games to 0.)

1943–45 (League suspended operations because of World War II.)

1946	*Erie	Steve Mizerak	91	39	.700
	Butler	Milton Rosner	78	52	.600
	Youngstown	Paul Birch	67	62	.519
	Niagara Falls	George Prochel	64	66	.492

(Playoffs: Erie defeated Youngstown 3 games to 1; Niagara Falls defeated Butler 3 games to 1. Finals: Erie defeated Niagara Falls 4 games to 3.)

1947	*Vandergrift	"Pat" Patterson	76	46	.623
	Niagara Falls	Charles Engle	68	55	.553
	Erie	Don Cross	68	56	.549
	Butler	Dallas Warren	62	62	.500

(Playoffs: Vandergrift defeated Erie 3 games to 0; Butler defeated Niagara Falls 3 games to 2. Finals: Vandergrift defeated Butler 4 games to 0.)

1948	Vandergrift	"Pat" Patterson– Lew Krausse	86	39	.688
	*Erie	Don Ramsay	80	44	.645
	Uniontown	Billy Mongiello	77	49	.611
	Johnstown	Roy Nichols	67	57	.540

* Asterisk indicates winning team.

Year	Championship Team	Manager	Won	Lost	Pct.

(Note: Patterson became ill in late July and was relieved as manager by Lew Krausse for the remainder of the season. Playoffs: Vandergrift defeated Uniontown 3 games to 1; Erie defeated Johnstown 3 games to 1. Finals: Erie defeated Vandergrift 4 games to 1.)

Year	Championship Team	Manager	Won	Lost	Pct.
1949	*Erie	Pete Pavich	85	53	.616
	Johnstown (1st half)	Roy Nichols	41	29	.586
	Erie (2nd half)	Pete Pavich	48	21	.696

(Erie defeated Johnstown in playoff 4 games to 3.)

Year	Championship Team	Manager	Won	Lost	Pct.
1950	Oil City	Jim Davis	70	44	.617
	*Butler	Marvin Olson	67	49	.578
	Erie	Pete Pavich	63	52	.548
	New Castle	Charles Cronin	64	54	.542

(Playoffs: Oil City defeated Erie 3 games to 0; Butler defeated New Castle 3 games to 2. Finals: Butler defeated Oil City 4 games to 3.)

Year	Championship Team	Manager	Won	Lost	Pct.
1951	Erie	Pete Appleton	85	40	.680
	*Niagara Falls	Jim Davis	74	47	.612

(Niagara Falls defeated Erie in playoff 4 games to 2.)

* Asterisk indicates winning team.

MIDDLE ATLANTIC LEAGUE BATTING CHAMPIONS

Year	Player and Club	G	AB	Hits	Pct.
1925	Mike Martineck, Johnstown	97	374	139	.372
1926	Deney Sothern, Cumberland	95	390	146	.374
1927	Doc Weber, Wheeling	119	456	155	.340
1928	Bill Pritchard, Clarksburg–Wheeling	106	373	138	.370
1929	Fred Lucas, Charleroi	113	437	178	.407
1930	Joe Medwick, Scottdale	75	332	139	.419
1931	Gordon "Babe" Phelps, Hagerstown	115	436	178	.408
1932	Fred Sington, Beckley	102	400	147	.368
1933	Pepper Barry, Johnstown	128	538	194	.361
1934	Vernon Mackie, Johnstown	95	354	129	.365
1935	Jimmy Wasdell, Zanesville	125	510	182	.357
1936	Barney McCosky, Charleston	108	407	163	.400

Year	Player and Club	G	AB	Hits	Pct.
1937	Frank Scalzi, Springfield	127	523	197	.377
1938	George "Whitey" Kurowski, Portsmouth	129	542	209	.386
1939	Ed Murphy, Portsmouth	106	392	147	.375
1940	Edward J. Tighe, Akron	117	449	146	.325
1941	Como Cotelle, Dayton–Erie	112	409	150	.367
1942	Como Cotelle, Erie	123	422	138	.327
1943–45	(Play was suspended.)				
1946	Cy Pfeifer, Johnstown	106	323	111	.344
1947	Alex Garbowski, Vandergrift	111	402	158	.396
1948	Art Seguso, Butler	119	442	158	.357
1949	Robert Betz, Youngstown	133	525	181	.345
1950	Robert Huddleston, Oil City	92	338	123	.364
1951	Walter Kowalski, New Castle	112	451	169	.375

14

BASEBALL IN MEXICO

The Mexican Baseball League declared war on both major leagues in 1946, when it raided the rosters of teams in both the American and National circuits for top players. Behind the Mexican organization was President Jorge Pasquel and his four brothers, who controlled a fortune said to be worth $60,000,000. The Pasquel brothers offered long-term six-figure contracts to such stars as Hank Greenberg, Bob Feller, and Stan Musial; but they were unsuccessful in luring them south of the border. However, they were able to sign a great number of established big league regulars, such as Sal Maglie and Danny Gardella of the New York Giants, Mickey Owen of the Brooklyn Dodgers, and Max Lanier of the St. Louis Cardinals.

Players who jumped contracts to sign with the outlaw Mexican League were suspended from Organized Baseball in the United States for a period of five years by Commissioner A. B. "Happy" Chandler.*

Most of the American players, however, soon found that they did not like the playing facilities, weather, altitude, food, and other conditions of the Mexican League. Jorge Pasquel himself became disenchanted when he discovered that it was not possible to turn a profit in operating

---

* A number of Mexican cities had been members of various leagues in the National Association for a number of years, however. Nogales, Sonora, for example, had been in the Arizona-Texas League as early as 1931, while a total of five Mexican towns, including Nogales, fielded entries in the Arizona-Texas League in the late 1940s and early 1950s.

the league, and in 1948, he pulled out of baseball completely and turned to such other diversions as big-game hunting and politics.

Finally, on June 5, 1949, Commissioner Chandler rescinded his ban on the big league contract jumpers, and they were free to rejoin their old teams. The Mexican League continued to operate with the use of native players only.

Eventually, the ill-feelings which existed between baseball magnates in Mexican and Organized Baseball interests in the United States were forgotten, and in 1955, the Mexican League joined the National Association as a Class AA circuit. In 1967, it achieved Class AAA status.

In 1956, the Class C Central Mexican League was the first of the lower classification circuits south of the border to join the National Association. And during the past two decades a total of six different professional leagues in Mexico have held membership in the National Association, including the two present members (the Class AAA Mexican League and the Class A Mexican Center).

According to current rules, teams in the Mexican League may have no more than 7 foreign-born players on their 21-man rosters, while all players on the 21-man rosters of teams in the Mexican Center circuit must be Mexicans.

Players in the Mexican professional circuits can be purchased by major league teams, and they can be sent to farm teams within the United States. A number of big league players in recent years gained their professional starts in various Mexican leagues, including Aurelio Rodriguez, Celerino Sanchez, Cecilio Acosta, Horacio Pina, Vincente Romo, and Luis Tiant.

CITIES IN MEXICO WHICH HAVE HAD TEAMS AFFILIATED WITH THE NATIONAL ASSOCIATION

Agua Prieta, Sonora

Aguascalientes, Aguascalientes

Caborca, Sonora

Campeche, Campeche

Cananea, Sonora

Celaya, Guanajuato

Chihuahua, Chihuahua

Ciudad del Carmen, Campeche

Ciudad de Valles, San Luis Potosi

Ciudad Juarez, Chihuahua

Ciudad Madero, Tamaulipas

Ciudad Mante, Tamaulipas

Ciudad Monclava, Coahuila

Ciudad Victoria, Tamaulipas

Coatzacoalcos, Veracruz

Cordoba, Veracruz

Durango, Durango

Ebano, San Luis Potosi

Ensenada, Baja California

Fresnillo, Zacatecas

Gomez Palacio, Durango

Guadalajara, Jalisco

Guanajuato, Guanajuato
Las Choapas, Veracruz
Leon, Guanajuato
Merida, Yucatan
Mexicali, Baja California
Mexico City, D. F.
Minatitlan, Veracruz
Monterrey, Nuevo Leon
Morelia, Michoacan
Naranjos, Veracruz
Nogales, Sonora
Nuevo Laredo, Tamaulipas
Orizaba, Veracruz
Poza Rica, Veracruz
Puebla, Puebla

Puerto Penasco, Sonora
Reynosa, Tamaulipas
Sabinas, Nuevo Leon
Salamanca, Guanajuato
Saltillo, Coahuila
San Luis Potosi, San Luis Potosi
San Luis Rio Colorado, Sonora
San Pedro de las Colonias, Coahuila
Tampico, Tamaulipas
Tamuin, San Luis Potosi
Tijuana, Baja California
Torreon, Coahuila
Veracruz, Veracruz
Villahermosa, Tabasco
Zacatecas, Zacatecas

ROSTER OF MEXICAN LEAGUE TEAMS
(CLASS AA, 1955–66; CLASS AAA, 1967—)

Team	Years in Operation
Chihuahua, Chihuahua	1973—
Cordoba, Veracruz	1972—
Guadalajara, Jalisco	1964—
Juarez, Chihuahua	1973—
Merida, Yucatan	1955–58, 1970—
Mexico City Tigers, Mexico City	1955—
Mexico City Reds, Mexico City	1955—
Monterrey, Nuevo Leon	1955—
Nuevo Laredo, Tamaulipas	1955–59
Poza Rica, Veracruz	1958—
Puebla, Puebla	1969#, 1970—
Reynosa, Tamaulipas	1963—
Sabinas, Coahuila	1971–73
Saltillo, Coahuila	1970—
Tampico, Tamaulipas	1971—
Union Laguna (Gomez Palacio), Durango	1970—
Veracruz (Club Aguila), Veracruz	1955–57, 1959—

ROSTER OF MEXICAN CENTER LEAGUE TEAMS
(CLASS C, 1960–62; CLASS A, 1963—)

Team	Years in Operation
Aguascalientes, Aguascalientes	1960–63, 1965–67, 1969—
Celaya, Guanajuato	1960–61
Ciudad Madero, Tamaulipas	1968–70
Ciudad Mante, Tamaulipas	1969—
Ciudad de Valles	1974—
Ciudad Victoria, Tamaulipas	1971, 1973—
Durango, Durango	1965–67, 1972—
Ebano, San Luis Potosi	1972—
Fresnillo, Zacatecas	1962, 1964–68
Guanajuato, Guanajuato	1960–67
Leon, Guanajuato	1960–71
Monterrey, Nuevo Leon	1970–72
Morelia, Michoacan	1966
Naranjos, Veracruz	1973
Nuevo Laredo, Tamaulipas	1968
Salamanca, Guanajuato	1960–62, 1964–65
Saltillo, Coahulla	1964, 1967–69
San Luis Potosi, San Luis Potosi	1960–66, 1967–71 *
San Pedro, Coahuila	1974—
Tampico, Tamaulipas	1967–70
Tamuin, San Luis Potosi	1973
Torreon, Coahuila	1968
Zacatecas, Zacatecas	1965–71, 1973—

* San Luis Potosi fielded two teams in the Mexican Center League in 1963, the "Reds" and the "Indians."

ROSTER OF MEXICAN SOUTHEAST LEAGUE TEAMS
(CLASS A, 1964–70)

Team	Years in Operation
Campeche, Campeche	1964–70
Carmen, Campeche	1968–70
Las Choapas, Veracruz	1967–68
Merida, Yucatan	1964–69

Team	Years in Operation
Minatitlan, Veracruz	1968–69
Orizaba, Veracruz	1966–67
Puerto Mexico (Coatzacoalcos), Veracruz	1964–70
Villahermosa, Tabasco	1964–70

ROSTER OF MEXICAN NORTHERN LEAGUE TEAMS
(CLASS A, 1968–69)

Team	Years in Operation
Caborca, Sonora	1969
Ensenada, Baja California	1968–69
Mexicali, Baja California	1968–69
Nogales, Sonora	1968–69
Puerto Penasco, Sonora	1969
San Luis Rio Colorado, Sonora	1968–69

ROSTER OF CENTRAL MEXICAN LEAGUE TEAMS
(CLASS C, 1956–57)

Team	Years in Operation
Aguascalientes, Aguascalientes	1956–57
Chihuahua, Chihuahua	1956–57
Ciudad Juarez, Chihuahua	1956–57
Durango-Laguna, Durango	1956–57
Fresnillo, Zacatecas	1956–57
Saltillo, Coahuila	1956–57

ROSTER OF MEXICAN ROOKIE LEAGUE TEAMS
(ROOKIE CLASSIFICATION, 1968)

Team	Years in Operation
Agua Prieta, Sonora	1968
Caborca, Sonora	1968
Cananea, Sonora	1968
Empalme (Region), Sonora	1968

PART THREE

15

GREAT MINOR LEAGUE PLAYERS

JOE HAUSER

Joe Hauser stood only 5-foot, 10½ inches, and never weighed more than 180 pounds during his playing days, but he ranks as one of the greatest —if not the greatest—of the home run hitters in the history of the minors. Regardless of the league Hauser happened to be playing in, he blasted home runs—lining balls over fences, on top of houses across the street from the various parks, breaking slats in bleacher and grandstand seats, and in general terrorizing opposing pitchers.

Hauser, who was born on January 12, 1899, at Milwaukee, Wisconsin, broke into Organized Baseball with Providence of the Eastern League in 1918. His start was a modest one, for he appeared in only 39 games as an outfielder, batted .277, and stroked only a single homer. In the following season with Providence he became a semiregular (107 games), hit .273, and banged out 6 homers.

In 1920, Hauser signed with the Milwaukee Brewers of the American Association, and he immediately became popular with the home fans, since he was both a native of the nation's "Beer Capital" and a slugger of growing repute. He belted 15 and 20 homers for the Brewers in 1920 and 1921, respectively, while averaging .284 and .316 during those two years. The Milwaukee fans affectionately called him "Unser Choe" (Our Joe), a tag that stayed with him throughout his career.

Based on his performance at Milwaukee, Hauser was promoted to the big leagues, signing a contract with the Philadelphia Athletics (with whom he was to spend the next five years). A left-hander all the way, by the time Hauser got to Philadelphia he was a first baseman. He remained at that position for the rest of his pro career. As a regular with the A's in 1922, 1923, and 1924, he batted .323, .307, and .288 respectively. He reached his peak in the majors in 1924, when he rapped 27 homers (including 3 in one game) and drove in 115 runs.

Hauser missed the entire 1925 season when he broke his kneecap in an exhibition game on April 7. He did not return to form the next year, batting only .192 and hitting 8 homers in 91 games. In 1927, he was sent to the Kansas City Blues of the American Association, where he turned on the power with a .352 average in 169 games and drove out 218 base hits, including 20 homers. This performance earned him another shot with the A's in 1928, where he batted a respectable .260 in 95 games and produced 16 roundtrippers. Nonetheless, the A's traded Hauser to Cleveland in 1929. He remained with the Indians for only half the season, being used mainly as a pinch hitter and batting .250 in 37 games. His 3 homers that year raised his big league total to 79.

"Unser Choe" spent the balance of the 1929 campaign at Milwaukee, his old stamping grounds, but he only managed a .238 average and 3 homers in 31 games. Hauser never played in the majors again (his American League average was a healthy .284 in 629 games). He was now past thirty years of age, and yet the phase of his career for which he is best remembered lay ahead of him. In the 1930s, he became one of the most celebrated minor league sluggers, first with Baltimore of the International League and then with Minneapolis of the American Association. Following is Joe Hauser's spectacular record from 1930 through 1936:

Year	Team	G	AB	R	H	HR	RBI	Pct.
1930	Baltimore	168	617	173*	193	63*	175	.313
1931	Baltimore	144	487	100	126	31*	98	.259
1932	Minneapolis	149	522	132	158	49*	129	.303
1933	Minneapolis	153	570	153*	189	69*	182*	.322
1934	Minneapolis	82	287	81	100	33	88	.348
1935	Minneapolis	131	409	74	107	23	101	.262
1936	Minneapolis	125	437	95	117	34	87	.268

* League Leader

The Minneapolis Millers' Nicollet Park had a short right field, only 278 feet to the fence, but Hauser could hit the ball out of any park when he laid the wood to it. Ted Williams, also a left-handed hitter, had a great season at Minneapolis in 1938 with a home run total of 43—yet 43 is not 69!

Hauser, who attacked the ball like a human jackhammer, belted 302 homers and had 860 RBI's during those seven years, solid power hitting in any league.

He retired from Organized Baseball for three years after the 1936 campaign, but he reentered the game in 1940 as player–manager of Sheboygan in the Class D Wisconsin State League. In his three playing years with Sheboygan, Hauser averaged about 78 games per season and hit a total of 32 homers. Thus, his home run total in the minors comes to 399 (when added to his 79 AL circuit clouts, the grand total is 478). No other player has hit that many homers in the minor leagues.

Moreover, Joe Hauser was a successful manager at Sheboygan and was popular with fans and players alike. He remained as a nonplaying manager at Sheboygan until league suspended operations after the 1953 season. He was a credit to the game in every respect.

IKE BOONE

Isaac Morgan "Ike" Boone, another of the great sluggers in the high minors, had the distinction of winning five batting titles in three different leagues over a period of 14 years. Boone (born at Samantha, Alabama, on February 17, 1897) attended the University of Alabama for two years, and then broke into pro baseball with Cedartown of the Class D Georgia State League in 1920. Unfortunately, no averages were issued for Cedartown for 1920, so we do not know what Boone did; but he landed with the New Orleans Pelicans of the Southern League in 1921, where he pounded out a solid .389 and copped the first of his batting crowns. A left-handed hitter and a right-handed thrower, Boone played the outfield. He stood 6 feet tall and weighed 195.

The following table lists Boone's record for those five years in which he posted championship averages, plus his 1930 log for a half season with Mission (where he batted a stratospheric .448 in 83 games before being called up by Brooklyn). Boone was about to break every Coast League record in the book before the Dodgers beckoned.

Year	Club and League	G	AB	R	H	2B	3B	HR	RBI	Pct.
1921	New Orleans, Southern	156	574	118	223	46	27	5	126	.389
1923	San Antonio, Texas	148	600	134	241	53	26	15	135	.402
1929	Mission, Pacific Coast	198	794	195	323	49	9	55	218	.407
1930	Mission, Pacific Coast	83	310	76	139	22	3	22	96	.448
1931	Newark, International	124	469	82	167	33	9	18	92	.356
1934	Toronto, International	136	500	87	186	32	9	6	108	.372

Boone is the only player in modern Texas League history (since 1900) to hit .400, and his 555 total bases for Mission in 1929 is the all-time Coast League mark. With Toronto in 1934, at the age of thirty-seven, he was selected as the International League's Most Valuable Player.

Boone's 1934 performance is all the more remarkable since he was named manager before the start of the season and led the Toronto Maple Leafs to the playoff championship (though Toronto lost the Little World Series to Columbus of the American Association 5 games to 4). Boone continued as the Leaf's playing manager through 1936 and then took over as a nonplaying manager of Jackson, Mississippi, in the Class B Southeastern League before retiring.

In-between winning minor league batting crowns, Boone made a number of trips up to the majors between 1922–1932, playing in a total of 355 games for the New York Giants, the Boston Red Sox, the Chicago White Sox and the Brooklyn Dodgers. His big league average was a very potent .319. However, he was a regular outfielder for only two of those years. With the Red Sox in 1924 and 1925, he hit .333 and .330 respectively.

Isaac Morgan Boone is still a legendary figure in baseball—anyone with the name of Boone who enters the professional baseball ranks is always immediately dubbed "Ike."

For his exploits with the Toronto Maple Leafs, Boone was elected to the International League's Hall of Fame in 1957.

Ike Boone's older brother Danny was also a long-time professional ball player. Danny, who pitched for a number of minor league teams, also saw big league mound service with Philadelphia, Detroit, and Cleveland in the American League between 1919–23.)

16

OUTSTANDING MINOR LEAGUE RECORDS

MINOR LEAGUE HOME RUN RECORDS

Joe Bauman's 72 home runs in 1954 for Roswell, New Mexico, in the Class C Longhorn League still stand as the all-time record for circuit blasts in U.S. professional baseball. Bauman's statistics for 1954 are eye-popping:

G	AB	R	H	2B	3B	HR	TB	RBI	Pct.
138	498	188	199	35	3	72	456	224	.400

He walked 150 times and compiled a stratospheric slugging average of .916. Babe Ruth's highest slugging average, compiled in 1920, was only a "measly" .847.

Bauman, a big left-handed hitting first baseman, is clearly the all-time homer champ in the *low minors*. With Amarillo in the Class C West Texas–New Mexico League in 1946–47, he belted 48 and 38 four-baggers, respectively. With Artesia in the Longhorn League in 1952–53, he socked 50 and 53 big ones, respectively. In 1955, with Roswell, following his really big year, he "fell" to 46 homers and 132 runs batted in.

Joe Bauman never swung a bat in the majors, but his place in the history of Class C baseball is secure. No one has a better record.

Bill Serena, twenty-two-year-old third baseman for Lubbock in the West Texas–New Mexico League, hit 57 home runs in 137 regular season games in 1947. Then he added a remarkable total of 13 four-baggers in 10 playoff games, giving him 70 for the entire season. In six years for the Chicago Cubs (1949–54) Serena hit 48 homers in 408 big league games.

MINOR LEAGUE PLAYERS WHO HIT 60 OR MORE HOME RUNS IN ONE SEASON

This list does not include performances in any of the Mexican professional leagues.

Year	Name	Team	League	Class	Number
1925	Tony Lazzeri	Salt Lake City	Pacific Coast League	AAA	60
1926	John Clabaugh	Tyler	East Texas	D	62
1930	Joe Hauser	Baltimore	International	AA	63
1933	Joe Hauser	Minneapolis	American Association	AA	69
1948	Bob Crues	Amarillo	West Texas–New Mexico	C	69
1954	Bob Lennon	Nashville	Southern Association	AA	64
1954	Joe Bauman	Roswell	Longhorn	C	72
1956	Ken Guettler	Shreveport	Texas	AA	62
1956	Dick Stuart	Lincoln	Western	A	66
1956	Forrest Kennedy	Plainview	Southwestern	B	**60**

NINE HOME RUNS IN ONE GAME— ONE BY EACH PLAYER IN THE LINEUP

An amazing home run feat never accomplished in Organized Baseball before or since was recorded by the Douglas Copper Kings against the Chihuahua Dorados in the Class C Arizona–Mexico League. In a game played at Chihuahua on August 19, 1958, every member of the Douglas lineup contributed one home run in a 22–8 rout of Chihuahua. The nine players hitting for the circuit were: Don Pulford, ss; Andy Prevedello, cf; Ron Wilkins, lf; Frank Van Burkleo, 1b; Luis Torres, 2b; Fred Filipelli, rf; Darrel McCall, 3b; Rich Binford, c; and Manager Bob Clear, p. In addition to the nine homers, the Copper Kings produced 14 other hits, with Wilkins pacing the barrage with a six-for-six performance. Douglas scored in all but one inning of the slugging bee, which was stopped after eight innings because of darkness.

THE LONGEST GAME IN ORGANIZED BASEBALL—
29 INNINGS

On the night of June 14, 1966, at Al Lang Field in St. Petersburg, two Florida State League (Class A) teams battled for 29 innings before a decision was reached. When the 6-hour and 59-minute game ended at 2:29 A.M., the visiting Miami Marlins had scored a 4–3 victory over the St. Petersburg Cardinals.

This was the longest game ever played in the history of Organized Baseball. The longest previous professional game occurred on May 8, 1965, in the Class AA Eastern League. The Elmira Pioneers took a 2–1 decision over the Springfield Giants in 27 innings.

Prior to 1965, there had been two 26-inning games in Organized Baseball. The Brooklyn Dodgers and the Boston Braves played a 26-inning 1–1 tie on May 1, 1920; while on May 31, 1909, a Three-I League game at Bloomington, Illinois, lasted 26 innings before Bloomington edged Decatur 2–1.

In the St. Petersburg battle, the score was knotted at 2–2 after the regulation nine frames. Both teams pushed over a run in the eleventh inning, and 17 successive scoreless innings followed.

Miami finally scored the deciding run in the twenty-ninth inning, just after the umpires announced the game would end after 30 frames if no decision was reached. Mike Hebert, the Marlins' sixth pitcher, opened the inning with a line drive double to right. Dennis Denning walked and Gary Carnegie beat out a bunt, loading the bases. Dick Hickerson, who had appeared as a pinch-hitter for Elmira in the previous season's 27-inning marathon, hit a grounder that struck Carnegie for an automatic out.

With the sacks still full and one away, Fred Rico lofted a long fly to center fielder Archie Wade, with Hebert tagging up at third and dashing across the plate after the catch. Hebert subsequently retired the Cardinals 1–2–3 to end the historic contest. About 150 bleary-eyed fans from the original crowd of 740 were still on hand at the game's conclusion.

Bill DeMars, now a Philadelphia Phillies coach, managed the victorious Marlins; while George "Sparky" Anderson, now manager of the Cincinnati Reds, piloted the losing Cardinals.

Box Score

Miami	AB	R	H	PO	A	E	St. Pet'burg	AB	R	H	PO	A	E
Denning, 3b	11	0	2	7	7	0	Wade, cf	12	0	2	10	1	0
Tepedino, lf	4	0	1	3	0	0	Taylor, lf	13	0	1	3	0	0
dCarnegle, lf	8	0	2	4	0	1	Coulter, 2b	12	0	2	8	10	1
Hickerson, 1b	12	0	2	31	0	0	Villar, rf	12	0	4	4	0	0
Rico, cf	10	1	2	5	1	0	Morgan, 3b	12	1	3	2	5	0
Cmejrek, rf–lf	12	0	5	4	0	1	Milani, 1b	12	1	4	33	3	1
Reed, 2b	10	0	2	8	7	0	Ruberto, c–ss	10	1	2	11	7	1
Myrshall, ss	12	0	1	3	5	2	Rodriguez, ss	3	0	2	1	4	0
Sands, c	12	1	2	20	0	1	bStone, c	9	0	3	15	1	0
Bardes, p	2	0	0	0	0	1	Bakenhaster, p	2	0	0	0	2	0
King, p	0	0	0	0	0	0	cDavis	1	0	0	0	0	0
aFourroux	1	1	1	0	0	0	Robertson, p	0	0	0	0	0	0
Rawls, p	1	0	0	0	2	0	Thompson, p	0	0	0	0	1	0
Thoms, p	2	0	0	2	4	0	eBraddock	0	0	0	0	0	0
Gilliford, p	3	0	0	0	7	0	Williamson, p	2	0	0	0	0	0
gDeptula	1	0	0	0	0	0	fFiore	1	0	0	0	0	0
Hebert, p	1	1	1	0	1	0	Bowlby, p	3	0	0	0	2	0
Totals	102	4	21	87	34	6	Totals	104	3	23	87	36	3

Pitching Summary

Miami	IP	H	R	ER	BB	SO	St. Pet'burg	IP	H	R	ER	BB	SO
Bardes	6	7	2	0	1	3	Bakenhaster	9	6	2	2	2	7
King	1	0	0	0	0	1	Robertson	1/3	2	0	0	0	1
Rawls	3	3	1	1	1	3	Thompson	3-2/3	4	1	1	0	2
Thoms	4	4	0	0	2	2	Williamson	8	3	0	0	1	8
Gilliford	11	7	0	0	2	7	Bowlby (L)	8	6	1	1	4	4
Hebert (W)	4	2	0	0	0	2							

Miami	000 000 020 010 000 000 000 000 000 01—4
St. Petersburg	000 000 200 010 000 000 000 000 000 00—3

aHomered for King In eighth. bStruck out for Rodriguez in ninth. cGrounded out for Bakenhaster In ninth. dStruck out for Tepedino in tenth. eSacrificed for Thompson in thirteenth. fStruck out for Williamson in twenty-first. gGrounded out for Gilliford In twenty-sixth. Runs batted in—Rico, Reed, Fourroux (2), Rodriguez. Two base hits—Carnegie, Cmejrek, Hebert, Villar, Morgan. Home run—Fourroux. Stolen base—Rodriguez. Caught stealing—Wade. Sacrifice hits—Carnegie, Rico, Coulter, Braddock. Sacrifice fly—Rico. Double plays—Denning, Reed, and Hickerson; Myrshall, Reed, and Hickerson; Coulter, Rodriguez, and Milani; Coulter and Milani; Wade, Coulter, and Stone. Left on bases—Miami, 21; St. Petersburg, 22. Passed ball—Sands. Umpires—Bonitiz and Molinari. Time of game—6:59.

ROCKY MOUNT PITCHERS HURL NO-HITTERS IN DOUBLEHEADER

Two no-hitters in a doubleheader? Veteran students of Organized Baseball history had never heard of such an unbelievable feat, nor did they ever expect to—until May 15, 1966. On that day, in Greensboro, North Carolina, two roommates on the Rocky Mount Leafs (a Detroit Tigers farm club in the Class A Carolina League) threw a pair of seven-inning no-hitters.

Joining forces for the double blanking were right-handers Dick Drago and Darrell Clark. Drago zipped the Greensboro Yankees 5–0 in the opener of the Sunday twin bill. While extending congratulations between games, Clark jokingly told him: "Now I guess I'll have to go out and pitch one too." Seven innings later it was no joke. Clark had his no-hitter and a 2–0 victory over the shocked Yankees.

Drago, a native of Toledo, Ohio, and then only twenty years old, came within four outs of a perfect game but issued a walk in the sixth inning and another in the seventh. Clark, who is twenty-four, from Chino, California, walked five.

Drago continued climbing the minor league ladder and graduated to the big leagues in 1969, when he became a regular starter for the Kansas City Royals.

The box scores for the doubleheader follow:

First Game Box Score

Rocky Mount	AB	R	H	PO	A	E	Greensboro	AB	R	H	PO	A	E
Woods, cf	4	0	1	2	0	0	Cantrell, cf	3	0	0	2	0	0
Sherer, rf	3	0	0	0	0	0	Warmsley, ss	3	0	0	1	4	1
Kelly, 2b	3	1	2	5	2	0	Covington, rf	2	0	0	1	0	0
Haggitt, lf	4	0	0	2	0	0	Freynik, 1b	3	0	0	9	2	0
Petranovich, 3b	1	3	0	2	1	0	MacClellan, c	2	0	0	5	0	1
Kalafatis, 1b	4	1	3	4	1	0	Monteleone, 3b	2	0	0	1	1	0
Lopez, ss	4	0	1	0	2	0	Otto, lf	2	0	0	0	0	1
Cernich, c	3	0	0	4	0	0	McLemore, 2b	2	0	0	1	4	1
Drago, p	3	0	0	1	0	0	Dunn, p.	1	0	0	0	2	0
Totals	29	5	7	20	6	0	aFeris	0	0	0	0	0	0
							Roberts, p	0	0	0	0	0	0
							Totals	20	0	0	20	13	4

Pitching Summary

Rocky Mount	IP	H	R	ER	BB	SO	Greensboro	IP	H	R	ER	BB	SO
Drago (W)	7	0	0	0	2	4	Dunn (L)	6	6	4	3	4	4
							Roberts	1	1	1	0	0	0

Rocky Mount	0 0 0	1 3 0	1—5
Greensboro	0 0 0	0 0 0	0—0

aWalked for Dunn in sixth. Runs batted in—Kelly, Kalafatis (2). Home runs—Kelly, Kalafatis. Caught stealing—Kelly. Double plays—Lopez, Kelly, and Kalafatis. Left on bases—Rocky Mount (8), Greensboro (1). Bases on balls—off Drago (2—Covington, Feris), off Dunn [4—Sherer, Kelly, Petranovich (2)], off Roberts (1—Petranovich). Strikeouts—by Drago [4—(Cantrell (2), Warmsley, Monteleone], by Dunn [4—Sherer, Drago (3)]. Umpires—Grygiel, Bowman. Time of game—1:42.

Second Game Box Score

Rocky Mount	AB	R	H	PO	A	E	Greensboro	AB	R	H	PO	A	E
Woods, cf	3	0	1	2	0	0	Cantrell, cf	3	0	0	1	0	0
Sherer, rf	4	0	2	2	1	0	Warmsley, ss	2	0	0	1	5	0
Kelly, 2b	2	0	1	1	1	0	Covington, rf	1	0	0	0	1	0
Haggitt, lf	2	0	0	1	0	0	Feris, 1b	3	0	0	7	0	1
Zalocha, lf	0	0	0	1	0	0	Monteleone, 3b	3	0	0	0	0	0
Petranovich, 3b	2	0	0	3	1	0	Siebel, c	2	0	0	8	1	0
Kalafatis, 1b	3	1	1	6	1	0	Otto, lf	3	0	0	0	0	0
Lopez, ss	3	0	0	2	4	0	McLemore, 2b	2	0	0	3	4	0
Leyland, c	0	1	0	2	0	0	Burbach, p	1	0	0	1	1	2
Clark, p	3	0	0	1	0	0	Roberts, p	0	0	0	0	0	0
Totals	22	2	5	21	8	0	Totals	20	0	0	21	12	3

Pitching Summary

Rocky Mount	IP	H	R	ER	BB	SO	Greensboro	IP	H	R	ER	BB	SO
Clark (W)	7	0	0	0	5	2	Burbach (L)	6-2/3	5	2	0	5	7
							Roberts	1/3	0	0	0	0	0

Rocky Mount	0 0 0	0 0 0	2—2
Greensboro	0 0 0	0 0 0	0—0

Run batted in—Leyland. Two base hits—Woods, Sherer, Kalafatis. Stolen bases—Kelly, Covington. Caught stealing—Petranovich. Sacrifice hits—Kelly, Leyland.

Double plays—Sherer and Lopez; Warmsley, McLemore, and Feris 2. Left on bases—Rocky Mount, 6; Greensboro, 4. Bases on balls—off Clark [5—Warmsley, Covington (2), Siebel, Burbach], Bases on balls off Burbach [5—Woods, Haggitt, Petranovich, Leyland (2)]. Strikeouts—by Clark (2—Covington, Otto), by Burbach [7—Kalafatis, Lopez (3), Clark (3)]. Wild pitches—Burbach, Roberts. Umpires—Bowman, Grygiel. Time of game—2:10.

17

CITIES AND TOWNS THAT HAVE HAD PROFESSIONAL BASEBALL TEAMS IN REGULARLY ORGANIZED LEAGUES

TEAMS IN THE UNITED STATES

Alabama—33

Abbeville
Albany
Alexander City
Andalusia
Anniston
Bessemer
Birmingham *
Brewton
Decatur
Dothan
Enterprise
Eufaula

Evergreen
Florence
Gadsden (also represented
    Attalla, Alabama City)
Geneva
Greenville
Headland
Huntsville
Lanett
Mobile
Montgomery *

Opelika
Ozark
Russellville
Selma
Sheffield
Talladega
Tallassee
Troy
Tuscumbia
Turkegee
Union Springs

Arizona—9

Bisbee
Douglass
Globe

Mesa
Miami
Nogales

Phoenix *
Tucson *
Yuma

    * An asterisk indicates that the city or town still has a professional team either in the majors or the minors.

Arkansas—23

Argenta
Batesville
Bentonville
Blytheville
Brinkley
Camden
El Dorado
Fayetteville

Fort Smith
Helena
Hot Springs
Huntsville
Jonesboro
Little Rock *
Marianna
Newport

Osceola
Paragould
Pine Bluff
Rogers
Siloam Springs
Texarkana
Van Buren

California—56

Alameda
Anaheim *
Bakersfield *
Berkeley
Calexico
Coalings
Coronado
El Centro
Elmhurst
Fresno *
Fruitvale
Hanford
Hayward
Healdsburg
Hollywood
Lodi *
Long Beach
Los Angeles *
Marysville (also repre-
    sented Yuba City)

Merced
Modesto *
Napa
Oakland *
Ontario
Orange
Oroville
Pasadena
Petaluma
Pittsburg
Pomona
Porterville
Redding
Redondo Beach
Richmond
Riverside
Roseville
Sacramento *
St. Helena
Salinas

San Bernardino
San Diego *
San Francisco *
San Jose *
San Leandro
San Rafael
Santa Ana
Santa Barbara
Santa Cruz
Santa Rosa
Stockton
Tulare
Vallejo
Ventura
Visalia *
Watsonville
Willows

Colorado—6

Canon City
Colorado Springs

Denver *
La Junta

Leadville
Pueblo

Connecticut—16

Bridgeport
Bristol *
Danbury
Derby (also represented
    Ansonia)
Hartford

Meriden
Middletown
New Britain
New Haven
New London
Norwich

Stamford
Torrington
Waterbury
West Haven *
Willimantic

Delaware—6

Dover
Laurel

Milford
Rehoboth Beach

Seaford
Wilmington

District of Columbia—1

Washington *

Florida—36

Bartow
Bradenton
Cocoa
Crestview
Daytona Beach
Deerfield Beach
DeLand
Fort Lauderdale *
Fort Myers
Fort Pierce
Fort Walton Beach
Gainesville

Graceville
Hollywood
Jacksonville *
Jacksonville Beach
Key West *
Lakeland *
Leesburg
Melbourne
Miami *
Miami Beach
Ocala
Orlando *

Palatka
Panama City
Pensacola
Pompano Beach
St. Augustine
St. Petersburg *
Sanford
Sarasota *
Tallahassee
Tampa *
West Palm Beach *
Winter Haven *

Georgia—38

Albany
Americus
Atlanta *
Augusta
Bainbridge
Baxley
Brunswick
Carrollton
Cedartown
Columbus *
Cordele
Donalsonville
Douglas

Dublin
Eastman
Fitzgerald
Griffin
Hazlehurst
Jesup
LaGrange
Lindale
Lyons
Macon
Moultrie
Newnan
Quitman

Rome
Sandersville
Savannah *
Sparta
Statesboro
Thomasville
Thomson
Tifton
Valdosta
Vidalia
Waycross
West Point

Hawaii—1

Honolulu *

Idaho—6

Boise
Caldwell

Idaho Falls *
Lewiston *

Pocatello
Twin Falls

(Note: Twin Falls, Idaho, in the Pioneer League in recent years has been called "Magic Valley," since the team also represented the towns in the surrounding area.)

Illinois—51

Alton	Freeport	Mount Vernon
Aurora	Galesburg	Murphysboro
Beardstown	Harrisburg	Ottawa
Belleville	Havana	Pana
Bloomington	Herrin	Pekin
Cairo	Jacksonville	Peoria
Canton	Joliet	Quincy
Centralia	Kankakee	Rockford
Champaign (Urbana)	Kewanee	Rock Island
Charleston	LaSalle (Peru)	Shelbyville
Chicago *	Lincoln	Springfield
Clinton	McLeansboro	Staunton
Danville *	Macomb	Sterling
Decatur *	Marion	Streator
East Moline	Mattoon	Taylorville
Eldorado	Moline	Waukegan
Elgin	Monmouth	West Frankfort

Indiana—25

Anderson	Huntington	Muncie
Auburn	Indianapolis *	Portland
Bluffton	Kokomo	Richmond
Decatur	Lafayette	South Bend
Elkhart	Linton	Terre Haute
Evansville *	Logansport	Vincennes
Fort Wayne	Marion	Wabash
Gary	Matthews	
Goshen	Michigan City	

Iowa—27

Bettendorf	Davenport *	Mason City
Boone	Des Moines *	Muscatine
Burlington *	Dubuque	Oskaloosa
Cedar Rapids *	Emmettsburg	Ottumwa
Charles City	Estherville	Rock Rapids
Clarinda	Fort Dodge	Sheldon
Clear Lake	Keokuk	Shenandoah
Clinton *	LeMars	Sioux City
Council Bluffs	Marshalltown	Waterloo *

Kansas—43

Abilene
Arkansas City
Atchison
Beloit
Blue Rapids
Chanute
Chapman
Cherryvale
Clay Center
Coffeyville
Concordia
El Dorado
Ellsworth
Emporia
Eureka

Fort Scott
Great Bend
Hiawatha
Holton
Horton
Hutchinson
Independence
Iola
Junction City
Larned
Leavenworth
Lyons
McPherson
Manhattan
Marysville

Minneapolis
Mulberry
Newton
Norton
Parsons
Pittsburg
Sabetha
Salina
Scammon
Seneca
Topeka
Wellington
Wichita *

Kentucky—30

Ashland
Bowling Green
Catlettsburg
Cynthiana
Dawson Springs
Frankfort
Fulton
Harlan
Hazard
Henderson

Hopkinsville
Jenkins
Lawrenceburg
Lexington
Louisville
Madisonville
Mayfield
Maysville
Middlesboro
Mount Sterling

Newport
Nicholasville
Owensboro
Paducah
Paris
Pineville
Princeton
Richmond
Shelbyville
Winchester

Louisiana—21

Abbeville
Alexandria *
Baton Rouge
Crowley
DeQuincy
DeRidder
Hammond

Houma
Jeanerette
Lake Charles
Leesville
Monroe
Morgan City
New Iberia

New Orleans
Oakdale
Opelousas
Rayne
Shreveport *
Thibodaux
West Monroe

(Note: Monroe and West Monroe combined to form the "Twin Cities" entry in the "Cotton States League.")

Maine—10

Augusta
Bangor (Brewer)
Biddeford
Calais

Lewiston (Auburn)
Millinocket
Old Town

Pine Tree
Portland
York Beach

Maryland—14

Baltimore *	Easton	Lonaconing
Cambridge	Federalsburg	Pocomoke City
Centreville	Frederick	Salisbury
Crisfield	Frostburg	Westernport
Cumberland	Hagerstown	

Massachusetts—23

Attleboro	Lawrence	Salem
Boston *	Lowell	Springfield
Brockton	Lynn	Taunton
Fall River	Malden	Waltham
Fitchburg	New Bedford	Watertown
Gloucester	Northampton	Wayland
Haverhill	Pittsfield *	Worcester
Holyoke	Quincy	

Michigan—36

Adrian	Hancock	Mount Clemens
Battle Creek	Holland	Muskegon
Bay City	Houghton	Niles
Belding	Ionia	Pontiac
Benton Harbor	Iron Mountain	Port Huron
Berrien Springs	Jackson	Saginaw
Boyne City	Kalamazoo	St. Joseph
Cadillac	Lake Linden	Saulte Ste. Marie
Calumet	Lansing	Tecumseh
Detroit *	Ludington	Traverse City
Flint	Manistee	Wyandotte
Grand Rapids	Menominee	Ypsilanti

Minnesota—17

Bloomington *	Little Falls	St. Cloud
Brainerd	Mankato	St. Paul
Breckenridge	Minneapolis	Virginia
Crookston	Moorhead	Winona
Duluth	Red Wing	Worthington
East Grand Forks	Rochester	

Mississippi—19

Aberdeen	Corinth	Laurel
Biloxi	Greenville	Meridian
Brookhaven	Greenwood	Natchez
Canton	Gulfport	Tupelo
Clarksdale	Hattiesburg	Vicksburg
Cleveland	Jackson	Yazoo City
Columbus		

Missouri—24

Brookfield
Cape Girardeau
Carthage
Caruthersville
Cassville
Chillicothe
Hannibal
Jefferson City

Joplin
Kansas City *
Kirksville
Macon
Maryville
Monett
Neosho
Nevada

Poplar Bluff
Portageville
St. Joseph
St. Louis *
Sedalia
Springfield
Webb City
West Plains

Montana—5

Billings *
Butte

Great Falls *
Helena

Missoula

Nebraska—22

Auburn
Beatrice
Columbus
Fairbury
Falls City
Fremont
Grand Island
Hastings

Holdrege
Humboldt
Kearney
Lexington
Lincoln
McCook
Nebraska City

Norfolk
North Platte
Omaha *
Red Cloud
Seward
Superior
York

Nevada—2

Las Vegas

Reno *

New Hampshire—8

Concord
Dover
Epping

Fremont
Kingston
Manchester

Nashua
Newton

New Jersey—13

Asbury Park
Atlantic City
Bloomfield
Bloomingdale
Camden

Jersey City
Long Branch
Newark
New Brunswick

Paterson
Perth Amboy
Trenton
Washington

New Mexico—6

Albuquerque *
Artesia

Clovis
Hobbs

Las Cruces
Roswell

New York—59

Albany
Amsterdam
Auburn *
Batavia *
Binghamton
Brooklyn
Buffalo
Catskill
Corning
Cortland
Elmira *
Endicott
Fulton
Geneva
Glens Falls
Gloversville
Hornell
Hudson
Ilion (Herkimer)
Jamestown

Johnson City
Johnstown
Kingston
Lockport
Lyons
Malone
Massena
Middleton
Newark *
Newburgh (Beacon)
New York City *
Niagara Falls
Nyack
Ogdensburg
Olean
Oneida
Oneonta *
Ossining
Oswego
Peekskill

Penn Yan
Plattsburgh
Port Chester
Potsdam
Poughkeepsie
Rochester *
Rome
St. Albans
Saugerties
Schenectady
Seneca Falls
Syracuse *
Troy
Utica
Walden
Watertown
Waverly
Wellsville
Yonkers

North Carolina—70

Albermarle
Angier
Ashville *
Ayden
Belmont
Burlington
Charlotte
Clinton
Conover
Cooleemee
Dunn
Durham
Edenton
Elizabeth City
Elkin
Erwin
Fayetteville
Forest City
Fuquay Springs
Gastonia * *
Goldsboro
Graham
Granite Falls
Greensboro

Greenville
Henderson
Hendersonville
Hickory
High Point
Kannapolis
Kinston *
Landis
Leaksville-Spray-Draper
Lenoir
Lexington
Lincolnton
Lumberton
Marion
Mayodan
Moorsville
Morganton
Mount Airy
New Bern
Newton
North Wilkesboro
Raleigh
Red Springs

Reidsville
Roanoke Rapids (Weldon)
Rockingham
Rocky Mount *
Rutherfordton
Salisbury
Sanford
Selma
Shelby
Smithfield
Snow Hill
Spencer
Spindale
Statesville
Tarboro
Thomasville
Wadesboro
Warsaw
Whiteville
Williamston
Wilmington
Wilson
Winston-Salem *

North Dakota—10

Bismarck (Mandan)   Grand Forks   Valley City
Cavalier   Jamestown   Wahpeton
Devils Lake   Minot   Warren
Fargo

Ohio—40

Akron   Hamilton   Piqua
Alliance   Ironton   Pomeroy
Canton   Lancaster   Portsmouth
Chillicothe   Lima   Salem
Cincinnati *   Mansfield   Sandusky
Cleveland *   Marion   Sebring
Columbus   Massillon   Springfield
Coshocton   Middleport   Steubenville
Dayton   Middletown   Tiffin
East Liverpool   Mount Vernon   Toledo *
Findlay   Newark   Warren
Fostoria   New Philadelphia (Dover) Youngstown
Fremont   Niles (Girard)   Zanesville
Gallipolis

Oklahoma—37

Ada   El Reno   Oklahoma City *
Altus   Enid   Okmulgee
Anadarko   Eufaula   Pauls Valley
Ardmore   Guthrie   Pawhuska
Bartlesville   Henryetta   Ponca City
Blackwell   Holdenville   Sapulpa
Bristow   Hugo   Seminole
Chickasha   Lawton   Shawnee
Clinton   McAlester   Tulsa *
Cushing   Maud   Vinita
Drumright   Miami   Wewoka
Duncan   Muskogee   Wilson
Durant

Oregon—9

Baker   Eugene *   Medford
Bend   Klamath Falls   Pendleton
Coos Bay (North Bend)   La Grande   Portland *

Pennsylvania—66

Allentown	Hazleton	Punxsutawney
Altoona	Homestead	Reading *
Bangor	Jeannette	Ridgway
Beaver Falls	Johnsonburg	St. Clair
Berwick	Johnstown	St. Marys
Braddock	Kane	Scottdale
Bradford	Lancaster	Scranton
Butler	Lansdale	Shamokin
Carbondale	Lebanon	Sharon
Chambersburg	McKeesport	Shenandoah
Charleroi (Donora)	Mahanoy City	Slatington
Chester	Monessen	Stroudsburg
Coatesville	Mount Carmel	Tamaqua
Connellsville	New Castle	Uniontown
Coudersport	Nazareth	Vandergrift
DuBois	Norristown	Warren
Erie	Oil City	Washington
Franklin	Patton	Waynesboro
Gettysburg	Philadelphia *	Waynesburg
Greensburg	Pittsburgh *	Wilkes-Barre
Hanover	Pottstown	Williamsport
Harrisburg	Pottsville	York

Rhode Island—6

Cranston	Pawtucket *	Taunton
Newport	Providence	Woonsocket

South Carolina—13

Anderson *	Darlington	Orangeburg *
Bennettsville	Florence	Rock Hill
Charleston *	Greenville	Spartanburg *
Chester	Greenwood *	Sumter
Columbia		

South Dakota—10

Aberdeen	Miller	Sioux Falls *
Flandreau	Mitchell	Watertown
Huron	Redfield	Wessington Springs
Madison		

Tennessee—26

Bristol
Chattanooga
Clarksville
Cleveland
Columbia
Dyersburg
Elizabethton *
Erwin
Greensville

Harriman
Jackson
Johnson City *
Kingsport *
Knoxville
Lexington
Maryville (Alcoa)
Memphis *
Milan

Morristown
Nashville
Newport
Oak Ridge
Paris
Springfield
Trenton
Union City

Texas—101

Abilene
Alpine
Amarillo *
Arlington *
Austin
Ballinger
Bartlett
Bay City
Beaumont
Beeville
Belton
Big Springs
Bonham
Borger
Brenham
Brownsville
Bryan
Cisco
Clarksville
Cleburne
Coleman
Corpus Christi
Corsicana
Crockett
Dallas
Del Rio
Denison
Donna
Eastland
Edinburg
El Paso *
Ennis
Fort Worth
Gainsville

Galveston
Georgetown
Gladewater
Gorman
Graham
Greenville
Hamlin
Harlingen
Henderson
Hillsboro
Houston *
Italy
Jacksonville
Kaufman
Kilgore
Kingsville
La Feria
Lamesa
Lampasas
Laredo
Longview
Lubbock
Lufkin
McAllen
McKinney
Marlin
Marshall
Mexia
Midland *
Mineral Wells
Mission
Monahans
Mount Pleasant
Nacogdoches

Odessa
Orange
Palestine
Pampa
Paris
Plainview
Port Arthur
Ranger
Refugio
Robstown
Rusk
San Angelo
San Antonio *
San Benito
Schulenberg
Sherman
Stamford
Sulphur Springs
Sweetwater
Taft
Temple
Terrell
Texarkana
Texas City
Tyler
Vernon
Victoria *
Waco
Waxahachie
Weslaco
West
Wichita Falls
Wink

Utah—5

Logan	Ogden *	Salt Lake City *
Murray	Park City	

Vermont—2

Montpeller	Rutland

Virginia—42

Abingdon	Franklin	Parksley
Bassett	Galax	Pennington Gap
Big Stone Gap	Hampton *	Petersburg
Blackstone	Harrisonburg	Portsmouth *
Bluefield	Hopewell	Pulaski *
Bristol *	Lawrenceville	Radford
Cape Charles	Lynchburg *	Roanoke
Charlottesville	Marion *	Richmond *
Clifton Forge	Martinsville	Salem *
Colonial Heights	Narrows (Pearisburg)	Schoolfield
Covington *	Newport News *	South Boston (Halifax)
Danville	Norfolk *	Staunton
Emporia	Northampton	Suffolk
Fieldale	Norton	Wytheville

(Notes: Norfolk and Portsmouth play under the name of "Tidewater" in the International League. Newport News and Hampton are represented as "Peninsula" in the Carolina League.)

Washington—23

Aberdeen	Hoquiam	Seattle *
Ballard	Kennewick *	South Bend
Bellingham	Longview (Kelso)	Spokane
Centralia	Montesano	Tacoma
Chehalis	Olympia	Walla Walla *
Clarkston	Pasco *	Wenatchee
Everett	Raymond	Yakima
Gray's Harbor (Region)	Richland *	

(Note: Kennewick, Pasco, and Richland are represented in the Northwest League as "Tri-Cities.")

West Virginia—17

Beckley	Grafton	Parkersburg
Bluefield *	Huntington	Piedmont
Charleston *	Logan	Point Pleasant
Clarksburg	Mannington	Welch
Fairmont	Martinsburg	Williamson
Follansbee	Montgomery	

Wisconsin—17

Appleton *
Beloit
Eau Claire
Fond du Lac
Freeport
Green Bay

Janesville
La Crosse
Madison
Marinette
Milwaukee *
Oshkosh

Racine
Sheboygan
Superior
Wausau
Wisconsin Rapids *

Wyoming—1

Cheyenne

TEAMS OUTSIDE OF THE UNITED STATES

Canada—64

Acton Vale, Quebec
Bassano, Alberta
Berlin, Ontario
Brandon, Manitoba
Brantford, Ontario
Brockville, Ontario
Burlington, Ontario
Calgary, Alberta
Cap de la Madeleine, Quebec
Cornwall, Ontario
Dominion, Nova Scotia
Drummondville, Quebec
Edmonton, Alberta
Farnham, Quebec
Fort William, Ontario
Fredericton, New Brunswick
Glace Bay, Nova Scotia
Granby, Quebec
Guelph, Ontario
Hamilton, Ontario
Hull, Ontario
Ingersoll, Ontario
Kingston, Ontario
Kitchener, Ontario
Lethbridge, Alberta
London, Ontario
Medicine Hat, Alberta
Montreal, Quebec *
Moose Jaw, Saskatchewan
New Waterford, Nova Scotia
New Westminster, British Columbia *
Niagara Falls, Ontario

Outremont, Quebec
Ottawa, Ontario
Perth, Ontario
Peterborough, Ontario
Port Arthur, Ontario
Quebec City, Quebec *
Red Deer, Alberta
Regina, Saskatchewan
St. Boniface, Manitoba
St. Catherines, Ontario
St. Croix, New Brunswick
St. Hyacinthe, Quebec
St. Jean, Quebec
St. Johns, New Brunswick
St. Stephens, New Brunswick
St. Thomas, Ontario
Sarnia, Ontario
Saskatoon, Saskatchewan
Sault Ste. Marie, Ontario
Sherbrooke, Quebec
Smiths Falls, Ontario
Sydney, Nova Scotia
Sydney Mines, Nova Scotia
Thetford Mines, Quebec *
Three Rivers, Quebec *
Toronto, Ontario
Valleyfield, Quebec
Vancouver, British Columbia
Victoria, British Columbia
Windsor, Ontario
Winnipeg, Manitoba
Woodstock, Ontario

Cuba—1

Havana

Puerto Rico—6

| Aguadilla | Mayaguez | San Juan |
| Caguas | Ponce | Santurce (San Juan) |

Panama—1

Panama City

Venezuela—1

Caracas

APPENDIX: ROSTERS OF THE MINOR
LEAGUES SINCE 1902

This section includes a nearly complete listing of all of the minor leagues that have held membership in the National Association of Professional Baseball Leagues since 1902 (that organization's first full year of operation).

It would be impossible to give anything resembling a complete listing of the leagues and league cities of professional baseball during the 1877–1901 period, since the information available is extremely scanty. (In the chapters on the International League and the Texas League, we listed all the member cities back to 1884 and 1888, respectively, when those two circuits were founded; but this could not be accurately done for many of the smaller circuits, especially in regard to recording mid-season franchise shifts.)

Even after the National Association took over as the governing body of the minors and introduced more efficient record-keeping methods, complete records were not always preserved. Various documents have been lost, thrown out, or on a couple of occasions, destroyed by fire. Moreover, those leagues that folded during the season often did not turn in reports of any kind to the National Association's headquarters.

In drawing up our league "profiles," we attempted to list all member cities and the period of time they remained in the league. Perhaps the most difficult part of the job was to indicate franchise shifts made during the season. In some instances one franchise was located in as many as three cities during the course of the season, as the result of two shifts. Where the exact date of the franchise shift is known, that information is given. Also, when the exact dates are known concerning a team's dropping out of the league, or the league's disbanding, that information is given.

In a scattering of cases, as in the North Texas League of 1906 and the Pennsylvania–West Virginia League of 1914 (both Class D circuits), sufficient information for drawing up a complete profile was not readily available; but we were able to list the league's "unofficial champion," plus the length of that league's existence, which in the case of both afore-mentioned circuits was less than two weeks. National Association records are dotted with stories of those leagues whose lives on the professional baseball scene lasted less than a month.

Moreover, there are a number of cases where we have the name of a short-lived league, but cannot with any degree of accuracy come up with the name of even the "unofficial champion," or *any* of the towns. For example, the Intermountain League of Colorado (1909), and the Massachusetts-Connecticut League (1912). With the assistance of members of the Society for American Baseball Research, we eventually hope to come up with complete profiles for all leagues, even if they lasted for a scant few days.

In all, this book lists some 225 minor leagues. The total would easily go over the 275 mark if all of the minors of the 1877–1901 era were included. And since 1902, professional baseball has been played under the National Association banner in more than 1,200 cities and towns throughout North America, the Caribbean, and South America.

This listing does not consider, however, the various Florida "Rookie" leagues that have been operated by the major leagues since 1963. The Rookie leagues, which are administered somewhat like the instructional leagues, generally are made up of four teams with all games being played in one or two cities. For example, the Cocoa Rookie League of 1964 was made up of four teams: the Melbourne Twins, the Florida Mets, the Cocoa Colts, and the Cocoa Tigers. The teams played their entire fifty-two-game schedules at Cocoa, Florida.

However, the Appalachian and Pioneer Rookie leagues are listed since they both developed out of established leagues. Moreover, teams in the Appalachian and Pioneer circuits travel from one town to another and do not center their play in one specific area. (The annual *Sporting News Official Baseball Guides* do give a complete listing of all Florida Rookie leagues.)

In many cases here, we had to resolve the problem concerning the time when one league passed out of existence and when another came onto the scene. Changes in league names also complicate this situation. The International League, for example, has undergone nine name changes in its ninety-year history, but we treat the International as a single league since its organization in 1884.

On the other hand, we have a situation like the Midwest League, a Class A circuit that has been operating since 1956. The Midwest loop began as the Illinois State League in 1947–48 and was reorganized as the Mississippi–Ohio Valley League in order to cover a wider territory for the 1949–55 period. In 1956, the Mississippi–Ohio Valley circuit was reorganized into the Midwest League. Again, the primary reason was to take in a wider territory.

We treated the Illinois State, the M.O.V., and the Midwest as three separate leagues, although a case could be made for regarding the Midwest's history as a continuous one dating back to 1947. In the course of this section, we do include explanatory notations in order to clarify particularly complex situations. And in conducting research, we found that old leagues usually do not completely fade away; they are merely reformed into new leagues.

We might also add that being completely *logical* in listing all of the minor leagues and minor league cities of the twentieth century is not a practical possibility. But we did base our organizational plan upon the counsel of a number of experts in the field and upon a series of widely used reference sources.

We were given a tremendous amount of assistance by Don Avery, research director of the National Association and a thirty-year veteran with the minor leagues' governing body. At the same time we take full responsibility for any errors of commission or omission.

Among the printed sources used were: *The Story of Minor League Baseball: 1901–52* (published by the National Association), *The Leagues and League Cities of Professional Baseball: 1910–41* (by Earle W. Moss), and the various annual official baseball guides (especially those published by the A. J. Reach Co., A. G. Spalding, and *The Sporting News*). We structured the league profiles in accordance with the information given in these sources, though we often had to make our own modifications in form and style in order to achieve a greater measure of consistency.

The league profiles go through the 1974 season.

In conclusion, we might reemphasize three figures that have already been set down in the course of this book: 275-plus minor leagues operated in 1,200-plus cities and towns, involving approximately 275,000 players. These numbers are a graphic indication that professional baseball in the Western Hemisphere has been a vast and mighty enterprise.

KEY TO ROSTER OF LEAGUE TEAMS

X—The letter X following a date indicates that the club or league disbanded during the season.

#—A quantity sign (#) following a date indicates that the city or league acquired its franchise after the beginning of season or for some reason began play after the season opened.

Team	Years in Operation

ALABAMA-FLORIDA LEAGUE (CLASS D, 1936–39, 1951–62)

Team	Years in Operation
Abbeville, Alabama	1936X
Andalusia, Alabama	1936X 1937–39, 1953, 1954 (held franchise jointly with Opp, 1962X
Columbus, Georgia	1957
Crestview, Florida	1954–56
Donalsonville, Georgia	1955–56
Dothan, Alabama	1936–37X, 1938–39, 1951–56, 1958–62
Enterprise, Alabama	1936, 1951–52X
Eufala, Alabama	1952–53
Evergreen, Alabama	1937#, 1938
Fort Walton Beach, Florida	1953–62
Graceville, Florida	1952#, 1953–58
Greenville, Alabama	1939
Headland, Alabama	1951–52
Montgomery, Alabama	1957–62
Ozark, Alabama	1936–#37 (franchise shifted to Evergreen in midseason), 1951–52, 1962X
Panama City, Florida	1936–39, 1951–61
Pensacola, Florida	1957–62
Selma, Alabama	1957–62
Tallahassee, Florida	1951
Tallassee, Alabama	1939
Troy, Alabama	1936–39
Union Springs, Alabama	1936–38

ALABAMA–MISSISSIPPI LEAGUE (CLASS D, 1936X)

Team	Years in Operation
Anniston, Alabama	1936X
Corinth, Mississippi	1936X
Decatur, Alabama	1936X
Gadsden, Alabama	1936X
Huntsville, Alabama	1936X
Sheffield, Alabama	1936X

Team	Years in Operation

ALABAMA STATE LEAGUE (CLASS D, 1940–41, 1946–50)

Andalusia, Alabama	1940–41, 1947–50
Brewton, Alabama	1940–41, 1946–50
Dothan, Alabama	1940–41, 1946–50
Enterprise, Alabama	1947–50
Geneva, Alabama	1946–50
Greenville, Alabama	1940–41, 1946–50
Headland, Alabama	1950
Ozark, Alabama	1946–50
Tallassee, Alabama	1940–41
Troy, Alabama	1940–41, 1946–49
Tuskegee, Alabama	1941

ALABAMA–TENNESSEE LEAGUE (OR TENNESSEE–ALABAMA LEAGUE) (CLASS D, 1904, 1921#)

Albany–Decatur, Alabama	1921#
Chattanooga, Tennessee	1904
Columbia, Tennessee	1904, 1921#
Decatur, Alabama	1904
Huntsville, Alabama	1904
Knoxville, Tennessee	1904
Russellville, Alabama	1921#
Sheffield, Alabama	1904, 1921#

ANTHRACITE LEAGUE (CLASS D 1928X)

Hazelton, Pennsylvania	1928X
Mahanoy City, Pennsylvania	1928X
Mount Carmel, Pennsylvania	1928X
Shamokin, Pennsylvania	1928X
Shenandoah, Pennsylvania	1928X
Tamaqua, Pennsylvania	1928X

APPALACHIAN LEAGUE (CLASS D 1911–14X, 1921–25X, 1937–55, 1957–62; ROOKIE 1963—)

Asheville, North Carolina	1911–12
Bluefield, West Virginia	1946–55, 1957—
Bristol, Virginia	1911–13, 1921–25X, 1940–55, 1969—
Cleveland, Tennessee	1911–12, 1921–22

Team	Years in Operation
Covington, Virginia	1966—
Elizabethton, Tennessee	1937–42, 1945–51, 1974—
Erwin, Tennessee	1940, 1943–44
Greenville, Tennessee	1921–25X, 1938–41X, 1942X
Harlan, Kentucky	1961–63, 1965
Harriman, Tennessee	1914#X
Johnson City, Tennessee	1911–13, 1921–24, 1937–55, 1957–61, 1964—
Kingsport, Tennessee	1921–25X, 1938–52, 1957, 1960–63, 1969—
Knoxville, Tennessee	1911–14X, 1921–24
Lynchburg, Virginia	1959
Marion, Virginia	1955#, 1965—
Middlesboro, Kentucky	1913–14X, 1961–63
Morristown, Tennessee	1911–14X, 1923–25X, 1959–61
Narrows, Virginia	1946–50
Newport, Tennessee	1937–42X
Pennington Gap, Virginia	1937–40
Pineville, Kentucky	1914X
Pulaski, Virginia	1946–50, 1952–55, 1957–58, 1969—
Rome, Georgia	1913
Salem, Virginia	1955, 1957–67
Welch, West Virginia	1946–55X
Wytheville, Virginia	1953–55, 1957–65, 1967, 1969, 1971–73—

ARIZONA–MEXICO LEAGUE (CLASS C, 1955–58)

Bisbee–Douglas, Arizona	1955
Cananea, Sonora, Mexico	1955–57
Chihuahua, Chihuahua, Mexico	1958
Douglas, Arizona	1956–58
Globe–Miami, Arizona	1955
Juarez, Chihuahua, Mexico	1958
Las Vegas, Nevada	1957
Mexicali, Baja California, Mexico	1955–57X, 1958
Nogales, Sonora, Mexico	1955–56, 1958
Phoenix, Arizona	1955–57
Tijuana, Baja California, Mexico	1956X (franchise suspended operations on June 28, 1956; the league finished with seven Clubs)
Tucson, Arizona	1955–58
Yuma, Arizona	1955–56

Team   *Years in Operation*

ARIZONA STATE LEAGUE (CLASS D 1928–30)

Bisbee, Arizona	1928–30
El Paso, Texas	1930
Globe, Arizona	1929–30
Mesa, Arizona	1929
Miami, Arizona	1928–30
Phoenix, Arizona	1928–30
Tucson, Arizona	1928–30

ARIZONA–TEXAS LEAGUE (CLASS D, 1931; CLASS C, 1932— DISBANDED JULY 24,1932; CLASS D, 1937–39; CLASS C, 1940–41, 1947–50, 1952–54)

Albuquerque, New Mexico	1932X, 1937–41
Bisbee, Arizona	1931–32X, 1937–41
Bisbee–Douglas, Arizona	1947–50, 1952–54
Cananea, Sonora, Mexico	1954
Chihuahua, Chihuahua, Mexico	1952
El Paso, Texas	1931–32X, 1937–41, 1947–50, 1952–54
Globe, Arizona	1931
Globe–Miami, Arizona	1947–50
Juarez, Chihuahua, Mexico	1947 (franchise shifted to Mesa on June 22, 1947), 1948–50, 1952–54
Mesa, Arizona	1947#
Mexicali, Baja California, Mexico	1953–54
Nogales, Sonora, Mexico	1931, 1954
Phoenix, Arizona	1931–32X, 1947–50, 1952–54
Tuscon, Arizona	1931–32X, 1937–41, 1947–50, 1952–54

ARKANSAS LEAGUE (CLASS D, 1908)

Argenta, Arkansas	1908
Brinkley, Arkansas	1908
Helena, Arkansas	1908
Hot Springs, Arkansas	1908
Newport, Arkansas	1908
Pine Bluff, Arkansas	1908
Poplar Bluff, Arkansas	1908

Team	Years in Operation

ARKANSAS–MISSOURI LEAGUE
(CLASS D, 1936–40X—DISBANDED ON JULY 1, 1940)

Bentonville, Arkansas	1936
Carthage, Missouri	1938–40X
Cassville, Missouri	1936
Fayetteville, Arkansas	1936–40X
Monett, Missouri	1936–39
Neosho, Missouri	1937–40X
Rogers, Arkansas	1936–38
Siloam Springs, Arkansas	1936–38, 1940X

ARKANSAS STATE LEAGUE (CLASS D, 1934–35)

Bentonville, Arkansas	1934–35
Cassville, Missouri	1935#
Fayetteville, Arkansas	1934–35
Huntsville, Arkansas	1935#
Rogers, Arkansas	1934–35
Siloam Springs, Arkansas	1934–35

ARKANSAS–TEXAS LEAGUE (CLASS D, 1906)

Camden, Arkansas	1906
Hot Springs, Arkansas	1906
Pine Bluff, Arkansas	1906
Texarkana, Arkansas	1906

ATLANTIC ASSOCIATION (CLASS D, 1908X)

Attleboro, Massachusetts	1908X
Lewiston, Maine	1908X
Newport, Rhode Island	1908X
Pawtucket, Rhode Island	1908X
Portland, Maine	1908X
Woonsocket, Rhode Island	1908X

Team   *Years in Operation*

ATLANTIC LEAGUE (CLASS D, 1914)

Asbury Park, New Jersey	1914#
Bloomfield, New Jersey	1914 (franchise shifted to Asbury Park in midseason)
Danbury, Connecticut	1914
Long Branch, New Jersey	1914#
Middletown, New York	1914
Newark, New Jersey	1914 (franchise shifted to Long Branch July 1)
Newburgh, New York	1914
Paterson, New Jersey	1914
Perth–Amboy, New Jersey	1914
Poughkeepsie, New York	1914

BIG STATE LEAGUE (CLASS B 1947–57)

Abilene, Texas	1956–57
Austin, Texas	1947–55
Beaumont, Texas	1956–57
Bryan, Texas	1953#, 1954 (franchise shifted to Del Rio on June 25, 1954)
Corpus Christi, Texas	1954–57
Del Rio, Texas	1954#
Gainesville, Texas	1947–51
Galveston, Texas	1954–55X
Greenville, Texas	1947–50, 1953 (franchise shifted to Bryan on June 25, 1953)
Harlingen, Texas	1954–55
Longview, Texas	1952–53#
Lubbock, Texas	1956 (franchise shifted to Texas City on July 7, 1956)
Paris, Texas	1947–48, 1952–53
Port Arthur, Texas	1955–57 (franchise shifted to Temple on May 30, 1957)
Sherman–Denison, Texas	1948–51
Sherman, Texas	1947
Temple, Texas	1949–54, 1957#X
Texarkana, Texas	1947–53
Texas City, Texas	1955–56#
Tyler, Texas	1951–55X
Victoria, Texas	1956–57
Waco, Texas	1947–53 (franchise shifted to Longview on May 29, 1953), 1954–56
Wichita Falls, Texas	1947–53, 1956–57X

Team   *Years in Operation*

BI-STATE LEAGUE (ILLINOIS–WISCONSIN)
(CLASS D, 1915X)

Aurora, Illinois	1915X
Elgin, Illinois	1915X
Freeport, Illinois	1915X
Ottawa, Illinois	1915X
Racine, Wisconsin	1915X
Streator, Illinois	1915X

(Note: See listing for the Wisconsin-Illinois League.)

BI-STATE LEAGUE (NORTH CAROLINA–VIRGINIA)
(CLASS D, 1915, 1934–42)

Bassett, Virginia	1935–40
Burlington, North Carolina	1942
Danville–Schoolfield, Virginia	1939–41
Danville, Virginia	1934–38, 1942
Fieldale, Virginia	1934–36
Leaksville–Spray–Draper, North Carolina	1934–42
Martinsville, Virginia	1934–41
Mayodan, North Carolina	1934–41
Mount Airy, North Carolina	1934–41
Reidsville, North Carolina	1935–40
Rocky Mount, North Carolina	1942
Sanford, North Carolina	1941–42
South Boston, Virginia	1937–40
Wilson, North Carolina	1942

BLUE GRASS LEAGUE (CLASS D, 1909–12, 1922–24)

Cynthiana, Kentucky	1922–24
Frankfort, Kentucky	1909–12
Lexington, Kentucky	1909–12, 1922–24
Maysville, Kentucky	1910#, 1911–12, 1922–23
Mount Sterling, Kentucky	1922–23
Nicholasville, Kentucky	1912#X
Paris, Kentucky	1909–12

Team	Years in Operation
Richmond, Kentucky	1909–12
Shelbyville, Kentucky	1909–10 (franchise shifted to Maysville late in 1910 season)
Winchester, Kentucky	1909–12 (franchise shifted to Nicholasville in midseason), 1922–24

(Note: Casey Stengel, in his first year in professional baseball in 1910, played the outfield for Shelbyville–Maysville and batted .223 in 69 games. Stengel joined Shelbyville–Maysville in July after the Kankakee, Illinois, team (of the Northern Association) folded.

BLUE RIDGE LEAGUE (CLASS D, 1915–18, 1920–30, 1946–50)

Abingdon, Virginia	1948#
Bassett, Virginia	1950#
Chambersburg, Pennsylvania	1915–17 (franchise shifted to Cumberland on June 30, 1917), 1920–30
Cumberland, Maryland	1917# (gained Chambersburg franchise on June 30)
Elkin, North Carolina	1949–50
Frederick, Maryland	1915–17, 1920–30
Galax, Virginia	1946–50
Gettysburg, Pennsylvania	1915–17
Hagerstown, Maryland	1915–17, 1920–30
Hanover, Pennsylvania	1915–17, 1920–29
Leaksville–Spray–Draper, North Carolina	1948X
Lenoir, North Carolina	1946–47
Martinsburg, West Virginia	1915–17, 1920, 1922–27, 1929
Martinsville, Virginia	1921, 1928
Mount Airy, North Carolina	1946–50
North Wilkesboro, North Carolina	1948–50
Radford, Pennsylvania	1946–50
Waynesboro, Pennsylvania	1920–30
Wytheville, Virginia	1948–50X

BORDER LEAGUE (MICHIGAN–ONTARIO)
(CLASS D, 1912–13)

Mount Clemens, Michigan	1912–13
Pontiac, Michigan	1912–13
Port Huron, Michigan	1912–13
Windsor, Ontario, Canada	1912–13
Wyandotte, Michigan	1913
Ypsilanti, Michigan	1913

(Note: The Border League was reorganized as the Eastern Michigan League for the 1914 season.)

Team	Years in Operation

BORDER LEAGUE (NEW YORK–ONTARIO–QUEBEC) (CLASS C, 1946–51X—DISBANDED ON JULY 15)

Auburn, New York	1946–51X
Cornwall, Ontario, Canada	1951X
Geneva, New York	1947–51X
Granby, Quebec, Canada	1946
Kingston, Ontario, Canada	1946–51X
Ogdensburg, New York	1946–51X
Ottawa, Ontario, Canada	1947–50
Sherbrooke, Quebec, Canada	1946
Watertown, New York	1946–51X

BUCKEYE LEAGUE (OHIO) (CLASS D, 1915X— DISBANDED ON JULY 5)

Akron, Ohio	1915X
Canton, Ohio	1915X
Findlay, Ohio	1915X
Lima, Ohio	1915X
Marion, Ohio	1915X
Newark, Ohio	1915X

CALIFORNIA LEAGUE (CLASS C, 1941–42—DISBANDED ON JUNE 28; CLASS C, 1946–62; CLASS A, 1963—)

Anaheim, California	1941
Bakersfield, California	1941–42X, 1946—
Fresno, California	1941–42X, 1946—
Las Vegas, Nevada	1958#
Lodi, California	1966—
Merced, California	1941
Modesto, California	1946–64, 1966—
Reno, Nevada	1955#, 1956–64, 1966—
Riverside, California	1941X
Salinas, California	1954–58, 1963–65, 1973—
San Bernardino, California	1941X
San Jose, California	1942X, 1947–58 (franchise shifted to Las Vegas on May 26)
Santa Barbara, California	1941–42X, 1946–53, 1962–67
Stockton, California	1941, 1946–72
Ventura, California	1947–55 (franchise shifted to Reno on July 1)
Visalia, California	1946–62, 1968—

Team	Years in Operation

CALIFORNIA STATE LEAGUE
(CLASS B, 1910X; CLASS D, 1913–14X, 1915X, 1929X)

Team	Years in Operation
Alameda, California	1915X
Bakersfield, California	1929X
Fresno, California	1910X, 1913–14X
Merced, California	1910X
Modesto, California	1914X, 1915X
Oakland, California	1915X
San Bernardino, California	1929X
San Diego, California	1929X
San Francisco, California	1915X
San Jose, California	1910X, 1913–14X, 1915X
Stockton, California	1910X, 1915X
Ventura, California	1929X
Watsonville, California	1913

(Note: The California State League operated from 1902 through 1909 as an outlaw league. The circuit joined the National Association in time for the 1910 season.)

CANADIAN–AMERICAN LEAGUE (CLASS C, 1936–42, 1946–51)

Team	Years in Operation
Amsterdam, New York	1938–42, 1946–51
Auburn, New York	1938, 1940
Brockville, Ontario	1936–37
Cornwall, Ontario	1938–39
Gloversville–Johnstown, New York	1937–42, 1946–51
Kingston, Ontario	1951
Ogdensburg, New York	1936–39
Oneonta, New York	1940–42, 1946–51
Oswego, New York	1936–40
Ottawa, Ontario	1936–40
Perth, Ontario	1936
Perth–Cornwall, Ontario	1937
Pittsfield, Massachusetts	1941–42, 1946–51
Quebec, Quebec	1941–42, 1946–50
Rome, New York	1937–42, 1946–51
Schenectady, New York	1946–50
Smith Falls, New York	1937
Three Rivers, Quebec	1941–42, 1946–50
Utica, New York	1939–42
Watertown, New York	1936

Team   *Years in Operation*

CANADIAN LEAGUE (CLASS C TO D, 1911;
CLASS C, 1912–13; CLASS B, 1914–15)

Team	Years in Operation
Berlin, Ontario	1911–13
Brantford, Ontario	1911–15
Erie, Pennsylvania	1914
Guelph, Ontario	1911–15
Hamilton, Ontario	1911–15
London, Ontario	1911–15
Ottawa, Ontario	1912–15
Petersboro, Ontario	1912–14
St. Thomas, Ontario	1911–15
Toronto, Ontario	1914

CAPE BRETON COLLIERY LEAGUE (CANADA)
(CLASS D, 1937–38; CLASS C, 1939)

Team	Years in Operation
Dominion, Nova Scotia	1937–38X
Glace Bay, Nova Scotia	1937–39
New Waterford, Nova Scotia	1937–39
Sydney, Nova Scotia	1937–39
Sydney Mines, Nova Scotia	1937–39

CAROLINA BASEBALL ASSOCIATION (CLASS D, 1908–12)

Team	Years in Operation
Anderson, South Carolina	1908–12
Charlotte, North Carolina	1908–12
Greensboro, North Carolina	1908–12
Greenville, South Carolina	1908–12
Spartanburg, South Carolina	1908–12
Winston–Salem, North Carolina	1908–12

CAROLINA LEAGUE (CLASS C, 1945–48; CLASS B,
1949–62; CLASS A, 1963—)

Team	Years in Operation
Asheville, North Carolina	1967
Burlington, North Carolina	1945–55, 1958–72
Danville, Virginia	1945–58
Durham, North Carolina	1945–67
Fayetteville, North Carolina	1950–56
Greensboro, North Carolina	1945–68
Hampton–Newport News, (Peninsula) Virginia	1974—

Team	Years in Operation
High Point–Thomasville, North Carolina	1954–58, 1968–69
Kinston, North Carolina	1956–57X, 1962—
Leaksville, North Carolina	1945
Leaksville–Spray–Draper, North Carolina	1946–47X
Lynchburg, Virginia	1966—
Martinsville, Virginia	1945–49
Newport News, Virginia	1963–68
Norfolk–Portsmouth (Tidewater), Virginia	1963–68
Raleigh, North Carolina	1945–53, 1958–67
Raleigh–Durham, North Carolina	1968–70
Red Springs, North Carolina	1969
Reidsville, North Carolina	1948–55
Rocky Mount, North Carolina	1962—
Salem, Virginia	1968—
Wilson, North Carolina	1956, 1957#, 1958–68, 1973—
Winston–Salem, North Carolina	1945—

CENTRAL ASSOCIATION (CLASS D, 1904–14; CLASS B, 1915; CLASS D, 1916–17X; CLASS C, 1947–49)

Boone, Iowa	1904–05
Burlington, Iowa	1904–16 (franchise shifted to Ottumwa in midseason 1916)
Cedar Rapids, Iowa	1913–17X, 1949
Charles City–Dubuque, Iowa	1917
Clinton, Iowa	1906, 1914–17X, 1947–49
Fort Dodge, Iowa	1904–06, 1916–17X
Galesburg, Illinois	1910–12, 1914#
Hannibal, Missouri	1909–12, 1947–48
Keokuk, Iowa	1904–15, 1947–49
Kewanee, Illinois	1908–13, 1948#, 1949
LaCrosse, Wisconsin	1917X
Marshalltown, Iowa	1904–07, 1914–17X
Mason City, Iowa	1915–17X
Moline, Illinois	1947–48 (franchise shifted to Kewanee on June 18, 1948)
Monmouth, Illinois	1910–13
Muscatine, Iowa	1911–16
Oskaloosa, Iowa	1904–08
Ottumwa, Iowa	1904–14, 1916#
Quincy, Illinois	1907–10

Team	Years in Operation
Rockford, Illinois	1947–49
Waterloo, Iowa	1904–09, 1913–17

(Note: The Central Association was known as the Iowa State League, 1904–07; Central Association, 1908–17, 1947–49.)

CENTRAL CALIFORNIA BASEBALL LEAGUE
(CLASS D, 1910–11)

Alameda, California	1910–11
Berkeley, California	1911
Elmhurst, California	1911
Fruitvale, California	1911
Hayward, California	1911
Healdsburg, California	1911
Napa, California	1910
Petaluma, California	1910
Richmond, California	1910–11
San Leandro, California	1911
San Rafael, California	1910–11
Santa Rosa, California	1910
St. Helena, California	1910
Vallejo, California	1910

CENTRAL INTERNATIONAL LEAGUE (CLASS C, 1912)

Duluth, Minnesota	1912
Fargo, North Dakota	1912
Grand Forks, North Dakota	1912
Superior, Wisconsin	1912
Virginia, Minnesota	1912
Winnipeg, Manitoba, Canada	1912

Team	*Years in Operation*

CENTRAL KANSAS LEAGUE (CLASS D, 1909–11X— LEAGUE DISBANDED JULY 5, 1911; 1912) (BECAME THE NUCLEUS OF THE KANSAS STATE LEAGUE IN 1913)

Abilene, Kansas	1909–10
Beloit, Kansas	1909–10
Clay Center, Kansas	1909–11X
Concordia, Kansas	1911X
Ellsworth, Kansas	1909–10
Great Bend, Kansas	1911X–1912
Junction City, Kansas	1909–11X, 1912
Lyons, Kansas	1911X–1912
Manhattan, Kansas	1909–11X, 1912
Minneapolis, Kansas	1909–10, 1912#
Newton, Kansas	1912 (franchise shifted to Minneapolis in midseason)
Salina, Kansas	1909–10, 1912

CENTRAL LEAGUE (CLASS B, 1903–17, 1920#, 1921–22, 1928–30, 1932, 1934—LEAGUE DISBANDED JUNE 10; CLASS A, 1948–51)

Akron, Ohio	1912, 1928–29, 1932X
Battle Creek, Michigan	1916#X
Canton, Ohio	1905–07, 1912, 1928–30, 1932#X
Charleston, West Virginia	1949–51
Dayton, Ohio	1903–17, 1928–30, 1932, 1948–51
Erie, Pennsylvania	1912, 1915, 1928–30, 1932
Evansville, Indiana	1903–11X, 1913–17
Flint, Michigan	1948–51
Fort Wayne, Indiana	1903–04, 1908–15, 1917, 1928–30, 1932, 1934X, 1948
Grand Rapids, Michigan	1903–11 (franchise shifted to Newark on June 28, 1911; reentered league on July 14 to replace South Bend), 1912–17, 1920#, 1921–22, 1948–51
Iona, Michigan	1921#, 1922
Jackson, Michigan	1921X
Kalamazoo, Michigan	1920#, 1921–22
Lansing, Michigan	1921–22
Lima, Ohio	1934X
Ludington, Michigan	1920#, 1921–22
Muskegon, Michigan	1916–17, 1920#, 1921–22, 1934X, 1948–51
Newark, Ohio	1911#
Peoria, Illinois	1917#, 1934X

Team	Years in Operation
Richmond, Indiana	1917, 1930
Saginaw, Michigan	1948–51
South Bend, Indiana	1903–11X, 1912, 1915X, 1916–17 (franchise shifted to Peoria on July 8), 1932X
Springfield, Ohio	1912–14X, 1916–17, 1928–30
Terre Haute, Indiana	1903–16
Wheeling, West Virginia	1903–12, 1915–16
Youngstown, Ohio	1912, 1915, 1932
Zanesville, Ohio	1908–12

CENTRAL NEW YORK LEAGUE (CLASS D, 1910)

Auburn, New York	1910
Cortland, New York	1910
Geneva, New York	1910
Oneida, New York	1910
Oswego, New York	1910
Rome, New York	1910

CENTRAL TEXAS LEAGUE: CENTRAL TEXAS TROLLEY (CLASS D, 1914#–1915X), CENTRAL TEXAS LEAGUE (CLASS D, 1916#–1917X)

Corsicana, Texas	1914#–1915X, 1917X
Ennis, Texas	1914#–1915X, 1916X–1917X
Hillsboro, Texas	1914#
Italy, Texas	1914#
Kaufman, Texas	1915#X
Marlin, Texas	1916X–1917X
Mexia, Texas	1915#X–1916#X, 1917X
Temple, Texas	1916X–1917X
Terrell, Texas	1915#X–1916X
Waxahachie, Texas	1914#–1915#X, 1916X–1917X

Team	*Years in Operation*

COASTAL PLAIN LEAGUE (CLASS D, 1937–41, 1946–52)

Ayden, North Carolina	1937–38
Edenton, North Carolina	1952
Goldsboro, North Carolina	1937–41, 1946–52
Greenville, North Carolina	1937–40, 1946–51X
Kinston, North Carolina	1937–41, 1946–52
New Bern, North Carolina	1937–41, 1946–52
Roanoke Rapids, North Carolina	1947–52
Rocky Mount, North Carolina	1941, 1946–52
Snow Hill, North Carolina	1937–40
Tarboro, North Carolina	1937–41, 1946–52X
Williamston, North Carolina	1937–41
Wilson, North Carolina	1939–41, 1946–52

COLONIAL LEAGUE (CLASS C, 1914; CLASS B, 1947–50X— DISBANDED ON JULY 16)

Bridgeport, Connecticut	1947–50X
Bristol, Connecticut	1949–50X
Brockton, Massachusetts	1914
Fall River, Massachusetts	1914
Kingston, New York	1948#, 1949–50X
New Bedford, Massachusetts	1914
New Brunswick, New Jersey	1947–48X
New London, Connecticut	1947
Pawtucket, Rhode Island	1914
Port Chester, New York	1947–48
Poughkeepsie, New York	1947–50X
Stamford, Connecticut	1947–49
Taunton, Massachusetts	1914
Torrington, Massachusetts	1950X
Waterbury, Connecticut	1947–50X
Woonsocket, Rhode Island	1914

(Note: Operated in 1915 outside the jurisdiction of the National Association— affiliated with the outlaw Federal League.)

CONNECTICUT ASSOCIATION (CLASS D, 1910)

Middletown, Connecticut	1910
New London, Connecticut	1910
Norwich, Connecticut	1910
Willimantic, Connecticut	1910

Team	Years in Operation

CONNECTICUT STATE LEAGUE (CLASS D, 1902–10)
CONNECTICUT LEAGUE (CLASS D, 1911–12—BECAME
THE EASTERN ASSOCIATION IN 1913)

Bridgeport, Connecticut	1902–12
Hartford, Connecticut	1902–12
Holyoke, Massachusetts	1903–11X, 1912
Meriden, Connecticut	1902#, 1903–05, 1908
New Britain, Connecticut	1911–12 (franchise shifted to Waterbury in midseason)
New Haven, Connecticut	1902–12
New London, Connecticut	1902#, 1903–07
Northampton, Massachusetts	1909–11X
Norwich, Connecticut	1902#, 1903–07
Springfield, Massachusetts	1902–12
Waterbury, Connecticut	1902, 1906–12#

COPPER-COUNTRY SOO LEAGUE (CLASS D, 1905)

Calumet, Michigan	1905
Hancock, Michigan	1905
Lake Linden, Michigan	1905
Sault Ste. Marie, Michigan	1905X

(Note: In 1906, the Copper-Country Soo League joined with the Northern League to form the Northern Copper Country League, a circuit which had a life of two seasons.)

COTTON STATES LEAGUE (1902–08; CLASS D, 1910–14X, 1921–23X; CLASS C, 1936–41, 1947–55)

Aberdeen, Mississippi	1914X
Alexandria, Louisiana	1925–30X
Baton Rouge, Louisiana	1902–05X, 1906, 1929#, 1930–32X
Brookhaven, Mississippi	1924–25
Clarksdale, Mississippi	1913, 1922–23X, 1936–41X, 1947–51
Cleveland, Mississippi	1936
Columbus, Mississippi	1907–08, 1912–14X
DeQuincy, Louisiana	1932#X
El Dorado, Arkansas	1929–32X, 1936–41, 1947–55
Greenville, Mississippi	1902–05X, 1922–23X, 1936–41, 1947–55

Team	Years in Operation
Greenwood, Mississippi	1910–12, 1922–23X, 1936–40, 1947–52
Gulfport, Mississippi	1906–08 (also represented Biloxi in 1908), 1926–28
Hattiesburg, Mississippi	1910–11, 1923X, 1924–29X
Helena, Arkansas	1936–41, 1947–49
Hot Springs, Arkansas	1938–41, 1947–55
Jackson, Mississippi	1902, 1905X, 1906–08, 1910–14X, 1922–23X, 1924–31, 1932X, 1936, 1953
Jackson, Tennessee	1914X
Lake Charles, Louisiana	1929#, 1930X
Laurel, Mississippi	1922–23X, 1924–29
Marshall, Texas	1941#
Meridian, Mississippi	1905X, 1906–08, 1910–14X, 1925–29 (franchise shifted to Lake Charles in midseason), 1952–55
Mobile, Alabama	1905X, 1906–07
Monroe, Louisiana	1902–04, 1908, 1924–32X, 1937–41, 1950–55
Natchez, Mississippi	1902–04, 1948–53
Opelousas, Louisiana	1932#X
Pensacola, Florida	1913
Pine Bluff, Arkansas	1903–04, 1930–32X, 1936–40, 1948–55X
Port Arthur, Texas	1932X
Selma, Alabama	1913
Texarkana, Texas	1941
Vicksburg, Mississippi	1902–05X, 1906–08, 1910–12X, 1922–23X, 1924–31, 1937, 1941, 1955
Yazoo City, Mississippi	1910–12X

DAKOTA LEAGUE (CLASS D, 1921–23X—LEAGUE DISBANDED ON JULY 13) (CALLED THE SOUTH DAKOTA LEAGUE IN 1923)

Aberdeen, South Dakota	1921–23X
Fargo, North Dakota	1922
Huron, South Dakota	1921
Jamestown, North Dakota	1922
Madison, South Dakota	1921
Mitchell, South Dakota	1921–23X
Redfield, South Dakota	1921
Sioux Falls, South Dakota	1921–23X
Valley City, North Dakota	1922
Wahpeton, North Dakota; Breckenridge, Minnesota	1921–22
Watertown, South Dakota	1921–23X

(Note: See entry for the South Dakota League of 1920.)

Team	Years in Operation

DELTA LEAGUE (CLASS D, 1904)

Team	Years in Operation
Brookhaven, Mississippi	1904
Canton, Mississippi	1904
Clarksdale, Mississippi	1904
Hattiesburg, Mississippi	1904
Jackson, Mississippi	1904
Yazoo City, Mississippi	1904

DIXIE LEAGUE (ARKANSAS, LOUISIANA, MISSISSIPPI, AND TEXAS) (CLASS C, 1933)

Team	Years in Operation
Baton Rouge, Louisiana	1933
El Dorado, Arkansas	1933
Henderson, Texas	1933
Jackson, Mississippi	1933
Longview, Texas	1933
Pine Bluff, Arkansas	1933#
Shreveport, Louisiana	1933
Tyler, Texas	1933
Waco, Texas	1933 (franchise shifted to Pine Bluff in midseason)

DIXIE LEAGUE (GEORGIA AND ALABAMA) (CLASS D, 1916#–1917X)

Team	Years in Operation
Bainbridge, Georgia	1916#–1917X
Dothan, Alabama	1916#–1917X
Eufaula, Alabama	1916#–1917X
Moultrie, Georgia	1916#–1917X
Quitman, Georgia	1916#–1917X
Tifton, Georgia	1917X
Valdosta, Georgia	1916#

EASTERN ASSOCIATION (CLASS B, 1913–14)

Team	Years in Operation
Bridgeport, Connecticut	1913–14
Hartford, Connecticut	1913–14
Holyoke, Massachusetts	1913
New Britain, Connecticut	1914
New Haven, Connecticut	1913–14
New London, Connecticut	1913–14
Pittsfield, Massachusetts	1913–14
Springfield, Massachusetts	1913–14
Waterbury, Connecticut	1913–14

Team	Years in Operation

EASTERN CANADA LEAGUE (CLASS B, 1922#–1923)

Montreal, Quebec	1922#, 1923#
Ottawa, Ontario	1922#, 1923
Quebec, Quebec	1923
Three Rivers, Quebec	1922#, 1923 (franchise shifted to Montreal on July 11)
Valleyfield (Cape Madeliene), Quebec	1922#

EASTERN CAROLINA LEAGUE (CLASS D, 1908–11, 1928–29)

Fayetteville, North Carolina	1909–11, 1928–29
Goldsboro, North Carolina	1908–09, 1928–29
Greenville, North Carolina	1928–29
New Bern, North Carolina	1908X
Raleigh, North Carolina	1908–11
Rocky Mount, North Carolina	1909–11, 1928–29
Wilmington, North Carolina	1908–09, 1928–29
Wilson, North Carolina	1908–11

(Note: Known as the Eastern Carolina Association in 1908–11.)

EAST DIXIE LEAGUE (CLASS C, 1934–35)

Baton Rouge, Louisiana	1934 (franchise shifted to Clarksdale in midseason)
Clarksdale, Mississippi	1934#, 1935
Cleveland, Mississippi	1935#
Columbus, Mississippi	1935 (franchise shifted to Cleveland in midseason)
El Dorado, Arkansas	1934–35
Greenville, Mississippi	1934–35
Greenwood, Mississippi	1935
Helena, Arkansas	1935
Jackson, Mississippi	1934–35
Pine Bluff, Arkansas	1934–35
Shreveport, Louisiana	1934X

Team	Years in Operation

EASTERN ILLINOIS LEAGUE (CLASS D, 1907–08X— LEAGUE DISBANDED AUGUST 20)

Centralia, Illinois	1907 (franchise shifted to Paris shortly after season opened)
Charleston, Illinois	1907–08X
Danville, Illinois	1908 # X (gained Staunton franchise during season)
Linton, Illinois	1908 (gained Pana franchise during season)
Mattoon, Illinois	1907–08X
Pana, Illinois	1907–08 (franchise shifted to Linton)
Paris, Illinois	1907–08X (gained Centralia franchise during 1907 season)
Shelbyville, Illinois	1907–08X
Staunton, Illinois	1908 (franchise shifted to Danville)
Taylorsville, Illinois	1908X
Vincennes, Indiana	1908X

EASTERN KANSAS LEAGUE (CLASS D, 1910–11X)

Atchison, Kansas	1911X
Blue Rapids, Kansas	1910
Hiawatha, Kansas	1910–11X
Horton, Kansas	1910–11X
Marysville, Kansas	1910
Sabetha, Kansas	1910
Seneca, Kansas	1910–11X

EASTERN LEAGUE (CLASS B, 1916–18X—SUSPENDED OPERATIONS JULY 22; 1919–32X—DISBANDED JULY 17)

Albany, New York	1920–32X
Allentown, Pennsylvania	1929–32X
Bridgeport, Connecticut	1916–18X, 1919–32X
Hartford, Connecticut	1916–18X, 1919–30X, 1931–32X
Lawrence, Massachusetts	1916X, 1917
Lowell, Massachusetts	1916X
Lynn, Massachusetts	1916
New Haven, Connecticut	1916–18X, 1919–30X, 1931–32X
New London, Connecticut	1916–18X
Norfolk, Virginia	1931–32X
Pittsfield, Massachusetts	1919–30X
Providence, Rhode Island	1918X, 1919, 1926–30X
Richmond, Virginia	1931–32
Springfield, Massachusetts	1916–18X, 1919–32X

Team   *Years in Operation*

EASTERN MICHIGAN LEAGUE (CLASS D, 1914X)

Ann Arbor, Michigan	1914X
Mount Clemens, Michigan	1914X
Port Huron, Michigan	1914X
Windsor, Ontario, Canada	1914X
Wyandotte, Michigan	1914X
Ypsilanti, Michigan	1914X

EASTERN SHORE LEAGUE (CLASS D, 1922–28, 1937–41, 1946–49)

Cambridge, Maryland	1922–28, 1937–41, 1946–49
Cape Charles, Virginia	1928
Centreville, Maryland	1937–41, 1946
Crisfield, Maryland	1922–28, 1937
Dover, Delaware	1923–26, 1937–40, 1946–48
Easton, Maryland	1924–28, 1937–41, 1946–49
Federalsburg, Maryland	1937–41, 1946–49
Laurel, Delaware	1922–23
Milford, Delaware	1923X, 1938–41, 1946–48
Northampton, Virginia	1927
Parksley, Virginia	1922–28
Pocomoke City, Maryland	1922–23X, 1937–40
Rehoboth Beach, Delaware	1947–49
Salisbury, Maryland	1922–28, 1937–41, 1946–49
Seaford, Delaware	1946–49

EAST TEXAS LEAGUE (CLASS D, 1916X, 1923–26, 1931X; CLASS C, 1936–40, 1946, 1949–50)

Bryan, Texas	1949–50X
Crockett, Texas	1916X
Gladewater, Texas	1936, 1949–50
Greenville, Texas	1923–26, 1946
Henderson, Texas	1931X, 1936–40, 1946, 1949–50
Jacksonville, Texas	1936–40X, 1946
Kilgore, Texas	1931X, 1936–40, 1949
Longview, Texas	1923–26, 1931X, 1936–40, 1949–50
Lufkin, Texas	1916X, 1946
Marshall, Texas	1923–26, 1936–40, 1949–50
Mount Pleasant, Texas	1923–25X
Nacogdoches, Texas	1916X
Palestine, Texas	1916X, 1936–40X

Team	Years in Operation
Paris, Texas	1923, 1946, 1949–50X
Rusk, Texas	1916X
Sherman, Texas	1946
Sulphur Springs, Texas	1923–25X
Texarkana, Texas	1924–26, 1937–40, 1946
Tyler, Texas	1924–26, 1931X, 1936–40, 1946, 1949–50

EMPIRE STATE LEAGUE (GEORGIA) (CLASS D, 1913)

Americus, Georgia	1913
Brunswick, Georgia	1913
Cordele, Georgia	1913X
Thomasville, Georgia	1913
Valdosta, Georgia	1913
Waycross, Georgia	1913

EMPIRE STATE LEAGUE (NEW YORK) (1905–07)

Auburn, New York	1906–07
Fulton, New York	1905–07
Geneva, New York	1905–07
Lyons, New York	1905, 1907
Oswego, New York	1905–07
Penn Yan, New York	1906X
Rome, New York	1905
Seneca Falls, New York	1905–07

Team	Years in Operation

EVANGELINE LEAGUE (CLASS D, 1934–42X—SUSPENDED OPERATIONS MAY 30, 1942; CLASS D, 1946–48; CLASS C, 1949–57)

Team	Years in Operation
Abbeville, Louisiana	1935–39, 1946–50, 1952
Alexandria, Louisiana	1934–42X, 1946–57
Baton Rouge, Louisiana	1946–57X
Crowley, Louisiana	1951–57
Hammond, Louisiana	1946–51
Houma, Louisiana	1940 (franchise shifted to Natchez, June 27), 1946–52
Jeanerette, Louisiana	1934–39
Lafayette, Louisiana	1934–42X, 1948–57X
Lake Charles, Louisiana	1935–42X, 1954–57
Monroe–West Monroe, Louisiana	1956
Natchez, Mississippi	1940#, 1941–42X, 1946–47
New Iberia, Louisiana	1934–42X, 1946–56X
Opelousas, Louisiana	1934–41
Port Arthur, Texas	1940–42X, 1954
Rayne, Louisiana	1934–41X
Texas City, Texas	1954X
Thibodeaux, Louisiana	1946–54X, 1956–57

FAR WEST LEAGUE (CLASS D, 1948–51)

Team	Years in Operation
Eugene, Oregon	1950–51
Klamath Falls, Oregon	1948–51
Marysville, California	1948–50
Medford, Oregon	1948–51
Oroville, California	1948
Pittsburg, California	1948X, 1949–51X
Redding, California	1948–51
Reno, Nevada	1950–51
Roseville, California	1948#
Santa Rosa, California	1948–49X
Vallejo, California	1949X
Willows, Califorina	1948–50

(Note: League finished the 1951 season with five clubs.)

FLORIDA EAST COAST LEAGUE (CLASS D, 1940–42X—DISBANDED ON MAY 14)

Team	Years in Operation
Cocoa, Florida	1941
DeLand, Florida	1942X

Team	Years in Operation
Fort Lauderdale, Florida	1940–41
Fort Pierce, Florida	1940–42X
Hollywood, Florida	1940
Miami, Florida	1940–42X
Miami Beach, Florida	1940–42X
Orlando, Florida	1942X
West Palm Beach, Florida	1940–42X

FLORIDA INTERNATIONAL LEAGUE (CLASS C, 1946–48; CLASS B, 1949–54X—DISBANDED ON JULY 27)

Fort Lauderdale, Florida	1947–52X, 1953
Havana, Cuba	1946–53
Key West, Florida	1952#
Lakeland, Florida	1946–52
Miami, Florida	1946–54X
Miami Beach, Florida	1946–54X
St. Petersburg, Florida	1947–54X
Tallahassee, Florida	1954X
Tampa, Florida	1946–54X
West Palm Beach, Florida	1946–54X

FLORIDA STATE LEAGUE (CLASS D, 1919–20; CLASS C, 1921–24X—SUSPENDED OPERATIONS ON AUGUST 8; CLASS D, 1925–27, 1936–41, 1946–62; CLASS A, 1963—)

Bartow, Florida	1919–20
Bradenton, Florida	1919–20, 1923#, 1924X, 1926
Cocoa, Florida	1951–58, 1965–72
Daytona Beach Florida	1920–24X, 1936–41, 1946–73
Deerfield Beach, Florida	1966 (franchise shifted to Winter Haven on June 27)
DeLand, Florida	1936–41, 1946–54, 1970
Fort Lauderdale, Florida	1962—
Gainesville, Florida	1936–41, 1946–52X, 1955–58
Jacksonville, Florida	1921–22, 1923X
Jacksonville Beach, Florida	1952–54
Key West, Florida	1969, 1971—
Lakeland, Florida	1919–24X, 1925–26, 1953#–55, 1960, 1962–64, 1967—
Leesburg, Florida	1937–41, 1946–53, 1956–57, 1960–61, 1965–68
Miami, Florida	1927, 1962—
Ocala, Florida	1940–41
Orlando, Florida	1919–24X, 1926–27, 1937–41, 1946–61, 1963–72
Palatka, Florida	1936–39, 1946–53X, 1956–62

Team	Years in Operation
Pompano Beach, Florida	1969–73
St. Augustine, Florida	1936–41, 1946–50, 1952X
St. Petersburg, Florida	1920–24X, 1925–27, 1955—
Sanford, Florida	1919–20, 1925–27, 1936–41X, 1946–53, 1955, 1959–60
Sarasota, Florida	1926–27, 1961–65
Tampa, Florida	1919–24X, 1925–27, 1957—
West Palm Beach, Florida	1955–56, 1965—
Winter Haven, Florida	1966#, 1967, 1969—

GEORGIA–ALABAMA LEAGUE (CLASS D, 1913–14, 1915–17X, 1928–30, 1946–51)

Team	Years in Operation
Alexander City, Alabama	1947–51X
Anniston, Alabama	1913–17X, 1928–30
Carrollton, Georgia	1928–30, 1946–50
Cedartown, Georgia	1928–30
Gadsden, Alabama	1913–14X, 1928–29
Gadsden (Tri-Cities, Gadsden-Attalla, Alabama City), Alabama	1917X
Griffin, Georgia	1915–17X, 1947–51
Huntsville, Alabama	1930
LaGrange, Georgia	1913–17X, 1946–51
Lanett, Alabama	1946–51
Lindale, Georgia	1928–30
Newnan, Georgia	1913–16, 1946–50
Opelika, Alabama	1913–14, 1946–51X
Rome–Lindale, Georgia	1914–17X
Rome, Georgia	1950–51
Selma, Alabama	1914
Talladega, Alabama	1913–17X, 1928–30
Tallassee, Alabama	1946–49

(Note: Known as the Georgia–Alabama Association in 1928.)

GEORGIA–FLORIDA LEAGUE (CLASS D, 1935–42, 1946–58, 1962; CLASS A, 1963)

Team	Years in Operation
Albany, Georgia	1935–42, 1946–58
Americus, Georgia	1935–42, 1946–51
Americus–Cordele, Georgia	1954
Brunswick, Georgia	1951–56, 1947#–58, 1962–63
Cordele, Georgia	1936–42, 1946–53, 1955
Dublin, Georgia	1958, 1962
Fitzgerald, Georgia	1953–54, 1956–57

Team	Years in Operation
Moultrie, Georgia	1935–42, 1946–52, 1955–57X (franchise shifted to Brunswick on June 1), 1962–63
Panama City, Florida	1935
Tallahassee, Florida	1935–42, 1946–50
Thomasville, Georgia	1935–41, 1946–50, 1952–58, 1962–63
Tifton, Georgia	1951–56
Valdosta, Georgia	1939–42, 1946–58
Waycross, Georgia	1939–42, 1946–58, 1963

GEORGIA STATE LEAGUE (CLASS D, 1906X, 1914–15X— SUSPENDED OPERATIONS ON MAY 31; 1920–21, 1948–56)

Albany, Georgia	1906X
Americus, Georgia	1906X, 1914–15X
Baxley, Georgia	1948
Baxley–Hazlehurst, Georgia	1949–50
Brunswick, Georgia	1914–15
Carrollton, Georgia	1920–21
Cedartown, Georgia	1920–21
Columbus, Georgia	1906X
Cordele, Georgia	1906X, 1914
Dothan, Alabama	1915X
Douglas, Georgia	1948–56
Dublin, Georgia	1949–56
Eastman, Georgia	1948–53
Fitzgerald, Georgia	1948–52
Gainesville, Florida	1915X
Griffin, Georgia	1920–21
Hazlehurst, Georgia	1952–56
Hazlehurst–Baxley, Georgia	1951
Jesup, Georgia	1950–53
LaGrange, Georgia	1920–21
Lindale, Georgia	1920–21
Rome, Georgia	1920–21
Sanderville, Georgia	1953–56
Sparta, Georgia	1948–49
Statesboro, Georgia	1952–55X
Thomasville, Georgia	1914–15X
Thomson, Georgia	1956
Tifton, Georgia	1949–50
Valdosta, Georgia	1906X, 1914–15X
Vidalia, Georgia	1952–56
Vidalia–Lyons, Georgia	1948–50
Waycross, Georgia	1906X, 1914–15X

(Note: In 1915, the Georgia State League was also called the "FLAG" League (for Florida, Louisiana, Alabama, and Georgia), although no team represented a Louisiana town.

Team	Years in Operation

GULF COAST LEAGUE (CLASS D, 1907–08X—DISBANDED ON JUNE 1; CLASS D, 1926#; CLASS C, 1950; CLASS B, 1951–53)

Team	Years in Operation
Alexandria, Louisiana	1907–08X
Beaumont, Texas	1908X
Brownsville, Texas	1951–53
Corpus Christi, Texas	1926#, 1951–53
Crowley, Louisiana	1908X, 1950
Galveston, Texas	1950–53
Harlingen, Texas	1951–53
Jacksonville, Texas	1950
Kingsville, Texas	1926#
Lafayette, Louisiana	1907
Lake Charles, Louisiana	1907–08X, 1950–53
Laredo, Texas	1926#, 1952–53
Leesville, Louisiana	1950#
Lufkin, Texas	1950 (franchise shifted to Leesville July 15)
Monroe, Louisiana	1907
Morgan City, Louisiana	1908X
Opelousas, Louisiana	1907
Orange, Texas	1907–08X
Port Arthur, Texas	1950–53
Texas City, Texas	1951–53
Victoria, Texas	1926X

HUDSON RIVER LEAGUE (CLASS D, 1903–07X— DISBANDED ON JUNE 20)

Team	Years in Operation
Catskill, New York	1903#
Glen Falls, New York	1906–07X
Hudson, New York	1903–07X
Kingston, New York	1903–07X
Newburgh, New York	1903–07X
Ossining, New York	1903 (franchise shifted to Catskill early in July)
Paterson, New York	1904–07X
Peekskill, New York	1903–05X
Pittsfield, Massachusetts	1905X
Poughkeepsie, New York	1903–07X
Saugerties, New York	1903–04
Schenectady, New York	1907X
Yonkers, New York	1905X, 1907X

(Note: Three teams—Peekskill, Pittsfield, and Yonkers—dropped out of the league in midseason 1905, and the circuit finished the year with five clubs.)

Team	Years in Operation

ILLINOIS–IOWA–INDIANA LEAGUE (THREE-I LEAGUE) (CLASS B, 1902–17X—SUSPENDED OPERATIONS ON JULY 8; 1919–32X—SUSPENDED OPERATIONS ON JULY 15; 1936, 1937, 1946–61)

Team	Years in Operation
Alton, Illinois	1917X
Appleton, Wisconsin	1958–61
Bloomington, Illinois	1902–11 (franchise shifted to Quincy in midseason), 1912–17X, 1919–31, 1935, 1937X, 1938–39
Burlington, Iowa	1952–61
Cedar Rapids, Iowa	1902–09, 1920–21, 1938–42, 1950–61
Clinton, Iowa	1907–08, 1937–41
Danville, Illinois	1910–14 (franchise shifted to Moline on June 14), 1922–32X, 1946–50
Davenport, Iowa	1902–06, 1909–16, 1946–52, 1957–58
Decatur, Illinois	1902–09, 1911#, 1912–15X, 1922–32X, 1935, 1937–42, 1946–50
Des Moines, Iowa	1959–61
Dubuque, Iowa	1903–15 (franchise shifted to Freeport in midseason)
Evansville, Indiana	1902, 1919–31, 1938–42, 1946–57
Fort Wayne, Indiana	1935
Freeport, Illinois	1915#
Green Bay, Wisconsin	1958–60
Hannibal, Missouri	1916–17X
Keokuk, Iowa	1952–57
Lincoln, Nebraska	1959–61
Madison, Wisconsin	1940–42
Moline, Illinois	1914#, 1915–17X, 1919–23, 1937–41
Peoria, Illinois	1905–17X, 1919–32X, 1935, 37, 1953–57
Quincy, Illinois	1911#, 1912–17X, 1925–32X, 1946–56
Rochester, Minnesota	1958 (franchise shifted to Winona on June 25)
Rockford, Illinois	1902–04, 1915–17X, 1919–23
Rock Island, Illinois	1902–11, 1916–17X, 1920–21
Sioux City, Iowa	1959–60
Springfield, Illinois	1903–11 (franchise shifted to Decatur in mid-season), 1912–14, 1925–32, 1935, 1938–42, 1946–49
Terre Haute, Indiana	1902, 1919–32X, 1935, 1937X, 1946–56X
Waterloo, Iowa	1910–11, 1938–42, 1946–56
Winona, Minnesota	1958#

Team	Years in Operation

ILLINOIS–MISSOURI LEAGUE (CLASS D, 1908–14)

Beardstown, Illinois	1909–10
Canton, Illinois	1908–13X
Champaign, Illinois	1911–14
Clinton, Illinois	1910–12
Galesburg, Illinois	1908–09
Hannibal, Missouri	1908
Havana, Illinois	1908
Kankakee, Illinois	1913–14X
LaSalle, Illinois	1914
Lincoln, Illinois	1910–14X
Macomb, Illinois	1908–10
Monmouth, Illinois	1908–09
Ottawa, Illinois	1914
Pekin, Illinois	1909–13X
Streator, Illinois	1912–14
Taylorville, Illinois	1911

ILLINOIS STATE LEAGUE (CLASS D, 1947–48)

Belleville, Illinois	1947–48
Centralia, Illinois	1947–48
Marion, Illinois	1947–48
Mattoon, Illinois	1947–48
Mount Vernon, Illinois	1947–48
Murphysboro, Illinois	1947X
West Frankfort, Illinois	1947–48

(Note: The Illinois State League was reorganized and renamed as the Mississippi–Ohio Valley League in time for the beginning of the 1949 season.)

INDIANA–MICHIGAN LEAGUE (CLASS D, 1910)

Benton Harbor, Michigan	1910
Berrien Springs, Michigan	1910
Elkhart, Indiana	1910
Gary, Indiana	1910
Goshen, Indiana	1910
Niles, Michigan	1910

Team	*Years in Operation*

INDIANA–OHIO LEAGUE (1907X)

Decatur, Indiana	1907X
Kokomo, Indiana	1907X
Portland, Indiana	1907X
Richmond, Indiana	1907X

(Note: Though there were no Ohio towns in the Indiana–Ohio League, the Indiana cities were close enough to the Ohio border so that crowds were expected to be drawn from the bi-state area.)

INDIANA STATE LEAGUE (CLASS D, 1909, 1911X— DISBANDED ON JULY 29)

Anderson, Indiana	1911X
Bluffton, Indiana	1909, 1911X
Huntington, Indiana	1909, 1911X
Kokomo, Indiana	1909
Lafayette, Indiana	1909, 1911X
Marion, Indiana	1909, 1911X
Wabash, Indiana	1909, 1911X

(Note: The Indiana State League apparently started play in the 1910 and 1912 seasons, but in both years the circuit suspended action after only a few games. There are no accurate records available, even as to the cities involved. The Indiana State League also was called the "Northern State of Indiana League.)

INTERMOUNTAIN LEAGUE (CLASS D, 1909X) (COLORADO)

No accurate records are available.

INTERNATIONAL LEAGUE (ONTARIO, CANADA–NEW YORK) (CLASS D, 1908X)

Hamilton, Ontaria	1908X
London, Ontario	1908X
Niagara Falls, New York	1908X
St. Thomas, Ontario	1908X

Team	*Years in Operation*

INTER-STATE ASSOCIATION (INDIANA, MICHIGAN, OHIO) (CLASS D, 1906)

Anderson, Indiana	1906
Bay City, Michigan	1906
Flint, Michigan	1906
Fort Wayne, Indiana	1906
Lima, Ohio	1906
Marion, Indiana	1906
Muncie, Indiana	1906
Saginaw, Michigan	1906

INTER-STATE LEAGUE (CLASS D, 1932X)

Stroudsburg, Pennsylvania was the unofficial league champion (won, 19; lost, 7; pct., 731). The league disbanded on June 29, 1932, after about four weeks of play.

INTER-STATE LEAGUE (OHIO, PENNSYLVANIA, WEST VIRGINIA) (CLASS B, 1913)

Akron, Ohio	1913X
Canton, Ohio	1913X
Erie, Pennsylvania	1913
Johnstown, Pennsylvania	1913
Steubenville, Ohio	1913X
Wheeling, West Virginia	1913
Youngstown, Ohio	1913
Zanesville, Ohio	1913X

INTER-STATE LEAGUE (CONNECTICUT, DELAWARE, MARYLAND, NEW YORK, NEW JERSEY, PENNSYLVANIA) (CLASS D, 1905–08X—SUSPENDED OPERATIONS ON JUNE 7; 1914–16; CLASS C, 1939; CLASS B, 1940–52)

Allentown, Pennsylvania	1939–52
Bradford, Pennsylvania	1905–08X, 1914–16
Bridgeport, Connecticut	1941
Coudersport, Pennsylvania	1905
DuBois, Pennsylvania	1905–07X
Erie, Pennsylvania	1905–08X, 1916X
Franklin, Pennsylvania	1907–08X
Hagerstown, Maryland	1941–52

Team	Years in Operation
Harrisburg, Pennsylvania	1940–42, 1946–52
Hazleton, Pennsylvania	1939–40X
Hornell, New York	1914–15
Jamestown, New York	1914–15
Johnsonburg, Pennsylvania	1916X
Kane, Pennsylvania	1905–07X
Lancaster, Pennsylvania	1940#, 1941–52
Oil City, Pennsylvania	1906–08X
Olean, New York	1905–07X, 1908X, 1914–16X
Patton, Pennsylvania	1906
Punxsutawney, Pennsylvania	1906–07X
Reading, Pennsylvania	1940–41
Ridgway, Pennsylvania	1906
St. Marys, Pennsylvania	1916
Salisbury, Maryland	1951–52
Sunbury, Pennsylvania	1939–40, 1946–52
Trenton, New Jersey	1939–50
Warren, Pennsylvania	1908X, 1914–16
Wellsville, New York	1914–16
Wilmington, Delaware	1940–52
York, Pennsylvania	1940, 1943–52

IOWA AND SOUTH DAKOTA LEAGUE (CLASS D, 1902–03)

Flandreau, South Dakota	1902
LeMars, Iowa	1902–03
Rock Rapids, Iowa	1902
Sheldon, Iowa	1902–03
Sioux City, Iowa	1902–03
Sioux Falls, South Dakota	1902–03

IOWA STATE LEAGUE (CLASS D, 1911X)

Fort Dodge, Iowa, was the unofficial league champion (won, 23; lost, 11; pct., .676). The league disbanded after six weeks.

Team	Years in Operation

KANSAS–OKLAHOMA–MISSOURI LEAGUE (KOM LEAGUE) (CLASS D, 1946–52)

Bartlesville, Oklahoma	1946–52 (franchise shifted to Pittsburg on June 28)
Blackwell, Oklahoma	1952
Carthage, Missouri	1946–51
Chanute, Kansas	1946–50
Independence, Kansas	1946–50, 1952
Iola, Kansas	1946–52
Miami, Oklahoma	1946–52
Pittsburg, Kansas	1946–51, 1952#
Ponca City, Oklahoma	1946–52

KANSAS STATE LEAGUE (CLASS D, 1905–06. 1909–11, 1913–14)

Arkansas City, Kansas	1909–10
Bartlesville, Oklahoma	1906
Chanute, Kansas	1905–06
Cherryvale, Kansas	1906
Clay Center, Kansas	1913
Coffeyville, Kansas	1905–06
El Dorado, Kansas	1911
Emporia, Kansas	1905#, 1914
Fort Scott, Kansas	1905 (franchise shifted to Emporia in midseason)
Great Bend, Kansas	1909–11, 1913–14
Hutchinson, Kansas	1909–11, 1914
Independence, Kansas	1905#, 1906
Iola, Kansas	1905 (franchise shifted to Independence in midseason)
Junction City, Kansas	1913
Larned, Kansas	1900–11
Lyons, Kansas	1909–11, 1913
McPherson, Kansas	1909–11
Manhattan, Kansas	1913
Newton, Kansas	1909–11
Parsons, Kansas	1905–06
Pittsburg, Kansas	1905
Salina, Kansas	1913–14
Wellington, Kansas	1909–11

Team	Years in Operation

KEYSTONE LEAGUE (CLASS D, 1935X)

Team	Years in Operation
Lancaster, Pennsylvania	1935X
Lebanon, Pennsylvania	1935X
Mount Carmel, Pennsylvania	1935X
Pottstown, Pennsylvania	1935X
Pottsville, Pennsylvania	1935X
York, Pennsylvania	1935X

KITTY LEAGUE (KENTUCKY, ILLINOIS, TENNESSEE) (1903–05X, 1906; CLASS D, 1910–14, 1916X, 1922–24, 1935#, 1936–42X—SUSPENDED OPERATIONS JUNE 19; 1946–55)

Team	Years in Operation
Bowling Green, Kentucky	1939–42X
Cairo, Illinois	1903–05X, 1906, 1911–14, 1922–54, 1946–50
Cape Girardeau, Missouri	1936 (franchise shifted to Fulton in midseason)
Central City, Tennessee	1954#
Clarksville, Tennessee	1903–04, 1910–14X, 1916X, 1946–49
Danville, Illinois	1906
Dawson Springs, Kentucky	1916X
Dyersburg, Tennessee	1923–24
Evansville, Indiana	1912
Fulton, Kentucky	1911, 1922–24, 1936#, 1937–42, 1946–55
Harrisburg, Illinois	1911#, 1913
Henderson, Kentucky	1903–04, 1910–11#, 1912–14, 1916X
Hopkinsville, Kentucky	1903–04, 1910–14, 1916X, 1922–23, 1935#–42X, 1946–54
Jackson, Tennessee	1903, 1911, 1924, 1935#–42X, 1950–54X
Jacksonville, Illinois	1906
Lexington, Tennessee	1935#–38
McLeansboro, Illinois	1911 (franchise shifted to Henderson in midseason)
Madisonville, Kentucky	1910, 1916X, 1922, 1946–55X
Mattoon, Illinois	1906
Mayfield, Kentucky	1922–24, 1936–41, 1946–55
Milan, Tennessee	1923# (franchise shifted to Trenton near the season's end)
Owensboro, Kentucky	1913–14, 1916X, 1936#, 1937–42, 1946–55
Paducah, Kentucky	1903–05X, 1906, 1910–14, 1922–23, 1935#, 1936–41, 1951–55
Paris, Tennessee	1922–24
Portageville, Missouri	1935#, 1936X
Princeton, Kentucky	1905X

Team	Years in Operation
Springfield, Tennessee	1923 (franchise shifted to Milan in mid-season)
Trenton, Tennessee	1922–23#
Union City, Tennessee	1935–42X, 1946–55
Vincennes, Indiana	1904–05X, 1906, 1910–11, 1913

LONE STAR LEAGUE (CLASS D, 1927–29X—DISBANDED MAY 16; CLASS C, 1947–48)

Bryan, Texas	1947–48
Corsicana, Texas	1927–28
Gladewater, Texas	1948
Henderson, Texas	1947–48
Jacksonville, Texas	1947
Kilgore, Texas	1947–48
Longview, Texas	1927X, 1947–48
Lufkin, Texas	1947–48
Marshall, Texas	1927X, 1947–48
Mexia, Texas	1927–28
Palestine, Texas	1927–29X
Paris, Texas	1927–28
Sherman, Texas	1929X
Texarkana, Texas	1927–29X
Tyler, Texas	1927–29X, 1947–48

LONGHORN LEAGUE (CLASS D, 1947–50; CLASS C, 1951–55)

Artesia, New Mexico	1951–55
Ballinger, Texas	1947–50
Big Spring, Texas	1947–53X, 1954–55
Carlsbad, New Mexico	1953–55
Del Rio, Texas	1948
Hobbs, New Mexico	1955
Lamesa, Texas	1953 (franchise shifted to Winters–Ballinger on June 3)
Midland, Texas	1947–55
Odessa, Texas	1947–55
Roswell, New Mexico	1949–55
San Angelo, Texas	1949–55
Sweetwater, Texas	1947–52, 1954#
Vernon, Texas	1947–52
Wichita Falls, Texas	1954 (franchise shifted to Sweetwater in May)
Winters–Ballinger, Texas	1953#X

Team	*Years in Operation*

LOUISIANA LEAGUE (CLASS D, 1920X— DISBANDED ON JULY 15)

Abbeville, Louisiana	1920X
Alexandria, Louisiana	1920X
Lafayette, Louisiana	1920X
New Iberia, Louisiana	1920X
Oakdale, Louisiana	1920X
Rayne, Louisiana	1920X

MAINE STATE LEAGUE (CLASS D, 1907–08X— DISBANDED ON AUGUST 28)

Augusta, Maine	1907X, 1908X
Bangor, Maine	1907–08X
Biddeford, Maine	1907–08X
Pine Tree, Maine	1907
Portland, Maine	1907–08X
Waterville, Maine	1907X

MASSACHUSETTS–CONNECTICUT LEAGUE (CLASS D, 1912X)

No accurate records available.

MICHIGAN–ONTARIO LEAGUE (CLASS B, 1919–25)

Battle Creek, Michigan	1919–21 (franchise shifted to Port Huron early in 1921 season)
Bay City, Michigan	1919–25
Brantford, Ontario	1919–22
Flint, Michigan	1921–25
Grand Rapids, Michigan	1923–24
Hamilton, Ontario	1919–25
Kalamazoo, Michigan	1923–24
Kitchener, Ontario	1919–22, 1925
London, Ontario	1919–25
Muskegon, Michigan	1923–24
Port Huron, Michigan	1921#
Port Huron, Michigan–Sarnia, Ontario	1922
Saginaw, Michigan	1919–25

Team	Years in Operation

MICHIGAN STATE LEAGUE (CLASS D, 1902)

Battle Creek, Michigan	1902
Flint, Michigan	1902
Jackson, Michigan	1902
Lansing, Michigan	1902
Muskegon, Michigan	1902

MICHIGAN STATE LEAGUE (CLASS D, 1910–14; CLASS B, 1926; CLASS C, 1940–41)

Bay City, Michigan	1926
Belding, Michigan	1914#
Boyne City, Michigan	1911–14X
Cadillac, Michigan	1910–14
Flint, Michigan	1926, 1940–41
Grand Rapids, Michigan	1926, 1940–41
Holland, Michigan	1910–11
Kalamazoo, Michigan	1926
Lansing, Michigan	1940–41
Ludington, Michigan	1912–14, 1926
Manistee, Michigan	1911–14 (franchise shifted to Belding on September 8)
Muskegon, Michigan	1910–14, 1926, 1940–41
Port Huron, Michigan	1926
Saginaw, Michigan	1926, 1940–41
St. Joseph, Michigan	1940–41
Traverse City, Michigan	1910–14X

(Note: The Michigan State League was called the Western Michigan League In 1910.)

MIDDLE TEXAS LEAGUE (CLASS D, 1914X—SUSPENDED OPERATIONS ON AUGUST 8; 1915X—LEAGUE DISBANDED ON JUNE 20)

Austin, Texas	1915 (franchise shifted to Taylor)
Bartlett, Texas	1914X–1915X
Belten, Texas	1914X–1915X
Brenham, Texas	1914X–1915X
Georgetown, Texas	1914X
Lampasas, Texas	1914X
Schulenburg, Texas	1915X
Tyler, Texas	1915#X
Temple, Texas	1914X–1915X

Team	*Years in Operation*

MIDWEST LEAGUE (CLASS D, 1956–62; CLASS A, 1963—)

Team	Years in Operation
Appleton (Fox Cities), Wisconsin	1962—
Burlington, Iowa	1962—
Cedar Rapids, Iowa	1956—
Clinton, Iowa	1956—
Danville, Illinois	1970—
Davenport (Quad Cities: Davenport, and Bettendorf, Iowa; Moline and Rock Island, Illinois)	1960—
Decatur, Illinois	1956—
Dubuque, Iowa	1956–68, 1974—
Keokuk, Iowa	1958–62 (Keokuk surrendered its franchise to the league on August 7 and played the remainder of its home games in Dubuque as the "Midwest Dodgers." Thus, Dubuque had two teams during the latter part of 1962.)
Kokomo, Indiana	1956–61
Lafayette, Indiana	1956–57
Mattoon, Illinois	1956–57
Michigan City, Indiana	1956–59
Paris, Illinois	1956–59
Quincy, Illinois	1960–73
Waterloo, Iowa	1958—
Wisconsin Rapids, Wisconsin	1963—

(Note: The Midwest League developed directly out of the Mississippi–Ohio Valley League.)

MINNESOTA–WISCONSIN LEAGUE (CLASS D, 1909–10; CLASS C, 1911; CLASS D, 1912X—DISBANDED EARLY IN THE 1912 SEASON AND RESUMED PLAY IN 1913 AS THE NORTHERN LEAGUE)

Team	Years in Operation
Duluth, Minnesota	1909–11
Eau Claire, Wisconsin	1909–12X
La Crosse, Wisconsin	1909–12X
Red Wing, Minnesota	1910–11X
Rochester, Minnesota	1910–12X
Superior, Wisconsin	1909–11
Wausau, Wisconsin	1909–11X
Winona, Minnesota	1909–12X

Team	*Years in Operation*

MISSISSIPPI-OHIO VALLEY LEAGUE (CLASS D, 1949–55)

Belleville, Illinois	1949
Canton, Illinois	1952
Centralia, Illinois	1949–52
Clinton, Iowa	1954–55
Danville, Illinois	1951–54
Decatur, Illinois	1952–55
Dubuque, Iowa	1954–55
Hannibal, Missouri	1952–55
Kokomo, Indiana	1955
Lafayette, Indiana	1955
Mattoon, Illinois	1949–55
Mount Vernon, Illinois	1949–54
Paducah, Kentucky	1949–50
Paris, Illinois	1950–55
Springfield, Illinois	1950
Vincennes, Indiana	1950–52 (franchise shifted to Canton on June 6)
West Frankfort, Illinois	1949–50

(Note: The Mississippi–Ohio Valley League was reorganized and renamed as the Midwest League in time for the beginning of the 1956 season.)

MISSISSIPPI STATE LEAGUE (CLASS D, 1921)

Clarksdale, Mississippi	1921
Greenwood, Mississippi	1921
Jackson, Mississippi	1921
Meridian, Mississippi	1921

(Note: All four teams shifted to the Cotton States League for the start of the 1922 season.)

MISSISSIPPI VALLEY LEAGUE
(CLASS D, 1922–32; CLASS B, 1933)

Burlington, Iowa	1924–32
Cedar Rapids, Iowa	1922–32
Davenport, Iowa	1929–33
Dubuque, Iowa	1922–32
Keokuk, Iowa	1929–33
Marshalltown, Iowa	1922–28
Moline, Illinois	1924–32
Ottumwa, Iowa	1922–28
Peoria, Illinois	1933

Team	*Years in Operation*
Quincy, Illinois	1933
Rock Island, Illinois	1922–33
Springfield, Illinois	1933
Waterloo, Iowa	1922–32

MISSOURI–IOWA–NEBRASKA–KANSAS LEAGUE (M.I.N.K. LEAGUE) (CLASS D, 1910–12)

Auburn, Nebraska	1910–12
Beatrice, Nebraska	1912
Clarinda, Iowa	1910–11
Falls City, Nebraska	1910–12
Hiawatha, Kansas	1912
Humboldt, Nebraska	1912
Maryville, Missouri	1910–11
Nebraska City, Nebraska	1910–12
Shenandoah, Iowa	1910–11

MISSOURI STATE LEAGUE (CLASS D, 1911X)

Brookfield, Missouri	1911X
Chillicothe, Missouri	1911X
Jefferson City, Missouri	1911X
Kirksville, Missouri	1911X
Macon, Missouri	1911X
Sedalia, Missouri	1911X

MISSOURI VALLEY LEAGUE (CHANUTE, KANSAS) (CLASS D, 1902–05)

Chanute, Kansas	1902
Fort Scott, Kansas	1902–05
Iola, Kansas	1902–04
Jefferson City, Missouri	1902
Joplin, Missouri	1902–04
Leavenworth, Kansas	1904
Muskogee, Oklahoma	1905
Nevada, Missouri	1902
Parsons, Kansas	1905
Pittsburg, Kansas	1903–05
Sedalia, Missouri	1902–04
South McAlester, Oklahoma	1905
Springfield, Missouri	1902–04
Topeka, Kansas	1904
Tulsa, Oklahoma	1905
Vinita, Oklahoma	1905
Webb City, Missouri	1905

Team	Years in Operation

MOUNTAIN STATES LEAGUE (CLASS D, 1911-12—X DISBANDED ON JULY 8; 1937–42, 1948–54X)

Team	Years in Operation
Ashland, Kentucky	1911, 1939–42
Ashland–Catlettsburg, Kentucky	1912X
Beckley, West Virginia	1937–38
Big Stone Gap, West Virginia	1949–53
Bluefield, West Virginia	1937–42
Charleston, West Virginia	1911–12X
Harlan, Kentucky	1948–54X
Hazard, Kentucky	1948#, 1949–52
Huntington, West Virginia	1911–12X, 1937–42
Jenkins, Kentucky	1948–51
Kingsport, Tennessee	1953–54X
Knoxville, Tennessee	1953
Lexington, Kentucky	1954X
Logan, West Virginia	1937–42
Maryville–Alcoa, Tennessee	1953–54X
Middleport–Pomeroy, Ohio	1911#
Montgomery, West Virginia	1911–12X
Morristown, Tennessee	1948–54X
Newport, Tennessee	1948–50
Norton, Virginia	1951–53
Oak Ridge, Tennessee	1948 (franchise shifted to Hazard on June 27), 1954X
Pennington Gap, Virginia	1948–51
Point Pleasant, West Virginia	1911 (franchise shifted to Middleport–Pomeroy on July 14)
Welch, West Virginia	1937–42
Williamson, West Virginia	1912X, 1937–42

NEBRASKA STATE LEAGUE (CLASS D, 1910–15X— DISBANDED ON JULY 18; 1922–23, 1928–38; ROOKIE, 1956–59)

Team	Years in Operation
Beatrice, Nebraska	1913#, 1914–15X, 1922–23, 1928, 1932–38
Columbus, Nebraska	1910–15X
Fairbury, Nebraska	1915X, 1922–23, 1928–30, 1936X, 1937
Fremont, Nebraska	1910–13
Grand Island, Nebraska	1910–15X, 1922–23, 1928–31, 1936–38, 1956–59
Hastings, Nebraska	1910–15X, 1922–23, 1956–59
Holdrege, Nebraska	1956–59
Kearney, Nebraska	1910–15X, 1956–59
Lexington, Nebraska	1956–58

Team	Years in Operation
Lincoln, Nebraska	1922–23, 1928–36X, 1938
McCook, Nebraska	1928–32, 1956–59
Mitchell, South Dakota	1936–37
Norfolk, Nebraska	1914–15X, 1922–23, 1928–38
North Platte, Nebraska	1928–32, 1956–59
Norton, Kansas	1929–30X
Red Cloud, Nebraska	1910
Seward, Nebraska	1910–13X
Sioux City, Iowa	1938
Sioux Falls, South Dakota	1933–38
Superior, Nebraska	1910–14
York, Nebraska	1911–15X, 1928–31

NEW BRUNSWICK AND MAINE LEAGUE (CLASS D, 1913X)

Bangor, Maine	1913X
Calais, Maine–St. Stephens,	1913X
New Brunswick, Canada	
Fredericton, New Brunswick, Canada	1913X
St. John, New Brunswick, Canada	1913X

NEW ENGLAND LEAGUE (CLASS B, 1902–15, 1919X— DISBANDED AUGUST 2; 1926–30X—DISBANDED JUNE 22, 1933, 1946–49)

Attleboro, Massachusetts	1928#
Brockton, Massachusetts	1907–13, 1928#, 1929, 1933#
Concord, New Hampshire	1902–05
Dover, New Hampshire	1902
Fall River, Massachusetts	1902–13, 1946–49X
Fitchburg, Massachusetts	1914X, 1915, 1919X, 1929#X
Gloucester, Massachusetts	1929#X
Haverhill, Massachusetts	1902–12, 1914, 1919X, 1926–29X
Lawrence, Massachusetts	1902–15, 1919X, 1926–27, 1933X, 1946–47X
Lewiston, Maine	1914–15, 1919X, 1926–30X
Lowell, Massachusetts	1902–04, 1906–15, 1919X, 1926 (franchise shifted to Salem on June 3), 1929 (franchise shifted to Nashua in midseason 1929), 1933, 1947#
Lynn, Massachusetts	1905–15, 1926–30X, 1946–49
Manchester, New Hampshire	1902–04, 1906, 1914#, 1915, 1926–30X, 1946–49X
Nashua, New Hampshire	1902–05, 1926–27, 1929#, 1930X, 1933X, 1946–49

Team	Years in Operation
New Bedford, Massachusetts	1903–13, 1929, 1933
Pawtucket, Rhode Island	1946–49
Portland, Maine	1913–15, 1919X, 1926–30X, 1946–49
Providence, Rhode Island	1946–49X
Quincy, Massachusetts	1933
Salem, Massachusetts	1926#, 1927–28, 1930#
Springfield, Massachusetts	1948–49
Taunton, Massachusetts	1905, 1933
Woonsocket, Rhode Island	1933#
Worcester, Massachusetts	1906–15, 1933

(Note: See entry for the Northeastern League.)

NEW HAMPSHIRE LEAGUE (CLASS D, 1907X— DISBANDED AFTER ABOUT TWO WEEKS OF PLAY)

Epplng, New Hampshire	1907X
Fremont, New Hampshire	1907X
Kingston, New Hampshire	1907X
Newton, New Hampshire	1907X

(Note: The New Hampshire League also was called the Southern New Hampshire League.)

NEW YORK–NEW JERSEY LEAGUE (CLASS D, 1913)

Danbury, Connecticut	1913#
Kingston, New York	1913
Long Branch, New York	1913
Middletown, New York	1913
Newburgh, New York	1913
Paterson, New Jersey	1913 (franchise shifted to Danbury in mid-season)
Poughkeepsie, New York	1913

NEW YORK–PENNSYLVANIA LEAGUE (CLASS D, 1957–62; CLASS A, 1963—)

Auburn, New York	1958—
Batavia, New York	1957–59, 1961—
Bradford, Pennsylvanla	1957 (franchise shifted to Hornell on May 23)
Corning, New York	1957–60, 1968–69

Team	Years in Operation
Elmira, New York	1957–50, 1973—
Erie, Pennsylvania	1957–63, 1967
Geneva, New York	1958–73
Hornell, New York	1957#
Jamestown, New York	1957X, 1961–73
Newark–Wayne, New York	1968—
Niagara Falls, New York	1970—
Olean, New York	1957–59, 1961–62
Oneonta, New York	1966—
Wellsville, New York	1957–61, 1963–65
Williamsport, Pennsylvania	1968–72

(Note: The New York–Pennsylvania League developed from the Pony League, 1939–56. Both of these leagues have roots in the old New York–Pennsylvania League (1923–37), which is now the Class AA Eastern League.)

NEW YORK STATE LEAGUE (CLASS B, 1902–17)

Albany, New York	1902–16 (franchise shifted to Reading on August 22)
Amsterdam–Johnstown–Gloversville, New York	1904–07
Binghamton, New York	1902–17
Elmira, New York	1908–17
Harrisburg, Pennsylvania	1916#, 1917X
Ilion, New York	1902–04
Johnstown, New York	1902–03
Reading, Pennsylvania	1916#, 1917
Schenectady, New York	1902–03
Scranton, Pennsylvania	1904–17
Syracuse, New York	1902–17
Troy, New York	1902–16 (franchise shifted to Harrisburg on June 17)
Utica, New York	1902–17X
Wilkes-Barre, Pennsylvania	1905–17

Team	Years in Operation

NORTH ATLANTIC LEAGUE (CLASS D, 1946–50)

Team	Years in Operation
Bangor, Pennsylvania	1950
Bangor–Berwick, Pennsylvania	1949
Berwick, Pennsylvania	1950
Bloomingdale, New Jersey	1946–48
Carbondale, Pennsylvania	1946–50
Hazleton, Pennsylvania	1949–50
Kingston, New York	1947
Lansdale, Pennsylvania	1947–48
Lebanon, Pennsylvania	1949–50
Mahanoy City, Pennsylvania	1949–50
Nazareth, Pennsylvania	1946–50
Newburgh, New York	1946 (franchise shifted to Walden in mid-season)
Nyack, New York	1946–48
Peekskill, New York	1946–49
Stroudsburg, Pennsylvania	1946–50
Walden, New York	1946#

NORTH CAROLINA LEAGUE (CLASS D, 1902X— DISBANDED ON JULY 15)

Team	Years in Operation
Charlotte, North Carolina	1902X
Durham, North Carolina	1902X
Greensboro, North Carolina	1902X
New Bern, North Carolina	1902X
Raleigh, North Carolina	1902X
Wilmington, North Carolina	1902X

NORTH CAROLINA STATE LEAGUE (CLASS D, 1913–17X— DISBANDED ON MAY 30; 1937–42, 1945–52)

Team	Years in Operation
Albemarle, North Carolina	1947–48
Asheville, North Carolina	1913–17X
Charlotte, North Carolina	1913–17X
Concord, North Carolina	1939–42, 1945–51
Cooleemee, North Carolina	1937–41
Durham, North Carolina	1913–17X
Elkin, North Carolina	1951#, 1952
Gastonia, North Carolina	1938#
Greensboro, North Carolina	1913–17X
Hickory, North Carolina	1942, 1945–50
High Point–Thomasville, North Carolina	1948–52
Kannapolis, North Carolina	1939–41
Landis, North Carolina	1937–42, 1945–51 (franchise shifted to Elkin on July 18)

Team	Years in Operation
Lexington, North Carolina	1937–42, 1945–52
Mooresville, North Carolina	1937–42, 1945–52
Newton–Conover, North Carolina	1937–38
Raleigh, North Carolina	1913–17X
Salisbury, North Carolina	1937–42, 1945–52
Shelby, North Carolina	1937–38 (franchise shifted to Gastonia on July 22)
Statesville, North Carolina	1942, 1945–52
Thomasville, North Carolina	1937–42, 1945–47
Winston–Salem, North Carolina	1913–17X

NORTH DAKOTA LEAGUE (CLASS D, 1923#)

Bismarck, North Dakota	1923#
Jamestown, North Dakota	1923#
Minot, North Dakota	1923#
Valley City, North Dakota	1923#

NORTHEAST ARKANSAS LEAGUE (CLASS D, 1909–11X— DISBANDED ON JULY 5; 1936–41)

Batesville, Arkansas	1936#, 1938–39, 1940#, 1941
Blytheville, Arkansas	1910–11X, 1937–38
Caruthersville, Missouri	1910, 1936#, 1937–40
Helena, Arkansas	1911X
Jonesboro, Arkansas	1909–11X, 1936–41
Marianna, Arkansas	1909
Newport, Arkansas	1909, 1936–41
Osceola, Arkansas	1936–37
Paragould, Arkansas	1909–11X, 1936–41
West Plains, Missouri	1936X

NORTHEASTERN LEAGUE (CLASS A, 1934)

Hartford, Connecticut	1934
Lowell, Massachusetts	1934
Malden-Worcester, Massachusetts	1934
Manchester, New Hampshire	1934
New Bedford, Massachusetts	1934
Springfield, Massachusetts	1934

(Note: The Northeastern League was actually the new name that the New England League adopted for the 1934 season. Most baseball historians, however, list the two as separate leagues.)

Team	Years in Operation

NORTHERN ASSOCIATION OF BASEBALL (CLASS C, 1910X)

Clinton, Iowa	1910X
Decatur, Illinois	1910X
Elgin, Illinois	1910X
Freeport, Illinois	1910X
Jacksonville, Illinois	1910X
Joliet, Illinois	1910X
Kankakee, Illinois	1910X
Muscatine, Illinois	1910X

NORTHERN COPPER COUNTRY LEAGUE (CLASS C, 1906–07)

Calumet, Michigan	1906–07
Duluth, Minnesota	1906–07
Fargo, North Dakota	1906
Houghton, Michigan	1906–07
Lake Linden, Michigan	1906
Winnipeg, Manitoba, Canada	1906–07

(Note: The league was reformulated and became the nucleus for the Northern League in 1908.)

NORTHERN LEAGUE (1902–05; CLASS D, 1908X; CLASS C, 1913–16; CLASS D, 1917X, 1933–40; CLASS C, 1941–42, 1946–62; CLASS A, 1963–71)

Aberdeen, South Dakota	1946–71
Bismarck–Mandan, North Dakota	1962–64, 1966
Brainerd, Minnesota	1933X, 1935
Brainerd–Little Falls, Minnesota	1934
Brandon, Manitoba, Canada	1908X, 1933#, 1934X
Cavalier, North Dakota	1902
Crookston, Minnesota	1902–05, 1933–41
Devil's Lake, North Dakota	1902
Duluth, Minnesota	1902–05, 1908X, 1913–16, 1934–42, 1946–55
Duluth, Minnesota–Superior, Wisconsin	1956–70
East Grand Forks, Minnesota	1933#, 1935
Eau Claire, Wisconsin	1933–42, 1946–62
Fargo, North Dakota–Moorehead, Minnesota	1902–05, 1908X, 1913–16, 1917X, 1933–42, 1946–60
Fort William, Ontario, Canada	1914
Fort William–Port Arthur, Ontario, Canada	1916X

Team	Years in Operation
Grand Forks, North Dakota	1902–05, 1913–15X, 1934–35, 1938–42, 1946–64
Huron, South Dakota	1965–70
Jamestown, North Dakota	1936–37
La Crosse, Wisconsin–St. Paul, Minnesota	1913
Little Falls, Minnesota	1933X
Mankato, Minnesota	1967–68
Minneapolis, Minnesota	1908–13
Minot, North Dakota	1917X, 1958–60, 1962
St. Boniface, Minnesota	1915
St. Cloud, Minnesota	1913, 1946–71
Sioux Falls, South Dakota	1942, 1946–53, 1966–71
Superior, Wisconsin	1902–05, 1913–15X, 1916, 1933–42, 1946–55
Virginia, Minnesota	1913–16X
Warren, North Dakota	1917X
Watertown, South Dakota	1970–71
Wausau, Wisconsin	1936–42, 1956–57
Winnipeg, Manitoba, Canada	1902–05, 1908X, 1913–16, 1917X, 1933–42, 1954–64, 1969
Winona, Minnesota	1913–14

(Note: In 1906–07; Northern League cities comprised the Northern Copper Country League, and in 1909–12 NL cities comprised the Minnesota–Wisconsin League. These two circuits are listed separately.)

NORTHERN MAINE LEAGUE (CLASS D, 1902X)

Millinocket, Maine	1902X
Old Town, Maine	1902X

(Note: The names of the two other cities in the short-lived Northern Maine League are not readily available.)

NORTHERN NEW YORK LEAGUE (CLASS D, 1902X)

Malone, New York	1902X
Plattsburg, New York	1902X
Potsdam, New York	1902X
St. Albans, New York	1902X

NORTH TEXAS LEAGUE (CLASS D, 1906X)

Corsicana, Texas, was the unofficial league champion (won, 7; lost, 2; pct., .778). The league disbanded after less than two weeks.

Team   *Years in Operation*

NORTHWESTERN LEAGUE (CLASS B, 1905–14X— SUSPENDED PLAY ON SEPTEMBER 13; 1915–17X— DISBANDED ON JULY 15)

Aberdeen, Washington	1907–09, 1915X
Ballard, Washington	1914#X
Bellingham, Washington	1905
Butte, Montana	1906–08, 1916–17X
Everett, Washington	1905
Gray's Harbor, Washington	1906
Great Falls, Montana	1916–17X
Portland, Oregon	1909, 1911–14 (franchise shifted to Ballard on July 18) 1973—
Seattle, Washington	1907–14X, 1915–17X
Spokane, Washington	1906–14X, 1915–17X
Tacoma, Washington	1906–14X, 1915–17X
Vancouver, Washington	1905, 1907–14X, 1915–17X
Victoria, British Columbia, Canada	1905, 1911–14X, 1915X

NORTHWEST LEAGUE (CLASS B, 1955–62; CLASS A, 1963—)

Bellingham, Washington	1973—
Bend, Oregon	1970–71
Coos Bay–North Bend, Oregon	1970–72
Eugene, Oregon	1955–68, 1974—
Lewiston, Idaho	1955—
Medford, Oregon	1967–71
New Westminster, British Columbia	1974—
Portland, Oregon	1973—
Salem, Oregon	1955–65
Seattle, Washington	1972—
Spokane, Washington	1972
Tri-Cities (Kennewick–Pasco–Richland), Washington	1955—
Walla Walla, Washington	1969—
Wenatchee, Washington	1955–65
Yakima, Washington	1955–65

OHIO–INDIANA LEAGUE (CLASS D, 1948–51)

Lima, Ohio	1948–51
Marion, Ohio	1948–51
Muncie, Indiana	1948–50
Newark, Ohio	1948–51X

Team	Years in Operation
Portsmouth, Ohio	1948–50
Richmond, Indiana	1948–51
Springfield, Ohio	1948–51
Zanesville, Ohio	1948–50

(Note: The league started the 1951 season with five clubs, an awkward number.)

OHIO–PENNSYLVANIA LEAGUE (CLASS C, 1905–11; CLASS D, 1912—DISBANDED ON JULY 6)

Akron, Ohio	1905–11
Alliance–Sebring, Ohio	1912X
Braddock, Pennsylvania	1905
Butler, Pennsylvania	1908 (franchise shifted to Erie in midseason)
Canton, Ohio	1908–11
Connellsville, Pennsylvania	1912X
East Liverpool, Ohio	1908–11X
Erie, Pennsylvania	1908#, 1909–11
Fairmont, West Virginia	1911#X
Follansbee, West Virginia	1912#X
Homestead, Pennsylvania	1905
Lancaster, Ohio	1905–07
McKeesport, Pennsylvania	1905, 1908–12X
Mansfield, Ohio	1906–07, 1910–12X
Marion, Ohio	1906–07
New Castle, Pennsylvania	1906–11X, 1912X
Newark, Ohio	1905–07
Niles, Ohio	1905
Salem, Ohio	1912#X
Sharon, Pennsylvania	1905–08, 1912X
Steubenville, Ohio	1909, 1911X, 1912X
Youngstown, Ohio	1911
Zanesville, Ohio	1905

Team	Years in Operation

OHIO STATE LEAGUE (CLASS D, 1908–16—DISBANDED ON JULY 19, 1936–41, 1944–47)

Canton, Ohio	1936
Charleston, West Virginia	1913–16X
Chillicothe, Ohio	1910–15
Coshocton, Ohio	1936X
Dayton, Ohio	1946–47
Findlay, Ohio	1937–41
Fostoria, Ohio	1936–41
Frankfort, Kentucky	1915–16X
Fremont, Ohio	1936–41
Hamilton, Ohio	1911, 1913
Huntington, West Virginia	1913–14X, 1915#X, 1916X
Ironton, Ohio	1913–15
Lancaster, Ohio	1908–11X
Lexington, Kentucky	1913–16X
Lima, Ohio	1908–12, 1939–41, 1944–47
Mansfield, Ohio	1908–09, 1912, 1936X, 1937, 1939–41
Marion, Ohio	1908–12X, 1937#, 1944–47
Maysville, Kentucky	1913–14X, 1915#, 1916X
Middletown, Ohio	1944–46
Muncie, Indiana	1946–47
Newark, Ohio	1908–09X, 1910–11 (franchise shifted to Piqua on June 22), 1912, 1936X, 1944–47
New Philadelphia, Ohio	1936X
Newport, Kentucky	1914 (franchise shifted to Paris June 15)
Paris, Kentucky	1914#X
Piqua, Ohio	1911#
Portsmouth, Ohio	1908 (franchise shifted to Springfield in midseason), 1909–16
Richmond, Indiana	1946–47
Sandusky, Ohio	1936–37 (franchise shifted to Marion in late June)
Springfield, Ohio	1908#, 1911, 1944–47
Tiffin, Ohio	1936–41
Zanesville, Ohio	1944–47

OKLAHOMA–ARKANSAS–KANSAS LEAGUE (1907)

Bartlesville, Oklahoma	1907
Coffeyville, Kansas	1907
Fort Smith, Arkansas	1907X
Independence, Missouri	1907
McAlester, Oklahoma	1907X
Muskogee, Oklahoma	1907X
Parsons, Kansas	1907X
Tulsa, Oklahoma	1907

Team	Years in Operation

OKLAHOMA–KANSAS LEAGUE (CLASS D, 1908)

Bartlesville, Oklahoma	1908
Independence, Missouri	1908
Muskogee, Oklahoma	1908
Tulsa, Oklahoma	1908

OKLAHOMA STATE LEAGUE (CLASS D, 1912X—DISBANDED ON JULY 1, 1922–24X—DISBANDED ON JULY 8; 1936X— DISBANDED IN MIDSEASON)

Ada, Oklahoma	1936X
Anadarko, Oklahoma	1912X
Ardmore, Oklahoma	1924X
Blackwell, Oklahoma	1924X
Bristow, Oklahoma	1923–24X
Chickasha, Oklahoma	1922
Drumright, Oklahoma	1922–23 (franchise shifted to Ponca City in midseason)
Duncan, Oklahoma	1922–24X
El Reno, Oklahoma	1922–23
Enid, Oklahoma	1912#X
Eufaula, Oklahoma	1912#X
Guthrie, Oklahoma	1912X, 1922–24X
Holdenville, Oklahoma	1912X
McAlester, Oklahoma	1912X, 1936X
Muskogee, Oklahoma	1912X
Oklahoma City, Oklahoma	1912X
Okmulgee, Oklahoma	1912X
Pawhuska, Oklahoma	1912X
Ponca City, Oklahoma	1923#, 1924X
Seminole, Oklahoma	1936X
Shawnee, Oklahoma	1923–24X
Tulsa, Oklahoma	1912X
Wewaka, Oklahoma	1936X
Wilson, Oklahoma	1922#

OLD DOMINION LEAGUE (VIRGINIA) (D 1908X)

Newport News, Virginia	1930X
Petersburg, Virginia	1930X
Phoebus, Virginia	1930X
Suffolk, Virginia	1930X

Team   *Years in Operation*

ONTARIO LEAGUE (CLASS D, 1930X—DISBANDED JULY 22)

Brantford, Ontario, Canada	1930X
Guelph, Ontario, Canada	1930X
Hamilton, Ontario, Canada	1930X
London, Ontario, Canada	1930X
St. Catherines, Ontario, Canada	1930X
St. Thomas, Ontario, Canada	1930X

OREGON STATE LEAGUE (CLASS D, 1904)

No accurate records are available.

PACIFIC COAST INTERNATIONAL LEAGUE (CLASS B, 1918, 1920), PACIFIC INTERNATIONAL LEAGUE (CLASS B, 1921)

Aberdeen, Washington	1918
Portland, Oregon	1918
Spokane, Washington	1918, 1920
Tacoma, Washington	1918, 1920–21
Vancouver, British Columbia, Canada	1918, 1920–21
Victoria, British Columbia, Canada	1920–21
Yakima, Washington	1920–21

PACIFIC NATIONAL LEAGUE (CLASS C, 1902–04)

Boise, Idaho	1904
Butte, Montana	1902–04
Helena, Montana	1902#–1903X
Los Angeles, California	1903#X
Portland, Oregon	1902, 1903 (franchise shifted to Salt Lake City)
Salt Lake City, Utah	1903#, 1904
San Francisco, California	1903X
Seattle, Washington	1902–03
Tacoma, Washington	1902–1903X

(Note: The Pacific National League, a charter member of the National Association, was known as the Pacific Northwest League when it joined that organization in September, 1901.)

Team   *Years in Operation*

PALMETTO LEAGUE (CLASS D 1931X)

Anderson, South Carolina	1931X
Augusta, Georgia	1931X
Florence, South Carolina	1931X
Greenville, South Carolina	1931X

PANHANDLE–PECOS VALLEY LEAGUE (CLASS D, 1923)

Amarillo, Texas	1923
Clovis, New Mexico	1923
Lubbock, Texas	1923
Roswell, New Mexico	1923

PENN–OHIO–MARYLAND LEAGUE (P.O.M. LEAGUE) (CLASS D, 1906–07)

Braddock, Pennsylvania	1906–07
Charleroi, Pennsylvania	1906–07
Cumberland, Maryland	1906
East Liverpool, Ohio	1906–07
McKeesport, Pennsylvania	1907
Steubenville, Ohio	1906–07
Uniontown, Pennsylvania	1906–07
Washington, Pennsylvania	1906–07
Waynesboro, Pennsylvania	1906
Zanesville, Ohio	1907

PENNSYLVANIA–ONTARIO–NEW YORK LEAGUE (CLASS D, 1939–56)

Batavia, New York	1939–53
Bradford, Pennsylvania	1939–42, 1944–56X
Corning, New York	1951–56
Erie, Pennsylvania	1944–45, 1954–56
Hamilton, Ontario, Canada	1939–42, 1946–56X
Hornell, New York	1942–56
Jamestown, New York	1939, 1940#, 1941–56
Lockport, New York	1942–50
London, Ontario, Canada	1940–41
Niagara Falls, New York	1939–40 (franchise shifted to Jamestown on July 13)
Olean, New York	1939–56
Wellsville, New York	1942–56

(Note: This circuit was popularly referred to as the "Pony League.")

Team   *Years in Operation*

PENNSYLVANIA STATE ASSOCIATION (CLASS D, 1934–42)

Beaver Falls, Pennsylvania	1937–41
Butler, Pennsylvania	1935–42
Charleroi, Pennsylvania	1934–36X
Greensburg, Pennsylvania	1934–39
Jeannette, Pennsylvania	1934–37X
Johnstown, Pennsylvania	1939–40
McKeesport, Pennsylvania	1934–37X, 1938–40 (franchise shifted to Oil City on July 15)
Monessen, Pennsylvania	1934–38X
Oil City, Pennsylvania	1940#, 1941–42
Warren, Ohio	1940–41
Washington, Pennsylvania	1934–36X, 1939–42

(Note: The Pennsylvania State Association was organized by Elmer M. Daily, president of the Class C Middle Atlantic League, as a type of informal "farm system" for the MAL. Daily served as president of the PSA for its entire nine-year history, while Russell Hockenbury, the MAL's secretary–treasurer, also served as secretary–treasurer for the PSA.)

PENNSYLVANIA STATE LEAGUE (CLASS D, 1902X— DISBANDED ON MAY 26)

Lancaster, Pennsylvania	1902X
Lebanon, Pennsylvania	1902X
Reading, Pennsylvania	1902X
Scranton, Pennsylvania	1902X
Wilkes–Barre, Pennsylvania	1902X
Williamsport, Pennsylvania	1902X

PENNSYLVANIA–WEST VIRGINIA LEAGUE (CLASS D, 1908–09)

Charleroi, Pennsylvania	1908, 1909 (franchise shifted to Parkersburg)
Clarksburg, West Virginia	1908–1909X
Connellsville, Pennsylvania	1908–09
Fairmont, West Virginia	1908–09
Grafton, West Virginia	1908–09
Parkersburg, West Virginia	1909#X
Uniontown, Pennsylvania	1908–09

Team   *Years in Operation*

PENNSYLVANIA–WEST VIRGINIA LEAGUE
(CLASS D, 1914X)

Connellsville, Pennsylvania was the unofficial league champion (won, 5; lost, 3; pct., .625). The league disbanded after one week.

PIEDMONT LEAGUE (CLASS D, 1920; CLASS C, 1921–31; CLASS B, 1932–55)

Team	Years in Operation
Asheville, North Carolina	1931, 1933X, 1934#, 1935–42
Charlotte, North Carolina	1931–35, 1937–42
Colonial Heights–Petersburg, Virginia	1954
Columbia, South Carolina	1935X
Danville, Virginia	1920–25
Durham, North Carolina	1920–33, 1936–43
Greensboro, North Carolina	1920–26, 1928–34, 1941–42
Hagerstown, Maryland	1953–55
Henderson, North Carolina	1929–31
High Point, North Carolina	1920–24, 1926–32X
Lancaster, Pennsylvania	1954–55
Lynchburg, Virginia	1943–55
Newport News, Virginia	1944–55
Norfolk, Virginia	1934–55X
Portsmouth, Virginia	1935–55
Raleigh, North Carolina	1920–32
Richmond, Virginia	1933–53
Roanoke, Virginia	1943–53
Rocky Mount, North Carolina	1927, 1936–40
Salisbury, North Carolina	1925–26
Salisbury–Spencer, North Carolina	1927–29
Sunbury, Pennsylvania	1955
Wilmington, North Carolina	1932–35
Winston–Salem, North Carolina	1920–32X, 1933, 1937–42
York, Pennsylvania	1953–55

Team   *Years in Operation*

PIONEER LEAGUE (CLASS C, 1939–42, 1946–62;
CLASS A, 1963; ROOKIE, 1964—)

Team	Years in Operation
Billings, Montana	1948–63, 1969—
Boise, Idaho	1939–42, 1946–63
Caldwell, Idaho	1964–71
Great Falls, Montana	1948–63, 1969—
Idaho Falls, Idaho	1940–42, 1946—
Lewiston, Idaho	1939
Missoula, Montana	1956–60
Ogden, Utah	1939–42, 1946–55, 1966—
Pocatello, Idaho	1939–42, 1946–65
Salt Lake City, Utah	1939–42, 1946–57, 1967–69
Twin Falls, Idaho	1939–41, 1946–58, 1961–66, 1968–71

POTOMAC LEAGUE (CLASS D, 1916X—
DISBANDED ON AUGUST 16)

Team	Years in Operation
Cumberland, Maryland	1916X
Frostburg, Maryland	1916X
Lonaconing, Maryland	1916X
Piedmont, West Virginia	1916X

PROVINCIAL LEAGUE (CLASS C, 1950–55)

Team	Years in Operation
Burlington, Vermont	1955
Drummondville, Quebec, Canada	1950–54
Farnham, Quebec, Canada	1950–51
Granby, Quebec, Canada	1951–55
Quebec, Quebec, Canada	1951–55
St. Hyacinthe, Quebec, Canada	1950–53
St. Jean, Quebec, Canada	1950–55
Sherbrooke, Quebec, Canada	1950–51, 1953–55
Thetford Mines, Quebec, Canada	1953–55
Three Rivers, Quebec, Canada	1951–55

QUEBEC–ONTARIO–VERMONT LEAGUE (CLASS B, 1924#)

Team	Years in Operation
Canadiens, Montreal, Canada	1924#
Montpelier, Vermont	1924#
Montreal, Quebec, Canada	1924#
Ottawa–Hull, Ontario, Canada	1924#
Quebec, Quebec, Canada	1924#
Rutland, Vermont	1924#

Team   Years in Operation

QUEBEC PROVINCIAL LEAGUE (CLASS B, 1940X)

Drummondville, Quebec, Canada	1940X
Granby, Quebec, Canada	1940X
Quebec, Quebec, Canada	1940
Sherbrooke, Quebec, Canada	1940X
St. Hyacinthe, Quebec, Canada	1940
Trois Rivieres, Quebec, Canada	1940

RIO GRANDE VALLEY LEAGUE (CLASS D, 1915X—LEAGUE DISBANDED ON JULY 5; 1931X—LEAGUE DISBANDED JULY 30, 1949; CLASS C, 1950)

Albuquerque, New Mexico	1915X
Brownsville, Texas	1949–50
Corpue Christi, Texas	1931X, 1949–50
Del Rio, Texas	1949–50
Donna–Robstown, Texas	1949X
Donna–Weslaco, Texas	1950X
Douglas, Arizona	1915X
El Paso, Texas	1915X
Harlingen, Texas	1931X, 1950
La Feria, Texas	1931X
Laredo, Texas	1949–50
Las Cruces, New Mexico	1915X
McAllen, Texas	1931X, 1949–50
Phoenix, Arizona	1915X
Robstown, Texas	1950#
San Benito, Texas	1931X
Tuscon, Arizona	1915X

ROCKY MOUNTAIN LEAGUE (COLORADO) (CLASS D, 1912X)

Canon City, Colorado	1912X
Colorado Springs, Colorado	1912X
La Junta, Colorado	1912X
Pueblo, Colorado	1912X

SAN JOAQUIN VALLEY LEAGUE (CLASS D, 1910X— DISBANDED AFTER APPROXIMATELY 28–30 GAMES)

Bakersfield, California	1910X
Coalinga, California	1910X
Tulare, California	1910X
Visalia, California	1910X

(Note: The San Joaquin Valley League apparently was reorganized for the 1911 season, but results of any action have never been recorded.)

Team   *Years in Operation*

SOONER STATE LEAGUE (CLASS D, 1947–57)

Team	Years in Operation
Ada, Oklahoma	1947–54
Ardmore, Oklahoma	1947–57
Chickasha, Oklahoma	1948–52
Duncan, Oklahoma	1947–50 (franchise transferred to Shawnee on August 18)
Gainesville, Texas	1953–55 (franchise transferred to Ponca City on May 21)
Lawton, Oklahoma	1947–57
McAlester, Oklahoma	1947–56
Muskogee, Oklahoma	1955–57
Paris, Texas	1955–57
Pauls Valley, Oklahoma	1948–54
Ponca City, Oklahoma	1955#, 1956–57
Seminole, Oklahoma	1947–51, 1954–57
Shawnee, Oklahoma	1950#, 1951–57
Sherman, Texas	1952–53

SOPHOMORE LEAGUE (CLASS D, 1958–61)

Team	Years in Operation
Albuquerque, New Mexico	1960–61
Alpine, Texas	1959–61
Artesia, New Mexico	1958–61
Carlsbad, New Mexico	1958–61
El Paso, Texas	1961
Hobbs, New Mexico	1958–61
Midland, Texas	1958–59
Odessa, Texas	1959–60
Plainview, Texas	1958–59
Roswell, New Mexico	1959#
San Angelo, Texas	1958–59 (franchise shifted to Roswell on June 1)

SOUTH CAROLINA LEAGUE (CLASS D, 1907–08)

Team	Years in Operation
Chester, South Carolina	1908
Florence, South Carolina	1907
Orangeburg, South Carolina	1907–08
Rock Hill, South Carolina	1908
Spartanburg, South Carolina	1907
Sumter, South Carolina	1907–08

Team   *Years in Operation*

SOUTH CENTRAL LEAGUE (ARKANSAS, OKLAHOMA) (CLASS D, 1906)

Fort Smith, Arkansas	1906
Guthrie, Oklahoma	1906
Muskogee, Oklahoma	1906
South McAlester, Oklahoma	1906

(Note: Guthrie, Muskogee, and South McAlester were actually in "Indian Territory," since Oklahoma did not achieve statehood until November 1907.)

SOUTH CENTRAL LEAGUE (TEXAS) (CLASS D, 1912)

Cleburne, Texas	1912X
Longview, Texas	1912
Marshall, Texas	1912
Paris, Texas	1912
Texarkana, Texas	1912
Tyler, Texas	1912X

SOUTH DAKOTA LEAGUE (CLASS D, 1920)

Aberdeen, South Dakota	1920
Huron, South Dakota	1920
Madison, South Dakota	1920
Miller, South Dakota	1920
Mitchell, South Dakota	1920
Redfield, South Dakota	1920
Sioux Falls, South Dakota	1920
Wessington Springs, South Dakota	1920

(Note: See entry for the Dakota League of 1921–23.)

SOUTHEASTERN KANSAS LEAGUE (CLASS D, 1911)

Fort Scott, Kansas	1911
Mulberry, Kansas	1911
Pittsburg, Kansas	1911
Scammon, Kansas	1911

Team	Years in Operation

SOUTHEASTERN LEAGUE (CLASS D, 1910–12X—DISBANDED ON JULY 20; 1926–30, 1932X—LEAGUE DISBANDED ON MAY 18, 1937–42, 1946–50)

Team	Years in Operation
Albany, Georgia	1926–28X
Anniston, Alabama	1911–12X, 1938–42, 1946–50
Asheville, North Carolina	1910
Bessemer, Alabama	1912X
Cedartown, Georgia	1912X
Columbus, Georgia	1926–32X
Decatur, Alabama	1911
Gadsden, Alabama	1910–12X, 1938–41, 1946–50
Huntsville, Alabama	1911–12X
Jacksonville, Florida	1926–30
Johnson City, Tennessee	1910
Knoxville, Tennessee	1910
Macon, Georgia	1932X
Meridian, Mississippi	1937–42, 1946–50
Mobile, Alabama	1932X, 1937–42
Montgomery, Alabama	1926–30, 1932X, 1937–42, 1946–50
Morristown, Tennessee	1910
Pensacola, Florida	1927–42, 1946–50
Rome, Georgia	1910–12X
Saint Augustine, Florida– Waycross, Georgia	1926–27
Savannah, Georgia	1926–28X
Selma, Alabama	1911–12X, 1927–32X, 1937–41, 1946–50
Talladega, Alabama	1912#X
Tampa, Florida	1928–30
Vicksburg, Mississippi	1946–50

SOUTHERN CALIFORNIA TROLLEY LEAGUE (CLASS D, 1910), SOUTHERN CALIFORNIA LEAGUE (CLASS D, 1913)

Team	Years in Operation
Long Beach, California	1913
Los Angeles, California (the "McCormicks")	1910
Los Angeles, California (the "Maires")	1913
Pasadena, California	1910, 1913 (franchise shifted to Santa Barbara in midseason)
Redondo Beach, California	1910
San Bernardino, California	1913
San Diego, California	1910
Santa Barbara, California	1913#

Team	Years in Operation

SOUTHERN ILLINOIS LEAGUE (CLASS D, 1910X—DISBANDED IN LATE MAY AFTER EACH TEAM PLAYED APPROXIMATELY 20–22 GAMES)

Eldorado, Illinois	1910X
Herrin, Illinois	1910X
Harrisburg, Illinois	1910X
McLeansboro, Illinois	1910X
Mount Vernon, Illinois	1910X

SOUTHERN MICHIGAN LEAGUE (CLASS D, 1906–10; (CLASS C, 1911–15X—DISBANDED ON JULY 7)

Adrian, Michigan	1909–14
Battle Creek, Michigan	1906–15X
Bay City, Michigan	1907–12X, 1913–15X
Flint, Michigan	1907–15X
Jackson, Michigan	1906–07X, 1908–15X
Kalamazoo, Michigan	1906–14
Lansing, Michigan	1907–14 (franchise transferred to Mount Clemens on July 10)
Mount Clemens, Michigan	1906–07, 1914#
Saginaw, Michigan	1906, 1908–12X, 1913–15X
South Bend, Indiana	1914
Tecumseh, Michigan	1906–08
Toledo, Ohio	1914

SOUTHWEST IOWA LEAGUE (CLASS D, 1903)

No reliable records are available.

Team	Years in Operation

SOUTHWESTERN LEAGUE (KANSAS, OKLAHOMA) CLASS D, 1921; CLASS C, 1922–23; CLASS D, 1924–26)

Arkansas City, Kansas	1924–26
Bartlesville, Oklahoma	1921–23
Blackwell, Oklahoma	1925–26
Coffeyville, Kansas	1921–24X
Cushing, Oklahoma	1925
Emporia, Kansas	1924
Enid, Oklahoma	1924–25 (franchise shifted to Shawnee in midseason), 1926
Eureka, Kansas	1924–1926#
Hutchinson, Kansas	1922–23
Independence, Kansas	1921–24X
Miami, Oklahoma	1921
Muskogee, Oklahoma	1921–23
Newton, Kansas	1924X
Ottawa, Kansas	1924X
Parsons, Kansas	1921
Pittsburg, Kansas	1921
Ponca City, Oklahoma	1926 (franchise shifted to Eureka in midseason)
Salina, Kansas	1922–26
Sapulpa, Oklahoma	1921–23
Shawnee, Oklahoma	1925#
Topeka, Kansas	1922–23, 1925–26

(Note: There was a Southwestern League organized in 1904, but the circuit disbanded early and no accurate records are available.)

SOUTHWESTERN LEAGUE (NEW MEXICO, TEXAS) (CLASS B, 1956–57)

Ballinger, Texas	1956–57
Carlsbad, New Mexico	1956–57
Clovis, New Mexico	1956–57
El Paso, Texas	1956–57X
Hobbs, New Mexico	1956–57
Lamesa, Texas	1957#
Midland, Texas	1956–57 (franchise shifted to Lamesa on August 1)
Pampa, Texas	1956–57 (franchise shifted to San Angelo on May 18)
Plainview, Texas	1956–57X
Roswell, New Mexico	1956
San Angelo, Texas	1956–57#X

Team   *Years in Operation*

SOUTHWEST INTERNATIONAL LEAGUE
(CLASS C, 1951–52)

Bisbee–Douglas, Arizona	1951
El Centro, California	1951–52X
El Paso, Texas	1951
Juarez, Chihuahua, Mexico	1951
Las Vegas, Nevada	1951–52
Mexicali, Baja California, Mexico	1951–52
Phoenix, Arizona	1951
Porterville, California	1952X
Tijuana, Baja California, Mexico	1951–52
Tucson, Arizona	1951
Yuma, Arizona	1951–52

(Note: The Class C Arizona-Texas and Sunset leagues were combined to form the Southwest International League in 1951. The Arizona-Texas League was reorganized in 1952 and continued play through 1954, while the Southwest International continued operations as a separate circuit in 1952.)

SOUTHWEST TEXAS LEAGUE (CLASS D, 1910–11X)

Bay City, Texas	1910–11X
Beeville, Texas	1910–11
Brownsville, Texas	1910–11
Corpus Christi, Texas	1910–11X
Laredo, Texas	1910–11
Victoria, Texas	1910–11X

SOUTHWEST WASHINGTON LEAGUE (CLASS D,
1903–04X, 1905X, 1906X)

Aberdeen, Washington	1903, 1905X
Centralia, Washington	1903
Hoquiam, Washington	1903, 1905X
Montesana, Washington	1905X
Olympia, Washington	1903, 1905X

(Note: No accurate records are available for 1904 and 1906.)

Team   *Years in Operation*

SUNSET LEAGUE (CLASS C, 1947–50)

Anaheim, California	1947–48X
El Centro, California	1947–50
Las Vegas, Nevada	1947–50
Mexicali, Baja California, Mexico	1948–50
Ontario, California	1947
Porterville, California	1949–50
Reno, Nevada	1947–49
Riverside, California	1947–50
Salinas, California	1949 (franchise shifted to Tijuana on August 8)
San Bernardino, California	1948#, 1949–50
Tijuana, Baja California, Mexico	1949#, 1950
Yuma, Arizona	1950

TAR HEEL LEAGUE (CLASS D, 1939–40, 1953–54X— DISBANDED ON JULY 1)

Forest City (Rutherford County), North Carolina	1953–54X
Gastonia, North Carolina	1939–40
Hickory, North Carolina	1939–40, 1953–54X
High Point–Thomasville, North Carolina	1953X
Lenoir, North Carolina	1939–40
Lexington, North Carolina	1953
Lincolnton, North Carolina	1953 (franchise shifted to Statesville July 7)
Marion, North Carolina	1953–54X
Mooresville, North Carolina	1953
Newton–Conover, North Carolina	1939–40X
Salisbury, North Carolina	1953
Shelby, North Carolina	1939–40X, 1953–54
Statesville, North Carolina	1939–40, 1953#

TEXAS ASSOCIATION (CLASS D, 1923–26)

Austin, Texas	1923–26
Corsicana, Texas	1923–26
Marlin, Texas	1923–24
Mexia, Texas	1923–26
Palestine, Texas	1925–26
Sherman, Texas	1923
Temple, Texas	1924–26
Terrell, Texas	1925–26
Waco, Texas	1923–24

Team   *Years in Operation*

TEXAS–OKLAHOMA LEAGUE (CLASS D, 1911–12X— CLOSED SEASON EARLY ON JULY 28; 1913–14, 1921–22X—DISBANDED EARLY IN 1922 SEASON)

Altus, Oklahoma	1911
Ardmore, Oklahoma	1911–12X, 1913–14X
Bonham, Texas	1911–12X, 1913–14X, 1921–22X
Cleburne, Texas	1911, 1921–22X
Corsicana, Texas	1922X
Denison, Texas	1912X, 1913–14
Durant, Oklahoma	1911–12X, 1913–14
Gainesville, Texas	1911
Graham, Texas	1921 (franchise shifted to Mineral Wells on May 28)
Greenville, Texas	1912X, 1922X
Hugo, Oklahoma	1913#, 1914X
Lawton, Oklahoma	1911X
McKinney, Texas	1912X
Mexia, Texas	1922X
Mineral Wells, Texas	1921#X
Paris, Texas	1913–14, 1921–22X
Sherman, Texas	1912X, 1913–14X, 1921–22X
Texarkana, Texas	1913–14
Wichita Falls, Texas	1911–12X, 1913 (franchise shifted to Hugo in midseason)

TEXAS VALLEY LEAGUE (CLASS D, 1927–28X, 1938)

Brownsville, Texas	1928X, 1938
Corpus Christi, Texas	1927–28X, 1938
Edinburg, Texas	1927
Harlingen, Texas	1938
Laredo, Texas	1927
McAllen, Texas	1928X, 1938
Mission, Texas	1927–28X
Refugio, Texas	1938
Taft, Texas	1938

Team	Years in Operation

TOBACCO STATE LEAGUE (CLASS D, 1946–50)

Team	Years in Operation
Angier–Fuquay Springs, North Carolina	1946
Clinton, North Carolina	1946–50
Dunn–Erwin, North Carolina	1946–50 (franchise shifted to Whiteville on June 16)
Fayetteville, North Carolina	1949
Lumberton, North Carolina	1947–50
Red Springs, North Carolina	1947–50
Rockingham, North Carolina	1950
Sanford, North Carolina	1946–50
Smithfield, North Carolina	1946
Smithfield–Selma, North Carolina	1947–50X
Warsaw, North Carolina	1947–48
Whiteville, North Carolina	1950#
Wilmington, North Carolina	1946–50

TRI-STATE LEAGUE (ARKANSAS, MISSISSIPPI, AND TENNESSEE) (CLASS D, 1925–26)

Team	Years in Operation
Blytheville, Arkansas	1925–26
Corinth, Mississippi	1925–26
Dyersburg, Tennessee	1925
Jackson, Tennessee	1925–26
Jonesboro, Arkansas	1925–26
Sheffield–Tuscumbia, Alabama	1926
Tupelo, Mississippi	1925–26

TRI-STATE LEAGUE (DELAWARE, PENNSYLVANIA, AND NEW JERSEY) (CLASS D, 1904–06; CLASS B, 1907–14)

Team	Years in Operation
Allentown, Pennsylvania	1912–14
Altoona, Pennsylvania	1904–06
Atlantic City, New Jersey	1912#, 1913
Camden, New Jersey	1904X
Chester, Pennsylvania	1912#
Coatesville, Pennsylvania	1904 (franchise shifted to Shamokin in midseason)
Harrisburg, Pennsylvania	1904–14
Johnstown, Pennsylvania	1905–12 (franchise shifted to Chester in early August)
Lancaster, Pennsylvania	1905–12, 1914#
Lebanon, Pennsylvania	1904–05 (franchise shifted to Wilmington in midseason)

Team	Years in Operation
Reading, Pennsylvania	1907–11, 1912#, 1914
Shamokin, Pennsylvania	1904#
Trenton, New Jersey	1907–14
Williamsport, Pennsylvania	1904–10
Wilmington, Delaware	1904–05#, 1907–08, 1911–14
York, Pennsylvania	1904–06, 1909–14 (franchise shifted to Lancaster on July 8)

(Note: The Tri-State League did not hold National Association membership In 1904–06; technically, therefore, it was an "outlaw" league during those three seasons.)

TRI-STATE LEAGUE (IOWA, NEBRASKA, AND SOUTH DAKOTA) (CLASS D, 1924X—SUSPENDED OPERATIONS ON JULY 17)

Beatrice, Nebraska	1924X
Grand Island, Nebraska	1924X
Hastings, Nebraska	1924X
Norfolk, Nebraska	1924X
Sioux City, Iowa	1924X
Sioux Falls, South Dakota	1924X

TRI-STATE LEAGUE (NORTH CAROLINA, SOUTH CAROLINA, AND TENNESSEE) (CLASS B, 1946–55)

Anderson, South Carolina	1946–54
Asheville, North Carolina	1946–55
Charlotte, North Carolina	1946–53
Fayetteville, North Carolina	1947–48
Florence, South Carolina	1948–50X
Gastonia, North Carolina	1952–53
Greenville, South Carolina	1951–52, 1954–55
Greenwood, South Carolina	1951
Knoxville, Tennessee	1946–52, 1954
Reidsville, North Carolina	1947
Rock Hill, South Carolina	1947–55
Shelby, North Carolina	1946
Spartanburg, South Carolina	1946–55
Sumter, South Carolina	1950

Team   *Years in Operation*

TWIN PORTS LEAGUE (CLASS E, 1943X—
DISBANDED ON JULY 26)

Duluth "Herald," Minnesota	1943X
Duluth "Dukes," Minnesota	1943X
Marion "Iron" Club (Duluth), Minnesota	1943X
Superior, Wisconsin	1943X

(Note: The Twin Ports League is the only circuit in National Association history to have the "E" classification.)

UNION ASSOCIATION (CLASS C, 1911; CLASS D,
1912–14X—DISBANDED ON AUGUST 5)

Boise, Idaho	1911, 1914X
Butte, Montana	1911–14X
Great Falls, Montana	1911–13
Helena, Montana	1911–14
Missoula, Montana	1911–13
Murray, Montana	1914X
Ogden, Utah	1912–14X
Salt Lake City, Utah	1911–14X

UTAH–IDAHO LEAGUE (CLASS C, 1926–28)

Boise, Idaho	1928
Idaho Falls, Idaho	1926–28
Logan, Utah	1926–27
Ogden, Utah	1926–28
Pocatello, Idaho	1926–28
Salt Lake City, Utah	1926–28
Twin Falls, Idaho	1926–28

VIRGINIA LEAGUE (CLASS C, 1906–17X—SUSPENDED PLAY
ON MAY 16, 1918X BECAUSE OF WORLD WAR I; 1919;
CLASS B, 1920–28X; CLASS D, 1939–40; CLASS C,
1941–42; CLASS D, 1948–51)

Blackstone, Virginia	1948
Colonial Heights–Petersburg, Virginia	1951
Danville, Virginia	1906–12X
Edenton, North Carolina	1951

Team	Years in Operation
Elizabeth City, North Carolina	1950–51
Emporia, Virginia	1948–51
Franklin, Virginia	1948–51
Harrisonburg, Virginia	1939#, 1940–41
Hopewell, Virginia	1916X, 1949–50
Kinston, North Carolina	1925–27
Lawrenceville, Virginia	1948
Lawrenceville–Blackstone, Virginia	1949
Lynchburg, Virginia	1906–12X, 1917X, 1939#, 1940–42
Newport News, Virginia	1912–17X, 1918X, 1919–22, 1941–42
Norfolk, Virginia	1906–17X, 1918X, 1919–28X
Petersburg, Virginia	1911–17X, 1918X, 1919–21X, 1922X, 1923–28X, 1941–42, 1948–50
Portsmouth, Virginia	1906–10, 1912–17X, 1919–28X
Pulaski, Virginia	1942
Richmond, Virginia	1906–14, 1918X, 1919–28X
Roanoke, Virginia	1906–13, 1914X
Rocky Mount, North Carolina	1915–17X, 1920–25
Salem–Roanoke, Virginia	1939#, 1940–42
Staunton, Virginia	1939#, 1940–42
Suffolk, Virginia	1915, 1919–22, 1948–51
Tarboro, North Carolina	1922#
Wilson, North Carolina	1920–27

VIRGINIA MOUNTAIN LEAGUE (CLASS D, 1914)

Charlottesville, Virginia	1914
Clifton Forge, Virginia	1914
Covington, Virginia	1914
Staunton, Virginia	1914

VIRGINIA–NORTH CAROLINA LEAGUE (CLASS D, 1905X)

Charlotte, North Carolina	1905X
Danville, Virginia	1905X
Greensboro, North Carolina	1905X
Winston-Salem, North Carolina	1905X

VIRGINIA VALLEY LEAGUE (CLASS D, 1910)

Ashland–Catlettsburg, Kentucky	1910
Charleston, West Virginia	1910
Huntington, West Virginia	1910
Montgomery, West Virginia	1910
Point Pleasant, West Virginia–Gallipolis, Ohio	1910
Parkersburg, West Virginia	1910

Team	*Years in Operation*

WASHINGTON STATE LEAGUE (CLASS D, 1910–11)

Aberdeen, Washington	1910
Centralia, Washington	1911
Chehalis, Washington	1910–11
Hoquiam, Washington	1910
Montesano, Washington	1910
Raymond, Washington	1910–11
South Bend, Washington	1911
Tacoma, Washington	1910

WEST DIXIE LEAGUE (CLASS C, 1934–35)

Gladewater, Texas	1935#
Henderson, Texas	1934–35
Jacksonville, Texas	1934–35
Longview, Texas	1934–35
Lufkin, Texas	1934#
Palestine, Texas	1934–35
Paris, Texas	1934 (franchise shifted to Lufkin on June 27)
Shreveport, Louisiana	1935 (franchise shifted to Gladewater in early June)
Tyler, Texas	1934–35

WESTERN ASSOCIATION (CLASS C, 1905–11X—SUSPENDED PLAY ON JUNE 20; CLASS D, 1914–17, 1920–21; CLASS C, 1922–26: CLASS B TO C, IN MIDSEASON 1927; CLASS B, 1928; CLASS C, 1929–32X—SUSPENDED PLAY IN MIDSEASON; 1934–42, 1946–54)

Ardmore, Oklahoma	1917#, 1923–24, 1925–26
Bartlesville, Oklahoma	1909–10, 1924, 1931–32, 1934–38
Blackwell, Oklahoma	1954
Carthage, Missouri	1941
Chickasha, Oklahoma	1920–21
Coffeyville, Kansas	1911X
Denison, Texas	1915–17
Drumright, Oklahoma	1920–21
Enid, Oklahoma	1908–10, 1920–23, 1950–51
Fort Smith, Arkansas	1911X, 1914–17, 1920–32X, 1938–42, 1946–53
Guthrie, Oklahoma	1905, 1909–10, 1914 (franchise shifted to Henryetta on July 22)
Henryetta, Oklahoma	1914#, 1920–23X
Hutchinson, Kansas	1906–08, 1924, 1932#X, 1934–42, 1946–48X, 1949–54

Team	Years in Operation
Independence, Kansas	1911X, 1925, 1928–32X
Iola, Kansas	1954
Joplin, Missouri	1905–08, 1910–11X, 1914 (franchise shifted to Guthrie on July 1), 1922–23, 1927#, 1928–32X, 1934–42, 1946–54
Leavenworth, Kansas	1905–07, 1946–49
McAlester, Oklahoma	1914–17, 1922–23X, 1926X
Maud, Oklahoma	1929
Muskogee, Oklahoma	1909–11X, 1914–17, 1924-26X, 1927–29 (franchise shifted to Maud in midseason 1929), 1932X, 1934–42, 1946–54
Oklahoma City, Oklahoma	1905–08, 1914–17
Okmulgee, Oklahoma	1920–27
Paris, Texas	1915–17 (franchise shifted to Ardmore early in 1917 season)
Pawhuska, Oklahoma	1920–22
Pittsburg, Kansas	1909
Ponca City, Oklahoma	1934–38, 1954 (franchise shifted to Joplin in midseason), 1939–41, 1946–51, 1953–54
St. Joseph, Missouri	
Salina, Kansas	1938–41, 1946–52
Sapulpa, Oklahoma	1909–11X
Sedalia, Missouri	1905
Shawnee, Oklahoma	1929–30
Sherman, Texas	1915–17
Springfield, Missouri	1905–09, 1911X, 1920–32X, 1933–42
Topeka, Kansas	1905–08, 1924, 1927, 1928, 1932#X, 1939–42, 1946–54
Tulsa, Oklahoma	1910–11X, 1914–17
Webb City, Missouri	1906–08
Wichita, Kansas	1905–08

WESTERN CANADA LEAGUE (CLASS B, 1907; CLASS C, 1909; CLASS D, 1910–11, 1912–14; CLASS C, 1919; CLASS B, 1920–21)

Bassano, Alberta	1912
Brandon, Manitoba	1909–11
Calgary, Alberta	1907, 1909–14, 1920–21
Edmonton, Alberta	1907, 1909–14, 1920–21
Lethbridge, Alberta	1907, 1909–11
Medicine Hat, Alberta	1907, 1909–10, 1913–14
Moose Jaw, Saskatchewan	1909–11, 1913–14, 1919–21
Red Deer, Alberta	1912
Regina, Saskatchewan	1909–11 (moved to Saskatoon in midseason), 1913–14, 1919–21
Saskatoon, Saskatchewan	1911 (picked up the Regina franchise in midseason), 1913–14, 1919–21
Winnipeg, Manitoba	1909–11, 1919–21

Team	Years in Operation

WESTERN CAROLINAS LEAGUE (CLASS D, 1948–52, 1960–62; CLASS A, 1963—)

Team	Years in Operation
Anderson, South Carolina	1970—
Belmont, North Carolina	1961
Charleston, South Carolina	1973
Charlotte, South Carolina	1972
Forest City (Rutherford County), North Carolina	1948, 1952, 1960
Gastonia, North Carolina	1950, 1960, 1963–70, 1972—
Granite Falls, North Carolina	1951
Greenville, South Carolina	1963–72
Greenwood, South Carolina	1968—
Hendersonville, North Carolina	1948–49
Hickory, North Carolina	1951–52, 1960
Lenoir, North Carolina	1948–51
Lexington, North Carolina	1960–61, 1963–67
Lincolnton, North Carolina	1948–52
Marion, North Carolina	1948–52
Monroe, North Carolina	1969#, 1971
Morganton, North Carolina	1948–52X
Newton–Conover, North Carolina	1948–51, 1960–62
Orangeburg, South Carolina	1973
Rock Hill, South Carolina	1963–68
Salisbury, North Carolina	1960–66, 1968
Shelby, North Carolina	1948–52, 1960–65, 1969
Spartanburg, South Carolina	1963—
Spindale, North Carolina	1949–51
Statesville, North Carolina	1960–64, 1966–67, 1969X
Sumter, South Carolina	1970–71
Thomasville, North Carolina	1965–66

WESTERN INTERNATIONAL LEAGUE (CLASS B, 1922X— SUSPENDED OPERATIONS ON JUNE 18; 1937–42, 1946–51; CLASS A, 1952–54)

Team	Years in Operation
Bellingham, Washington	1938–39
Bremerton, Washington	1946–49
Calgary, Alberta, Canada	1953–54X
Edmonton, Alberta, Canada	1922X, 1953–54
Kennewick–Richland–Pasco, Washington	1950–54
Lewiston, Idaho	1937, 1952–54
Salem, Oregon	1940–42, 1946–54
Spokane, Washington	1937–42, 1946–54X
Tacoma, Washington	1922X, 1937–42, 1946–51
Vancouver, British Columbia, Canada	1922X, 1937–42, 1946–54

Team	Years in Operation
Victoria, British Columbia, Canada	1946–54X
Wenatchee, Washington	1937–41, 1946–54
Yakima, Washington	1937–41, 1946–54

WESTERN LEAGUE (CLASS A, 1902–18X—SUSPENDED PLAY JULY 7 BECAUSE OF WORLD WAR I, 1919–37; CLASS D, 1939–41; CLASS A, 1947–58)

Albuquerque, New Mexico	1956–58
Amarillo, Texas	1927–28, 1956–58
Bartlesville, Oklahoma	1933#
Beatrice, Nebraska	1939X
Cedar Rapids, Iowa	1934–37
Cheyenne, Wyoming	1941
Colorado Springs, Colorado	1902–04, 1950–58
Council Bluffs, Iowa	1935#
Davenport, Iowa	1934–37
Denver, Colorado	1902–17, 1922–32, 1941, 1947–54
Des Moines, Iowa	1902–18X, 1919–37, 1947–58
Hutchinson, Kansas	1917#, 1918, 1933 (franchise shifted to Bartlesville in midseason)
Joplin, Missouri	1917–18X, 1919–21, 1933
Kansas City, Missouri	1902–03
Keokuk, Iowa	1935
Lincoln, Nebraska	1906–17, 1924–27, 1939–40, 1947–58
Milwaukee, Wisconsin	1902–03
Mitchell, South Dakota	1939–40#
Muskogee, Oklahoma	1933#
Norfolk, Nebraska	1939–41
Oklahoma City, Oklahoma	1918#X, 1919–22
Omaha, Nebraska	1902–18X, 1919–35 (franchise shifted to Council Bluffs on May 25), 1936, 1947–54
Peoria, Illinois	1902–03
Pueblo, Colorado	1905–09, 1911#, 1928–32, 1941, 1947–58
Rock Island, Illinois	1934–35X, 1936, 1937X
Sioux City, Iowa	1904–18X, 1919–23, 1934–40 (franchise shifted to Mitchell on July 21), 1941, 1947–58
Sioux Falls, South Dakota	1939–41
St. Joseph, Missouri	1902–05, 1910–17 (franchise shifted to Hutchinson on July 24), 1918X 1919–26, 1930–35
Springfield, Missouri	1933
Topeka, Kansas	1909–16, 1918#X, 1928–31#, 1933–34, 1956–58
Tulsa, Oklahoma	1919–29, 1931X, 1932
Waterloo, Iowa	1936–37
Wichita, Kansas	1909–11X, 1912–18X, 1919–33 (franchise shifted to Muskogee in midseason), 1950–55
Worthington, Minnesota	1939–40

Team   *Years in Operation*

WESTERN PENNSYLVANIA LEAGUE (PENNSYLVANIA AND WEST VIRGINIA) (CLASS D, 1907)

Beaver Falls, Pennsylvania	1907X
Butler, Pennsylvania	1907
Clarksburg, Pennsylvania	1907
Connellsville, Pennsylvania	1907
Fairmont, West Virginia	1907
Greensburg, Pennsylvania	1907
Piedmont, West Virginia	1907X
Scottdale, Pennsylvania	1907

WEST TEXAS LEAGUE (CLASS D, 1920–22, 1928–29)

Abilene, Texas	1920–21, 1928–29
Amarillo, Texas	1922
Ballinger, Texas	1921#, 1929
Big Springs, Texas	1929
Cisco, Texas	1920–21 (franchise shifted to Ballinger on May 5)
Clovis, New Mexico	1922
Coleman, Texas	1928–29
Eastland, Texas	1920
Gorman, Texas	1920
Hamlin, Texas	1928
Lubbock, Texas	1922, 1928
Midland, Texas	1928–29
Mineral Wells, Texas	1920
Ranger, Texas	1920–22
San Angelo, Texas	1921–22, 1928–29
Stamford, Texas	1922
Sweetwater, Texas	1920–22

WEST TEXAS–NEW MEXICO LEAGUE (CLASS C, 1937–42X, 1946–54; CLASS B, 1955)

Abilene, Texas	1939 (franchise shifted to Borger on June 7), 1946–55
Albuquerque, New Mexico	1942X, 1946–55
Amarillo, Texas	1939–42X, 1946–55
Big Springs, Texas	1938–40 (franchise shifted to Odessa on June 20), 1941–42#X
Borger, Texas	1939#, 1942X, 1946–54X
Clovis, New Mexico	1938–42X, 1946–55

Team	Years in Operation
El Paso, Texas	1955
Hobbs, New Mexico	1937–38
Lamesa, Texas	1939–42X, 1946–52
Lubbock, Texas	1938–42X, 1946–55
Midland, Texas	1937X, 1938–40
Monahans, Texas	1937
Odessa, Texas	1937X, 1940#
Pampa, Texas	1939–42X, 1946–55
Plainview, Texas	1953–55
Roswell, New Mexico	1937
Wichita Falls, Texas	1941–42X
Wink, Texas	1937–38

WESTERN TRI-STATE LEAGUE (IDAHO, OREGON, AND WASHINGTON) (CLASS D, 1912–14)

Baker, Oregon	1913X, 1914
Boise, Idaho	1912–13
La Grande, Oregon	1912–1913X
North Yakima, Washington	1913–14
Pendleton, Oregon	1912–14
Walla Walla, Washington	1912–14

WESTERN TRI-STATE LEAGUE (OREGON) (CLASS D, 1902X, 1908X)

The Western Tri-State League was known as the Inland Empire League and then became the nucleus for the Western Tri-State League of 1912–14.

1902: Pendleton, Oregon was the unofficial league champion (won, 19; lost, 13; pct., .594). The league disbanded after about six weeks.

1908: La Grande, Oregon was the unofficial league champion (won, 19; lost, 12; pct., .613). The league disbanded after about five weeks.

WEST VIRGINIA LEAGUE (CLASS D, 1910X)

Clarksburg, West Virginia	1910X
Fairmont, West Virginia	1910X
Grafton, West Virginia	1910X
Mannington, West Virginia	1910X

Team	*Years in Operation*

WISCONSIN–ILLINOIS LEAGUE
(CLASS D, 1907–10; CLASS C, 1911–14)

Appleton, Wisconsin	1909–14
Aurora, Illinois	1910–12
Eau Claire, Wisconsin	1907#
Fond du Lac, Wisconsin	1907–11, 1913 (part of schedule was played in Milwaukee)
Freeport, Illinois	1907–09, 1914 (franchise shifted to Wausau, Wisconsin, and the Freeport and Wausau teams combined in midseason)
Green Bay, Wisconsin	1907–14
La Crosse, Wisconsin	1907X–08
Madison, Wisconsin	1907–14
Marinette–Menominee, Wisconsin	1914
Milwaukee, Wisconsin	**1913 (shared team with Fond du Lac)**
Oshkosh, Wisconsin	1907–14
Racine, Wisconsin	1909–14
Rockford, Illinois	1908–14
Wausau, Wisconsin	1907–08, 1912–14 (with Freeport, Illinois in 1914)

(Note: A Wisconsin–Illinois Class D league, known as the "Bi-State League," was organized for the 1915 season.)

WISCONSIN STATE LEAGUE (CLASS D, 1905–06,
1940–42, 1946–53)

Appleton, Wisconsin	1940–42, 1946–53
Beloit, Wisconsin	1905
Eau Claire, Wisconsin	1906
Fond du Lac, Wisconsin	1940–42, 1946–53
Freeport, Illinois	1905–06
Green Bay, Wisconsin	1905–06, 1940–42, 1946–53
Janesville, Wisconsin	1941–42, 1946–53
La Crosse, Wisconsin	1905–06, 1940–42
Oshkosh, Wisconsin	1905–06, 1941–42, 1946–53
Sheboygan, Wisconsin	1940–42, 1946–53
Wausau, Wisconsin	1905–06, 1946–53
Wisconsin Rapids, Wisconsin	1940–42, 1946–53

BIBLIOGRAPHY

GENERAL REFERENCE BOOKS

Agreement, National Association of Professional Baseball Leagues, 1972 edition. St. Petersburg, Florida: Baseball Blue Book, Inc., 1972.

The Baseball Encyclopedia: The Complete and Official Record of Major League Baseball. New York: Macmillan Publishing Co., Inc., and Information Concepts, Inc., 1969.

Danzig, Allison, and Reichler, Joe. *The History of Baseball: Its Great Players, Teams and Managers.* Englewood Cliffs, New Jersey: Prentice-Hall, Inc., 1959.

Finch, Robert L.; Addington, L. H.; and Morgan, Ben M. *The Story of Minor League Baseball: A History of the Game of Professional Baseball in the United States with Particular Reference to Its Growth and Development in the Smaller Cities and Towns of the Nation. The Record of Championship Performances from 1901 to 1952.* Columbus, Ohio: Published by the National Association of Professional Baseball Leagues, 1952. (This 744-page book is an extremely useful reference and was of particular value in the preparation of the section on the administration of William G. Bramham, National Association President, 1932–46.)

Friend, J. P. *Cotton States League Golden Anniversary, 1902–51.* Blytheville, Arkansas: Published by The Cotton States League, 1951.

Graham, Frank. *The New York Yankees, An Informal History.* New York: G. P. Putnam's Sons, 1948.

Lieb, Frederick G. *The St. Louis Cardinals.* New York: G. P. Putnam's Sons, 1944.

Moss, Earle W. *The Leagues and League Cities of Professional Baseball, 1910–41.* Fort Wayne, Indiana: Heilbroner Baseball Bureau, 1941.

Musial, Stan, and Broeg, Bob. *Stan Musial: "The Man's" Own Story.* Garden City, New York: Doubleday & Co., Inc., 1964.

Ritter, Lawrence S. *The Glory of Their Times: The Story of the Early Days of Baseball Told by the Men Who Played It.* New York: Macmillan Publishing Co., Inc., 1966.

401

Smith, Don. *The Glory Years of Baseball.* New York: Stadia Sports Publishing, Inc., 1972.

Smith, Robert. *Baseball's Hall of Fame.* New York: Grosset & Dunlap, Inc., 1965.

Spalding, Albert Goodwill. *Historic Facts Concerning the Beginning, Evolution, Development and Popularity of Base Ball With Personal Reminiscences of Its Vicissitudes, Its Victories and Its Votaries.* New York: American Sports Publishing Co., 1911.

Williams, Ted, and Underwood, John. *My Turn at Bat, The Story of My Life.* New York: Simon & Schuster, Inc., 1969

GENERAL REFERENCE
MAGAZINES AND NEWSPAPER ARTICLES

Fisher, Eddie. "Mr. Minor League, That's George Trautman, Columbus' Major Contribution to Organized Baseball." *The Columbus Dispatch Sunday Magazine,* April 1, 1962.

Hern, Gerry. "There are Still *Too Many* Minors!" *Baseball Digest,* April 1954.

Koppett, Leonard. "The Golden Apple, A Strange Business, Baseball." *The New York Times Magazine,* September 2, 1973.

Miller, Dick. "Dalton Asks Winkles to Put Twinkle in Angels." *The Sporting News,* October 28, 1972.

Pepe, Phil. "Anderson: Rickey's Touch Still Paying Off in N.L." *The New York Daily News,* July 28, 1973.

"West Haven Yankees: The Team Is Good and So Are the Crowds." *The New York Times,* September 3, 1972.

CHAPTER 7. THE AMERICAN ASSOCIATION

French, Robert A. *Fifty Golden Years in the American Association of Professional Baseball Clubs: 1902–51.* Minneapolis: Published by The American Association, 1951. *All-Time Records and Highlights of the American Association,* 65th ed. Wichita: Published by The American Association, 1972.

CHAPTER 8. THE INTERNATIONAL LEAGUE

International League of Professional Baseball Clubs, White Book, 36th ed. Rochester, New York: Published by The International League, 1972.

Remington, John. *The Red Wings—A Love Story: A Pictorial History of Professional Baseball in Rochester, New York.* Rochester: The Christopher Press, 1969.

Weber, Ralph E. L., ed. *The Toledo Baseball Guide of the Mud Hens: 1883–1943.* Toledo: Published by The Toledo Mud Hens Baseball, Co., 1944.

CHAPTER 9. THE PACIFIC COAST LEAGUE

Lange, Fred W. *History of Baseball in California and Pacific Coast Leagues, 1847–1938.* Oakland: Privately published, 1938.

O'Brien, Robert. "San Francisco—April 18, 1906: It Happened 50 Years Ago." *Collier's,* March 30, 1956.

Weiss, William J. *Pacific Coast Baseball League Record Book, 1903–69.* Phoenix, Arizona: Published by the Pacific Coast Baseball League, 1969.

CHAPTER 10. THE TEXAS LEAGUE

Friend, J. P., ed. *Texas League Record Book, 1888–1972.* Blytheville, Arkansas: Published by The Texas League, 1972.

Ruggles, William B. *The History of the Texas League of Professional Baseball Clubs, 1888–1951.* Dallas: Published by The Texas League, 1951.

CHAPTER 11. THE SOUTHERN ASSOCIATION
AND THE SOUTHERN LEAGUE

Gammon, Wirt. *Your Chattanooga Lookouts Since 1885.* Chattanooga, Tennessee: Chattanooga Publishing Co., 1953.

Hurth, Charles A. *Baseball Records, The Southern Association, 1901–47.* New Orleans: Published by The Southern Association, 1947.

Southern League Records Book. Chicago: Compiled and edited for the Southern League by the Howe News Bureau, 1973.

The Southern League of Professional Baseball Clubs, 1973 Press, Radio and T.V. Guide. Opelika, Alabama: Published by The Southern League, 1973.

CHAPTER 12. THE EASTERN LEAGUE

Keyes, Ray, Ed. *Eastern League Record Book, Silver Anniversary, 1923–47.* Williamsport, Pennsylvania: Published by The Eastern League, 1947.

The Eastern League of Professional Baseball Clubs, 1973 Record Book. Paoli, Pennsylvania: Published by The Eastern League, 1973.

CHAPTER 13. THE MIDDLE ATLANTIC LEAGUE

Hockenbury, Russell. *A Sketch History of The Middle Atlantic League, 1925–47.* Scottdale, Pennsylvania: Published by The Middle Atlantic League, 1947.

Kramer, Charles F., ed. *The Middle Atlantic League, 25th Anniversary, 1925–49, Souvenir Book.* Johnstown, Pennsylvania: Published by The Middle Atlantic League, 1949.

We also relied heavily on the various official baseball guides published from the early 1880s to the present. For the earlier period of minor league history, we utilized guides published by J. D. Shibe, the A. J. Reach Co., and Albert G. Spalding. For the period of the last forty years or so, we made liberal use of the annual *Sporting News Official Baseball Guides*

Moreover, we used a number of other publications issued by *The Sporting News,* including the annual *Official Baseball Register* (which has been appearing since 1940) plus various editions of *Daguerreotypes of Great Stars of Baseball* (published during the past twenty-five years). Finally, we were able to keep abreast of current developments on the minor league baseball scene by gleaning *The Sporting News,* published weekly, which for several generations now has been called "The Bible of Baseball."

INDEX OF NAMES

Aaron, Hank, 57, 108
Aaron, Tommie, 108
Acosta, Cecilio, 288
Adams, Charles (Babe), 274
Akin, Roy, 148, 190
Alcarez, Luis, 79
Alexander, Bill, 187
Allen, Colonel Bob, 229
Alston, Walt, 71, 128–29, 277, 278
Anderson, George (Sparky), 44, 301
Archdeacon, Maurice (Comet), 127
Archibald, Ray, 271–72, 273
Archie, George, 155
Arlett, Russell, (Buzz), 104, 140
Armour, Bill, 69
Arntzen, Orie (Old Folks), 258
Atz, Jake, 192
Averill, Earl, 153
Avery, Don, 13, 322

Ball, Phil, 40–41

Barbisch, Joseph A., 182
Barnes, Donald, 41
Barrow, Edward Grant (Ed), 12, 69, 99, 100
Bates, Johnny, 231
Baugh, Sammy, 129
Baum, Allan T., 145
Bauman, Joe, 77, 299
Baumholtz, Frankie, 156
Beauchamp, Jim, 197
Beck, Walter (Boom Boom), 229–30
Belanger, Mark, 132
Bender, Charles (Chief), 274–75
Berra, Yogi, 72
Bert, Eugene F., 144
Bigelow, Elliot, 231
Bilko, Steve, 156
Binford, Rich, 300
Blades, Ray, 128
Blankenship, Cliff, 68
Blefary, Curt, 107

Block, Morris, 191
Bloodworth, Jimmy, 225
Bodie, Frank (Ping), 149
Boone, Danny, 298
Boone, Isaac (Ike), 231, 297–98
Borchert, Otto, 76
Bragan, Bobby, 195
Bramham, Judge William G., 20–22, 24, 47, 278
Breadon, Sam, 41, 43, 127
Bresnahan, Roger (Duke), 69
Brief, Anthony (Bunny), 76
Brown, Jimmy, 128
Brown, Joe (Poison), 105
Brown, Lloyd, 225
Bulkeley, Morgan G., 8
Bumbry, Alonza, 132
Burge, Les, 230
Burke, John, 256
Burns, Tom, 6
Burwell, Bill, 73–74
Bush, Owen (Donie), 70–71, 72, 76

Cabell, Enos, 197
Campanella, Roy, 78
Campau, Charley (The Count), 208
Cantillon, Joe (Pongo Joe), 68
Cantillon, Mike, 68
Carlisle, Walter, 148
Carmichael, Chester, 103
Carnegie, Gary, 301
Carpenter, Bob, 29
Carr, Joe F., 21
Carson, Al, 148
Case, I. H., 22
Cassini, Jack, 232
Castro, Fidel, 101
Chadwick, Henry, 15
Chandler, A. B. (Happy), 25, 287, 288
Chapman, Ben, 22
Chozen, Harry, 231
Christian, Tyler, 147
Cicero, Joe, 257
Clark, Darrell, 303
Clarke, Fred C., 183
Clarke, Justin (Nig), 187, 188–89

Clear, Bob, 300
Clemente, Roberto, 44
Clines, Gene, 259
Clyde, David, 57
Coan, Gil, 225, 231, 232
Cobb, Ty, 49–50, 57, 74, 153, 227
Coffman, Dick, 225
Colavito, Rocky, 258
Colbert, Nate, 197
Coles, Chuck, 232–33
Collins, James (Rip), 105, 128, 273
Comiskey, Charles A. (Old Roman), 65, 98
Conley, Jim, 256
Conlon, Jocko, 75
Connolly, Tom, 75
Corcoran, Tommy, 7
Corriden, John (Red), 75
Coveleski, Harry, 227–28
Coveleski, Stan, 227
Covington, Chet, 257
Cox, Bobby, 255
Crabtree, Estel, 129
Cravath, Clifford (Cactus), 144, 149
Crawford, Sam, 12, 150
Cronin, Joe, 29, 72, 225, 273
Crowder, Alvin, 225
Cullenbine, Roy, 23
Cullinane, Joe, 125
Cullop, Nick (Tomato Face), 76
Cummings, Arthur (Candy), 5–6

Dahlgren, Ellsworth (Babe), 105
Daily, Elmer, M., 273
Davis, John, (Red), 196
Davis, Willie, 157
Deal, Ellis (Cot), 78
Dean, Jay Hanna (Dizzy), 193
Dees, Charlie, 196–97
Delahanty, Ed, 12
Demaree, Frank, 154
DeMars, Bill, 301
Denning, Dennis, 301
DeRose, Carl, 77
Derringer, Paul, 128
Derry, Russ, 130
DeWitt, C. B., 187, 189

DeWitt, William O., 29
DiMaggio, Joe, 57, 154
DiMaggio, Vince, 77, 154
Dobbs, Johnny, 223, 228
Doljack, Frank, 275
Donald, Atley, 105
Donovan, Patsy, 7
Doubleday, Abner, 22
Drago, Dick, 303
Drake, James M., 185
Dressen, Chuck, 72, 76, 225
Drugmond, Joe, 275
Duke, Audrey, 256
Duke, Ron, 255–56
Dunn, Jack, 26, 100, 104, 127
Dunn, Jack, Jr., 107
Durocher, Leo, 72
Durst, Cedric, 130
Dwyer, Joe (Double Joe), 230
Dyer, Eddie, 128
Dykes, Jimmy, 228

Easter, Luke, 107
Easterling, Paul, 193–94
Embree, Charles (Red), 257
Engel, Joe, 224–26
Ermer, Cal, 233
Essick, Bill, 150
Evans, William G. (Billy), 75, 231
Ewing, J. Cal, 149
Fabian, Henry, 150
Fanzone, Carmen, 259
Farrell, John H., 14, 251
Farrell, Kerby, 231
Farrell, Perry B., 253
Feller, Bob, 57, 287
Filipelli, Fred, 300
Fine, Tommy, 258
Finley, Charles O., 54
Fitzgerald, Jack, 148
Flaherty, Pat, 74
Fleming, Les, 195, 230
Foxx, Jimmy, 57
Freed, Roger, 108
Frick, Ford, 25
Futch, Ike, 197

Galbreath, John W., 29
Galvin, James (Pud), 6
Ganzel, John, 126
Garagiola, Joe, 72–73
Gardella, Danny, 287
Gardner, J. Alvin, 20
Gardner, Joe, 191
Gehrig, Lou, 57, 154
Gehringer, Charlie, 154
Galbert, Charley, 127
George, Tom (Lefty), 256
Gilbert, Charlie, 222
Gilbert, Harold (Tookie), 222
Gilbert, Larry, 222–23, 229, 232
Giles, Warren C., 127, 128
Gilliam, James (Junior), 106
Gomez, Vernon (Lefty), 153
Gonder, Jesse, 157
Good, Wilbur, 229
Gordon, Joe (Flash), 105, 156
Goslin, Leon (Goose), 225
Gray, Pete, 219, 231
Greenberg, Hank, 193, 194, 287
Greenberg, Joe, 194
Grey, Reddy, 126
Grey, Zane, 126
Grich, Bobby, 108, 132, 197
Griffith, Clark C., 224, 225
Grimes, Burleigh, 130
Groh, Heinie, 127
Grimm, Charlie, 71
Grove, Robert (Lefty), 26, 104
Guettler, Ken, 196
Guy, Dick, 270–72, 274

Haas, George (Mule), 252
Hack, Stan, 158
Haggerly, H. L., 146
Hallums, Tommy, 33
Hamilton, Billy, 7
Haney, Fred, 71, 155–56
Harrelson, Ken (Hawk), 258
Hauser, Joe (Unser Choe), 77, 295–
   97
Hayes, Jackie, 225
Head, Lee, 230
Heath, Jeff, 277

Hebert, Mike, 301
Heilmann, Harry, 149
Helm, Ross, 191
Henley, Clarence (Cack), 147, 148
Henrich, Tommy, 23, 276
Herman, Billy, 74
Hern, Gerry, 28
Heslet, Harry, 195
Hess, Otto, 227
Hickerson, Dick, 301
Hickey, Thomas Jefferson, 13–14, 16, 64, 65, 66, 67
Hill, Bill (Still Bill), 226
Hill, Hugh, 226
Hinchman, Bill, 252
Hinchman, Harry, 252
Hitchcock, Billy, 221
Hockenbury, Russell, 279
Holland, James, 186
Holmes, Howard (Ducky), 276
Hopp, Johnny, 128
Hornsby, Everett (Pep), 190–91
Hornsby, Rogers, 43, 57, 190, 195
Houck, Ralph, 71
Houston, Lieutenant Gordon, 24
Howard, Elston, 107
Hubbell, Carl, 57
Hudlin, Willis, 230
Hudson, Sid, 225
Huggins, Miller, 71–72, 73
Hulbert, William A., 8–10
Hulvey, Hank, 230
Hunter, Gordon (Billy), 195
Hutchinson, Fred, 155
Hutton, Tom, 197

Jackson, Joe (Shoeless Joe), 227
Jackson, Roy, 249
Jansen, Larry, 155
Jennings, Hugh, 12
Johnson, Arnold, 29
Johnson, Ban, 13, 66, 99
Johnson, George H. (Tiny), 75–76
Johnson, Harry (Steamboat), 228
Johnson, Larry, 197
Johnson, Roy, 153
Johnson, Walter, 57, 68, 224

Jolley, Smead, 153
Jones, Johnny, 227
Judge, Joe, 225
Juran, Tim, 32

Kaline, Al, 57
Kamm, Willie, 150
Kaufmann, Tony, 129
Kavanaugh, Judge William, 219
Keane, Johnny, 130
Keller, Charley, 105
Kelley, Joe, 7
Kelley, Mike, 69, 70
Kerr, Dickie, 228
Kiel, Herman, 279
Killifer, Bill (Reindeer Bill), 150
Killifer, Wade, 150
Kiner, Ralph, 257
King, Quay, 272
Kitchens, Frank, 191
Klem, Bill, 74–75
Klimkowski, Ron, 108
Koestner, Elmer, 148
Konetchy, Ed, 192
Kopacz, George, 108
Kraft, Clarence (Big Boy), 192, 196
Krausse, Lew, Sr., 278
Krist, Howie, 128
Kuhel, Joe, 225
Kurowski, George (Whitey), 277

Lajoie, Napoleon (Larry), 7, 71
Lane, Bill, 153
Landis, Judge Kenesaw Mountain, 18, 19, 20, 22–23, 25, 42, 68, 219
Lange, Fred W., 142
Lanier, Max, 287
Lary, Lynn, 153, 225
Lazzeri, Tony, 152
Leach, Tommy, 12
Leard, Bill (Wild Bill), 148
Lelivelt, Jack, 154
Lennon, Bob, 107–08, 232
Lewis, Buddy, 225
Lieb, Frederick G., 42
Liebhardt, Glenn, 226

Lively, Jack, 148
Lombardi, Ernie, 153
Lopat, Eddie, 230–31
Lopez, Al, 71
Lucas, Fred, 275
Lucas, W. H., 14
Lucchesi, Frank, 233
Lucier, Lou, 277–78
Lund, Don, 231–32
Lush, Billy, 126
Lyons, Ted, 232

McBride, Algie, 185
McCall, Darrell, 300
McCarthy, Joe, 71, 76
McCloskey, John J., 180–84, 185
McConnell, George (Slats), 126
McCoskey, Barney, 277
McCovey, Willie, 196
McCoy, Benny, 23
McDermott, Maurice, 78
McDonald, Joe, 32, 33
McDougald, Gil, 195
McGaha, Mel, 233
McGinnity, Joe (Iron Man), 103, 183
McGraw, John, 69, 74, 139, 183
McGuire, Jimmy, 271
Mack, Connie, 10, 12, 26, 252, 253
McKechnie, Bill, Jr., 142
McKechnie, Bill, Sr., 128
McKeon, Jack, 71
MacLeod, Bill, 258
McNeely, Earl, 225
McNeill, Norman, 274
MacPhail, Lee, Jr., 131
McQuinn, George, 257
Maglie, Sal, 287
Maranville, Walter (Rabbit), 127, 257
Marberry, Fred, 225
Marichal, Juan, 258
Marion, Marty, 128
Markley, George, 187
Marlowe, Dick, 103
Marquard, Rube, 75
Martin, Judge John D., 219

Martin, John Leonard (Pepper), 128, 129
Martineck, Mike, 272, 273
Medich, George (Doc), 250, 255
Medinger, George, 29
Medwick, Joe (Ducky), 275
Meehan, Harry, 274
Merkle, Fred (Bone Head), 127
Metzger, George, 148
Miller, Bing, 154, 225
Miller, John (Dots), 150
Mills, Colonel A. G., 10
Mize, Johnny, 128
Mizell, Wilmer (Vinegar Bend), 195
Mogridge, George, 127
Molesworth, Carleton, 226
Monday, Rick, 54
Montague, Eddie, 273
Moore, Charles, 148
Morgan, Bobby, 106
Morgan, Joe, 197
Mueller, Ray, 129
Mulligan, Eddie, 141–42
Murnane, T. H., 14
Murtaugh, Danny, 194
Musial, Stan, 129, 228, 287

Nelson, Glenn (Rocky), 107
Newburg, Louis, 182
Nicholson, Bill, 225
Nolan, James, 185, 189
Novikoff, Lou (Mad Russian), 155

O'Brien, Dan, 152
O'Connor, Mike, 186–87
O'Doul, Frank (Lefty), 150, 152, 155–56
Olson, Marvin, 279
O'Malley, Walter, 29
Orth, Al, 12
O'Toole, Marty, 75
Ott, Mel, 57
Owen, Mickey, 287

Packard, Si, 183
Parnell, Mel, 258
Partridge, Jay, 229

Pasquel, Jorge, 287
Pate, Joe, 192
Patterson, Floyd (Pat), 277, 278
Paul, Gabe, 29
Pavich, Pete, 279
Peel, Homer, 194
Pendleton, Ike, 187
Penner, Ken, 129–30
Pete, Bill, 270–71
Peters, Henry J., 25, 55–57
Phelps, Gordon (Babe), 275–76
Piersall, Jimmy, 232
Pina, Horacio, 288
Piton, Phil, 25
Pizarro, Juan, 78
Poole, Jim, 229
Powell, Charles Abner, 217–18
Powell, John (Boog), 107, 132
Powers, Patrick T., 14, 98
Prevedello, Andy, 300
Prothro, James T. (Doc), 229
Pulford, Don, 300

Quebbedeaux, W. E., 191

Radbourne, Charles (Old Hoss), 65
Reach, Alfred J., 3
Reeder, Ed, 182
Reese, Jimmy, 153
Reichardt, Rick, 54
Remington, John L., 131
Rettenmund, Merv, 108, 132
Reynolds, Allie, 257
Richardson, Thomas H. (Tommy),
    249, 253–55
Richbourg, Lance, 225
Rickey, Branch, Jr., 43
Rickey, Branch, Sr., 15, 20, 39–45,
    106, 127, 128, 129, 189–90
Rickey, Emily, 39
Rickey, Jacob Franklin, 39
Rico, Fred, 301
Rigney, Bill, 71
Rizzuto, Phil, 72
Robbie, Dr. W. R., 189
Roberts, Dave, 57
Roberts, J. Doak, 189, 192, 193

Robinson, Jackie, 44, 106
Robinson, Wilbert, 7
Rolph, James, Jr., 152
Romo, Vincente, 288
Rooney, Art, 272
Rooney, Dan, 272
Roosevelt, Franklin D., 23, 254
Rosar, Buddy, 105
Rose, Eddie, 230
Rosen, Al (Flip), 195
Roth, Arthur H., 32
Rowland, Clarence (Pants), 71
Ruth, George Herman (Babe), 57,
    69, 74, 75, 99, 104, 299
Ruggles, Bill, 186, 188, 189
Ryba, Mike, 129

Sanchez, Celerino, 288
Sand, Heinie, 105
Sauer, Hank, 106
Scarborough, Ray, 225
Schalk, Ray, 75
Scheffing, Bob, 129
Schneider, Pete, 151
Schoendienst, Albert (Red)', 106
Score, Herb, 78
Schulte, Fred, 76
Seeds, Bob, 105–06
Seghi, Phil, 31
Senger, Charles G., 132–34
Sensheimer, Joseph, 182
Serena, Bill, 299–300
Severeid, Hank, 194
Sexton, Michael H., 14, 19
Sharman, Ralph, 192
Shaughnessy, Frank, 21, 46–48, 105
Shaute, Joe, 257
Shaw, Roy, 147–48
Sheely, Earl, 149–50
Shellenback, Frank, 140
Shotton, Burt, 71, 128
Sick, Emil, 154
Simmons, Hack, 126
Sisler, George H., Jr., 131, 135–36
Sisler, George H., Sr., 128
Smith, Frank, 227
Somers, Charles W., 68, 76

Southworth, Billy, 127, 128, 129
Spalding, Albert G., 8–9, 64–65
Speaker, Tris, 190, 226–27
Spencer, Jim, 197
Spikes, Charlie, 250, 255
Stallings, George, 75, 127
Stanky, Eddie, 57, 72
Statz, Arnold (Jigger), 139–40
Stengel, Charles Dillon (Casey), 52, 71, 155, 330
Stewart, Harry, 148
Stockton, Roy, 43
Stoneham, Horace, 29
Strong, Ken, 256
Stuart, Marlin, 78
Sudakis, Bill, 197
Sullivan, Ted, 184
Sundra, Steve, 105

Tanner, Chuck, 232
Tauby, Fred, 230
Taylor, Danny, 231
Taylor, Harry L., 98
Tedesco, Rocky, 279
Thomassie, Pete, 231
Thompson, Gus, 274
Tiant, Luis, 288
Toporcer, George (Specs), 105, 127–28
Torchia, Tony, 259
Torres, Luis, 300
Trautman, George M., 24–25, 29
Travis, Cecil, 225
Trice, Bob, 107
Truby, Harry (Bird Eye), 182

Van Burkleo, Frank, 300
Vance, Dazzy, 57, 228
Van Haltren, George, 143

Veeck, Bill, 77
Vincent, Al, 195
Vitt, Oscar, 105

Wachtel, Paul, 192
Wade, Archie, 301
Walker, Fred (Dixie), 130
Walker, Harry, 130, 196
Wagner, John Peter (Honus), 10–11, 69
Walsh, Ed, Jr., 154
Waner, Lloyd, 152
Waner, Paul, 150, 152
Wasdell, Jimmy, 276
Watt, Eddie, 132
Weaver, Earl, 132
Weintraub, Phil, 230
Weiss, George, 49–54
Weiss, William J., 151
Whitfield, James, 66, 67
Wiggs, Jimmy, 147
Wilkins, Ron, 300
Williams, Davey, 78
Williams, J., 4
Williams, Nick, 147
Williams, Ted, 69–70, 71, 140, 297
Williams, W., 4
Wiltse, George (Hooks), 105
Winkles, Bobby, 58, 196
Workman, Charley, 232
Works, Bill (Farmer), 182
Wynn, Early, 225

Yastrzemski, Carl, 259
York, Rudy, 194, 279
Young, Denton (Cy), 12
Young, Irving (Young Cy), 103

Zeider, Rollie, 147

INDEX OF THE MINOR LEAGUES

Alabama-Florida League, 323
Alabama-Mississippi League, 323
Alabama State League, 324
Alabama-Tennessee League, 324
American Association, 7, 14, 15, 17, 25, 34, 46–47, 48, 58, 59, 61–93, 140, 157, 184, 225, 229, 295, 296, 298
  league roster of teams, 62
  history, 62–79
  league presidents, 79
  league champions, 80–88
  batting champions, 88–90
  individual batting and pitching records, 90–91
  Junior World Series, 91–93
Anthracite League, 324
Appalachian League, 37, 217, 324–25
Arizona-Mexico League, 300, 325
Arizona State League, 326
Arizona-Texas League, 287, 326
Arkansas League, 326
Arkansas-Missouri League, 42, 327
Arkansas State League, 327
Arkansas-Texas League, 327
Atlantic Association (pre–1900), 11
Atlantic Association (post–1900), 327
Atlantic League (pre–1900), 11, 12
Atlantic League (post–1900), 184, 328

Big State League, 180, 328
Bi-State League (Illinois-Wisconsin), 329

Bi-State League (North Carolina-Virginia), 329
Blue Grass League, 329–30
Blue Ridge League, 104, 330
Border League (Michigan-Ontario), 330
Border League (New York-Ontario-Quebec), 331
Buckeye League, 331

California League, 35, 58, 140–41, 331
California State League, 142–43, 144, 145, 332
Canadian-American League, 332
Canadian League (pre–1900), 11, 12
Canadian League (post–1900), 48, 333
Cape Breton Colliery League, 333
Carolina Baseball Association, 333
Carolina League, 35, 216, 303, 333–34
Central Association, 141, 334–35
Central Atlantic League, 11
Central California Baseball League, 335
Central International League, 335
Central Inter-State League, 11
Central Kansas League, 336
Central League, 40, 48, 70, 73, 184, 230, 271, 336–37
Central New York League, 337
Central Pennsylvania League, 11
Central Texas League, Central Texas Trolley League, 180, 337
Coastal Plain League, 338

Colonial League, 338
Connecticut Association, 338
Connecticut League (pre–1900), 14
Connecticut State League, Connecti-
    cut League (post–1900), 339
Copper-Country Soo League, 399
Cotton States League, 16, 339–40

Dakota League, 340
Delta League, 341
Dixie League (Arkansas–Louisiana–
    Mississippi–Texas), 341
Dixie League (Georgia–Alabama),
    341

Eastern Association, 341
Eastern Canada League, 342
Eastern Carolina League, 342
Eastern Championship Association,
    7–8
East Dixie League, 342
Eastern Illinois League, 343
Eastern Inter-State League, 11, 12
Eastern Kansas League, 343
Eastern League (operated 1916–32),
    52, 250, 253, 295, 343
Eastern League (1923–37, known as
    the New York–Pennsylvania
    League), 35, 47, 61, 248–68
league roster of teams, 248–49
history, 249–59
league presidents, 259
league champions, 259–65
batting champions, 266–67
individual batting and pitching rec-
    ords, 267–68
Eastern Michigan League, 344
Eastern Shore League, 156, 344
East Texas League, 24, 180, 344–45
Empire State League, 345
Empire State League (Georgia), 345
Empire State League (New York),
    345
Evangeline League, 346

Far West League, 346
Florida East Coast League, 346–47

Florida International League, 347
Florida State League, 36, 216, 233,
    301, 347–48

Georgia-Alabama League, 348
Georgia-Florida League, 348–49
Georgia State League, 297, 349
Gulf Coast League, 180, 350
Gulf Coast Rookie League, 37, 58,
    216

Hudson River League, 350

Illinois-Iowa-Indiana League (Three–I
    League), 11, 13, 14, 58, 74,
    129, 141, 229, 301, 351
Illinois-Missouri League, 352
Illinois State League, 352
Indiana-Michigan League, 352
Indiana-Ohio League, 353
Indiana State League, 353
Intermountain League, 353
International Association, 4–6, 125
International League, 10, 14, 15, 17,
    21, 33, 46, 47, 48, 94–136, 157,
    220, 221, 224, 229, 251, 257,
    271, 296, 298
league roster of teams, 95–96
history, 96–108
league presidents, 109
league champions, 109–20
batting champions, 121–22
individual batting and pitching rec-
    ords, 123–24
Rochester Red Wings, 124–32
Toledo Mud Hens, 132–35
designated hitter rule, 135–36
International League (Ontario–New
    York), 353
Inter-State Association (Indiana–
    Michigan–Ohio), 354
Inter-State League (Connecticut–
    Delaware–Maryland–New York–
    New Jersey–Pennsylvania), 230,
    256, 354–55
Inter-State League (Ohio–Pennsylva-
    nia, pre–1900), 12

Inter-State League (Ohio–Pennsylvania–West Virginia), 354
Inter-State League (Pennsylvania, 1932X), 354
Iowa and South Dakota League, 16, 40, 355
Iowa State League, 355
Iron and Oil Association, 11
Iron and Oil League, 11, 12

Kansas–Oklahoma–Missouri League (KOM League), 356
Kansas State League (pre–1900), 11
Kansas State League (post–1900), 356
Keystone League, 357
Kitty League (Kentucky–Illinois–Tennessee), 357–58

League Alliance, 6, 9
Lone Star League, 180, 358
Longhorn League, 77, 180, 299, 358
Louisiana League, 359

Maine State League, 359
Massachusetts-Connecticut League, (1912), 359
Mexican Professional Leagues:
  Central Mexican League, 291
  Mexican Center League, 38, 290
  Mexican League, 38, 64, 108, 196, 287–89
  Mexican Northern League, 291
  Mexican Rookie League, 291
  Mexican Southeast League, 290–91
Michigan-Ontario League, 359
Michigan State League (pre–1900), 11, 12
Michigan State League (1902), 360
Michigan State League (1910–14, 1926, 1940–41), 360
Middle Atlantic League, 15, 47, 61, 252, 257, 269–86
  league roster of teams, 269–70
  history, 270–79
  major league players from the Middle Atlantic League, 279–81

league champions, 281–85
batting champions, 285–86
Middle Texas League, 180, 360
Midwest League, 361
Minnesota-Wisconsin League, 361
Mississippi-Ohio Valley League, 362
Mississippi State League, 362
Mississippi Valley League, 103, 362–63
Missouri-Iowa-Nebraska-Kansas League (M.I.N.K. League), 363
Missouri State League, 363
Missouri Valley League, 16, 363
Mountain States League, 364

Nebraska State League (pre–1900), 11
Nebraska State League (post–1900), 42, 364–65
New Brunswick and Maine League, 365
New England League (pre–1900), 7, 14
New England League (post–1900), 365–66
New Hampshire League, 366
New York-New Jersey League, 366
New York-Pennsylvania League, 135, 366–67
New York State League, 14, 74, 251, 367
North Atlantic League, 368
North Carolina League, 14, 368
North Carolina State League, 368–69
North Dakota League, 369
Northeast Arkansas League, 369
Northeastern Connecticut State League, 11
Northeastern League, 369
Northern Association of Baseball, 370
Northern Copper Country League, 370
Northern League, 16, 73, 74, 370–71
Northern Maine League, 371
Northern New York League, 371

North Texas League, 180, 371
Northwestern League (pre–1900; be-
    gan in 1879), 7, 10, 64, 65
Northwestern League (pre–1900; be-
    gan in 1895), 11
Northwestern League (post–1900),
    372
Northwest League, 36–37, 372

Ohio-Indiana League, 372–73
Ohio–Pennsylvania League, 373
Ohio State League (pre–1900), 11,
    12
Ohio State League (post–1900), 374
Oklahoma-Arkansas League, 374
Oklahoma-Kansas League, 375
Oklahoma State League, 375
Old Dominion League, 375
Ontario League, 376
Oregon State League, 376

Pacific Coast League, 11, 15, 16, 17,
    34, 46, 61, 79, 91, 105, 108,
    137–76, 183, 197, 221, 230,
    249, 258, 277, 297
  league roster of teams, 137–38
  history, 138–58
  league presidents, 159
  league champions, 159–65
  batting champions, 165–67
  individual batting and pitching rec-
    ords, 167–76
  league attendance records, 176
Pacific Coast International League,
    376
Pacific National League (Pacific
    Northwest League), 11, 14, 183,
    376
Palmetto League, 377
Panhandle League, 184
Panhandle-Pecos Valley League, 377
Penn-Ohio-Maryland League (P.O.M.
    League), 377
Pennsylvania-Ontario-New York
    League (Pony League), 377
Pennsylvania State Association, 15,
    129, 276, 279, 378

Pennsylvania State League (pre–
    1900), 11
Pennsylvania State League (1902),
    16, 378
Pennsylvania-West Virginia League
    (1908–09), 378
Pennsylvania-West Virginia League
    (1914), 379
Piedmont League, 129, 379
Pioneer League, 37, 380
Pony League. See Pennsylvania-On-
    tario-New York League
Potomac League, 380
Provincial League, 380
Puget Sound League, 183

Quebec, Ontario-Vermont League,
    380
Quebec Provincial League, 381

Rio Grande Valley League, 180,
    184, 381
Rocky Mountain League, 381

San Joaquin Valley League, 381
Sooner State League, 382
Sophomore League (New Mexico–
    Texas), 382
South Carolina League, 382
South Central League (Arkansas–
    Oklahoma), 383
South Central League (Texas), 383
South Dakota League, 383
Southeastern Kansas League, 383
Southeastern League, 230, 298, 384
Southern Association (and the South-
    ern League), 10, 11, 12, 14, 15,
    23, 34, 46, 58, 61, 108, 184,
    185, 214–47, 297
  Southern Association roster of
    teams (1901–61), 214
  South Atlantic League roster of
    teams (1904–63), 215
  Southern League roster of teams
    (1964—), 215–16
  Southern Association and South-
    ern League history, 216–21

Larry Gilbert's managerial career, 222–23
Johnny Dobbs' managerial career, 223
Joe Engel ("Champion ivory hunter"), 224–26
Southern Association highlights, 226–33
Southern Association and Southern League presidents, 233
Southern Association and Southern League champions, 234–43
Southern Association and Southern League batting champions, 243–45
Dixie Series, 245–47
Southern California Trolley League (Southern California League), 384
Southern Illinois League, 385
Southern Michigan League, 385
Southwest Iowa League, 385
Southwestern League (Kansas–Oklahoma), 184, 386
Southwestern League (New Mexico–Texas), 386
Southwest International League, 387
Southwest Texas League, 387
Southwest Washington League, 387
Sunset League, 388

Tar Heel League, 388
Tennessee–Alabama League. See Alabama–Tennessee League.
Texas Association, 180, 229, 388
Texas League, 11, 15, 16, 34, 39, 40, 41, 44, 46, 58, 61, 157, 177–213, 217, 229, 230, 232, 252, 298
  league roster of teams, 177–78
  South Texas League, roster of teams, 179
  Texas League history, 179–97
  league presidents, 198
  league champions, 199–210
  batting champions, 210–12

individual batting and pitching records, 212–13
Texas-Oklahoma League, 180, 389
Texas Valley League, 180, 389
Tobacco State League, 390
Three–I League. See Illinois–Iowa–Indiana League.
Tri-State League (Arkansas–Mississippi–Tennessee), 390
Tri-State League (Delaware–Pennsylvania–New Jersey), 390–91
Tri-State League (Indiana–Ohio–West Virginia, pre–1900), 11, 12
Tri-State League (North Carolina–South Carolina–Tennessee), 391
Twin Ports League, 15, 392

Union Association, 184, 392
Utah-Idaho League, 392

Virginia League (pre-1900), 11, 12, 13
Virginia League (post-1900), 48, 392–93
Virginia Mountain League, 393
Virginia-North Carolina League, 393
Virginia Valley League, 393

Washington State League, 394
West Dixie League, 394
Western Association (pre-1900), 14
Western Association (post-1900), 41, 73, 394–95
Western Canada League, 395
Western Carolinas League, 35, 216, 396
Western International League, 396–97
Western League (pre-1901), 7, 13, 14, 16, 65, 66–67, 99, 134
Western League (post-1902), 58, 73, 74, 186, 229, 397
Western Pennsylvania League, 398
West Texas League, 398

West Texas-New Mexico League, 299–300, 398–99

Western Tri-State League (Idaho–Oregon–Washington, 1912-14), 399

Western Tri-State League (Oregon and others, 1902, 1908), 399

West Virginia League, 399

Wisconsin-Illinois League, 400

Wisconsin State League, 297, 400

GENERAL INDEX

American Association (pre-1900 major league), 4, 8, 10, 134, 216

Arizona State University, 57–58, 196

Baseball Digest, 28

Baseball Encyclopedia, The (Macmillan), 135

Baseball Register, 139

Batavia Trojans, 32, 135

Cincinnati Red Stockings, 3, 4

Continental League, 44

Designated hitter rule, 135

Dixie Series, 245–47

Federal League (outlaw major league, 1914-15), 99–100

Free Agent Draft, 32, 53–54

Genesee County Baseball Club, Inc., 32

Instructional Leagues, 15, 32–33

Junior World Series, 47, 91, 92–93

Kansas City Royals Baseball Academy, 37, 58

Kodak World Baseball Classic, 91

Ladies' Day, 217

Minor League Cities, 306–19

Minor League Records, 299–305

Minor League Stabilization Fund, 28–29

Minor Leagues in 1973 and their Major League Affiliations, 33–38

National Agreement, 10, 13

National Association of Professional Baseball Players (the first professional baseball league, 1871-75), 3–4, 6

National Association of Professional Baseball Leagues, 3–4, 12–13, 14, 15, 16, 17, 18, 19, 20, 21, 22, 23, 24, 25, 28, 29, 30, 55–56, 67, 79, 103, 108, 158, 320–22

National Commission, 17

New York Mets' farm system, 31–33

Ohio Wesleyan University, 40

Pan-American Association, 196

Player Development Contract, 30–31

Players' League (pre-1900 major league), 65, 98

Reserve Clause, 9, 15

Rochester Community Baseball, Inc., 130

Rochester Red Wings, 124–32

San Francisco earthquake of 1906,
    145–46
Shaughnessy Playoffs, 46–48, 77, 100
Spanish-American War, 185
Sporting News, The, 13, 45, 72, 77,
    78, 106, 108, 139, 258

Texas A & M, 179
Toledo Mud Hens, 132–35
Tripartite Agreement, 10
Tokyo Giants, 154

Union Association (pre-1900 major
    league), 65, 97
University of Texas, 179